Microsoft® 365 Excel®

Microsoft®
365 Excel®

by David H. Ringstrom, CPA

A Wiley Brand

Microsoft® 365 Excel® For Dummies®

Published by: **John Wiley & Sons, Inc.**, 111 River Street, Hoboken, NJ 07030-5774, www.wiley.com

For general information on our other products and services, please contact our Customer Care Department within the U.S. at 877-762-2974, outside the U.S. at 317-572-3993, or fax 317-572-4002. For technical support, please visit https://hub.wiley.com/community/support/dummies.

Wiley publishes in a variety of print and electronic formats and by print-on-demand. Some material included with standard print versions of this book may not be included in e-books or in print-on-demand. If this book refers to media that is not included in the version you purchased, you may download this material at http://booksupport.wiley.com. For more information about Wiley products, visit www.wiley.com.

Library of Congress Control Number: 2025934653

ISBN 978-1-394-31710-3 (pbk); ISBN 978-1-394-31727-1 (ehk); ISBN 978-1-394- 31726-4 (ebk)

Printed and bound by CPI Group (UK) Ltd, Croydon, CR0 4YY
C9781394317103_171025

The manufacturer's authorized representative according to the EU General Product Safety Regulation is Wiley-VCH GmbH, Boschstr. 12, 69469 Weinheim, Germany, e-mail: Product_Safety@wiley.com.

Contents at a Glance

Table of Contents

Introduction

Welcome to Microsoft 365 Excel! My goal in this book is to help you build efficient spreadsheets while maintaining data integrity, whether you're new to Excel or already have experience. For beginners, I guide you through getting oriented, and for experienced users, I aim to help you close any gaps in your knowledge. In my webinars, I often say, "Either you work Excel, or it works you!" Unfortunately, many users learn just enough to use Excel like a blunt instrument, so I chose the topics in this book specifically to help you move beyond that.

REMEMBER

Microsoft 365 Excel is an application you install on your desktop computer. In contrast, Excel for the Web (available at www.office.com/launch/Excel/) runs directly in your browser, and Excel Mobile is designed for use on phones or tablets. While there is significant overlap between these versions, this book focuses specifically on the Windows and macOS versions of Excel.

Microsoft Excel was first released for the Apple Macintosh on September 30, 1985. The AI-infused application we use today only faintly resembles that early version. While it's highly unlikely that anyone still uses a nearly 40-year-old version of Excel, you may still be working with Excel 2021, Excel 2019, or an even earlier version. Much of what I cover in this book applies to those versions, but in some chapters, you may find yourself reading about features you'll have access to only after you upgrade to a newer version of Excel.

About This Book

Microsoft Excel remained relatively static until 2010, when the Office 365 platform was first introduced, later rebranded as Microsoft 365 in 2017. Before then, new features were introduced in Excel every two to three years, a long and often frustrating wait (at least for me). Those days are behind us, as Microsoft 365 now provides ongoing updates with new features and improvements. However, not everyone receives updates at the same time, as users are divided into different channels:

>> **Current Channel:** Users receive monthly updates, with occasional out-of-band updates for critical fixes or security patches.

- **>> Monthly Enterprise Channel:** Like the Current Channel, this provides monthly updates for business users.

- **>> Semi-Annual Enterprise Channel (Preview):** This offers first access to features that will later be included in the Semi-Annual Enterprise Channel.

- **>> Semi-Annual Enterprise Channel:** Updates are released twice a year, ensuring that only thoroughly evaluated, stable features are introduced.

- **>> Beta Channel:** The cutting-edge channel where users who opt into the Microsoft 365 Insider program get early access to features still in development and testing.

- **>> Current Channel (Preview):** A more stable version of the Beta channel — for users that are edgy, but not quite that edgy.

To check which channel you're in:

- **>> Windows:** Go to File ➪ Account — your channel and build appears next to the About Excel button.

- **>> macOS:** Choose Help ➪ Check for Updates, then click Advanced. Your channel (but not build number) appears in the Preferences dialog box.

TECHNICAL STUFF

As you can see, Microsoft 365 Excel is a constantly evolving program. My editors and I have done our best to keep up with these changes and describe what, at times, has been a moving target. Think of it as Excel's way of keeping track of its ever-evolving self — one incremental update at a time.

WARNING

Because updates occur so often in Excel, by the time this book is published, some features and screens may have changed. (On second thought, make that *will* have changed.)

Then there's the matter of the subscription levels:

- **>> Individuals and Families:** Microsoft 365 Personal and Family

- **>> Businesses:** Business Basic (web/mobile only), Business Standard, and Business Premium, Apps for Business

- **>> Enterprises:** E1 (web/mobile only), E3, E5

- **>> Education:** A1 (web/mobile only) A3, A5

- **>> Government:** G1, G3, G5 are like E1, E3, and E5, but add additional compliance for governmental requirements

All Microsoft 365 users have the same feature set for the most part, but some differences can arise, such as the Inquire add-in in the Enterprise versions that creates detailed reports on workbooks, can compare two versions of a workbook, can improve performance by cleaning up workbooks, and can build diagrams that show how cells and worksheets relate together. I discuss how to enable this add-in in Chapter 10.

TIP

If you'd prefer a one-time purchase for Excel, Microsoft Office 2024 provides static versions of Excel and other Office apps. However, this version does not include access to the artificial intelligence features available in Microsoft 365 and will not receive any future feature or function updates.

Here's how the book is broken down:

» Part 1, "Explaining Excel Fundamentals," helps you get oriented in Excel, covering basic calculations, formatting, data sorting and filtering, as well as the often-overlooked Table feature, which can enhance spreadsheet integrity and drop repetitive tasks.

» Part 2, "Mastering Formulas and Functions," introduces lookup functions for retrieving data within a workbook, transforming text without retyping, and incorporating decision-making into formulas. You also learn how to create dynamic formulas that spill into additional cells and explore formula tracing and debugging tools.

» Part 3, "Expanding Beyond the Basics," teaches you to navigate both small and large workbooks efficiently, create refreshable reports with PivotTables and PivotCharts, and apply data visualizations with conditional formatting. You also learn how to secure sensitive data and formulas.

» Part 4, "Automating Analysis," introduces Excel's AI-driven features and teaches you to streamline tasks by recording macros.

» Part 5, "The Part of Tens," provides ten useful keyboard shortcuts and equips you with ten disaster recovery techniques.

Before diving in, I must get some technical conventions out of the way:

» Text that you're meant to type exactly as it appears in the book is formatted in monofont (which looks like text typed on an old typewriter).

» Web addresses and programming code are also displayed in monofont. If you're reading a digital version of this book on a device connected to the internet, you can tap or click a web address to visit the site, like this: www.dummies.com.

>> To use Microsoft 365 Excel effectively, the minimum recommended technical requirements vary slightly depending on whether you're using a Windows or macOS device. For Windows users, a dual-core processor with a speed of 1.6 GHz or faster is needed, along with at least 4 GB of RAM for 64-bit systems (or 2 GB for 32-bit systems). You'll also need 4 GB of available hard disk space, a display with a resolution of at least 1280 x 768, and a DirectX 9-compatible graphics card with WDDM 2.0 or higher for Windows 10. The software is compatible with Windows 10, Windows 11, and recent versions of Windows Server, and an internet connection is needed for product activation, updates, and cloud features.

For macOS users, Microsoft 365 Excel needs an Intel processor or Apple Silicon (M1, M2, or later), with at least 4 GB of RAM and 10 GB of available disk space. A display resolution of 1280 x 800 or higher is recommended, and the operating system should be one of the three most recent versions of macOS. Like Windows, an internet connection is necessary for activation, updates, and some online features. Additionally, users on both platforms will need a current browser (such as Microsoft Edge, Chrome, Safari, or Firefox) and a Microsoft account to access all the features of Microsoft 365.

For best performance, particularly when working with large datasets or advanced tools like Power Query or PowerPivot, higher specifications — such as faster processors and added RAM — are recommended.

>> When I discuss a command to choose, I separate the elements of the sequence with a command arrow that looks like this: ⇨ . For example, when you see Data ⇨ Sort, it means you should activate the Data tab in Excel's ribbon interface and then choose the Sort command. Some ribbon commands have drop-down menus, and I'll often include the corresponding keyboard shortcuts for added convenience.

REMEMBER

The ribbon interface sometimes collapses command groups based on your screen resolution or the size of the Excel window. If a command you're looking for seems to be missing, try expanding the window or clicking the drop-down arrow in the collapsed group to reveal hidden options.

Foolish Assumptions

I had to make some assumptions about you while authoring this book, so here are my educated guesses:

>> You want to learn how to use a spreadsheet or improve how you already use spreadsheets.

>> You may want to analyze your data using Excel features and/or worksheet functions, and perhaps automate repetitive tasks.

>> You have a personal computer running Windows 10 or 11 (I drafted this book in Windows 10 because I have my reasons) or a Mac running macOS 12 Monterey or later.

>> Ideally, you have Microsoft 365 Excel on your computer, but much of this book also applies to older versions of Excel. In fact, a good part of this book can be used with Excel for the Web or even Google Sheets.

Icons Used in This Book

Throughout the book, I use icons to draw your attention to key concepts that I don't want you to miss. Sometimes these icons highlight tips to help you save time, while in other cases, they focus on keeping your spreadsheets safe and secure.

TIP

This icon points out time-saving tricks or nuances that you may come across in Excel.

REMEMBER

This icon highlights tricky aspects of Excel that you should be aware of and keep in mind as you work.

WARNING

Caution: Contents Hot. Oh, wait — wrong type of warning! You won't burn yourself if this book falls into your lap but do pay close attention to the warnings you encounter. They're here to help you avoid issues that could cause problems in your spreadsheets or, more commonly, lead to unnecessary frustration.

TECHNICAL STUFF

At times, I may include some geeky details about Excel, your web browser, or your computer. If technical stuff isn't your cup of tea, feel free to skip over it without missing out on the main content.

CROSS REFERENCE

Think of this as an "oh, by the way" that points you to more details elsewhere in the book.

Beyond the Book

This book comes, with two bonus chapters on automating data transformation with Power Query and dealing with many of Excel's frustrating prompts. You can find the bonus chapters here: www.dummies.com/go/excelfd.

In addition, this book comes with a free access-anywhere Cheat Sheet, which includes extra tips; a list of features available in Excel for Windows, but not in macOS; and a couple of macOS-exclusive features. To get this Cheat Sheet, simply go to www.dummies.com and type Microsoft 365 Excel For Dummies Cheat Sheet in the Search box.

Where to Go from Here

Part 1 covers the basics of Microsoft Excel, and even experienced users may uncover blind spots they didn't realize they had. Continue to Part 2 for an in-depth look at using worksheet formulas to automate calculations and transform data. Part 3 takes you beyond the basics, showing how to manage large spreadsheets, visualize data, and user-proof your work. Part 4 focuses on automation, including artificial intelligence and Visual Basic for Applications (VBA) macros. The book wraps up with Part 5, where you learn to turbo-charge your work with keyboard shortcuts and protect your spreadsheets from the many things that can go wrong.

1

Explaining Excel Fundamentals

Get started with spreadsheets.

Carry out basic calculations.

Format cells and ranges.

Sort, filter, and sift through data.

Enhance your spreadsheets with Excel tables.

IN THIS CHAPTER

» **Getting oriented in Excel**

» **Creating and saving workbooks**

» **Working with spreadsheet templates**

» **Entering and editing data**

» **Sharing workbooks with others**

Chapter **1**

Getting Started with Spreadsheets

O rienteering is an outdoor sport where participants navigate between way-points on an unfamiliar course using nothing but a map and a compass. Think of it as a real-world treasure hunt — except instead of gold, you might find a mud puddle or a tree you're pretty sure you've seen before. If that sounds a little too outdoorsy, consider the IKEA alternative: winding through an endless maze of bookshelves and meatballs, desperately searching for the exit.

Unlike both of those scenarios, this Excel adventure won't leave you lost or questioning your life choices. No map, no compass — just a series of waypoints to guide you through the wilds of worksheets:

» Using screenshots to draw your attention to various parts of Excel

» Entering and editing data in an Excel worksheet

» Creating and saving Excel workbooks, both from scratch and by way of prebuilt Excel templates

» Sharing spreadsheets, collaborating in real-time, and keeping the conversation going

Our first stop is a Rosetta Stone of sorts, decoding what you're seeing onscreen when you launch Excel.

Exploring Excel's User Interface

Whenever you launch Excel, it eagerly greets you with a blank workbook featuring a single worksheet tab — like a fresh notepad just waiting for you to scribble all over it. You also see a tabbed menu interface across the top that Microsoft insists on calling the ribbon — because apparently "menu bar" wasn't fancy enough. The ribbon includes a set of static tabs, along with other contextual tabs that pop up when Excel deems them necessary (whether you agree or not). Just above this ribbon spectacle sits a collection of icons known as the Quick Access Toolbar — your personal stash of frequently used commands, which I cover in the "Customizing the Quick Access Toolbar" section later in this chapter.

Below the ribbon, shown in Figure 1-1, you see a row composed of three sections, because two wouldn't be enough, and four would be excessive:

>> **Name Box:** Most users rely on this area to see the address of the currently selected worksheet cell.

TIP

You can do a surprising number of things in the Name Box — more than two dozen! No need to feel overwhelmed; think of this as a peek into just how much Excel can do. Chapter 11 provides more details.

>> **Insert Function button:** Excel's real power comes from its hundreds of worksheet functions, which let you crunch numbers from simple sums to complex calculations using inputs called arguments. Clicking this button opens a search-friendly dialog box, followed by another that walks you through building the formula step by step. The "Leveraging worksheet functions" section later in this chapter offers a straightforward way to get started.

>> **Formula Bar:** This expandable section shows what's inside the selected worksheet cell. If a cell has a formula, you see the result in the cell, while the Formula Bar reveals the formula itself. You can edit cell contents directly in the formula bar or within the cell itself. To do so, double-click on a cell or press F2 (Windows) or Cmd+U (macOS).

TECHNICAL
STUFF

Cells can contain up to 32,000 characters, including text, numbers, symbols, non-printable characters like carriage returns, or formulas.

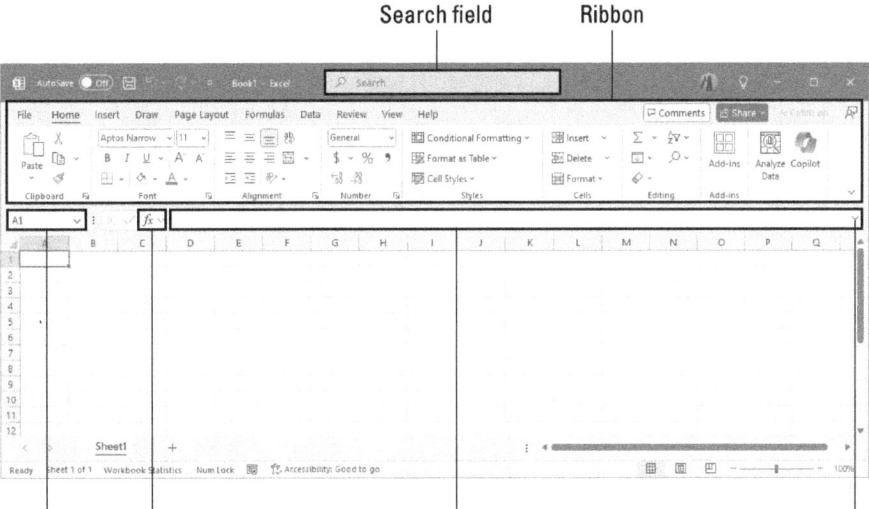

Search field   Ribbon

FIGURE 1-1:
Microsoft Excel's
user interface.

Name Box   Insert Function command   Formula Bar   Expand Formula Bar button

TIP

The Expand Formula Bar button sits on the right-hand side of the Formula Bar. Clicking it — or pressing Ctrl+Shift+U (Windows) or Cmd+Shift+U (macOS) — expands the Formula Bar to show up to 11 rows. Just keep in mind that this reduces the number of visible worksheet rows. You can also resize the Formula Bar by dragging its bottom edge, balancing the need to see more cell contents and keeping more of the worksheet in view.

Below the Formula Bar lies the worksheet grid, made up of a fixed number of rows and columns. Rows are numbered from 1 to 1,048,576, while columns follow a lettered system: A through Z for the first twenty-six, AA through AZ for the next set, continuing on until the final column, XFD.

TECHNICAL
STUFF

Every worksheet contains 1,048,576 rows and 16,384 columns — over 17 billion cells in total — giving you plenty of room to get lost in data.

Traversing the ribbon

The ribbon in Excel is divided into two groups: the headliners — main tabs that are always present — and the special guests, known as tool tabs. The rock star tabs that never leave the road, er screen, include:

>> **File:** Opens the Backstage View, where Excel handles all the behind-the-scenes business — opening, saving, printing, sharing workbooks, and tweaking settings.

>> **Home:** There's no place like the Home tab — it's where Excel keeps the most-used commands for formatting, editing, sorting, and filtering. Check here before you start clicking around like a lost tourist.

TIP

If all those icons are starting to blur together, think of ScreenTips as little cue cards. Hover over any ribbon or toolbar command, and Excel will remind you what it does. Windows users even get keyboard shortcuts — macOS users, not so much.

>> **Insert:** Think of this as Excel's "Add Stuff" tab. Drop in PivotTables, PivotCharts, and slicers (see Chapter 12), or spice things up with shapes, images (safe-for-work only, please), and text boxes (see Chapter 3).

>> **Page Layout:** Fine-tunes how your worksheet looks when printed — margins, scaling, and other settings that help you wrestle Excel into submission — *on paper, at least* (see Chapter 3).

>> **Formulas:** The command center for Excel's number-crunching wizardry. Dig into function libraries, troubleshoot formulas, and tweak calculation settings — because sometimes, Excel needs a little nudge to do the math right (see Chapters 6 through 10).

>> **Data:** Where Excel turns into a data-guzzling machine. The Get & Transform Data and Queries & Connections sections let you pull in info from just about anywhere using Power Query (see the bonus chapter "Automating Data Transformation with Power Query" available at www.dummies.com/go/excelfd). The Data Types feature (see Chapter 15) adds self-updating "smart" cells — because why settle for static data that just sits there? The rest of the tab wrangles sorting, filtering (see Chapter 4), and what-if analysis, like scenario management (see Chapter 18).

>> **Review:** This tab is like Excel's safety net — catching typos, flagging accessibility issues (see Chapter 3), adding comments (see the "Collaborating with Others" section of this chapter), and locking down spreadsheets to protect them from *ahem* enthusiastic but error-prone users (see Chapter 14).

>> **View:** The toolkit for controlling what's visible in Excel. Freeze rows and columns in place (see Chapter 4), switch between custom views and adjust zoom levels (see Chapter 11), or step into the world of automation with macros and Excel's Macro Recorder (see Chapter 16). Because sometimes, seeing is believing.

>> **Help:** Need somebody? Not just anybody? This tab (or, on macOS, the Help menu) connects users to support resources, troubleshooting information, and usage tips for Excel — so you can get by with a little help from this tab (or menu).

SEARCHING EXCEL'S MENUS

If you're feeling adrift, get back on firm ground with Excel's multipurpose Search feature. Access it in one of the following ways:

- Click the Search field in Excel's title bar.

- Press Alt+Q (Windows) or Cmd+Ctrl+U (macOS).

Choose from suggestions based on recent or common actions, or start typing to generate a dynamic list of commands. To search within the worksheet, enter a term and select Find in Worksheet (Windows) or Find (macOS).

A second Search the Menus field appears when you right-click the worksheet frame or any cell. This search is limited to ribbon commands — use Find instead when hunting for data (covered in Chapter 11).

TECHNICAL STUFF

Depending on your rights and licensing, the Automate tab may appear, granting access to Office Scripts for automating repetitive tasks with JavaScript-based scripts. Any user can enable the Developer tab, packed with tools for creating and editing macros (see Chapter 16) — perfect for those ready to tinker under Excel's hood.

Despite its name, the ribbon isn't particularly fluid — the built-in commands refuse to budge. If it's making you feel tied up in knots, cut through the clutter by adding new command groups to existing tabs or creating entirely new tabs. Here's how to try your hand at menu design:

1. **Open the Customization dialog box:**

    - **Windows:** Choose File ⇨ Options ⇨ Customize Ribbon or right-click the ribbon and select Customize the Ribbon (opens the Excel Options dialog box).

    - **macOS:** Choose Excel ⇨ Preferences ⇨ Ribbon & Toolbar (opens the Ribbon & Toolbar dialog box).

2. **Show or hide tabs by toggling the checkboxes in the Customize the Ribbon list.**

3. **Edit an existing tab:**

    a) **Select a tab from the Customize the Ribbon list (defaults to Main Tabs). Select Tool Tabs or All Tabs to explore further.**

    b) **Click New Group (+ then New Group on macOS) to add a custom group.**

c) **Rename it by clicking Rename (. . . then Rename on macOS).**

d) **Add commands by selecting them from the Choose Commands list and clicking Add >> (> on macOS). Use << Remove (< on macOS) to remove commands.**

4. **To create a new tab, click New Tab (+ then New Tab on macOS), then rename it and add groups and commands as needed.**

Here's a peek at some of the tool tabs that may make special appearances — stepping on stage when a task calls for them:

» **Header & Footer:** This tab takes the stage when you decide what should grace the top or bottom of each page — because every sheet deserves a proper introduction and a grand finale (see Chapter 3).

» **Analyze:** This tab steps into the spotlight for PivotTables and PivotCharts (see Chapter 12), giving you tools to connect, explore, and wrangle your data.

» **Design:** This tab makes a stylish appearance when you select a cell in an Excel table (see Chapter 5), a PivotTable, or click on a chart or PivotChart (all covered in Chapter 12). While "Design" may not always be in the name, similar variations appear for Sparklines, slicers, and Timelines (you guessed it, all in Chapter 12).

» **Format:** This feature-specific tab appears for charts, PivotCharts, shapes, and images — because sometimes your data needs a little wardrobe upgrade.

» **Query:** This tab enables you to edit, load, reuse, combine, and share data connections through Power Query — because why do the heavy lifting when you can make Excel do it for you? See the bonus chapter "Automating Data Transformation with Power Query" (available at www.dummies.com/go/excelfd).

TECHNICAL STUFF

Enterprise and government users can — and frankly should — enable the Inquire add-in. This powerhouse of a tool helps document workbooks, compare workbook versions, and fine-tune performance, making it a must-have for anyone wrangling complex spreadsheets.

Customizing the Quick Access Toolbar

The Quick Access Toolbar is like Excel's junk drawer — full of useful stuff, but only if you take the time to set it up. You can stash your favorite commands above or below the ribbon. By default, it includes AutoSave, Save, Undo, and Redo, which I cover later in the chapter. In Excel for Windows, tapping Alt turns your screen into an eye chart of alphanumeric shortcuts for every command on the toolbar and ribbon — macOS users must use their mouse. To make it your own:

- **»** **Add a single command:**
  - **Windows:** Right-click a ribbon command and select Add to Quick Access Toolbar
  - **macOS:** Unfortunately, you can't add commands on the fly, but you can use the Finetuning instructions
- **»** **Finetuning:**
  - **Windows:** Go to File ⇨ Options ⇨ Quick Access Toolbar to open the Excel Options dialog box.
  - **macOS:** Go to Excel ⇨ Preferences ⇨ Ribbon & Toolbar to open the Ribbon & Toolbar dialog box.

  From there, you can shuffle icons, relocate the toolbar, and decide whether command labels should appear as ScreenTips.
- **»** **Starting over** (if your customizations spiral into chaos):
  - **Windows:** In the Excel Options dialog box, click Rest and choose whether to restore just the Quick Access Toolbar or reset all ribbon customizations.
  - **macOS:** Click . . . in the Ribbon & Toolbar dialog box then reset the toolbar or include the ribbon in your do-over.

TECHNICAL STUFF

You already know that Ctrl is the go-to key for most keyboard shortcuts in Windows. Alt has some quirks, especially when numbers get involved. Tapping Alt lets you trigger Quick Access Toolbar shortcuts using either the number pad or the numbers row up top. However, hold down Alt while pressing a number on the number pad summons special characters instead — like Alt+7 giving you a bullet (·). Other numbers conjure up different symbols, which is either a handy trick or an unexpected detour, depending upon what you are trying to do.

One of my favorite areas to explore is Commands Not in the Ribbon list within the Choose Commands From list. This hidden trove contains hundreds of commands left off the ribbon — either due to space constraints or feature deprecation. Here are a few gems I often add to my Quick Access Toolbar:

- **»** **AutoFilter:** A one-click wonder that filters a normal range of cells based on whatever's in the selected cell. But don't get any wild ideas — this trick doesn't work within Excel tables (see Chapter 5).

>> **Custom Views:** Think of this as Excel's version of quick-change artist, letting you swap between saved worksheet and workbook layouts. I cover Custom Views in Chapter 11.

>> **Full Screen:** Clears away the ribbon, Formula Bar, and Status Bar so you can focus on your data — or just make Excel look extra dramatic. Press Escape to bring everything back.

TIP

The Customize Quick Access Toolbar drop-down lets you decide whether to apply changes For All Documents (customizing the toolbar on this device) or for a specific workbook. Workbook-specific toolbars stick with the file, so they can follow you to other computers — like a loyal sidekick.

Activating worksheets

Chapter 11 takes a deep dive into navigating worksheets and workbooks, so I'll keep things brief here. Each document you create in Excel is called a workbook, which consists of one or more worksheets — each represented by a tab at the bottom of the worksheet grid. Think of worksheets as pages in a ledger, neatly (or not so neatly) organized within your workbook.

Here are a few ways that you can activate a worksheet tab:

>> **Click the tab:** Simple and straightforward.

>> **Sheet navigation arrows:** Found just above the Status Bar, these let you nudge the visible tabs to the left or right — provided you have more tabs than can fit comfortably on screen.

>> **Activate dialog box:** Right-click the sheet navigation arrows to summon the Activate dialog box (Figure 1-2). Pick a worksheet from the list and click OK — or double-click a sheet name to skip the extra step.

REMEMBER

The Activate dialog box only lists visible worksheets — so if a sheet is playing hide-and-seek, it won't show up there. To track down hidden worksheets, use the Navigation task pane (covered in Chapter 11). For more on making sheets disappear (or reappear), check out the upcoming "Hiding or unhiding worksheets" section.

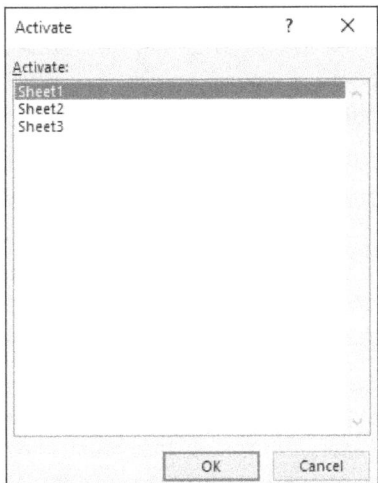

FIGURE 1-2:
The Activate
dialog box.

Exploring the Status Bar

The Status Bar — Excel's command center that hides out in plain sight — keeps you in the loop with various feedback mechanisms and quick-access tools. Here's a rundown of the default options (as shown in Figure 1-3):

>> **Cell Mode Indicator**: Your cell's current mood, expressed in one word:

- **Ready:** Just sitting there, minding its own business.

- **Enter:** Actively receiving data or a formula.

- **Point:** Waiting for you to pick cells for a formula, like a kid in a dodgeball lineup.

- **Edit (Windows Only):** Mid-editing, hoping you don't regret your choices.

Chapter 17 gets into the nitty-gritty of Enter, Point, and Edit modes.

CROSS REFERENCE

>> **AutoFilter Status:** Tells you how many records match your filter criteria — so you're not left wondering why half your data mysteriously vanished. Filtering gets the full treatment in Chapter 4.

>> **Calculate Status:** Signals that some values may be outdated because Automatic Calculation is turned off or when Excel enters Manual Calculation mode due to a large data set. Clicking it or pressing F9 (Windows only) recalculates outdated formulas in the open workbook.

TECHNICAL STUFF

Press Ctrl+Alt+F9 (Windows) or Cmd+Shift+= (macOS) to force a full recalculation of all formulas across all open workbooks. Windows users can also press Ctrl+Shift+Alt+F9 to rebuild the dependency tree — an internal structure that tracks relationships between formulas and the cells they reference — and then recalculate everything. Mac users can achieve a similar result by toggling Manual Calculation mode (via Excel ➪ Preferences ➪ Calculation) and then switch back to Automatic to force a full recalculation.

REMEMBER

Unlike most Status Bar features, the AutoFilter and Calculate settings cannot be toggled on or off — they appear only when relevant, like pop-up guests in your spreadsheet party.

>> **Accessibility Assistant:** Indicates if an accessibility issue has been detected — click the icon to open the Accessibility Checker (Chapter 3) where you can review and fix potential concerns so that your workbook is inclusive and easy to navigate for all users.

>> **AutoCalculate Functions:** Instantly crunches numbers when you select multiple cells, serving up average, count, numerical count, minimum, maximum, and sum — like a tiny data butler.

TIP

Click any calculation in the Status Bar to copy the value to the clipboard, letting you paste it elsewhere like the Excel wizard you are.

>> **View Modes:** Located out on the right-hand side, these buttons let you switch between Normal (standard spreadsheet view), Page Layout (Excel's best guess at how your data will break across pages), and Page Break Preview (a true print preview, complete with headers and footers, so you can see exactly what will make it on the printed page).

>> **Zoom Slider:** Don't worry, this won't pull you into yet another online meeting. Located on the far right, this lets you zoom in until your data takes over the screen or zoom out until it vanishes into microscopic oblivion. In Windows, percentage zoom level appears next to it — click the number to open the Zoom dialog box for precise control.

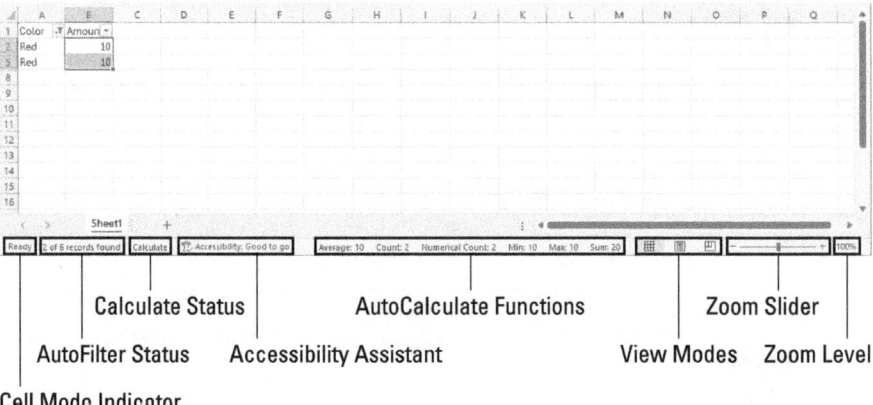

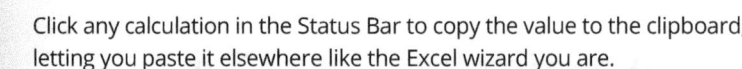

Calculate Status		AutoCalculate Functions	Zoom Slider
AutoFilter Status	Accessibility Assistant		View Modes Zoom Level

FIGURE 1-3:
The Status Bar.   Cell Mode Indicator

You can customize the Status Bar by turning features on or off. Just right-click anywhere on it and toggle the options you want. For example, I often disable the Zoom Slider because I inevitably graze it while using the horizontal scroll bar — instantly throwing my worksheet into either billboard mode or microscopic territory, neither of which is particularly helpful. Other options you may wish to enable include:

>> **Sheet Number:** Displays where the current worksheet stands in the lineup — along with the total number of sheets in the workbook. It's a handy way to confirm whether you're on Sheet 3 of 27 or just hopelessly lost.

>> **Workbook Statistics:** Click to open a dialog box that provides a quick summary of key details of the workbook, including the number of sheets, cells with data, tables, charts, and more.

>> **Caps Lock, Num Lock, Scroll Lock Indicators:** Letting you know if you've purposefully engaged one of these settings — or if you're typing LIKE YOU'RE SHOUTING and wondering why.

WARNING

Scroll Lock is Excel for Windows's little gremlin, waiting for the perfect moment to ruin your day. When active, the arrow keys stop moving the selection and instead sends the whole worksheet gliding around like a greased-up air hockey puck. To disable it, press ScrLk again — if your keyboard even has one. If not, search for "On-Screen Keyboard" in Windows, and click ScrLk to wrestle back control.

>> **Macro Recording:** When enabled, a button appears that allows you to start or stop the Macro Recorder — because why not make Excel do the heavy lifting? More on that in Chapter 16.

Entering and Editing Data

If you're itching to create a spreadsheet from scratch, you're in luck — after touring the Excel interface, it's time to build a simple task tracker. This example introduces basic data entry, formatting, and formulas while providing a preview of features explored in more detail later in the book.

Starting a task tracker

Here's how to get started with building a task tracking spreadsheet:

1. **Add the following column titles (referred to as headers in Excel) to a blank Excel worksheet — if you don't already have one open, try closing**

and reopening Excel, or check the "Creating new workbooks" section later in this chapter:

- **Cell A1:** Task
- **Cell B1:** Due Date
- **Cell C1:** Priority
- **Cell D1:** Status
- **Cell E1:** Time Spent (Hours)

TIP

Column headers organize data, make the spreadsheet easier to read, and improve ease of use with certain Excel features, such as sorting lists (Chapter 4) and report writing with PivotTables (Chapter 12).

2. **Enter the following example tasks (inspired by "The Jersey Shore") into the cells below:**

- **A2:** Gym
- **A3:** Tan
- **A4:** Laundry
- **A5:** Party

3. **In column B, add due dates for each task:**

a) **Type** 1/1 (the one day of the year that some folks actually go to the gym) **in cell B2, then press Enter.**

In unformatted cells, Excel converts entries in m/d or mm/dd format to d-mmm, with the hidden year defaulting to the current year. To display the full date in m/d/yyyy format, select Home ⇨ Number Format drop-down ⇨ Short Date.

TIP

Applying the Short Date format in advance to cells allows you to save keystrokes by omitting the year for dates within the current year.

b) **Type** 04/01/2026 **in cell B3, then press Enter.**

Excel pranks you by dropping the leading zeroes — see Chapter 2 for how to display them if needed.

c) **Overwrite the values in cells B2:B3 with yesterday's date and today's date, respectively, using the m/d format.**

Excel adds the current year automatically since both cells have date formats applied.

d) **Drag the Fill Handle from B2, shown in Figure 1-4, to cell B5 to fill the series of dates.**

TIP

To create a series of month-end dates, enter two consecutive month-end dates in adjacent cells, select both, and then drag the Fill Handle down. Excel will recognize the pattern and extend it accordingly. This works for any data where Excel can identify a logical sequence.

4. **Use column C to track priority:**

- **C2:** High
- **C3:** Medium
- **C4:** Low
- **C5:** High

TIP

As you may have noticed in cell D5, Excel can autofill entries based on similar entries within the current column of the current region ⇨ simply press Enter when the desired entry appears after typing matching characters.

5. **Use column D to track status:**

- **D2:** Completed
- **D3:** In Progress
- **D4:** Pending
- **D5:** Never Ending

TIP

Chapter 14 covers creating in-cell drop-down lists with the Data Validation feature, streamlining data entry and ensuring consistent inputs.

6. **Use column E to track hours:**

- **E2:** 2
- **E3:** 1.5
- **E4:** 3
- **E5:** 4

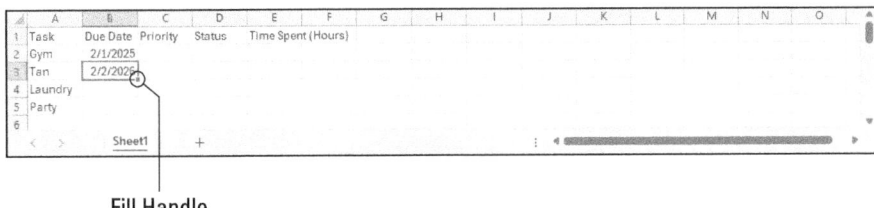

FIGURE 1-4:
Use the
Fill Handle.

Fill Handle

Applying basic formatting

A common next step is to dress up data:

1. **Select the header cells (a necessary step before applying formatting):**

   - **Mouse action:** Click once on cell A1, hold down the left mouse button, and drag across to cell E1.

   - **Keyboard action:** Use the Up Arrow key to return to cell A1, hold down Shift, and the Right Arrow to select across to cell E1.

   TIP

     To select the entire contiguous block of cells that surround the active cell, press Ctrl+A (Windows) or Cmd+A (macOS) to select the current region. If you press the shortcut again, Excel selects the entire worksheet.

2. **Apply basic formatting (see Chapter 2 for more advanced formatting options):**

   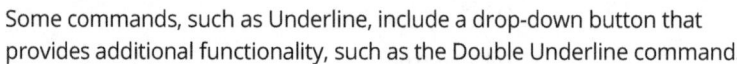

   - **Bold:** Choose Home ⇨ Bold or press Ctrl+B (Windows) or Cmd+B (macOS).

   - **Underline:** Choose Home ⇨ Underline or press Ctrl+U (Windows) or Cmd+U (macOS).

   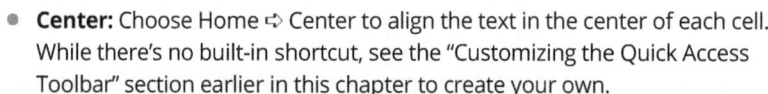
   TIP

     Some commands, such as Underline, include a drop-down button that provides additional functionality, such as the Double Underline command.

   - **Center:** Choose Home ⇨ Center to align the text in the center of each cell. While there's no built-in shortcut, see the "Customizing the Quick Access Toolbar" section earlier in this chapter to create your own.

     Many formatting commands function as toggles, such as Bold or Underline, while others require selecting an alternative option, such as Left Align when choosing not to center text in a cell.

3. **Select cell E1, then choose Home ⇨ Wrap Text.**

   Excel automatically adjusts the row height to ensure all data within the cell is visible.

   Line breaks for wrapped text are based on the column width. To insert a manual line break, press Alt+Enter (Windows) or Option+Return (macOS).

   TECHNICAL
   STUFF

4. **To format the hours with two decimal places, select cells E2:E5, and then choose Home ⇨ Comma Style.**

   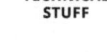

   If necessary, adjust the decimal places by clicking Home ⇨ Increase Decimal or Home ⇨ Decrease Decimal.

5. **To adjust the width of column D, click the letter D at the top of the worksheet to select the entire column, and then go to Home, and then choose Home ⇨ Format ⇨ AutoFit Column Width.**

REMEMBER

Sometimes Excel misinterprets your intent. For example, selecting cell D4 and choosing Home ➪ Format ➪ AutoFit Column Width *reduces* the column width to fit the seven characters in Pending, instead of displaying Never Ending in full, as you might have expected. To avoid this, select the entire column or the relevant range first, or double-click the column's right edge when the double-headed arrow appears to auto-fit to the widest cell contents. See Chapter 3 for more on adjusting column widths.

Leveraging worksheet functions

Worksheet functions are Excel's built-in magic tricks — prepackaged formulas that crunch numbers, manipulate data, and make your life easier. They work by using specific values called arguments, which you feed into the function like ingredients in a recipe. Whether you're doing simple math or wrangling a monster-sized data set, these functions have your back. You'll find them hanging out in the Function Library group of the Formulas tab of the ribbon. Some standout examples include:

>> **Arithmetic:** SUM, AVERAGE (Chapter 2)

>> **Lookups:** VLOOKUP, HLOOKUP, XLOOKUP (Chapter 6)

>> **Text manipulation:** UPPER, LOWER, TEXTSPLIT, SUBSTITUTE (Chapter 7)

>> **Logical operations:** IF, IFS, SWITCH, CHOOSE (Chapter 8)

>> **Data analysis:** UNIQUE, SORT, FILTER (Chapter 9)

TECHNICAL STUFF

Most worksheet functions are a single string of alphanumeric characters, but some functions come in two parts separated by a period, followed by parentheses. Most worksheet functions require at least one argument — a cell reference, text, numbers, or another even formula — neatly tucked inside the parentheses like a well-wrapped data burrito.

For instance, the SUM function is an ideal way to add a total to cell E6. This can be done in two ways. The first is using the AutoSum command:

1. **Select the cell where the total should appear; for example, E6.**

2. **Choose Home ➪ AutoSum.**

The second way is to use a manual formula:

1. **Type =SUM(in cell E6 to start the formula.**

2. **Select cells E2:E5 using one of these methods:**

- Drag the mouse across E2:E5

- Use the Up Arrow key to navigate to cell E5, hold Shift, then navigate to cell E2

- Manually type E2:E5 or E5:E2

3. Type) to close the formula, and then press Enter.

Using either approach, the completed formula =SUM(E2:E5) appears. The SUM function has 255 arguments, but most users only use the first one:

>> **number1:** The first range or amount to include in the total, for example, E2:E5.

>> **number2..255:** Optional additional ranges or amounts.

REMEMBER

Always reference cell ranges when possible, such as =SUM(E2:E6) instead of going full-on manual with =SUM(E2,E3,E4,E5) or, worse, writing a formula that screams inefficiency =SUM(E2+E3+E4+E5). Using a range ensures that if you insert a row between rows 2 and 5, the new value is automatically included in the total — sparing you from a future forehead-smacking moment when your total is mysteriously off.

TIP

>> The Table feature (Chapter 5) includes a Total Row option, which creates total rows without manual formulas — and better yet, it automatically updates when additional amounts are added to the list. No extra effort (or forehead-smacking) required!

Here's how to create a slightly more complex formula:

1. Type Completion % in cell G1.

2. Add this formula to cell G2: =COUNTIF(D2:D5,"Completed")/ COUNTA(A2:A5).

The COUNTIF function (Chapter 8) counts the number of instances of the word "Completed" in cells D2:D5, while the COUNTA function counts the number of non-blank cells in A2:A5. As covered in Chapter 2, the / operator performs division.

REMEMBER

Similarly named worksheet functions can return wildly different results, so don't let Excel lull you into a false sense of security. Take COUNT, for example — it only tallies up numeric values, meaning =COUNT(A2:A5) would return a big fat zero if the range contains nothing but text. So, if you were expecting a number and got ghosted instead, now you know why.

3. Select cell G2 and then choose Home ➪ Percent Style to format the result as a percent.

Handling Workbook Operations

As noted earlier in this chapter, launching Excel conjures up a blank workbook featuring a single worksheet tab. You can dive straight into data entry or open an existing workbook instead. If you open an existing workbook, Excel discreetly sweeps that initial blank workbook away, like a magician making a coin disappear, no dramatic hand flourish required. Because you've likely put some effort into building a worksheet, let's make sure it's saved for later use.

Saving Excel workbooks

The more time I spend working, the greater the odds a workbook will mysteriously close without saving. It's all too easy to get lost in a spreadsheet rabbit hole and forget to hit save — until it's too late. If you're used to online tools like Google Sheets, Excel's file management can feel like a rude awakening when you realize your hard work isn't automatically preserved. Here's how to make sure that doesn't happen:

TIP

>> **File menu:** Choose File ⇨ Save or Save As. If you've already saved the workbook, Save updates the existing version, while Save As allows you to save a copy under a new name.

If you save your workbook to OneDrive or SharePoint, you can toggle AutoSave on via the Quick Access Toolbar. Once enabled, your work is automatically saved every few seconds to a minute, ensuring you don't lose progress — even if Excel (or life) throws a curveball.

>> **Quick Access Toolbar:** Click Save or tap the Alt key in Windows and then type the shortcut that appears in a screentip.

>> **Keyboard shortcut:** Press Ctrl+S (Windows) or Cmd+S (macOS). If you've already saved the workbook at least once, this shortcut updates the saved version. Otherwise, it opens the Save As dialog box, allowing you to specify the name and location for the workbook.

TIP

Chapter 18 details ten disaster recovery techniques that, with any luck, you should never need. Spoiler alert: One of the best defenses is to save your work to a cloud-based drive like OneDrive.

Opening existing workbooks

Excel doesn't expect you to start from nothing each time — you can open an existing workbook in a couple of ways:

>> **Menu commands:** Choose File ⇨ Open ⇨ Browse (Windows) or File ⇨ Open (macOS) to display the Open dialog box or Finder window, respectively.

>> **Keyboard shortcut:** Press Ctrl+O (Windows) or Cmd+O (macOS) to skip the menu and select a file to open.

You can also check out File ⇨ Home (Windows) or File ⇨ Open Recent (macOS) to browse recent workbooks and folders — because even Excel knows you're just trying to find that file you swore you saved yesterday.

If you have multiple workbooks open, Excel typically shows only one at a time, but you're not stuck with that — you can view more than one simultaneously. Here's how to switch between workbooks or arrange them onscreen:

>> **Keyboard shortcut:** Press Ctrl+Tab (Windows).

>> **View ⇨ Switch Windows ⇨ [Window Name]:** Lists all open workbooks, except the sneaky hidden ones, like the Personal Macro Workbook (covered in Chapter 16).

>> **View ⇨ Arrange All:** Opens the Arrange All dialog, where you can choose how to display your workbooks:

   ● **Tiled:** Workbooks arranged in non-overlapping boxes

   ● **Horizontal:** Workbooks stacked in rows, one above the other

   ● **Vertical:** Workbooks placed in columns, side by side

   ● **Cascade:** Workbooks stacked with overlapping windows, like a deck of cards

Creating new workbooks

Need a new workbook? Here are a couple of ways to start fresh:

>> **Menu commands:** Windows users can select File ⇨ Home ⇨ New Blank Workbook or File ⇨ New ⇨ Blank Workbook, while macOS users must choose File ⇨ New.

>> **Keyboard shortcut:** Press Ctrl+N (Windows) or Cmd+N (macOS).

Any of these approaches create a new, blank workbook with a single worksheet tab — a clean slate, ready for whatever data you throw at it.

Using Excel templates

Excel workbook templates are like training wheels for your spreadsheets — ready-made designs spare you from starting from scratch. They also double as cheat sheets for good spreadsheet design, with formatting and formulas baked in to keep things running smoothly. Here's how to grab one:

>> **File menu:**

1. **Choose File ⇨ New (Windows) or File ⇨ New from Template (macOS).**

   The Template screen or Microsoft Excel dialog box opens.

2. **Scroll through the suggested templates — macOS users have to scroll down more than one screen — or perform a keyword search using the Search for Online Templates field (Windows) or Search field (macOS).**

3. **Click any template that seems to be a good match, and then click Create to generate a new workbook based on the template.**

>> **Worksheet tab context menu:** Windows users can right-click any worksheet tab, select Insert, choose a template from the General or Spreadsheet Solutions tabs (shown in Figure 1-5), and click OK to add it to the workbook.

>> **Microsoft website:** Head over to create.microsoft.com to explore a vast library of templates for Excel and other Microsoft 365 applications.

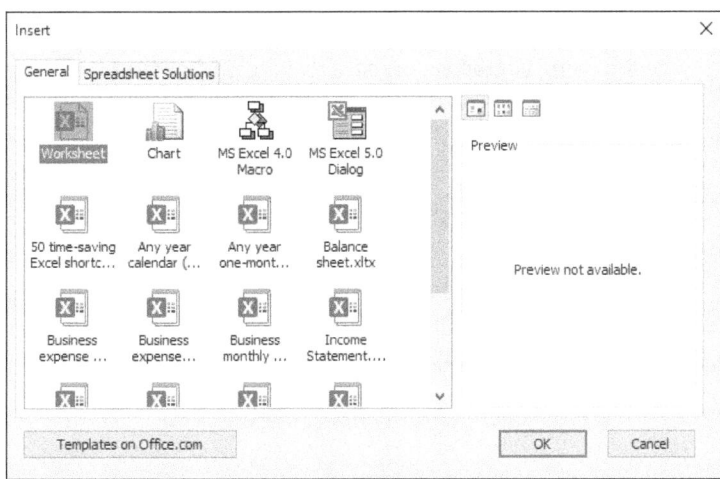

FIGURE 1-5:
The Insert
dialog box.

Managing Worksheet Tasks

Now it's time to dive into the many ways that you can wrangle worksheets within an Excel workbook. A workbook must always have at least one visible worksheet — Excel won't let you delete the last sheet, no matter how determined you are to start from absolute zero. You can rename, insert, remove, move, or copy worksheets, because sometimes spreadsheets need a little rearranging to keep the chaos in check.

TIP

You can perform most of these actions on multiple sheets at once. Check out the upcoming "Grouping Worksheets" section to corral them, because herding unruly worksheets one by one is no way to live.

Renaming Excel worksheets

Each tab name can be up to 31 characters long, but how many tabs you can see at once depends on their length and your screen resolution. Cram in long names, and you'll be scrolling like a hamster on a wheel. Keep them short, and you can fit more in view. You have three ways to rename an Excel worksheet:

>> Choose Home ⇨ Format ⇨ Rename Sheet.

>> Right-click a worksheet tab and then choose Rename.

>> Double-click on a worksheet tab.

Any of these approaches enable you to edit a worksheet tab, which must have at least a single character. Press Enter or click any worksheet cell or into the Formula Bar to apply your change or press Escape if you change your mind.

TECHNICAL
STUFF

The following characters are strictly banned from worksheet names: asterisk (*), colon (:), question mark (?), slashes (\ /), and square brackets ([ ]). But beyond that, Excel is surprisingly openminded — even emojis are fair game. Try typing an invalid character, though, and Excel won't bother with a warning; it'll just silently toss your keystroke like it never happened.

REMEMBER

Excel won't let you name a worksheet "History" — not because it has a grudge against the past, but because Track Changes has already claimed it. And while we're at it, each worksheet tab must have a unique name within a workbook — no duplicates allowed no matter how much you want two sheets called "Stuff."

Moving or copying worksheets

You can shuffle worksheets within a workbook just by dragging their tabs to a new spot — if only rearranging your living room were that easy! One of my favorite disaster recovery methods in Excel is duplicating a worksheet — an instant fall-back in case things go sideways. My go-to move for this is holding down the Ctrl (Windows) or Options (macOS) key while dragging a worksheet (or the first worksheet within a group of worksheets) into a new position, creating a copy without the hassle of menu diving. But if you prefer menus:

1. **Right-click the tab of the worksheet you want to move or copy, and then choose Move or Copy. . ., or select the worksheet and choose Home ⇨ Format ⇨ Move or Copy Sheet. . ..**

   The Move or Copy dialog box appears, as shown in Figure 1-6.

2. **To move the worksheet to another open workbook, select from the To Book list, or choose (new book).**

   You can move or copy worksheets only into a new workbook or an existing workbook that is currently open in Excel — no sneaky teleporting into a closed file.

3. **To specify the worksheet's position, choose a location from the Before Sheet list.**

   If no selection is made, the worksheet is moved or copied to appear before the first sheet in the workbook.

4. **To make a copy of the worksheet or worksheets, click the Create a Copy checkbox.**

   Excel moves worksheets to the specified or default location if you do not click Create a Copy.

   Moving or copying a worksheet cannot be undone, but other prior actions remain reversible.

   Take care when moving or copying worksheets between workbooks to prevent data loss. If you choose a destination in the To Book field without selecting Create a Copy, the worksheet is moved, not copied, and removed from the original workbook. The destination workbook becomes active, making it easy to overlook the change. Moving the last worksheet from a workbook causes Excel to close the workbook without a Save prompt.

5. **Click OK to apply the change.**

If you try to move the first worksheet within a workbook but skip selecting an option from the To Book or Before Sheet fields, Excel just shrugs and does nothing — like a cat refusing to come when you call its name.

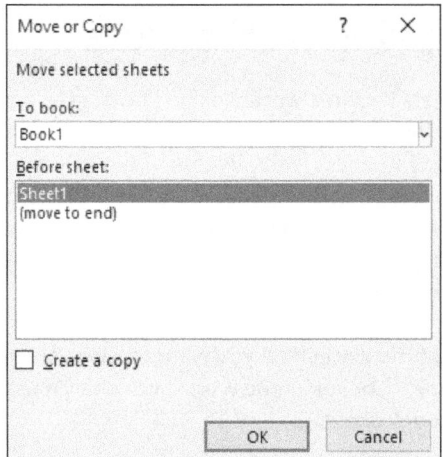

FIGURE 1-6:
The Move or
Copy dialog box.

Adding or deleting worksheets

The number of worksheets that you can add to an Excel workbook depends on your computer's memory — in theory, you can keep adding them until your machine freezes. But just because you can doesn't mean you should. Stuffing a workbook with too many sheets can turn navigation into a nightmare and tank your efficiency. There are four ways to mindfully insert worksheets:

>> Choose Home ➪ Insert drop-down ➪ Insert Sheet.

>> Right-click any worksheet tab, choose Insert, then click OK (Windows) or choose Insert Sheet (macOS).

 >> Click the New Sheet button that appears just above Excel's Status Bar, and to the right of the furthest onscreen worksheet tab.

>> Press Shift+F11 (Windows) or Fn+Shift+F11 (macOS and some Windows keyboards).

**TECHNICAL
STUFF**

Pressing F11 (or Fn+F11 if needed) creates a chart sheet, a dedicated worksheet that stores a single chart within your workbook.

You can delete a worksheet in two ways:

>> Choose Home ➪ Delete drop-down ➪ Delete Sheet.

>> Right-click on a worksheet tab, and then choose Delete.

Blank worksheets that haven't been edited vanish instantly upon deletion, no questions asked. However, if a worksheet contains any edits, Excel puts on the brakes and warns you that it is about to be permanently deleted, asking if you're sure you wish to proceed.

Deleting a worksheet is irreversible — you can't undo it or any actions taken before its deletion. Once it's gone, it's truly gone.

WARNING

Hiding or unhiding worksheets

If your workbook contains two or more worksheets, you can hide all but one. Formulas and features that reference hidden worksheets keep working as usual, since hiding a sheet doesn't impact its functionality. Here's how to hide a worksheet:

1. **Right-click on a worksheet tab (or the first worksheet within a group) and select Hide, or choose Home ➪ Format ➪ Hide & Unhide ➪ Hide Sheet.**

   The selected worksheet vanishes from view, and you can no longer navigate to it — but don't worry, it's just hiding, not gone for good.

You cannot undo hiding or unhiding a worksheet — but you can manually reverse the action by unhiding a hidden sheet or hiding it again.

REMEMBER

Use the following steps to unhide a worksheet within a workbook:

1. **Right-click on a worksheet tab (or the first worksheet within a group) and select Unhide, or choose Home ➪ Format ➪ Hide & Unhide ➪ Unhide Sheet.**

   The Unhide dialog box opens.

   The Unhide command stays grayed out if there are no hidden worksheets lurking in the workbook.

REMEMBER

2. **Select a worksheet from the list and then click OK.**

   To unhide two or more worksheets, hold down Ctrl (Windows) or Cmd (macOS) and then select the sheet names. To display all hidden worksheets, hold down the Shift key while you click on the last worksheet.

In Chapter 11, I discuss how you can hide and unhide worksheets via the Navigation task pane.

TIP

Grouping worksheets

The Group Sheets technique lets you boss around multiple worksheets at once, applying changes across all selected sheets in one go. It's a huge time-saver when you need to make identical updates to several worksheets, whether it's entering the same data, applying formatting, or crunching sets of numbers. You can also use this technique to hide multiple worksheets at once — because sometimes data is better left in the shadows. Here's how:

>> **All worksheets:** Right-click any tab and choose Select All Sheets.

>> **Selected worksheets:**

- **Adjacent worksheets:** Select the first worksheet you wish to group, then hold down the Shift key and click the last sheet in the group.

- **Non-adjacent worksheets:** Hold down the Ctrl (Windows) or Cmd (macOS) key while clicking individual worksheet tabs.

When worksheets are grouped, the word Group appears in Excel's Title Bar, signaling that any changes you make apply to all selected sheets — proceed with caution!

After completing your task, right-click on any worksheet and choose Ungroup Sheets, or simply click on a worksheet tab that isn't part of the group to break up the band, er, selection.

WARNING

Editing grouping worksheets comes with a considerable risk of accidental data loss. Any action performed on one sheet is applied to all sheets in the group, which means you could unknowingly overwrite data in worksheets you're not even looking at. Always double-check that you are working on the intended sheets before making edits while the worksheets are grouped.

Collaborating with Others

Your spreadsheets don't have to be solitary, as Excel makes sharing and collaborating easy. You can email versions back and forth like it's 1999, or you can embrace co-authoring — inviting anyone around the globe to work on your spreadsheet in real time, without the endless email attachments.

Sharing static copies of workbooks

To send a non-collaborative copy of a workbook, choose File ⇨ Share and then choose between the Workbook or PDF options. Workbooks can still be edited in Excel, and changes won't affect your copy. You cannot directly edit PDF files in Microsoft Excel, though. However, in the bonus chapter "Streamlining Data Transformation (available at www.dummies.com/go/excelfd), I discuss how you can extract data from PDF files with Power Query.

Co-authoring simultaneously

Simultaneous co-authoring allows multiple users to work on the same workbook at the same time, making collaboration easy. However, not every workbook is a good candidate. Workbooks containing any of the following features cannot be co-authored:

>> Workbooks saved locally (as opposed to OneDrive or SharePoint)

>> Macros (see Chapter 16)

>> Worksheet or workbook protection (Chapter 14)

>> Legacy data connections (OLAP, Query Tables, Linked Tables)

>> Data Model/PowerPivot

In addition, AutoSave must be enabled. Here's how to get started in Excel for Windows:

1. **In Excel for Windows, open the workbook you wish to share.**

2. **Choose File ➪ Share or Share ➪ Share....**

    The Share command appears in the upper right-hand corner of the Excel window.

One or two dialog boxes appear. Choose the option you prefer:

>> **Share:** This dialog prompts you to save the workbook to a Microsoft cloud platform, like OneDrive or SharePoint. After you select a platform and name the workbook, the Send Link dialog box appears.

>> **Send Link:** This dialog box contains three sections:

- **Send Link:** Enter email addresses, draft a message, and control access. Use the Can Edit icon to toggle sharing permissions or click Sharing Settings to limit sharing to specific people, set an expiration date, or add a password.

    The password that you set here applies only to users with whom you share the workbook and is separate from the workbook passwords that I discuss in Chapter 18. Type this password carefully because you won't be prompted to confirm it.

- **Copy Link:** Click Copy to generate a link to the workbook. Use the Anyone With The Link Can Edit option to manage permissions.

- **Send a Copy:** Choose Excel workbook to share a noncollaborative copy or send the workbook as a PDF.

REMEMBER

If you're on a Mac, choose or File ➪ Share ➪ Share or click Share. If necessary, you are prompted to save your workbook to the cloud. After you've done so, choose File ➪ Share or Share again, and then choose a sharing option.

REMEMBER

You can spy on changes made by others in real time. Excel highlights the cells being edited and shows the name of the editor. If you want to take control later, in Windows choose File ➪ Info ➪ Manage Workbook ➪ Manage Access to update permissions or stop sharing. In macOS, a Manage Access command may appear on the Share menu, or you may have to manage access via OneDrive.

Commenting collectively

Comments let you leave your brilliant thoughts in a spreadsheet and even invite others to chime in. Here's how to add one:

1. **Use one of these methods:**

   - Right-click on a cell and select New Comment.

   - Choose Review ➪ New Comment.

   - Click New in the Comments task pane (choose Review ➪ Show Comments if needed).

   A comment box appears on the worksheet grid, or in the Comments task pane.

2. **Type your message and then click Post Comment or press Ctrl+Enter.**

   To bring someone into the discussion, use an @mention by typing @ followed by their name. If they do not have access, Excel prompts you to share the workbook with them.

REMEMBER

Your workbook must be saved to OneDrive or SharePoint for @mentions to work.

When a comment is added, a purple indicator appears in the top-right corner of the cell. Hover over or click the cell to display the comment. Any user can add a reply to an existing comment. Replies are threaded, and each comment or reply is tagged with the author's name, helping collaborators track who said what and when.

To view all comments in a workbook, choose Review ➪ Show Comments or click the Comments button in the upper right-hand corner of Excel. The Comments task pane appears, listing all comments and replies. Click a comment to activate the corresponding cell.

Use any of the following methods to edit a comment:

>> Hover over the cell that contains a comment, and then click Edit Comment.

>> Select a comment from the Comments task pane, and then click Edit Comment.

>> Right-click the underlying cell, and then choose Edit Comment from the context menu.

To mark a comment as resolved, click More Thread Options within the comment or Comments task pane, and then choose Resolve Thread. The in-cell comment indicator turns gray, and the comment is marked as Resolved in the Comment task pane. This keeps the discussion history intact while distinguishing it from active conversations. Click Reopen (which looks like the Undo command) to reactivate a comment.

To delete a comment:

>> Hover over the cell that contains a comment, click More Thread Options then choose Delete Comment.

>> Select a comment from the Comments task pane, choose More Thread Options, and then click Delete Comment.

>> Right-click on the underlying cell, and then choose Delete Comment.

>> Click Delete Thread on a resolved comment in the Comments task pane

TIP

You can filter comments by @mentions, active threads, or resolved threads using the Filter button at the top of the Comments task pane.

NOTES VERSUS COMMENTS

In the good old days of Excel, what's now known as Notes used to be Comments. But here's the catch — Notes are one-way messages, like a sticky note that can't argue back, while Comments let you actually have a conversation. You can tell them apart by their indicators: Active Comments have a purple flag in the top-right corner of the cell, while Notes sport a red triangle in the top-left. Resolved Comments have a gray flag.

To manage your Comments and Notes, head to the Review tab on the ribbon. To upgrade your Notes to Comments, choose Review ➪ Notes ➪ Convert To Comments. To print all Comments and Notes, choose Page Layout ➪ Print Titles, select from the Comments and Notes field of the Sheet tab of the Page Setup dialog box, and then click Print.

IN THIS CHAPTER

» **Performing mathematical operations**

» **Contrasting cell reference types**

» **Filling cells with formulas**

» **Summing and averaging**

» **Finding lowest and highest values**

Chapter **2**

Carrying Out Basic Calculations

Quick question: "Why did the telephone operator break up with the calculator? Because it just couldn't handle the long distance!" But don't worry — understanding operators in Excel doesn't cost a quarter!

Operators are essential for calculating and analyzing data, but misapplying an operator may have your formula dialing — er, returning — zero. This chapter covers operators, the symbols that guide Excel in crunching numbers; cell references, which save time and reduce frustration when used correctly; filling cells with formulas — both the hard and easy ways; and powerful statistical worksheet functions, preparing you for analytical adventures in later chapters.

Understanding Operators

As the saying goes, the best place to start is at the beginning, which means the primary use of the = (equal sign). Every formula begins with this character, putting Excel on notice that a calculation is about to happen. If it's missing, Excel doesn't treat the entry as a formula; instead, it sees it as just a series of characters — basically, "Nuthin' to see here, so I'm movin' along."

TIP

To disable a formula without deleting it, type a ' (single quote) before the equal sign to convert the formula into text. This technique also helps preserve leading zeros in a number, ensuring Excel treats the entry as text rather than dropping the zeros.

Analyzing arithmetic operators

Like a DJ throwing down beats, Excel mixes in these characters to make arithmetic happen:

>> **+ (plus):** Addition, for example, =1+1 or =A1+B1.

>> **– (minus):** Subtraction, for example, =5–4 or =A1–B1, and negation, for example, =–8 or =–C1.

>> *** (asterisk):** Multiplication, for example, =10*10 or =A1*B1.

>> **/ (forward slash):** Division, for example, =13/14 or = A1/B1.

REMEMBER

Excel displays the #DIV/0! error value when a formula attempts to divide by zero. I discuss how to handle this situation in Chapter 8 and discuss other error values in the bonus chapter "Ten Frustrating Prompts (available at www.dummies.com/go/excelfd).

>> **% (percent):** Percent, for example, 17% as a cell input or =18% within a formula.

REMEMBER

In Excel, typing the percent symbol in a cell with the General format (the default number format) applies percentage formatting. However, using the percent symbol within a formula converts the number to its decimal form.

Now that you're in the know, there's no need to whip out your cell phone's calculator to crunch numbers before typing them into your spreadsheet. Strange but true — people who don't quite get Excel actually do this!

Comparing values with operators

There's no need to compare yourself to others — you're truly incomparable! But your data? Now, that's a different kettle of fish. Chapter 8 dives deep into logic functions, but I'm listing the comparison operators here to give you a bird's-eye view of all the options in one place. Whether within a logic function like IF or SUMIF, or directly in formulas, comparison operators return either TRUE or FALSE, based on whether the comparison holds. Here's the rundown on comparison operators:

>> **= (equal sign):** Equal to, for example, =A1=B1

>> **> (greater than sign):** Greater than, for example, =A1>B1

>> **< (less than sign):** Less than, for example, =A1<B1

>> **>= (greater than or equal to sign):** Greater than or equal to, for example, =A1>=B1

>> **<= (less than or equal to sign):** Less than or equal to, for example, =A1<=B1

>> **<> (not equal to sign):** Not equal to, for example, =A1<>B1

These examples use cell references, but you can apply these operators just as easily to compare the results of worksheet functions. Who says there's no comparison? When it comes to data, Excel is ready to dig in and determine whether one piece of data is or isn't like the other!

Combining text

Toot, toot! All aboard the data train! We're about to get busy coupling some data together. This section is going to be short and sweet, because there's only one operator to discuss:

& (ampersand): Combines text together, for example, =A1&B1

Think of the ampersand as the connector between pieces of data — it brings together content from worksheet cells, results generated by worksheet functions, text within double-quotes, or even plain numbers. Here are a few more examples:

>> **Inserting text:** Any text that isn't located within a worksheet cell must be enclosed in double quotes. For instance, if cell A1 contains my first name and B1 contains my last name, the formula =A1 & " " & B1 returns David Ringstrom. Similarly, the formula ="Jolly Good Fellow: "&A1&" "&B1 returns Jolly Good Fellow: David Ringstrom — which, at least from a formula stand-point, nobody can deny!

>> **Mixing cell contents and numeric values:** When referencing numeric values, formulas return unformatted numbers. For example, if cell A1 contains 2025, the formula ="Year: " & A1 simply displays Year: 2025. Now, if cell A1 has a quantity of 7 and B1 contains a total price of 37.43, the formula ="Unit Price: " & B1/A1 produces something like Unit Price: 5.347142, as Excel calculates values up to 15 decimal places. Chapter 7 covers the TEXT function, which can help format this output to a cleaner value, such as Unit Price: 5.35.

>> **Mix cell contents and static numbers:** When adding static numbers without leading zeros, you can skip the double quotes. For example, if cell A1 contains 123, the formula =A1 & 456 returns 123456. Easy-peasy! But Excel's handling of leading zeros? Don't get me started. If cell A2 contains an account number like 1000 and you want to append a subaccount with leading zeros, such as

0020, you need double quotes: =A2&"-0020". Without the quotes — =A2&-0020 — Excel returns 1000-20, doing its best to eliminate leading zeros like they're going out of style.

As you can see, the ampersand's job is all about making connections, one formula at a time!

TIP

The & operator is an alternative to the CONCAT and CONCATENATE functions, which Chapter 7 covers in detail. It's a simpler way to link text, numbers, or cell contents without needing a function, making it perfect for those quick data connections!

Linking cells across sheets and workbooks

Home, home on the range . . . whoops, there I go again, oversharing my innermost thoughts! Now, our discussion turns to the operators that connect cells, worksheets, and files. These little connectors are the backbone of linking data across your workbook and beyond, making complex calculations and references a breeze.

Exploring range operators

In Excel, ranges are cell references that span two or more cells. Of the four range operators, you most likely encounter the first two almost daily. The third one arises if you work with formulas that reference Excel tables, which I cover in Chapter 5. The fourth one is so rarified that you can't even see it, and might never have a need to use it:

>> **: (colon):** Indicates a range of cells or worksheets. Some examples include

TECHNICAL STUFF

- **Referencing a range of cells:** =A1:A10 returns the information that currently appears in cells A1:A10 into a range of 10 cells based upon where the formula is entered.

  Cell references such as =A1:A10 are known as *dynamic arrays* or *spilled ranges*, which are covered in Chapter 9. Entering a formula like this into a single cell results in multiple cells being filled automatically.

- **Summing a range of cells:** =SUM(A1:A10) totals the values contained in cells A1 through A10 of the current worksheet.

>> **$ (dollar sign):** Makes formulas transferable through mixed or absolute references. This operator is money — it can save you time (and maybe even money!). It's such a crucial concept that the "Contrasting Cell References" section explores it in detail later in this chapter.

- **, (comma):** Enables you to combine two or more non-contiguous ranges in a single formula, treating each range as a distinct argument for functions like SUM, AVERAGE and so on, for example, =SUM(A1:A10,C1:C10) and =AVERAGE(B2:M2,B12:M12).

- **@ (at sign):** Serves two purposes — to force an implicit intersection in formulas by returning a single value from a range or array and to retrieve data from the current row in an Excel table (see Chapter 5).

TECHNICAL STUFF

Implicit intersection refers to extracting data from a range based on the current position of the formula. In older versions of Excel, when entered in row 1, the implicit intersection formula =A1:A10+B1:B10 is equivalent to =A1+B1; in modern Excel, the formula must explicitly include the @ symbol as =@A1:A10+@B1:B10 to achieve the same effect. Otherwise, the formula adds the values of column A and B together across a dynamic array (see Chapter 9) of 10 rows, regardless of the row in which the formula is entered.

- **(space):** Creates a range comprised of an intersection of common cells between two ranges, for example, =A3:C3 B1:B5 would return the value of cell B3, which is the only cell that overlaps between the two ranges.

In short, range operators enable you to build formulas that reference straightforward cell ranges, merge noncontiguous areas, or pinpoint intersecting cells.

Navigating sheet operators

It's time to get between the sheets! Hey now, not those kind of sheets — I'm talking worksheets! If the previous deep dive into range operators felt overwhelming, I'm happy to report there's only one essential sheet operator to focus on, with a second one that might come in handy:

- **! (exclamation mark):** Indicates a worksheet reference — for instance, the formula =Sheet1!A1 refers to cell A1 on the Sheet1 worksheet, while the formula =SUM(Sheet1!B2:M12) totals the values of cells B2 through M12 on Sheet1.

- **: (colon):** Indicates a worksheet drill-through reference, where a formula refers to the same cell or cells across multiple worksheets. Accordingly, the formula =SUM(Sheet1:Sheet5!B2) totals the values of cell B2 on Sheet1 through Sheet5. You can also reference a range of cells across worksheets, such as =SUM(Sheet1:Sheet5!B2:B12).

As you can see, the ! operator is used to separate worksheet names from cell references.

REMEMBER

If a worksheet name contains spaces, it must be enclosed in single quotes — for example, `='Worksheet Name'!A1` or `=SUM('Worksheet Name'!B2:M12)`. Excel automatically adds these single quotes if you navigate to another worksheet with your mouse, but remember to include them if you're typing a cell reference manually for a worksheet with spaces in its name.

Interpreting workbook operators

Now we're going to hit the links — workbook links, that is. Feel free to breeze past this section if you don't create formulas that reference other workbooks.

A *workbook link* is a reference in a formula that connects to data in another workbook (and yes, folks sometimes confuse workbooks with worksheets). Workbook links create a dynamic connection between files, so formulas in Workbook B that reference cells in Workbook A automatically update to reflect changes in Workbook A.

This brings us to the one set of workbook operators that I want to share the lowdown on: **[] (square brackets).** Workbook names appear within square brackets before a worksheet name, such as `='[Source Workbook.xlsx]Sheet1'!A1`. Notice how both the workbook name and the worksheet name appear within single quotes. This formula returns the value of cell A1 on a worksheet named Sheet1 from a workbook named `Source Workbook.xlsx`. Alternatively, a formula that sums cells B2:M12 from Sheet1 of `Source Workbook.xlsx` takes the form `=SUM('[Source Workbook.xlsx]Sheet1'!B2:M12)`.

TECHNICAL STUFF

Workbook links undergo a bit of shapeshifting depending on whether the referenced workbook is currently open in Excel. The examples above show how workbook links look when the referenced workbook is open. However, if the workbook is closed, the Windows file path appears in the link as something like this:

`='C:\Users\David\Documents\[FruitSales.xlsx]Fruit Sales'!$A$1`

This includes the full path to the file, enabling Excel to locate and pull in data from a closed workbook.

REMEMBER

Some operators serve multiple roles in Excel formulas. For instance, the equal sign (=) starts formulas but also acts as a comparison operator. Similarly, square brackets ([]) offset workbook names, enclose column names in structured references (see Chapter 5), and have yet another use touched on in the "Contrasting Cell References" section later in this chapter.

In short, workbook links enable automatic data transfer between workbooks.

Exploring the Order of Operations

Excel doesn't just calculate formulas randomly; it computes each formula from left to right but deviates as needed to follow the sacred sequence of PEMDAS (Parentheses, Exponents, Multiplication and Division, Addition and Subtraction). This sequence, also known as the order of operations (remember this from high school math?), dictates exactly how calculations are performed in mathematical expressions and formulas. Here's how it works at a high level:

1. **Parentheses:** Excel calculates anything inside parentheses — including worksheet functions — first, ensuring key parts of a formula are prioritized.

2. **Exponents:** Any powers or roots are computed next.

3. **Multiplication and Division:** These operations follow, processed from left to right.

4. **Addition and Subtraction:** Finally, Excel handles addition and subtraction, also from left to right.

By following this sequence, Excel ensures formulas are evaluated systematically, helping you avoid unexpected or, worse, incorrect results.

TIP

To visually track the order of operations, check out the Evaluate Formula feature in Chapter 10.

To apply the concept: imagine you've got $10,000 burning a hole in cell B1, ready to grow at 7% for one year. Follow these steps to create a formula that intentionally computes incorrectly, illustrating just how crucial Excel's order of operations can be:

1. **Enter the word** `Principal` **in cell A1 of a blank worksheet.**

2. **Enter** `$10,000` **in cell B1.**

3. **Enter the word** `Rate` **in cell A2.**

4. **Enter** `7%` **in cell B2.**

TIP

Here's how to input percentages like a boss: type a number with the % sign when entering a percentage — skip the hassle of decimal values like 0.07 and manual formatting. Excel handles both the input and formatting in one smooth move!

TIP

Include the dollar sign and comma as you enter that value to get another two-for-one deal — both entering the number and formatting it in one swift move. Excel handles the heavy lifting, and your $10,000 looks as polished as your investment plan.

5. Enter the words `Initial Formula` in cell A3.

6. Enter this formula into cell B3: `=1+B2*B1`.

Since Excel computes formulas from left to right, you might think it would add 1 and the value in cell B2 (7%) first, then multiply that result by the value in cell B1 ($10,000), returning $10,700. But because of the order of operations, the formula returns $701 instead. Here's why: Excel first multiplies the value in cell B2 (7%) by cell B1 ($10,000), yielding $700, and then adds 1 to that result. This highlights the need for parentheses to ensure calculations flow as intended.

Prioritizing with parentheses

Portions of a formula wrapped in parentheses get the VIP treatment — they're calculated first. Worksheet functions, such as SUM, AVERAGE, or PMT, are also top priority, thanks to their parentheses Remove entourage. To create a beefed-up and accurate version of the formula that we just created:

1. Enter the words `Revised Formula` in cell A4.

2. Enter this formula in cell B4: `=(1+B2)*B1`

This time, the formula returns $10,700. The parentheses force Excel to add 1 plus the value in cell B2 (7%) first, resulting in 1.07. This intermediate result is then multiplied by the value in cell B1 ($10,000), producing the correct answer. Parentheses ensure that Excel processes calculations in the intended order, giving you the expected outcome.

TIP

I rearranged the order of the cell references to demonstrate that the order of operations always takes precedence over Excel's default left-to-right calculation sequence. Regardless of the cell reference order, Excel still follows PEMDAS to ensure accurate calculations, applying exponents, multiplication, and other operations in the correct order before moving left-to-right.

REMEMBER

Users who don't fully grasp the true purpose of parentheses often overcompensate by piling on extra ones, like this: =((1+B1)*B2). In this example, the outer parentheses are unnecessary and can make formulas harder to understand and edit.

Elevating with exponents

Exponentiation is a mathematical operation that raises a number, known as the base, to the power of another number, known as the exponent. In short, the exponent tells you how many times to multiply the base by itself. For instance, the formula =2^3 is equivalent to =2*2*2, with both returning 8. As a reminder, exponents in Excel are represented by the ∧ (caret) symbol.

Join me on a quick side quest to illustrate this concept before diving back into our investment calculations:

1. **Enter the word** Base **in cell D1.**

2. **Enter** 2 **into cell E1.**

3. **Enter the word** Exponent **in cell D2.**

4. **Enter** 3 **into cell E2.**

5. **Enter the word** Static **in cell D3.**

6. **Enter the formula** =2^3 **into cell E3.**

    The formula returns 8.

7. **Enter the word** Dynamic **into cell D4.**

8. **Enter the formula** =E1^E2 **into cell E4.**

    The formula also returns 8.

You can now calculate the power of any number by entering new values into cells E1 and E2. "That's fine," you say, "but show me the money!" I hear you! With the side quest complete, exponents can work to grow that $10,000 in cell B1 by 7% per year for 30 years.

1. **Enter the words** Annual Compounding **in cell A5.**

2. **Enter this formula in cell B5:** =(1+B2)^30*B1.

    The formula, which assumes annual compounding, should return $76,122.55. It adds 1 to the value in cell B1 (representing the growth rate of 7%), raises this sum to the 30th power, and then multiplies that result by the initial investment in cell B2. This demonstrates the impact of compounding over 30 years at a consistent 7% growth rate.

The order of operations cuts both ways, as a misplaced exponent can lead to a comically oversized result:

1. **Type** Exponential Error **in cell A6.**

2. **Enter this formula in cell B6:** =(1+B2)*B1^30

    Excel first adds 1 to the growth rate in cell B2 (7%), giving an interim value of 1.07. But next it raises the value in cell B1 to the 30th power — before multiplying by 1.07. This yields a colossal number that could be presented in a couple of different ways:

- **Currency format:** If cell B1 is formatted with a currency symbol, the resulting number starts with $1,070, followed by 118 zeros!

- **Scientific notation:** If cell B1 has the General number format assigned, the result will be 1.07E+120.

To avoid such exponential slip-ups, ensure that the exponent applies only to the 1+B2 portion, not the B1 portion.

Multiplying and dividing with precision

At this point, if you're thinking, "Wait a minute, most investments compound monthly instead of annually," you're spot on. The goal of this section is to build a purposeful progression, giving you a full grasp of how the order of operations works in Excel. Out of necessity, we've already been tackling multiplication and addition, but now it's time to bring in a little division to step things up a notch.

Confession time: I committed what I consider a cardinal sin in Excel by embedding the exponent as a static value in this formula: =(1+B1)^30*B2. Hardcoding the 30 can make it tricky for users to understand the logic and edit as needed.

Using a cell reference for the 30 exponent, rather than embedding it directly in the formula, makes future adjustments easier and provides transparency into what the formula is based on. This approach enhances both flexibility and readability, making the workbook more user-friendly over time. But fear not — clean-up is around the corner in our next iteration, making it flexible and ready for any adjustments you might need:

1. Enter the words `Timeframe (years)` in cell A7.

2. Enter the number `30` in cell B7.

3. Enter the words `Monthly Compounding` in cell A8.

4. Enter this formula into cell B8: `=B1*(1+B2/12)^(B7*12)`.

   The formula, which allows for monthly compounding, should return $81,164.97. This setup takes advantage of compounding each month, slightly increasing the growth over 30 years at a 7% annual rate.

   Time to break it on down:

   a) **Parenthesis:** Excel evaluates the expression within the parentheses (1+B2/12) first.

b) **Division:** Following the order of operations within the parentheses, Excel divides the annual growth rate in cell B2 (7%) by 12 to compute a monthly growth rate.

c) **Addition:** Excel adds the monthly growth rate to 1.

d) **Exponent:** Excel moves to the exponent, which is also enclosed in parentheses.

e) **Multiplication:** The expression (B7*12) multiplies the number of years (in cell B7) by 12, converting it into months. This monthly count represents the power to which we want to raise the monthly growth rate.

f) **Applying the Exponent**: Now that the exponent has been computed, Excel raises (1+B2/12) to the power of (B7*12), giving the compounded growth factor over the entire investment period.

g) **Multiplying the Principal:** Finally, Excel multiplies the result of the exponentiation by the principal amount in cell B1 (for example, $10,000). This yields the final investment value after compounding monthly for the specified period.

Adding and subtracting with ease

So far, our sequence of formulas has demonstrated how addition is handled within the order of operations, but we haven't yet subtracted anything. The series closes out with subtracting our initial investment from the future value we calculated — giving us a clear view of the gravy our future self will be feasting on.

1. **Enter the words** Return on Investment **in cell A9.**

2. **Enter this formula into cell B9:** =B1*(1+B2/12)^(B7*12)–B1, **or if that feels like too much math,** =B7–B2.

   Either way, the formula should return $71,164.97. This result comes from the future value of our investment, $81,164.97, minus the initial $10,000 — a tidy sum for our future selves!

REMEMBER

If you decide to be clever and copy the formula from cell B7 into cell B8, then add -B2, you might get stopped in your tracks with a #NUM! error value. The next section dives into why this happens and shows how creating absolute or mixed cell references can help you sidestep issues like this in the future.

TIP

If retyping the formula isn't on your agenda, click on cell B7, select the entire formula in the formula bar, right-click, and choose Copy. This allows you to paste the formula into cell B8 without triggering auto-adjustments in the cell references — which is what causes that #NUM! error value. Then simply add -B2 at the end of the formula to complete the step.

Contrasting Cell References

Don't be afraid to ask for references — Excel has plenty! In fact, it's got the whole lineup, from free agents to lockdowns. Cell references are typically composed of a column letter and a row number, unless you're a true Excel aficionado who appreciates — and can wrap your head around — the R1C1 reference style! In short, correctly placed reference operators ($ and :) ensure your formulas stay on target, whether you're working with relative, absolute, mixed, or structured references to individual cells or ranges.

TECHNICAL STUFF

The R1C1 style in Excel refers to a cell reference format where rows and columns are indicated by numbers (for example, R1C1 refers to Row 1, Column 1). This format is especially useful for creating dynamic formulas because it allows for relative references by indicating the number of rows or columns from the current cell, such as R[1]C[2] for one row down and two columns to the right.

Recognizing relative references

Relative references, like =A1 or =Sheet1!A1, are the free agents of Excel formulas — they adjust row and column references automatically when you copy a formula to a new location. This feature is helpful, saving you from manually updating countless cells. However, as the previous section illustrates, this convenience can sometimes backfire. For instance, copying a formula from cell B7 to B8 and encountering the #NUM! error value highlights how relative references can produce unintended results.

Mastering mixed references

Unlike people who send mixed signals just to keep you guessing, Excel's mixed references play it straight — they let you lock either the row or the column without the mind games. For example, copying =$A1 across a row keeps a fixed reference to column A; while copying it down a column allows the row number to adjust based on the formula's location. Likewise, =A$1 fixes the reference to row 1 when copied down a column, but the column reference adjusts when the formula is copied across a row.

Applying absolute references

Absolute references are like heat-seeking missiles, locking onto specific cells with precision. Just double-down on those dollar signs to create an absolute reference. For instance, =$A$1 always refers to cell A1, no matter where you copy the formula to within a worksheet. Even better, you don't have to painstakingly insert dollar signs in cell references by hand — there's a keyboard shortcut for that:

1. **Type =A1+A2 in cell B1, and then press Enter.**

2. **Double-click on cell B1 or press F2 (Windows) or Cmd+U (macOS) to edit the formula.**

3. **Select A1 or the entire formula, and then press F4 (Windows) or Cmd+T (macOS):**

   - **First press:** =$A$1+A2 (absolute reference for A1) or =$A$1:$A$2 (absolute reference for A1 and A2).

   - **Second press:** =A$1+A2 or =A$1+A$2 (row frozen).

   - **Third press:** =$A1+A2 or =$A1+$A2 (column frozen).

   - **Fourth press:** =A1+A2 (relative reference).

4. **Press Enter or continue editing.**

REMEMBER

Absolute references without a worksheet name behave relatively when copied to other worksheets. For instance, copying =$A$1 from Sheet1 to Sheet2 keeps it as =A1, referencing A1 on Sheet2, not Sheet1. To ensure accuracy, include the worksheet name in formulas you plan to copy across sheets (for example, =Sheet1!$A$1).

Replicating Formulas

Unlike in grade school, copying your homework — er, formulas — is both expected and encouraged in Excel! As we covered in the previous section, the $ operator ensures that formulas remain intact, even when Excel's helpfulness might otherwise get in the way. There are several efficient ways to transfer formulas from one place to another.

Copying with keyboard shortcuts

Formulas can be transferred between cells with ease:

>> **Copy and paste:** The Copy and Paste commands are on the Home tab. Select one or more cells and click Copy, and then navigate to the new location and then click Paste. To automate this repetitive task, press Ctrl+C (Windows) or Cmd+C (macOS) to copy, and then press Ctrl+V (Windows) or Cmd+V (macOS) to paste.

TIP

To paste like a pro, press Enter — just note that this shortcut clears the clipboard after pasting.

>> **Fill Formula from Above:** Like manna from heaven, press Ctrl+' (apostrophe) to copy the formula or cell contents — without the formatting — from the cell

directly above into the current cell. This action pastes what's in the cell above into the current cell, making it a quick way to replicate formulas or values.

>> **Fill Right:** You've likely been told some version of "You've gotta do right to be right." Select any range of cells that span two or more columns and then press Ctrl+R (Windows) or Cmd+R (macOS) to copy the contents of the first column into the adjacent columns to the right.

>> **Fill Down:** Get down! Yeah, baby! Select a range of cells spanning two or more rows, then press Ctrl+D (Windows) or Cmd+D (macOS) to copy the contents of the first row into the rows below.

Automating with AutoFill

The AutoFill feature in Excel is an often overlooked timesaver with multiple uses across different contexts. This chapter focuses on formulas, so start by setting the scene:

TIP

1. **Select the cell containing the formula you want to copy.**

   Hypothetically, call it cell A1, and say that the formula is =ROW().

   The ROW function returns the row number of the cell where the formula resides. You can also insert a cell reference, such as =ROW(A5), to return the row number of a specific cell.

2. **Choose Home ⇨ Copy or press Ctrl+C (Windows) or Cmd+C (macOS).**

   The cell contents are copied to the clipboard.

3. **Select the cells where you want to paste the formula.**

   If you're still along for the ride in my fever dream, select cells A2:A10 — where hypothetical formulas live their best lives.

4. **Choose Home ⇨ Paste or press Ctrl+V (Windows) or Cmd+V (macOS).**

Four steps, that's not too bad. But to riff off a TV show that originated in 1952, and is back on the air again, "I can copy that formula with one step":

1. **Navigate to cell A1 and then double-click the Fill Handle.**

   The state of cells A2:A10 determine the outcome:

   ● **A2:A10 are blank:** Double-clicking the Fill Handle in A1 has no effect, because AutoFill references the current region, defined as the contiguous block of nonblank cells.

   ● **A2:A10 are nonblank:** Double-clicking the Fill Handle in A1 copies the contents of cell A1 down through cell A10.

2. **Enter a formula in cell B1, such as =COLUMN( ), and then double-click the Fill Handle in B1.**

   The contents of cell B1 are copied down to cell B10. Uh-huh, I know what you're thinking: "Is that two steps or only one?" Well, to tell you the truth, in all the excitement I kinda lost track myself.

The takeaway? Double-clicking the Fill Handle is a huge time-saver. Many users know how to drag the Fill Handle down (say, from B1 to B10), which is fine for a few cells but quickly becomes tedious when copying a formula down dozens, hundreds, or even thousands of rows.

And, as hinted, copying formulas is just one way to use AutoFill. Other uses arise when Excel detects a pattern in two or more selected cells:

» **Number series:** Select cells containing the numbers 1 and 2, then double-click the Fill Handle to create a series. You can also drag the Fill Handle with the right mouse button to reveal the elusive context menu shown in Figure 2-1 — a menu that only seasoned Excel pros know about.

» **Date series:** Select two dates and double-click the Fill Handle to create a date series. Figure 2-1 shows several date-related options that appear when you right-drag the Fill Handle over a date range.

» **Text patterns:** Pick a card, any card . . . I mean, select a month name or day of the week and drag down. Excel will use the Custom List feature (covered in Chapter 4) to populate a series of months or days. Numeric patterns also work — like Day 1, Week 1, or Quarter 1, with or without spaces — to create a series (for example, Day 1, Day 2, Week 1, Week 2, Quarter 1, Quarter 2, and so on).

FIGURE 2-1: Context menu options for the Fill Handle.

Calculating Sums

Cue the ominous shark-movie music: SUM, SUM. . . SUM, SUM! Don't worry — that's not a great white lurking in your worksheet; it's just the function many users rely on most often in Excel. You can apply the SUM function manually or let Excel do the work with the AutoSum command.

Feel free to try these techniques with your own data, but here's a quick way to set up some sample data you can use in this section:

1. **Type 1 in cell A1 of a blank worksheet.**

2. **Type 3 in cell A2.**

3. **Select cells A1:A2 and then drag the Fill Handle down through cell A10.**

   A series of odd numbers from 1 to 19 appears in the cells, adding up to a nice round total of 100.

Computing amounts with AutoSum

Toga! Toga! Okay, that might be a throwback for some, but I couldn't resist it as a lead-in to the Greek letter Σ (Sigma) on the AutoSum command in Excel. You find this command in the Home's Editing group or the Formulas tab's Function Library group. In math, Sigma represents summation, and in Excel it's your go-to for quickly adding up a range of numbers. So whenever you see Σ, think of it as Excel's shorthand for 'Let's add these up!' Here's how to try it out:

1. **Select a range of cells that contain numeric values, such as A1:A10.**

2. **Click the Σ command on the Home tab or press Alt+= (equal sign) (Windows) or Cmd+Shift+T (macOS).**

   The SUM function appears in the nearest blank cell to the selection. For example, =SUM(A1:A10) appears in cell A11.

You can also sum rows and columns simultaneously:

1. **Select cells A1:A10, and then drag the Fill Handle to cell E10.**

2. **Select cells A1:F11, and then use AutoSum.**

   Excel adds totals to cells A11:F11 as well as cells F1:F10.

Totaling with SUM

The SUM function has the following arguments:

» **number1:** The first number, cell reference, or range that you want to reference.

» **number2..255:** Optional additional numbers, cell references, or ranges to include in the summation.

Improving the integrity of totals

Users unfamiliar with Excel often use the SUM function in, shall we say, less than ideal ways. The preferred method is to reference a range of cells, like A1:A10, using a formula like =SUM(A1:A10). A less efficient approach is to reference each cell individually, like =SUM(A1, A2, A3, A4, A5, A6, A7, A8, A9, A10). It may sound dramatic but trust me — I've seen formulas written exactly like this!

REMEMBER

Using cell ranges ensures that any rows inserted between the first and last cell in the range are included in the total automatically. In contrast, listing each cell individually with commas requires manually updating the formula whenever a new row is added to include that row's amount. Even worse, deleting a referenced row replaces the cell reference with #REF!, which must be manually removed.

Although using cell ranges is best practice, there's still some risk: rows inserted immediately above or below the range may be unintentionally excluded from the total. Chapter 10 covers the "Formulas that omit cells in a region" error-checking rule, which may sometimes alert you to potential issues — but in my experience, it's not foolproof. And depending on the size of your data set, you might miss the error alert entirely if it appears offscreen.

You can, however, create a resizable range:

1. **Click on the first row in the range that you are summing, and then choose Home ⇨ Insert ⇨ Insert Sheet Rows.**

   If you're using the sample data from earlier in this section, row 1 is now blank and your amounts span cells A2:A11.

TIP

   For a keyboard-based approach, press Shift+Spacebar to select the row, then press Ctrl+Plus on the number pad (Windows) or Cmd+Shift+Plus (macOS) to insert a new row.

2. **Choose Home ⇨ Format ⇨ Row Height.**

   The Row Height dialog box opens.

3. **Enter 7.5 in the Row Height field and then click OK.**

Row 1 is now half the height of a traditional row, helping discourage users from entering data there.

4. **Click the row just below your range, insert a new row, and change the row height as before.**

If you're using the sample data, the SUM function that originated in cell A11 will now be in cell A13.

5. **Click the cell just below the lower buffer row, such as A13, and then click AutoSum or press Alt+= (equal sign) (Windows) or Cmd+Shift+T (macOS).**

Excel creates a preview, highlighting the range it detects as relevant for summing, marked with a dashed outline to review or adjust before confirming.

6. **Drag the upper selector handle within the AutoSum outline up one cell to include the upper buffer row, and then press Enter.**

The SUM function now has better integrity, encouraging users to insert new rows within the formula range rather than just outside it.

REMEMBER

Solving one problem in Excel can sometimes create another. A green error indicator may appear in the cell containing the expanded range due to the "Formulas referring to empty cells" rule. Chapter 10 explains how to ignore this error on a cell-by-cell basis or turn the rule off entirely.

Adding numbers stored as text

One surefire way to pull your hair out is unexpectedly encountering numeric values stored as text. The SUM function treats these cells as blank, while formulas with arithmetic operators treat them as numeric values.

TIP

Chapter 7 covers the Text to Columns wizard, which has a lesser-known use as a quick way to convert numbers stored as text into numeric values.

Here's a quick example that illustrates the nuance of numbers stored as text:

1. **Enter '1 into cell A1 of a blank worksheet and '2 into cell A2.**

The apostrophe before each number instructs Excel to store the values as text.

2. **Click on cell A3 and either use AutoSum, or type =SUM(A1:A2).**

The formula returns zero.

3. **Enter this formula into cell A4: =A1+A2.**

The formula returns three.

This works in reverse for cells with non-numeric characters. The SUM function still treats such cells as blank, while arithmetic operators referencing them cause formulas to return #VALUE!.

Adding or subtracting dates and times

In Excel, time "began" on December 31, 1899, which it treats as day zero, with January 1, 1900, as day 1. Each day adds 1 to the serial value, creating a system that tracks dates seamlessly. So, when you enter a date like 1/1/2026 into a cell, Excel displays it as entered, but behind the scenes, it gives a sly chuckle, thinking, "Pah! Silly humans, that's actually 46023."

This explains why you might occasionally see a series of seemingly random numbers instead of dates — Excel has simply removed the date formatting. To get your dates back in line, select the cells and choose Short Date from the Number Format drop-down on the Home tab. This drop-down typically shows General unless a different format has been applied to the active cell or selection.

To calculate dates in the future or past, simply add or subtract a whole number. You can also utilize a date-related worksheet function. Some examples include:

>> **TODAY():** Returns the current date, updating automatically each day

>> **NOW():** Returns the current date and time, updating when the worksheet recalculates

>> **DATE(year, month, day):** Enables you to combine separate components into a date

>> **YEAR(date), MONTH(date), DAY(date):** Extracts the year, month, or day from a given date

>> **WEEKDAY(date, [return_type]):** Returns the day of the week (By default Sunday is day 1, but you can adjust the start day.)

>> **EDATE(start date, months):** Calculates a date a specified number of months before or after a given start date

>> **EOMONTH(start date, months):** Returns the last day of the month for a specified start date and months forward or backward

Add 1 to the value returned by EOMONTH to calculate the first day of a month.

I can feel my editor looking askance at this date-related side quest, so to close out, here is a shoutout to other related functions: DATEDIF, NETWORKDAYS, WORKDAY, DATEVALUE, and TIMEVALUE.

Analyzing Data with Statistical Functions

Excel isn't just for tallying expenses or managing inventory — it's packing some serious statistical muscle under the hood. In this section, we dig into the stats functions that help you slice, dice, and overanalyze data to your heart's content. With apologies to my college statistics professor (whose class I somehow survived), this discussion steers clear of the geekier side of stats and focuses on the mainstream analytics to give you a sense of what's possible.

As always, you can crunch your own numbers, but if you don't have any lying around, here's a how to generate a quick data set:

REMEMBER

1. **Type Sunday in cell A1 of a blank worksheet.**

2. **Click once on cell A1, and then drag the Fill Handle down through cell A21.**

   Every day of the week should now appear three times in column A.

3. **Enter your three favorite fruits into cells B1:B3.**

   If you're feeling uninspired, just go with Apple, Banana, and Cherry.

4. **Select cells B1:B3 and then double-click the Fill Handle.**

   The series of three fruits repeats all the way down to cell B21. Sneaky, isn't it?

5. **Enter this formula into cell C1: =RANDBETWEEN(1000,5000)**

   A random number between 1000 and 5000 appears.

TECHNICAL STUFF

   RANDBETWEEN is a volatile function, meaning it recalculates automatically whenever a change occurs anywhere in the workbook. As a result, the contents of cell C1 keep changing as you work through this example.

6. **Select cell C1 and then double-click the Fill Handle.**

   The contents of cell C1 will be copied down to cell C21, creating a random set of numbers you can reference throughout the rest of this chapter.

TIP

   If you prefer to have a static set of numbers to work with, copy cells C1:C21 to the clipboard and then press Ctrl+Shift+V in Windows, or choose Home ⇨ Paste Special drop-down ⇨ Values.

Calculating averages with AVERAGE

As a reader of this book, you know you're far from average. OK, all flattery aside, the AVERAGE function calculates the arithmetic mean by adding up a group of numbers and dividing by the count of those numbers. The AVERAGE function includes the following arguments:

>> **number1:** The first number, cell reference, or range that you want to reference.

>> **number2..255:** Optional additional numbers, cell references, or ranges to include in the average calculation.

Though it may seem a bit ironic, here's how to use the AutoSum command to implement the AVERAGE function:

1. **Enter the word AVERAGE into cell E1.**

2. **Select cell F1, and then choose Home ⇨ AutoSum drop-down ⇨ Average.**

   A default formula, such as =AVERAGE(C1:E1), appears in Excel's formula bar.

3. **Adjust the range by selecting cells C1:C21 and then pressing Enter.**

   The formula =AVERAGE(C1:C21) appears in cell F1, providing the arithmetic mean of the numbers in cells C1:C21.

If you consider yourself a rugged individualist, feel free to type the AVERAGE function directly into a cell or the Formula bar instead.

REMEMBER

Calculating a weighted average

Be prepared — this next formula has some heft to it. A weighted average is like a regular average but with a twist: some values carry more weight, or importance, than others. Instead of just adding up all the numbers and dividing by how many there are, a weighted average considers how significant each value is.

Picture this: you're in a statistics class (of all things), and the grading breakdown looks like this:

>> **Final exam:** Your score of 95 is 40% of your grade.

>> **Homework:** Your score of 90 is 30%.

>> **Group project:** Your score of 85 is 20%.

>> **Class participation:** Your score of 80 is 10%.

In this setup, your final exam grade counts much more toward your overall grade than your class participation. To calculate the weighted average, you multiply each score by its weight, add the results together, and then divide by the sum of the weights, like so:

$$\text{Weighted Average} = \frac{(95 \times 0.4) + (90 \times 0.3) + (85 \times 0.2) + (80 \times 0.1)}{0.4 + 0.3 + 0.2 + 0.1}$$

The result of this calculation is 90, whereas a simple average of 95, 90, 85, and 80 would be 87.5. As you can see, the weighted average reflects the importance of each component.

Now that you've seen this on paper, whether physical or virtual, you can take it to the streets — I mean sheets:

1. **Enter the categories — meaning** `Final exam`, `Homework`, `Group project`, and `Class participation` — into cells H1:H4.

2. **Enter the scores — meaning** 95, 90, 85, 80 — into cells I1:I4.

3. **Enter the weights — meaning** 0.4, 0.3, 0.2, 0.1 — into cells J1:J4.

4. **Select cells I1:I4 and then use the AutoSum command to add the average of the scores to cell I5.**

   The AVERAGE function returns 87.5.

5. **Enter formula into cell J5:** `=SUMPRODUCT(I1:I4,J1:J4)/SUM(J1:J4)`.

   The weighted average formula returns 90, and breaks down as follows:

   - **SUMPRODUCT(I1:I4,J1:J4):** The SUMPRODUCT multiplies corresponding values in up to 255 ranges of cells and then adds up the results. In this case, the scores in cells I1:I4 are multiplied by the weights in cells J1:J4, and then SUMPRODUCT returns the sum of the multiplied amounts, providing the numerator for the division calculation that yields a weighted average.

   - **SUM(J1:J4):** The SUM function adds up the weights in cells J1:J4, providing the denominator for the weighted average calculation.

   This formula calculates the weighted average by dividing the weighted sum by the total weight, giving a balanced result that reflects each score's importance.

Calculating conditional averages

When is an average not so average? When it comes with conditions! The AVERAGEIF function lets you calculate an average for values that meet a single condition. If you're ready to take it up a notch, the AVERAGEIFS function allows you to apply up to 127 conditions. How about them apples?

The AVERAGEIF function includes the following arguments:

>> **range:** Two or more cells to average — because the average of a single cell is simply the value of that cell.

>> **criteria:** Specifies which cells are averaged. This can be text, like "apples"; numbers, like 42 (or "42" if you enjoy typing extra characters); or comparison operators, like ">42" (in which case, the double quotes are required).

>> **average_range:** An optional range of cells to average — Excel uses the range unless you specify otherwise.

Here's a quick rundown:

1. **Enter the word** AVERAGEIF **into cell E2.**

2. **Enter your favorite day of the week into cell E3.**

   TGIF, right?

   Be sure to spell the day of the week in full, with no extra spaces at the end. Functions that rely on matches in Excel are, to say the least, exacting.

REMEMBER

3. **Enter this formula in cell F3:** =AVERAGEIF(A1:A35,E3,C1:C35).

   The formula returns the average amount for your favorite day of the week.

Easy enough, eh? Kick it up a notch by adding a second criterion with AVERAGEIFS, which has the following arguments:

>> **average_range (required):** The range of two or more cells to average

>> **criteria_range1 (required):** The first range where Excel looks for the corresponding criteria

>> **criteria1 (required):** The condition to match in criteria_range1

>> **criteria_range2..127 (optional):** Additional ranges where Excel searches for additional criteria

>> **criteria2..127 (optional):** Additional conditions to apply

To put it into action:

1. **Enter the word** AVERAGEIFS **into cell E5.**

2. **Enter the fruit of your choice in cell E6.**

   Any item that you typed in cells B1:B3 will do.

3. **Enter this formula in cell F5:** =AVERAGEIFS(C1:C35,A1:A35, E3,B1:B35,E5)

   The formula returns the average amount for the fruit of your choice on your favorite day of the week.

Finding the smallest and largest values

It is indeed a small world after all — for the MIN function. I choose to skip the argument breakdown — not because I'm phoning it in, but because MIN uses the same arguments as SUM and AVERAGE. As you'd expect, MIN stands for minimum, pulling the smallest value from a range of numbers. And watch out — a pattern might be emerging here. You can use MINIF to retrieve the smallest value based on a single criterion and MINIFS for two or more criteria, just like AVERAGEIF and AVERAGEIFS. Or go to the other extreme with MAX, MAXIF, and MAXIFS.

You can get more nuanced and retrieve the second smallest or third largest values. For this, you can use the SMALL or LARGE functions. Both functions share the same arguments:

» **Array:** The range of two or more cells from which you want to return the k-th value

» **k:** The position (for example, second smallest, third largest) you'd like to retrieve from the array

IN THIS CHAPTER

» **Formatting cells**

» **Incorporating text boxes and images**

» **Managing rows and columns**

» **Hiding and unhiding worksheets and workbooks**

» **Improving worksheet accessibility**

» **Adjusting page layout settings**

Chapter **3**

Formatting Cells and Worksheets

This chapter dives into the essential tools and techniques for *Extreme Makeover: Spreadsheet Edition*, where drab, lifeless worksheets get transformed into data masterpieces. Inspired by the reality show *Extreme Makeover*, which gave homes (and sometimes people) dramatic overhauls, this edition focuses on giving your spreadsheets the glow-up they deserve. It begins with sprucing up cells to improve readability and dazzle the eye, offering tips on using text boxes to manage wordier rambles and jazzing things up with images and shapes. Formatting often acts as a double-edged sword — solving one problem while introducing others — but the Accessibility Checker helps manage some of these challenges. Later sections tackle the art of hiding (and unhiding) rows, columns, worksheets, and even entire workbooks, because some things aren't meant for prying eyes. The chapter winds up with page layout tweaks that result in polished printouts screaming "I know what I'm doing!"

Applying Basic Formatting Commands

The Font section of the Home tab contains a collection of the most frequently used formatting commands in Excel:

>> **Font drop-down:** Displays a list of fonts available for use in your workbooks.

>> **Font Size drop-down:** Displays a list of font sizes, with the option to type a custom size.

TIP

The Increase Font Size and Decrease Font Size commands, located to the right of the Font Size drop-down, allow you to ratchet font sizes up or down with a single click.

B

>> **Bold:** When your text needs to make a statement, select a range of cells and choose Home ⇨ Bold or press Ctrl+B (Windows) or Cmd+B (macOS).

I

>> **Italics:** Add a touch of flair by applying italics with Home ⇨ Italics or Ctrl+I (Windows) or Cmd+I (macOS).

U

>> **Underline:** Emphasize your data by drawing a line beneath it with Home ⇨ Underline or Ctrl+U (Windows) or Cmd+U (macOS), or to double-down on your data, choose Home ⇨ Underline drop-down ⇨ Double Underline.

>> **Borders:** Set some boundaries around your data with Home ⇨ Borders drop-down, then select a border option. If you need more customization, choose More Borders to open the Format Cells dialog and activate the Borders tab. The Borders command is "sticky," meaning it remembers the last border you applied within the active workbook.

>> **Fill Color:** Add a splash of color to your cells with Home ⇨ Fill Color. Like Borders, it's a sticky command, though it doesn't have a built-in keyboard shortcut.

A

>> **Font Color:** Draw attention by changing the font color of your data with Home ⇨ Font Color.

TIP

A dialog box launcher, labeled Font Settings, appears in the lower-right corner of Excel's Font group on the ribbon. It opens the Format Cells dialog box to the Font tab. Other dialog box launchers on the ribbon provide similar access to additional settings.

If formatting doesn't look right, remember that commands like Bold, Italic, and Underline are toggles. Choosing the command, or pressing the keyboard shortcut, a second time removes the formatting. Another way to remove formatting is to choose Home ⇨ Clear ⇨ Clear Formatting, which removes all borders, fonts, colors, and number formatting, but retains any data or formulas. To have granular control over formatting, see the next section.

Exploring the Format Cells Dialog Box

Excel's ribbon includes commands — and a healthy dose of keyboard shortcuts for Windows users — for common formatting needs. But sometimes you've just got to get down to the nitty-gritty and grab the reins — I mean, fine-tune your formatting. That's where the Format Cells dialog box comes in, giving you control over all the details. Two common ways to open this dialog box are Home ⇨ Format ⇨ Format Cells or pressing Ctrl+1 (Windows) or Cmd+1 (macOS).

Formatting numbers

The Format Cells dialog box comprises several tabs, but most of the tabs are self-explanatory and only worth exploring if the ribbon's formatting commands don't meet your needs. Except for the Number tab, that is. Very often, you may find that what Excel does with your numbers just doesn't match your intent. The Number tab (see Figure 3-1) can help you display numbers the way that you want.

>> **General:** This is the unimaginative blank slate of Excel, where numbers roam raw and unformatted, exactly as they're entered or computed — untamed and untouched by formatting frills.

>> **Number:** Use this format to display digits in their purest form — no currency symbols, no fuss. You can choose anywhere from 0 to 30 decimal places, enable the 1000 separator if you'd like to keep those larger numbers readable, and choose an approach for formatting negative numbers.

REMEMBER

If others will be using your workbook, avoid using red formatting to indicate negative numbers, as this can create accessibility challenges for users with color vision deficiencies.

>> **Currency:** If you're carrying cash, this might be the number format for you. The Currency format lets you specify decimal places, currency symbols, and negative number styles, with the currency symbol positioned right next to the number.

>> **Accounting:** Tomato, to-mah-to, right? Not quite. But unlike Currency, the Accounting format displays the currency symbol aligned to the left edge of the cell and indents the numbers so that the digits align, even if negative values are shown in parentheses.

>> **Date:** Unlike dried fruit, these dates stay fresh! Use this section to display your numbers as actual dates, choosing from a variety of formats (no raisins or prunes involved). Whether you need a short format like "3/15/26" or something more formal like "March 15, 2026" to document the Ides of March, beware — the Date section has you covered.

>> **Time:** If you've got the time, I've got the b . . . best number format for you! All formats include hours and minutes; you can optionally add seconds, AM/PM, or even go full drill sergeant with military time.

>> **Percentage:** This format lets you display interest rates, completion rates, investment returns — so many ways to make your numbers pop.

REMEMBER

Excel makes a distinction between percents and percentages. The Percent Style command, prominently placed on the Home tab, quickly adds a percent symbol but hides all decimal places. If needed, you can then use the Increase Decimal command next to it to reveal decimal places. Alternatively, to format numbers as a percentage with two decimal places via the Ribbon, go to Home ⇨ Number Format drop-down ⇨ Percentage.

>> **Fraction:** This is one of those categories I can't recall ever using in a spreadsheet. The Type list offers nine different fractional formats — ideal if you're calculating your share of a timeshare or divvying up a pizza in complex fractions.

>> **Scientific:** I like to think of this as the format Excel foists on me when I enter, say, a 16-digit number — perhaps a credit card account number. In lieu of sharing my credit card number with you, try entering this number into any unformatted cell: 1234567890123456. The result? 1.23457E+15. Clear as mud, right? Scientific notation is a way to express very large or very small numbers using powers of 10, simplifying calculations and making the numbers easier to read and work with — if you're a scientist, that is.

>> **Text:** This is the format used by two consenting adults who love each other very much — ack! Wrong word! The Text format calls cell contents as it sees it, meaning dates are shown as serial numbers, numbers are unformatted, and formulas are displayed instead of their results.

>> **Special:** These deluxe number formats enable you to transform unformatted numeric values into ZIP codes, phone numbers, and Social Security Numbers.

TECHNICAL STUFF

Number formats visually change what you see in a worksheet cell but don't alter the actual cell content. For example, if you save an Excel worksheet as a comma-separated values (CSV) file with a list that includes ZIP codes or Social Security Numbers, Excel drops leading zeros. Even if the cell appears with the zero in Excel, the CSV file doesn't retain it. Chapter 7 guides you on truly transforming your text to preserve those leading zeros.

>> **Custom:** Hold the pickle, hold the lettuce — you can truly create a number format your way in this section. Custom number formats consist of four segments separated by semicolons: positive numbers, negative numbers, zero values, and text. You don't have to spell out all four formats, though; the previous segment applies to any missing segments.

REMEMBER

Custom number formats are only applied to cells that contain data. Empty cells remain unaffected by the format settings.

Crafting custom number formats

Geekiness alert! If you're not a number formatting enthusiast — like, *really* into formatting numbers — you might want to skip this section, because we're about to dive into some serious details here. Here's a list of some (but not all) of the characters that you can use when rolling your own custom number formats:

>> **0 (zero):** Displays insignificant zeros — also known as leading zeros — when a number has fewer digits. For instance, 000 displays three digits, turning 7 into 007 — elegance worthy of an international spy.

>> **# (hash sign):** Displays only significant digits. For example, #,##0 displays 5 as 5, but 5000 as 5,000 — camouflaging those extra zeros with the finesse of a spy slipping through security.

>> **, (comma):** As shown above, the comma can be used with the hash sign to add a thousands separator, or to scale numbers. For example, the number format #, drops the thousands digits, displaying 10,000 as 10 or 10,000,000 as 10,000.

>> **_ (underscore):** Adds space equal to the width of the next character, commonly for alignment purposes. For instance, _) aligns numbers with parentheses for negative values, mimicking the neat precision of the Accounting number format.

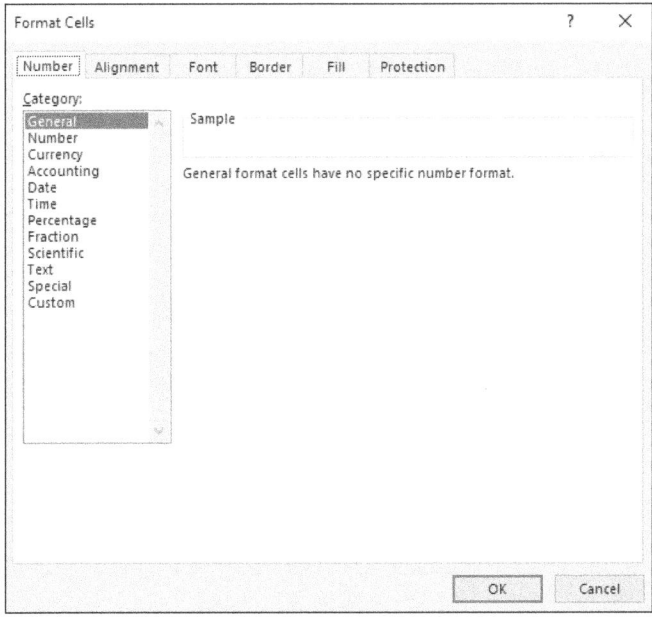

FIGURE 3-1:
The Format Cells
dialog box.

>> **"Text" (quotation marks):** Enclose text in double quotes and use zeros or hash signs to format numbers (such as 0" Years"), which displays 30 Years if you type 30 in a cell. Any formulas referencing cells formatted this way still treat the cell contents as numeric values, not text.

>> **d:** Represents the day of the week within date formats:

- **d:** Returns the day of the month (e.g., 5).

- **dd:** Includes a leading zero when applicable (e.g., 05).

- **ddd:** Displays the first three letters of the day of the week (e.g., Wed).

- **dddd:** Spells out the day of the week in full (e.g., Wednesday).

>> **m:** Represents the day of the month of the year within date formats, or minutes within time formats:

- **m:** Returns the day of the month (e.g., 1).

- **mm:** Includes a leading zero when applicable (e.g., 01).

- **mmm:** Displays the first three letters of the day of the month (e.g., Jan).

- **mmmm:** Spells out the day of the week in full (e.g., January).

>> **hh:mm:** Returns hours and minutes (e.g., 05:27 for 5 hours and 27 minutes).

>> **hh:mm:ss:** Returns hours, minutes, and seconds (e.g., 05:27:38 for 5 hours, 27 minutes, and 38 seconds).

>> **m:ss:** Returns minutes and seconds (e.g., 27:38 for 27 minutes and 38 seconds).

>> **y:** Represents the year portion within date formats:

- **y or yy:** Returns a two-digit year (e.g., 26).

- **yyyy:** Returns a four-digit year (e.g., 2026).

TIP

You can mix and match date format characters. For instance, dddd, mmmm d, yyyy returns Saturday, July 4, 2026, if a cell contains 7/4/2026, while "Balance Sheet As of" mmmm d, yyyy causes Balance Sheet as of December 31, 2026, to appear within a cell that contains 12/31/2026.

>> **[Color]:** Applies color to a number format, say [Blue]0 to format numbers in blue. To take things further, use [Green]0;[Black]-0;[Blue]0;[Yellow]@ to format positive numbers in green, negative numbers in black, zero values in blue, and text in yellow. Common colors include [Red], [Blue], [Green], [Yellow], [Cyan], [Magenta], and [White].

>> **Conditions ([>value] or [<value]):** Sets conditions for displaying specific formats based on values — how fancy is this? For example, [>=1000]0.0,"K";0

displays values 1000 or greater in thousands (so 1.5K appears when a cell contains 1500).

REMEMBER

Excel allows only up to two conditions within a custom number format. This means you can set formats for specific values or ranges but are limited to two conditional options within the format.

Custom number formats are saved at the workbook level. This means that any custom formats you create in, say, Workbook A won't be available in Workbook B unless you copy and paste cells between workbooks that use the format. In the Format Cells dialog box, any custom number formats appear at the bottom of the Type list within the Number tab. As a reference, your custom formats start about five positions below the [h]:mm:ss format.

TIP

The upcoming "Applying Cell Styles" section explains how you can embed cell formatting, including custom number formats, into styles that can then be merged into other workbooks. This allows you to reuse consistent formatting across different workbooks seamlessly.

Applying Cell Styles

The Cell Styles feature provides a straightforward way to apply consistent formatting across a workbook. Admittedly, I overlooked this feature for years, mainly because I hadn't taken the time to explore it fully. Most of the 47 built-in styles seemed unlikely candidates for my own workbooks. Another drawback is that custom styles are confined to the workbook where they're created, though there is a method for transferring styles between workbooks. With that said, there is much more to the Cell Styles feature, shown in Figure 3-2, than meets the eye.

Modifying predefined styles

One often overlooked aspect of the Cell Styles feature is that, while built-in styles cannot be renamed, they can be modified or deleted. In fact, I only discovered while researching this book that changes to the Normal style affect every unformatted cell across the entire workbook. Cells with any existing formatting remain unaffected by updates to the Normal style, though you can manually apply the Normal style to these cells if needed.

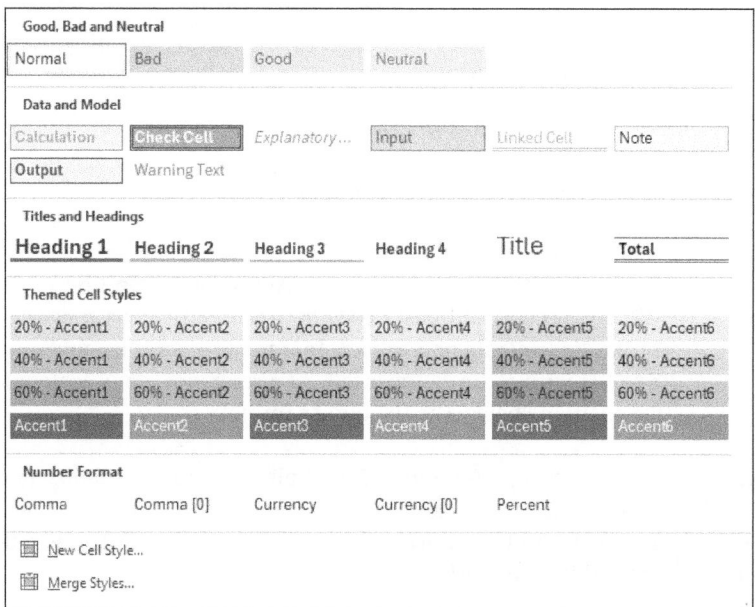

Good, Bad and Neutral			
Normal	Bad	Good	Neutral

Data and Model					
Calculation	Check Cell	Explanatory...	Input	Linked Cell	Note
Output	Warning Text				

Titles and Headings

Heading 1	Heading 2	Heading 3	Heading 4	Title	Total

Themed Cell Styles

20% - Accent1	20% - Accent2	20% - Accent3	20% - Accent4	20% - Accent5	20% - Accent6
40% - Accent1	40% - Accent2	40% - Accent3	40% - Accent4	40% - Accent5	40% - Accent6
60% - Accent1	60% - Accent2	60% - Accent3	60% - Accent4	60% - Accent5	60% - Accent6
Accent1	Accent2	Accent3	Accent4	Accent5	Accent6

Number Format

Comma	Comma [0]	Currency	Currency [0]	Percent

New Cell Style...
Merge Styles...

FIGURE 3-2:
The Cell
Styles gallery.

Here's how to format all worksheets within an Excel workbook by customizing the Normal style:

1. **To modify the Normal style, either choose Home ⇨ Cell Styles, then right-click on Normal, or right-click directly on Normal if it's visible within the Styles group on Excel's Home tab. Select Modify from the context menu.**

   The Style dialog box opens.

2. **Styles are combinations of settings from every tab in the Format Cells dialog box. Here's how to make changes:**

   - **Disabling unwanted style elements:** Deselect any checkbox within the Style Includes list to exclude that type of formatting from the style. This allows you to apply only certain attributes without overwriting other formatting you may have already set.

   - **Customizing a style:** Click Format to open the Format Cells dialog box, make any desired changes across the tabs, then click OK.

3. **Click OK to close the Styles dialog box.**

   The customizations you made now apply to every unformatted cell within the workbook.

   You can modify, but not rename, any of the predefined styles.

REMEMBER

Creating custom styles

If you'd like a style that's entirely your own, Excel allows you to create custom cell styles:

1. **Use either of the following techniques to start a custom style:**

    - **Select Home ➪ Cell Styles drop-down, right-click an existing style, then choose Duplicate.**

       This approach copies the formatting of the selected style, allowing you to apply a custom name.

    - **Choose Home ➪ Cell Styles drop-down ➪ New Cell Style.**

       This approach uses the formatting of the active cell as a starting point, which you can override as needed.

2. **Use the Style Name field to assign a name to the style.**

    You can enter up to 255 characters, though only the first dozen or so display within the Styles Gallery. Hover over the style name to view the full name.

3. **Adjust style elements as needed, or click the Format button to open the Format Cells dialog box and further customize your style.**

4. **Click OK as needed to close the Style dialog box.**

REMEMBER

Custom cell styles are initially only available in the workbook where they were created. The upcoming "Transferring Cell Styles Between Workbooks" section shows how to move styles to other workbooks.

Applying and identifying cell styles

To apply a cell style, select one or more cells and then choose the desired style from the gallery. As you navigate through your workbook, the style applied to the active cell is highlighted in the Styles gallery, allowing you to identify it instantly.

While Excel doesn't allow a direct keyboard shortcut for specific styles, Windows users can say, "Look, Ma! No mouse!" with these steps:

1. **Press Alt+H+J.**

    The Cell Styles gallery opens.

2. **Use the arrow keys to navigate to the desired style, then press Enter.**

You can delete all styles except for Normal from the Cell Styles gallery, though manually removing the remaining 46 might be tedious. Additionally, these deletions apply only to the active workbook.

Transferring cell styles between workbooks

You can transfer custom cell styles to another workbook by copying and pasting one or more cells that use a custom cell style. While this is quick, it does not work for built-in styles. However, customizations to built-in styles can be transferred this way:

1. **Open the workbook containing the cell styles you wish to transfer.**

Styles can only be transferred between open workbooks.

2. **Open the workbook into which you want to transfer cell styles.**

3. **Choose Home ⇨ Cell Styles drop-down ⇨ Merge Styles.**

The Merge Styles dialog box opens.

4. **Choose the workbook you want to merge styles from, then click OK.**

5. **If any built-in styles have been customized, or if any custom styles share the same name between the two workbooks, a prompt asks,** `Merge Styles That Have the Same Names?` **Choose one of the following responses:**

- **Yes:** Overwrites all cell styles, both built-in and customized, in the current workbook.

- **No:** Leaves existing styles intact and only adds new styles not present in the current workbook.

- **Cancel:** Cancels the transfer of styles between workbooks.

The cell styles can now be used in the new workbook. Any differences within the imported styles automatically apply to existing cells with a style applied, including unformatted cells, which default to the Normal style.

Merging Cells

Sometimes folks get wildly excited about corporate mergers, but in Excel, merging cells can open a can of worms. Merged cells present a paradox for Excel users: they're both immensely helpful and incredibly frustrating. Essentially, merging combines two or more worksheet cells into a single mega-cell. The bonus chapter

"Ten Frustrating Prompts (available at www.dummies.com/go/excelfd) covers the dark side of merged cells, so we'll keep it light here. Here's how to use the Merge & Center command:

1. **Drop** `The Greatest Financial Report of All Time` **into cell A1 of a blank worksheet — because every masterpiece needs a grand title, right?**

   If you're feeling more reserved, simply type `Report Title` instead.

2. **Select cells A1:E1.**

   The cells that you select comprise a merged cell.

3. **Choose Home ⇨ Merge & Center.**

   Cells A1:E1 are now merged, and the report title is centered across cells A1:E1.

   Be cautious when using Merge & Center on selections spanning multiple rows or columns. Excel displays a warning because merging non-blank cells in this manner retains only the contents of the top-left cell, discarding data in all other rows and columns within the selection.

4. **To unmerge cells, select any cell within the merged range, and then choose Home ⇨ Merge & Center again.**

   Just like bold, italic, and underline, the merge format in Excel toggles on and off with a single click.

Merging across columns

Excel users often take one germ of information about a feature and then dash off to the races. Case in point: when centering content across multiple rows, it's tempting — but unnecessary — to merge columns one row at a time. Here's a better approach:

1. **Plunk** `Authored by a Most Excellent Spreadsheet User` **into cell A2 — because if we don't toot our own horn, who will?**

   If you'd rather keep it low-key, simply type `Report Subtitle` instead. Don't worry; I won't judge.

2. **Select cells A1:E2.**

   These selected cells form two merged sections.

3. **Choose Home ⇨ Merge & Center drop-down ⇨ Merge Across.**

   Cells A1:E1 and A2:E2 are now merged.

4. **Choose Home ⇨ Center.**

   Merging and centering data across multiple rows requires this two-step process.

The Merge & Center drop-down menu includes two other options: Merge combines cells without centering, and Unmerge Cells separates merged ranges back into individual cells. Simply clicking Merge & Center also unmerges cells if they're already merged. Additionally, you can merge or unmerge cells using the Merge checkbox on the Alignment tab in the Format Cells dialog box. However, when merging cells across two or more rows, you need to use the Merge Across command.

TIP

Check out the upcoming "Wrapping Text" section if you'd like to wrap text within a merged cell — but don't miss the "Tapping into Text Boxes" section after that for a more refined text-management solution.

Center across selection

If the blaring TV commercials are to be believed, light beer has all the taste of "normal" beer but with fewer calories. Think of the Center Across Selection format as the light-beer equivalent of merged cells — all the formatting, but none of the side effects.

Center Across Selection is a formatting option in Excel that centers text across a selected range of cells without merging them. Unlike merged cells, which combine multiple cells into one, Center Across Selection keeps each cell in the range separate. This allows you to visually center content across the selection without the structural issues that come with merging, such as difficulty in sorting, autofilling, or selecting individual cells within the range. Even better, you can apply Center Across Selection across multiple rows simultaneously without losing any data.

So pop that tab, baby, and take a swig of Center Across Selection:

1. **Select the range of cells where you want the text centered.**

   I don't know about you, but I'm gonna select cells A1:E2 and then click Merge & Center to undo the havoc that I wreaked in the previous section.

2. **Open the Format Cells dialog box by pressing Ctrl+1 (Windows) or Cmd+1 (macOS) or selecting Home ⇨ Alignment Settings (the small arrow in the lower-right corner of the Alignment section).**

   Alternatively, if you have some time to kill, you can choose Home ⇨ Format ⇨ Format Cells.

3. **If the Alignment tab isn't already active, click on it.**

4. **Choose Center Across Selection from the Horizontal list.**

5. **Click OK to apply the format and close the Format Cells dialog box.**

This approach provides a visually centered effect while keeping each cell independent, making it a cleaner alternative to merging for certain layouts. The bonus chapter "Ten Frustrating Prompts (available at www.dummies.com/go/excelfd) offers some sharp critiques of merged cells — just in case you're not already convinced of the value of this format.

Wrapping Text

Put the tape and scissors away; we're not talking about that kind of wrapping here. The Wrap Text command enables you to display long text within a single cell by wrapping it onto multiple lines, making it easier to read without spilling into adjacent cells. Users often utilize this feature in conjunction with Merged Cells to display a sentence, paragraph, or more text within a spreadsheet, although the next section of this chapter spills the beans on a far more efficient and elegant approach. Wrapping text is easy as pie:

1. **Select the range for which you want to apply the Wrap Text format.**

   If you're feeling uninspired, type `Dang it, David, now you have me wanting a piece of pie.` into a worksheet cell, and then select that cell.

2. **Choose Home ➪ Wrap Text, or Home ➪ Format Cells --> Alignment Tab, turn the Wrap Text checkbox on, and then click OK.**

   Excel wraps text within a cell and automatically adjusts the row height to ensure that all the text is displayed at once. This feature allows for easier readability of longer entries without needing to manually adjust row dimensions.

Always wrap text for column headings to keep your data organized and readable, while keeping headings in a single row to avoid unwanted side effects with certain Excel features.

REMEMBER

Tapping into Text Boxes

The Text Box feature in Excel allows you to add a floating object — which resembles a scaled-down Word document — that can be positioned anywhere on your worksheet, independent of cell boundaries. This is especially useful for adding commentary, labels, or instructions. Text boxes eliminate the hassle of fitting text into merged cells; you can even choose whether a text box appears only on screen or is included on printouts. Unlike text in worksheet cells, text boxes can be freely moved and resized — a godsend when the boss says, "Hey, add the lyrics to "Blank Space" to that block of text on the Taylor Swift spreadsheet."

To sum up (hee-hee, Excel pun intended), text boxes create a "blank space" that makes adding and manipulating text much easier than trying to work within a worksheet cell. So slap on your favorite friendship bracelet, and brace yourself for the wonders of text boxes:

1. **Choose Insert ⇨ Text Box or Insert ⇨ Text ⇨ Text Box.**

2. **Choose one of the following options:**

   - Click once on your worksheet to create a transparent text box that automatically expands as you type within it.

   - Click and drag on your worksheet to create a text box of your desired size with a solid white background.

   - Hold down the Alt key while clicking and dragging to create a text box that aligns exactly over one or more cells.

3. **Type directly in the text box and adjust font, color, alignment, and other formatting as needed.**

   Select any text within the text box to display a formatting toolbar, select formatting from the Home tab, or press Ctrl+1 (Windows) or Cmd+1 (macOS to open the Font dialog box.

   Unlike merged cells, which require you to enable the Wrap Text format, text wraps automatically within text boxes.

REMEMBER

   To format paragraphs within a text box, right-click inside the text box or on the selected text, then choose Paragraph. Similarly, to create a bulleted list, right-click inside the text box or on the selected text and choose an option from the Bullets submenu.

TIP

4. **To exit the text box, click on any worksheet cell or another object.**

   To reactivate, click once on the text box. Use the selection handles to resize the text box or drag its edge to move it to a new location on your worksheet.

If you really want to get your glam on, text boxes can also be customized with borders, fill colors, and effects, giving them a polished appearance — or not. You do you; mine is not to question why. Here's how:

1. **Click once on a text box to select it.**

    The Shape Format tab appears on Excel's ribbon.

2. **To change the background color, choose Shape Format ⇨ Shape Fill and select an option.**

3. **To add or remove a border, choose Shape Format ⇨ Shape Outline and select an option.**

4. **To really trick out your text box, choose Shape Format ⇨ Shape Effects and then select an option.**

    Options include shadow, reflection, 3-D formatting, and more.

5. **To precisely adjust the size of the text box, use the Height and Width fields on the Shape Format tab.**

Text boxes resize automatically by default when you insert or delete cells beneath them or when you sort or filter data. Additionally, text boxes appear on printouts if they're in the visible area. To control these characteristics:

1. **Choose Shape Format ⇨ Rotate ⇨ More Rotation Options or right-click on the text box and choose Format Shape.**

    The Format Shape task pane opens.

2. **Click Size & Properties to open the Size & Properties page of the task pane.**

3. **To keep the text box anchored in a specific location, expand the Properties section and select Don't Move or Size with Cells.**

    No matter what happens beneath, that text box should stay put.

4. **To prevent the text box from appearing on printouts, clear the Print Object checkbox in the Properties section.**

    This is helpful for creating instructions that the user can view onscreen but won't see on paper.

Inserting Images

Picture this: You want to display an image in your worksheet to jazz things up, much like a teenager hanging posters in their room, or maybe you have a staider purpose in mind. Either way, Excel has you covered:

1. **Choose Insert ⇨ Illustrations (if needed) ⇨ Pictures ⇨ Place in Cell (inserts an image within a worksheet cell) or Place Over Cells (image floats over the worksheet).**

2. **Choose one of the following options:**

   - **This Device:** Opens the Insert Picture dialog box, from which you can select an image that is stored locally.

   - **Stock Images:** Opens the Stock Images window from which you can choose images, icons, cutout people, stickers, illustrations, and cartoon people.

   - **Online Pictures:** Opens the Online Pictures window, from which you can choose images from across the internet.

REMEMBER

Online pictures may be subject to copyright limitations. A Creative Commons Only option appears once you enter a search term, which limits your search to images that are generally free to use, but you should still consider reviewing licensing terms, which may require attribution, a link to the license, noting modifications, or other limitations.

Images placed within a worksheet cell may be too small to be recognizable. To resize such images, increase the row height and/or column width, or merge two or more cells to create a larger space within which the image can appear. To resize an image that floats above the worksheet, click once on the image, and then use the selection handles.

Toggle picture placement between embedding it within a cell or floating above the worksheet by clicking the picture and selecting the Place in Cell icon in the upper right corner of the image, or by clicking within the cell and choosing Place Over Cell. The icons are similar.

Enhancing Accessibility

Accessibility within spreadsheets refers to designing and formatting spreadsheets so that they are usable and understandable for all users, including those with disabilities. Accessible spreadsheets improve readability, navigation, and interaction, making it easier for users with — or without — visual, auditory, motor, or cognitive impairments to work with the content effectively.

Improving accessibility benefits everyone, not just those with disabilities, by enhancing overall usability and clarity. To support this effort, the Accessibility Assistant helps you identify and resolve accessibility issues within your spreadsheets, making your data more usable for everyone, including people with disabilities. This tool scans the active workbook for common accessibility issues — such as missing alt text, merged cells, and low color contrast — and provides step-by-step guidance for fixing them.

Here's how to launch the Accessibility Assistant:

1. **Choose Review ⇨ Check Accessibility or click Accessibility: Investigate when it appears on Excel's status bar.**

   The Accessibility Assistant task pane and Accessibility ribbon tab appear.

2. **Click on any task pane section that displays a numeric count of issues.**

   The task pane highlights the affected area of the workbook and provides suggestions for resolving the issues.

REMEMBER

The Accessibility Assistant is helpful but imperfect, much like the Spelling and Error Checking features. Excel's spell check catches the most obvious errors but may miss contextual ones. For example, the Spelling feature won't flag a typo where "principle" is used instead of "principal" in an amortization schedule, as both are correctly spelled words. Such features in Excel are much better than nothing, but a word to the wise: "trust, but verify."

Key aspects of accessibility in spreadsheets include:

>> **Clear and descriptive column headers:** Proper labeling helps screen readers identify content and structure, while also ensuring that features like PivotTables and other Excel tools function correctly.

>> **Alternative text (alt text):** Adding descriptive text to images, charts, and other non-text elements provides context for users relying on screen readers. To add alt text, select a worksheet object that supports alt text, such as a chart or image, choose Accessibility ⇨ Alt Text, and then add one or two detailed sentences or mark the object as decorative.

REMEMBER

The Alt Text task pane becomes accessible only when a worksheet object is selected.

>> **Limiting the use of merged cells:** Merged cells can disrupt navigation for assistive technology users. The bonus chapter "Ten Frustrating Prompts

(available at www.dummies.com/go/excelfd) offers additional insights on why to minimize the use of merged cells.

>> **Ensuring sufficient color contrast:** Using distinct colors improves readability, especially for users with color vision deficiencies. To select accessible colors, toggle the High Contrast Only option on when choosing fill or font colors.

Adjusting Row Heights and Column Widths

Life is full of competing, perhaps even Byzantine, measurement standards — metric versus imperial, tall coffee versus medium-sized; the list goes on. It's probably no surprise, then, that Excel applies two different measurements for row heights and column widths, each with its own logic — much like so many other choices in life. Here's the lowdown:

>> **Rows:** Row heights are based upon a typographic standard called *points*, which are equivalent to $\frac{1}{72}$ of an inch. This means that the standard row height of 15 points in Excel is equal to just over one-fifth of an inch.

REMEMBER

In Excel, increasing the font size within cells automatically increases the row height to fit the larger text. However, column widths remain unchanged, meaning wider text may spill over into adjacent columns. If you decrease the font size, Excel automatically reduces the row height, but never below the default height of 15. This ensures that the rows are always tall enough for standard readability.

>> **Columns:** Column widths in Excel roughly correspond to the number of characters that can fit within a cell, based on the default font and size. A standard column width of 8.43 typically displays 8 to 9 characters in a cell. To accommodate additional characters, you'll need to widen the column.

TECHNICAL STUFF

Microsoft periodically updates Excel's default font to enhance readability and align with modern design standards. In 2022, Microsoft introduced Aptos Narrow as the default font, allowing slightly more text to appear in a cell without adjusting the column width.

TIP

To set your preferred default font and size, go to File ⇨ Options (Windows) or Excel ⇨ Preferences ⇨ General (macOS) Adjust the Default Font and Font Size fields, then click OK. These settings apply to new workbooks you create from this point onward. To adjust the default column width for the active worksheet, choose Home ⇨ Format ⇨ Default Width, enter a number, and then click OK.

You can let Excel decide how tall your rows and how wide your columns should be, or you can flex your muscle and tell Excel exactly how it's going to be. Adjusting row heights and column widths is an either/or proposition — you can't change both at the same time — but the techniques are so similar that we can cover both in one fell swoop:

>> **Manual Adjustments:** Excel provides a couple of ways to automatically adjust row heights and column widths:

- **Ribbon command:** Choose Home ⇨ Format ⇨ Row Height or Column Width, enter the desired height or width in the dialog box, and click OK. Alternatively, you can right-click on a row or column heading and select Row Height or Column Width to adjust manually.

- **Mouse:** Select one or more rows or columns, then click and hold the bottom edge of a selected row or the right edge of a selected column. Drag to adjust the height or width as needed.

>> **Automatic adjustments:** Excel provides two ways to automatically adjust row heights and column widths:

- **Ribbon command:** Select one or more rows and/or columns, and then choose Home ⇨ Format ⇨ Autofit Row Height or Autofit Column Width.

REMEMBER

You can also adjust row height or column width based on an individual cell, but this can lead to unintended results. For instance, if the selected cell has fewer characters than others in the column, the column width shrinks to fit that cell, rather than expanding to accommodate the cell with the most characters. This may create a disconnect between what you intend for Excel to do and the actual result.

- **Mouse:** Select one or more rows or columns, then double-click the worksheet frame at the bottom of any selected row or the right edge of any selected column. Unlike the Ribbon command, double-clicking ensures that the tallest entry in each row or the widest entry in each column is fully displayed.

TECHNICAL STUFF

If you're aiming to create square cells in Excel, set the column width to 2.14 and the row height to 15. This combination generally produces cells that appear square on most screens, though display settings and font choices may introduce slight variations.

Hiding and Unhiding Rows and Columns

Hidden columns are like household items tucked away in storage — just in case you need that Flowbee, er, data one day! For rows and/or columns you're not ready to delete, the Hide Rows and Hide Columns commands let you keep data out of sight but readily accessible when needed.

Hiding rows and columns

Here's how to hide rows or columns by selecting cells:

1. **Select one or more cells within a worksheet.**

2. **Choose Home ⇨ Format ⇨ Hide & Unhide ⇨ Hide Rows or Hide Columns.**

   The rows or columns containing the selected cells will be hidden.

If step 2 has too many clicks for your liking, try these shortcuts:

» Select one or more rows or columns on the worksheet frame, right-click the selection, and then choose Hide.

» Select cells, rows, or columns, and then press Ctrl+9 (Windows) or Cmd+9 (macOS) to hide rows; press Ctrl+0 (zero) (Windows) or Cmd+0 (zero) (macOS) to hide columns.

Unhiding rows and columns

If the words of that immortal Chambers Brothers song, "Time Has Come Today," have come true and it's time to unhide rows or columns, here's how to get your groove on:

1. **Select surrounding rows or columns.**

   Highlight the rows or columns on both sides of the hidden ones.

2. **Choose Home ⇨ Format ⇨ Hide & Unhide ⇨ Unhide Rows or Unhide Columns.**

   Presto chango! The hidden rows or columns reappear as easily as a magician pulling a rabbit from a hat — unless the column isn't truly hidden, which we'll get to momentarily.

Nonetheless, if time is of the essence:

>> Select an area that encompasses the hidden rows or columns, right-click on the worksheet frame, and then choose Unhide.

>> Select the hidden range and then press Ctrl+Shift+9 (Windows) or Cmd+Shift+9 (macOS) to unhide rows; for columns use Ctrl+Shift+0 (Windows) or Cmd+Shift+0 (macOS).

Die-hard Excel enthusiasts might be thinking, "Wait a minute, didn't Windows 10 usurp the Ctrl+Shift+0 keyboard shortcut?" That's very astute of you! Indeed, the shortcut was overridden in Windows 10 but has since been restored in Microsoft 365.

Hang with me on this next part — it could save you some frustration! Hidden rows and columns have a height or width of zero, which is key when it seems like the Unhide Rows or Unhide Columns commands are pranking you by not revealing the hidden areas. It's not that the commands are malfunctioning; rather, the column widths or row heights might be slightly above zero, creating the illusion of being hidden. When that happens, select an area around the hidden rows or columns and use the steps from the previous section to adjust their row height or column width.

Here's how to unhide only certain rows or columns within a group of hidden rows or columns, while keeping others hidden:

1. **Choose Home ⇨ Find & Select ⇨ Go To or press Ctrl+G (Windows) or Cmd+G (macOS).**

   The Go To dialog box opens.

2. **Type the address of a cell in a hidden row or column (e.g., D1 to unhide column D) and click OK or press Enter.**

   You can also specify a range, like D1:E1 to unhide columns D and E, or 3:5 to unhide rows 3 through 5.

   If the Go To dialog box feels unwieldy, strut your stuff by typing a cell address or range directly into the Name Box and pressing Enter. The Name Box in Excel is located to the left of the formula bar and displays the cell reference or defined name of the currently selected cell, allowing you to quickly navigate to any cell or range by typing its address and then pressing Enter.

3. **Choose Home ⇨ Format ⇨ Hide & Unhide ⇨ Unhide Rows or Unhide Columns or use the unhide keyboard shortcuts from earlier in this section.**

   This lets you reveal specific rows or columns without exposing the entire hidden group.

Grouping rows and columns

Hiding and unhiding columns can be tedious and may inadvertently obscure data when users miss hidden columns within a range. Excel's Group feature addresses both issues, allowing you to hide or unhide columns and rows with a single click or keystroke. Expand (+) and Collapse (−) buttons appear next to or above the worksheet frame when rows or columns are grouped, making it easy to control data visibility.

Here's how to group individual rows or columns within a worksheet:

1. **Select cell(s), row(s), or column(s) within a worksheet.**

2. **Choose Data ⇨ Group or press Shift+Alt+Right (Windows).**

   The selection is grouped, with outline controls appearing in the top left corner, along with a collapse button for the group.

REMEMBER

   You can also select one or more cells instead of entire rows or columns before choosing Data ⇨ Group. In this case, Excel displays a Group dialog box, prompting you to specify Rows or Columns for the grouping.

WARNING

   Excel allows up to eight levels of grouping for both rows and columns. If you try to create a ninth level, you won't see an error prompt; instead, your clicks seem to disappear into the abyss, like your own private version of Dante's *Inferno*.

If you're feeling lucky, you can give Excel a shot at outlining your worksheet:

1. **Select any cell within the area of the worksheet that you wish to group columns and rows.**

REMEMBER

   Most Excel commands, such as Group, operate on the current region, the contiguous block of rows and columns surrounding the active cell, unless you specifically select a range of two or more cells. For more details on working with the current region, see Chapter 17.

2. **Choose Data ⇨ Group drop-down ⇨ Auto Outline.**

   The rows and/or columns within the current region or selection are grouped.

Certain aspects of Excel are just flat-out Kafkaesque, and the Group feature is Exhibit A. One tricky aspect of the Group and Auto Outline commands is that their actions can't be undone with the Undo command. To reverse grouping, you need to manually ungroup the rows or columns:

1. **Select one or more columns or rows within a group.**

2. **Choose Data ⇨ Ungroup or press Shift+Alt+Left (Windows).**

   The selected columns or rows are ungrouped, allowing you to remove specific rows or columns from a group without clearing the entire grouping.

To remove all groups from an area of the worksheet:

1. **Select any cell within the area of where you want to ungroup rows and columns.**

2. **Choose Data ⇨ Ungroup drop-down ⇨ Clear Outline.**

   All grouped rows or columns are removed from the selected area.

WARNING

Here's where things get truly surreal. Not only can you not undo the Ungroup or Clear Outline commands, but they also wipe out the entire undo stack, erasing your ability to reverse any previous actions. And you thought I was being hyperbolic when I tossed around the term Kafkaesque.

Hiding and Unhiding Worksheets

Hiding worksheets is a handy way to protect sensitive data and reduce workbook clutter by tucking away less essential sheets. While there's no limit to the number of worksheets a workbook can contain, at least one worksheet must always remain visible. Here are a couple of ways to hide a worksheet:

1. **Activate the worksheet that you wish to hide.**

2. **Choose Home ⇨ Format ⇨ Hide & Unhide ⇨ Hide Sheet or right-click the worksheet tab, then choose Hide.**

   The active worksheet is hidden, unless it's the only visible worksheet within the workbook. In that case, Excel rewards your transgression with an error prompt.

REMEMBER

You cannot undo worksheet-related tasks, such as hiding worksheets. Unlike some worksheet-related actions, you can still undo prior tasks — but any hidden worksheets need to be manually unhidden.

TIP

Chapter 1 covers how you can group two or more worksheets before performing actions like the Hide command. Grouping lets you apply changes across multiple worksheets simultaneously, streamlining tasks like hiding, formatting, or data entry.

If you want to unhide one or more worksheets, here are the steps:

1. **Choose Home ⇨ Format ⇨ Hide & Unhide ⇨ Unhide Sheet or right-click on a worksheet tab and then choose Unhide.**

   The Unhide dialog box opens.

2. **Select from the Unhide One or More Sheets list:**

   - Click on any worksheet or use the arrow keys to navigate to the worksheet that you wish to unhide.

   - To unhide all worksheets, click on the first worksheet on the list, scroll down to the bottom of the list, and then hold down the Shift key while you click on the last worksheet on the list.

   - To unhide noncontiguous worksheets, hold down the Ctrl key while you select individual worksheets.

3. **Click OK.**

   The worksheet(s) are unhidden.

TIP

Chapter 11 introduces the Navigation task pane, which displays all visible and hidden worksheets. You can easily unhide a sheet by right-clicking on any hidden worksheet name in the pane and selecting Unhide.

REMEMBER

Chapter 14 covers how to password-protect the structure of Excel workbooks. This feature prevents users from making structural changes, such as unhiding worksheets, among other restrictions.

Hiding and Unhiding Workbooks

I won't be offended if you skip over this next section — it's here for the sake of completeness. In some cases, you might want to keep an Excel workbook open but hidden to reduce workspace clutter as you navigate between files. Chapter 16 covers one key example: the Personal Macro Workbook, which stores macros — code routines that automate repetitive tasks — and must remain open for the macros to run. Another instance is hiding workbooks that are referenced by workbook link formulas involving functions like SUMIF or SUMIFS, as these functions may return #VALUE! error values if the linked workbook isn't open in Excel.

It's easy to hide a workbook:

1. **Activate the workbook that you wish to hide.**

2. **Choose View ⇨ Hide.**

   The formal name of the command is Hide Window. Each open workbook is a window in Excel.

REMEMBER

It's easy to lose track of hidden workbooks since they're out of sight. Rest assured, though — Excel prompts you to save any changes within hidden workbooks when you close the application. However, if you save a workbook while it's hidden, it reopens hidden, which can be confusing, especially if a colleague opens it unaware that it's hidden. You might even trigger a minor panic — I've managed to do it to myself!

Unhiding a workbook is just as easy. If the Unhide command on the View tab is disabled, you can stop here — no hidden workbooks are open on your computer. Otherwise, carry on:

1. **Choose View ⇨ Unhide.**

   The Unhide dialog box opens.

2. **Select from the Unhide Workbook list and click OK.**

   Most users see only one hidden workbook — unless they are power users of this feature.

Modifying Page Setup

Page setup in Excel generally refers to adjusting the layout and appearance of a worksheet in preparation for printing. Most, but not all, page setup settings can be applied to multiple worksheets at once:

1. **Right-click any worksheet tab, then choose Select All Sheets.**

   All visible worksheets are selected.

   The Select All Sheets command is one of those double-edged features in Excel that can save you a ton of time — but also cause a ton of grief if not respected. This command enables Group mode, as indicated by the word "Group" in Excel's title bar. Any change you make to one worksheet applies to all worksheets in the group — a huge time saver for setting print options, but pure havoc if you forget that Group mode is still on when making changes meant for just one specific worksheet. Ask me how I know.

2. **Modify the page layout settings as described later in this section.**

Certain settings, such as defining the Print Area and specifying rows or columns to repeat at the top or left, must be set individually for each worksheet. More details on these features are just around the corner in this section.

The Page Layout tab on Excel's ribbon includes several commands related to managing page setup:

TIP

>> **Margins:** Options include Last Custom Setting, Normal, Wide, and Narrow, along with Custom Margins, which displays the Margins tab of the Page Setup dialog box.

Some inkjet printers offer edge-to-edge (borderless) printing, while most laser printers print within ¼ inch of the page edge. High-end models — yes, the fancy ones — can go as close as ⅛ inch.

>> **Orientation:** This drop-down menu lets you toggle printouts between Portrait and Landscape — a choice that ultimately comes down to personal preference.

>> **Size:** Use Page Layout ⇨ Size to pick a paper size. And don't be fooled by the More Sizes command at the bottom in Windows — every size that's fit to print is already right there in the drop-down.

>> **Print Area:** Set or clear the section of the worksheet you want to print. See "Setting print ranges and page breaks" for the scoop.

>> **Breaks:** I hate to disappoint, but there are no smoke, vape, or coffee breaks here — just page breaks. This drop-down menu lets you set or remove them.

>> **Print Titles:** Opens the Page Setup dialog box, which offers far more options than the ribbon-based commands. And yes, it's a bit of an oxymoron — this command lets you adjust way more than just titles.

>> **Width:** Specifies the number of printed pages across that you'd like the print area to span.

>> **Height:** Specifies the number of printed pages that you'd like the print area to span.

>> **Scale:** This field is disabled when either the Width or Height fields are set to anything other than Automatic but otherwise can used to control the percentage that Excel zooms in (or out) when printing.

TIP

There are always exceptions to every rule, particularly in Excel, but I generally recommend keeping the print scale at 64% or higher if you plan to share your printout with others. Their eyes — and probably yours too — will surely thank you.

>> **Print Gridlines:** Turn on this checkbox to include gridlines on your printouts.

>> **Print Headings:** Select this checkbox to include row numbers and column letters along the left and top edges of your printout.

Setting print ranges and page breaks

Print ranges in Excel let you specify areas of a worksheet to be printed, helping you focus on relevant sections and exclude unnecessary data. By default, Excel's print area extends from cell A1 to the last nonblank cell, but you can limit the printable area in two main ways:

>> **Set Print Area:** Here's how to use the Page Layout tab of Excel's ribbon to manage your print area:

1. **Select the range of cells you want to print.**

   Don't be afraid to play favorites here — it's all about saving the trees.

2. **Choose Page Layout ⇨ Print Area ⇨ Set Print Area.**

   Any cells outside this selected range are excluded from printouts.

>> **Page Break Preview:** Alternatively, use drag-and-drop to adjust the print area visually:

1. **Choose View ⇨ Page Break Preview.**

2. **The print area is outlined by a bold blue border, which you can adjust by dragging with your mouse.**

   Page numbers in light gray help you see how pages are divided.

3. **Choose View ⇨ Normal to return to Normal View.**

   Normal View is the default worksheet view, optimized for data entry and editing.

TIP

A third way to view or adjust the cell coordinates in the Print Area field is on the Sheet tab of the Page Setup dialog box, which appears when you select Page Layout ⇨ Print Titles.

Savvy shoppers know to "try before you buy" — a philosophy you can apply to printouts by double-checking settings in two ways:

>> **Page Layout:** Now we're talking about View ⇨ Page Layout (not the Page Layout tab). Confusing, right? Page Layout View gives you a detailed, bird's-eye

view of how your data will look on paper or in PDF, showing cells alongside the actual layout.

>> **Print Preview:** Choose File ⇨ Print to access a motherlode of print settings. Most settings can be modified, except for the pesky print range, and those dang rows and columns that you want to include on every page. Rest assured, the suspense is almost over, that feature is coming up in the very next section.

Adding headers, footers, and print titles

No need to look out below here! We're focused on keeping page headers and footers in line, not bracing for unexpected tumbles — though Chapter 18 covers strategies to protect good spreadsheets from bad outcomes. But I digress . . . again. Ahem.

In Excel, page headers and footers are sections (left, center, right) at the top and bottom of each printed page, providing consistent labels across pages, such as document titles, page numbers, dates, or custom text. Headers appear above the top margin, while footers are below the bottom margin.

To establish headers and/or footers, follow these steps:

1. **Choose Insert ⇨ Header & Footer.**

Excel enters Page Layout mode, displaying the Header & Footer tab on the ribbon. Or, if a dialog box like Figure 3-3 appears, click OK to unfreeze worksheet panes, or Cancel to open the Header/Footer tab in the Page Setup dialog box.

Chapter 4 begins with a discussion on the Freeze Panes feature, used to lock specified rows and columns at the top or left side of the screen.

FIGURE 3-3:
The dreaded
Page Layout
View/Freeze
Panes conflict
prompt.

Microsoft Excel

⚠ Page Layout View is not compatible with Freeze Panes. If you continue, the panes on this sheet will be unfrozen. Would you like to continue?

OK   Cancel

2. **The next steps depend on what's on your screen:**

- **Header & Footer ribbon tab:** If you're new to Excel, restoring frozen worksheet panes may be a minor trade-off for header/footer access:

  1. **Click Add Header at the top to show three header sections.**

  2. **Select the section where you'd like to place a header.**

  3. **Use commands from the Header & Footer tab:**

- **Header:** A list of predefined headers. Options with commas span multiple sections.

- **Footer:** Mirrors header options but inserts content into footer sections.

- **Page Number:** Inserts the &[Page] placeholder for page numbers; you can add text around it, e.g. Page &[Page].

- **Page Numbers:** Inserts the &[Pages] placeholder, which show the total number of pages of the printout, and can be combined with the Page Number placeholder, e.g. Page &[Page] of &[Pages].

- **Current Date:** Inserts &[Date] placeholder, which displays the date that the printout was created.

- **Current Time:** Inserts the &[Time] placeholder, which displays the time that the printout was created.

TIP

  Consider adding both date and time for clarity — for instance, &[Date] - &[Time] will place a dash between the date and time.

- **File Path:** Inserts the &[Path]&[File] placeholders, which together display the file path and file name of the workbook on the printout.

- **File Name:** Inserts the &[File] placeholder, which displays the workbook name on the printout.

- **Sheet Name:** Inserts the &[Tab] placeholder, which displays the worksheet name on the printout.

REMEMBER

  Add a space or wrap the &[Tab] placeholder in parentheses/square brackets to separate it from other text.

- **Picture:** Adds the &[Picture] placeholder for logos or watermarks, covered in the next section.

- **Page Setup dialog box:** The Header/Footer tab offers the same functionality as the Headers & Footers ribbon, albeit in a more inscrutable form. For instance, the Header and Footer fields offer the same predefined headers and footers. Click Custom Header to display the Header dialog box, which has buttons that correspond to the ribbon commands, and insert the same place holders — Custom Footer works in the same fashion.

Inserting pictures and watermarks

To add a dash of flair to your headers and footers, why not throw in a logo or even a watermark? Yes, you can make your spreadsheets look like they came from a high-end design agency (or at least like you spent more than five minutes on them). Inserting pictures here isn't just about aesthetics — it's about making your mark on the page:

1. **Choose Insert ⇨ Header & Footer or Insert ⇨ Text ⇨ Header & Footer.**

   Either the Header & Footer tab appears on the ribbon, Page Layout mode is activated, and the worksheet displays header and footer sections for editing, or the prompt shown in Figure 3-3 appears. Click Cancel to preserve your frozen panes by proceeding via the Page Setup dialog box.

2. **The next step depends on your current view:**

   - **Header & Footer ribbon tab:** Choose Picture.
   - **Page Setup dialog box:** Click Insert Picture.

     Either option summons the Insert Pictures window, like summoning a trusty a sidekick.

3. **Select a location from the Insert Pictures window and then browse for the picture you wish to use.**

   The &[Picture] placeholder marks the spot in your header or footer.

   Sadly, Excel guards your image's identity like a secret handshake — you won't be able to recognize it later without visiting File ⇨ Print for a preview.

   REMEMBER

4. **To customize the image, the next step will depend on your current view:**

   - **Header & Footer ribbon tab:** Choose Header & Footer ⇨ Format Picture.
   - **Page Setup dialog box:** Click Format Picture.

   You can now carry out one or both of the following actions:

   - **Resize image:** By default, the picture is inserted at full scale, which may overlap data outside the header. Use the Size options in the Format Picture dialog box to adjust the dimensions.

- **Create watermark:** Activate the Picture tab, and feel free to laugh maniacally as you bellow, "Wipeout!" — ahem, or just select Washout from the Color field (Windows) or Color Mode field (macOS) and click OK. Theatrics aside, your watermark adds a polished and professional touch.

5. **Preview your masterpiece by choosing File ⇨ Print and then bask in the glory of your well-placed image.**

REMEMBER

Images added to worksheet headers and footers are only visible in Print Preview and Page Layout mode; they remain hidden in Normal and Page Break Preview modes.

TIP

To remove the image or watermark, just delete the &[Picture] placeholder from its header or footer field.

IN THIS CHAPTER

» **Locking your view**

» **Sorting data effectively**

» **Eliminating duplicates**

» **Filtering data efficiently**

» **Tallying with precision**

» **Outlining and subtotalling lists**

» **Jump-starting analysis**

Chapter **4**

Sifting Through Data

R ing-a-ring-of rows (and columns) — Excel helps you pinpoint data without running in circles. You can even keep your pocket full of posies (or PivotTables)! Start with freezing panes to stay grounded, and then tackle the sort versus filter debate. Accelerate your data-sifting process with tools like Subtotal, Remove Duplicates, and Quick Analysis. You can also save time by naming cells and objects, and use the underrated Custom Lists feature to simplify data entry and speed up sorting tasks.

This seemingly nonsensical data set serves as a reference throughout the chapter (don't worry, there's a method to my madness):

1. **Type** Random **and** Data **into cells A1:B1 of a blank worksheet, respectively.**

REMEMBER

Lists should always have a single row of headers. The Sort feature might treat two header rows as one, while other features, like PivotTables and PivotCharts (see Chapter 12), may not support multiline or missing headers.

2. **Type the formula** =RAND() **in cell A2 and then copy the formula down to cell A20.**

Random numbers between 0 and 1 appear in cells A2:A20, recalculating whenever the worksheet changes.

3. Type 1, 2, and 3 in cells B2:B4.

4. Type 10, 20, and 30 in cells B5:B7.

5. Select cells B5:B7, and then choose Text from the Home ⇨ Number Format drop-down.

6. Type a, b, c (lowercase) cells B8:B10 and A, B, C (uppercase) in cells B11:B13.

7. Type #, $, and "Leading Space" (with an actual leading space) into cells B14:B16.

8. Leave cell B17 blank.

9. Type TRUE and FALSE into cells B18:B19.

10. Type the formula =NA() into cell B20.

This sample data set expands further in the chapter to illustrate additional techniques.

Freezing Panes

Feeling lost in your data? With 16,384 columns and 1,048,576 rows per worksheet, it's easy to lose your place. Freezing panes locks rows and/or columns onscreen, keeping you oriented without affecting editing. (For more info on cell protection, see Chapter 14.) Here's how to get your freeze on:

1. Scroll down to row 10 using the vertical scrollbar.

   Rows 10 through 20 now appear without context.

2. Press Ctrl+Home (Windows) or Cmd+Fn+Left Arrow (macOS) to activate cell A1.

3. Click a cell below the row and/or to the right of the column(s) that you want to keep visible, such as A2 or B2.

4. Choose View ⇨ Freeze Panes ⇨ Freeze Panes (Windows) or View ⇨ Freeze Panes (macOS).

   Row 1 stays visible. Positioning the cursor in cell B2 also keeps column A onscreen.

5. To unfreeze panes within a worksheet, choose View ⇨ Freeze Panes ⇨ Unfreeze Panes (Windows) or View ⇨ Unfreeze Panes (macOS).

The View ⇨ Freeze Panes drop-down (Windows) or View tab (macOS) includes two additional options:

>> **Freeze Top Row:** Freezes the first visible row of the worksheet.

>> **Freeze First Column:** Freezes the first visible column of the worksheet.

The View ⇨ Page Layout command unfreezes worksheet panes, although it asks you for permission via a confirmation prompt first.

To freeze panes on multiple worksheets simultaneously, first group the worksheets, as explained in Chapter 1.

Utilizing the Sort Feature

Sort is one of Excel's most-used features, as shown by its representation on the Home tab. Within a spreadsheet, a basic sort refers to organizing data in a specific order based on specific criteria. By default, Excel applies the following hierarchy when sorting in ascending order:

>> **Numbers**: Smallest to largest

>> **Numbers Stored as Text**: Smallest to largest

>> **Dates:** Oldest to newest

>> **Special Characters:** Spaces, non-alphanumeric characters, and punctuation marks in Excel's determined order

>> **Text:** A to Z, case insensitive

>> **Logical values (explored in Chapter 8):** FALSE to TRUE

>> **Error Values:** #N/A, #REF!, etc.

>> **Blank cells:** Always sorted to the bottom of the list

For descending sorts, the order is reversed, except for blank cells, which remain at the bottom.

Getting started with basic sorting

Here's how to get some firsthand experience with sorting mixed data:

1. **Select any cell within cells A1:A20 and then choose Data ⇨ Sort A to Z or Home ⇨ Sort & Filter ⇨ Sort A to Z.**

   Column A is now sorted smallest to largest, causing the data in column B to appear in an even more random order.

2. **Select any cell within cells B1:B20 and then choose Data ⇨ Sort A to Z or Home ⇨ Sort & Filter ⇨ Sort A to Z.**

   Column B is now sorted according to the default hierarchy described earlier, while column A is randomized.

3. **Select any cell within cells B1:B20 and then choose Data ⇨ Sort Z to A or Home ⇨ Sort & Filter ⇨ Sort Z to A.**

   The hierarchy is now reversed.

Feel free to expand on this structure to gain hands-on experience with Excel's sorting nuances.

Resolving sorting mishaps

If a sort goes awry, click Undo on the Quick Access Toolbar or press Ctrl+Z (Windows) or Cmd+Z (macOS). Then try these techniques:

>> **Overcoming blank rows or columns:** Excel sorts data within the current region (contiguous cells around the selected one). For data with blank rows or columns, select the entire range before sorting.

>> **Converting numbers or dates stored as text:** Select the data, choose Data ⇨ Text to Columns ⇨ Finish. Though intended for splitting text into columns, this wizard also transforms data formats.

>> **Unmerging Cells:** Merged cells block sorting, with one triggering a prompt like Figure 4-1. To unmerge, select the range and choose Home ⇨ Merge & Center.

>> **Leading or trailing spaces:** Extra spaces disrupt sorting, but can be removed with the TRIM function (see Chapter 7).

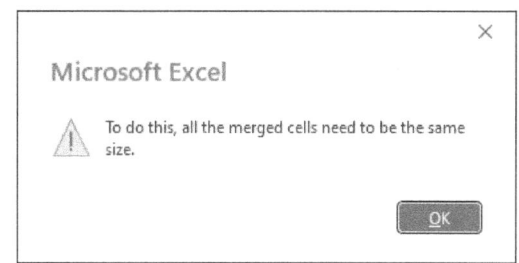

FIGURE 4-1:
The merged cells
need to be the
same size.

Creating custom sorts

Excel allows sorting on up to 64 columns or criteria. Sixty-four! That's the same number of squares on a chessboard — but hopefully your sorting game won't end in a stalemate. Here's how to expand the reference data for this chapter in anticipation of a more complex sort:

1. **Type** Non-text **in cell C1.**

2. **Type** =NONTEXT(A2:A20) **in cell C2.**

   TRUE indicates non-text values in column A, while FALSE identifies text.

3. **Type** Month **in cell D1.**

4. **Type** January **in cell D2 and double-click the Fill Handle to extend the series of months down to cell D20.**

 5. **Select cell C2 and then choose Data ⇨ Sort A to Z or Home ⇨ Sort & Filter ⇨ Sort A to Z.**

   An error prompt states You can't change part of an array. The formula =ISNONTEXT(A2:A20) creates a dynamic array (see Chapter 9), making the data unsortable.

6. **Convert the list to static values:**

   a) **Press Ctrl+A (Windows) or Cmd+A (macOS) to select the entire list.**

    b) **Choose Home ⇨ Copy or press Ctrl+C (Windows) or Cmd+C (macOS).**

    c) **Choose Home ⇨ Paste drop-down ⇨ Values or press Ctrl+Shift+V (Windows).**

   The random numbers in column B are now static values, which is fine for this demonstration.

 7. **Select cells A2:D8, and then choose Home ⇨ Fill Color to apply a color.**

 8. **Select cells A14:D20, and then choose Home ⇨ Fill Color drop-down and select another color.**

You're now ready to explore sorting in greater depth:

1. **Select any cell within A1:D20.**

2. **Choose Data ⇨ Sort or Home ⇨ Sort & Filter ⇨ Custom Sort.**

   The Sort dialog box opens, as shown in Figure 4-2.

3. **If necessary, turn on My Data has Headers.**

   Excel often detects headers but may miss those spanning multiple rows.

4. **From the Sort By drop-down, choose Non-Text.**

   The Sort On field defaults to Cell Values with other options, including Cell Color, Font Color, or Conditional Formatting Icon (referred to in Excel as Cell Icon; see Chapter 13). The Order field defaults to Smallest to Largest, but you can also choose Largest to Smallest, or Custom List.

   TRUE and FALSE are Boolean values equivalent to 1 and 0, respectively.

TECHNICAL STUFF

5. **Click Add Level, and then choose Month from the Then By drop-down.**

   The Sort On field defaults to Cell Values, and the Order field defaults to A to Z since the Month field is text-based.

6. **Click Add Level, and then choose Random from the second Then By drop-down.**

7. **Choose Cell Color from the third Sort On drop-down, and then choose a color from the No Cell Color drop-down.**

8. **Click Copy Level, and then choose the other color from the No Cell Color drop-down.**

   Copy Level provides a quick start for adding similar criteria to a sort.

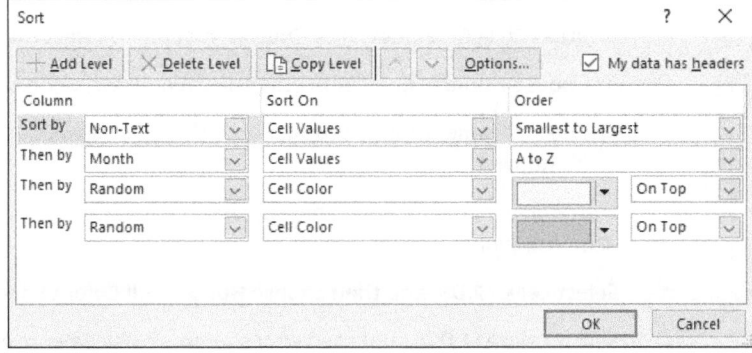

FIGURE 4-2:
The Sort dialog box.

9. Click OK to apply the sort.

If your data looks like Figure 4-3, with months sorted alphabetically, that's expected — for now. No need to worry, we'll get this sorted out in just a moment (pun intended). At least column C and the colors sorted correctly!

Excel often frustrates users by following instructions literally, as seen with alphabetically sorted months.

	A	B	C	D	E	F	G	H	I	J	K	L	M
1	Random	Data	Non-Text	Month									
2	0.785597	#	FALSE	August									
3	0.791547	b	FALSE	December									
4	0.386811	c	FALSE	February									
5	0.690228	B	FALSE	January									
6	0.207419	Leading S	FALSE	July									
7	0.412529	C	FALSE	March									
8	0.782686	A	FALSE	November									
9	0.549716	a	FALSE	October									
10	0.676627	$	FALSE	September									
11	0.104322	10	TRUE	April									
12	0.83831	TRUE	TRUE	April									
13	0.743239	2	TRUE	February									
14	0.852904	1	TRUE	January									
15	0.450305		TRUE	July									
16	0.259514	30	TRUE	June									
17	0.295451	#N/A	TRUE	June									
18	0.584357	3	TRUE	March									
19	0.788767	20	TRUE	May									
20	0.05691	TRUE	TRUE	May									

< > Sheet1 +

FIGURE 4-3: Sort results with the months arranged alphabetically, instead of sequentially.

10. Click on any cell within the list and then choose Data ⇨ Sort or Home ⇨ Sort & Filter ⇨ Custom Sort.

The Sort dialog box opens.

11. From the second Order drop-down, choose Custom List.

The Custom Lists dialog box opens.

12. Select the list that begins with January, February, March and then click OK.

The Custom Lists dialog box closes, and the Order field now displays a list of month names.

13. Click OK to apply the sort.

Your months are now sorted in calendar order as intended. Column C still groups non-text values first, followed by column D sorting by month. Cells D14:D19 show examples of the color order being applied.

Manual sorting can be automated using the SORT and SORTBY functions, covered in Chapter 9.

Leveraging custom lists

If you've dragged the Fill Handle after typing a month or day, you've unknowingly used Excel's Custom Lists — like discovering your favorite fries are from a Michelin-starred restaurant! To be fair, this feature is buried so deeply in Excel's options it feels like you need a diving certification to find it:

1. **Choose File ⇨ Options ⇨ Advanced (Windows) or Excel ⇨ Preferences (macOS).**

2. **Windows users, breathe in a good lung full of air and pull the scroll bar all the way to the bottom.**

   You're in the right place when you see Lotus Compatibility settings — no yoga poses here, just a nod to Lotus 1-2-3, Excel's predecessor.

3. **Click Edit Custom Lists (Windows) or Custom Lists (macOS).**

   The Custom Lists dialog box opens, as shown in Figure 4-4.

   Days and months are listed in read-only form, so you can't add an 8th day of the week (not even for the Beatles' *Eight Days a Week*) or a 13th month.

4. **To create a new custom list, type up to 255 items into the List Entries field (pressing Enter after each one), or select a cell range and click Import.**

5. **Click OK twice (Windows) or close the Custom Lists dialog box (macOS).**

   In Windows, it's a bit like initialling a car rental agreement: the first OK saves your custom list, and the second exits the Excel Options dialog box.

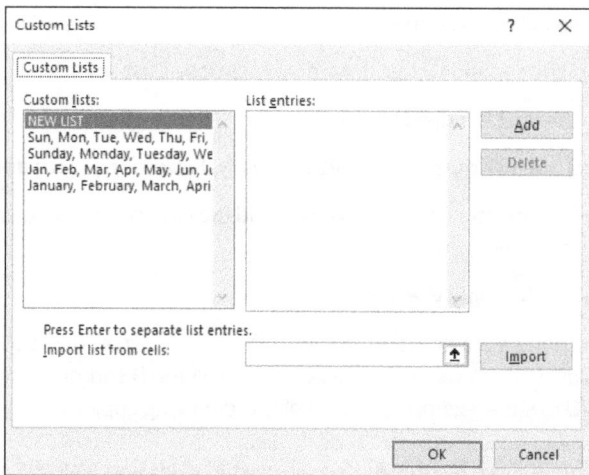

FIGURE 4-4: The Custom Lists dialog box.

You can use custom lists like days or months: Type an item into a cell and drag with the Fill Handle or use them to control the sort order of ranges and PivotTables (see Chapter 12).

Applying sort options

As noted earlier, text-based sorts are case-insensitive, so you may find that sometimes a lowercase instance will lead, while in others an uppercase instance will prevail. To confirm this behavior:

1. **Select any cell within B1:B20.**

2. **Choose Data ⇨ Sort A to Z or Home ⇨ Sort & Filter ⇨ Sort A to Z.**

   The order of uppercase and lowercase letters (A, a, B, b, C, c) is random.

   The Sort A to Z and Sort Z to A commands reset and override any options previously set in the Custom Sort dialog box.

REMEMBER

Here's how to force lowercase letters to appear before uppercase:

1. **Select any cell within your data.**

2. **Choose Data ⇨ Sort or Home ⇨ Sort & Filter ⇨ Custom Sort.**

   The Sort dialog box opens.

3. **Click Options.**

   The Sort Options dialog box opens, as shown in Figure 4-5.

4. **Enable the Case Sensitive option, then click OK twice.**

   The order of lowercase and uppercase letters is now structured.

The Sort Options dialog box lets you sort data from left to right (by column instead of by row). When enabled, the Sort By drop-downs in the Sort dialog box prompt you to select a row number rather than a column heading.

TIP

FIGURE 4-5:
The Sort Options
dialog box.

Removing Duplicates

Out, damned duplicates! With apologies to Lady Macbeth, Excel's Remove Duplicates feature swiftly banishes those pesky repetitions, leaving your dataset spotless and guilt-free. The key word here is *remove*, so be sure to work on a copy of your data if preserving the original list is important.

Removing duplicates from a single column

It's usually not ideal to be seeing double — unless you're trying to escape reality — so here's how to clear the clutter by removing duplicates from a single column:

1. **Select cells D1:D20.**

2. **Press Ctrl+C (Windows) or Cmd+C (macOS) or choose Home ⇨ Copy to copy the selected cells to the clipboard.**

3. **Navigate to cell F1, and then choose Home ⇨ Paste drop-down ⇨ Values or press Ctrl+Shift+V (Windows).**

   A copy of the data from A1:A20 should now appear in F1:F20.

   Always position your cursor within the list to remove duplicates. When pasting data into Excel, all cells are selected automatically; otherwise, selecting a single cell in the list suffices.

   REMEMBER

4. **Choose Data ⇨ Remove Duplicates.**

   The Remove Duplicates dialog box, shown in Figure 4-6, opens.

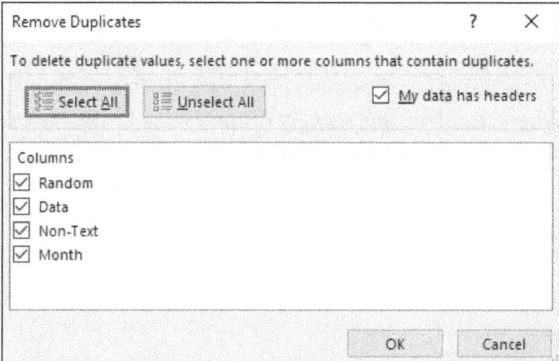

FIGURE 4-6:
The Remove Duplicates dialog box.

5. **If applicable, turn the My Data has Headers checkbox on, and then click OK.**

Excel displays one of two prompts:

- **Summary of Action:** Shows the number of duplicates removed and the count of unique items that remain, with a note about empty cells and blanks.

- **No Duplicate Values Found:** Indicates the list consists entirely of unique items, such as when removing duplicates from a copy of cells A1:A20.

   As noted, Remove Duplicates can shrink your original list unexpectedly. To backtrack, press Ctrl+Z (Windows) or Cmd+Z (macOS), or click the Undo command on the Quick Access Toolbar.

REMEMBER

Eliminating duplicates across multiple columns

Duplicate data sneaks into lists as quickly as weeds sprout in a garden. You won't need a hoe, but removing duplicates across multiple columns demands care to avoid leaving behind any unwanted items. Here's how potential issues can arise:

1. **Copy cells A1:D20 and paste to cell H1 as values.**

2. **Choose Data ⇨ Remove Duplicates.**

The Remove Duplicates dialog box opens.

3. **If applicable, turn the My Data has Headers checkbox on, and then click OK.**

Excel reports that no duplicate values were found because it treats each row as a separate record.

4. **Choose Data ⇨ Remove Duplicates again.**

5. **Click Unselect All, check Non-Text and Month, and then click OK.**

This removes five duplicate rows, leaving fourteen. Columns J and K now contain each combination of TRUE or FALSE and a month name, while Columns H and I show the values from the first instance of each combination.

CROSS REFERENCE

Dynamically remove duplicates in real-time with the UNIQUE function, discussed in Chapter 9.

Finessing the Filter Feature

Modern life might be unfiltered, but your data doesn't have to be. With Excel's Filter feature, you can swiftly cut through the noise to focus on what matters — no earplugs required! In-cell buttons help you temporarily hide rows that don't meet your criteria. Here's a quick tour of the drop-down menu that appears when you click one:

>> **Sorting commands:** Sort A to Z, Sort Z to A, Sort by Color.

>> **Sheet view commands:** Create individualized views for collaborative work on shared worksheets (covered in Chapter 11).

>> **Filtering options:** Clear Filter, Filter by Color, and context-specific submenus like Text, Date, or Value filters.

CROSS
REFERENCE

When Cell Icons (see Chapter 13) are applied in a column, the Filter by Cell Icon option appears below Filter by Color.

>> **Search field and checkboxes:** Type full or partial criteria in the search field and refine your displayed data with checkboxes.

Here's how to finesse and finagle the Filter feature:

1. **Click any cell within cells A1:D20.**

For lists with blank rows or columns, select the entire range instead.

2. **To turn on the Filter feature, choose Data ⇨ Filter, Home ⇨ Sort & Filter ⇨ Filter, or press Ctrl+Shift+L (Windows) or Cmd+Shift+L (macOS).**

A filter button appears at the top of each column in the list.

3. **Click the filter button in cell D1, or select cell D1 and press Alt+Down (Windows) or Option+Down (macOS).**

4. **To narrow your view:**

a) Clear the (Select All) checkbox.

b) Turn on the January, February, and March checkboxes.

c) Click OK (Windows) or Close (macOS).

TIP

Keyboard aficionados can navigate the Filter drop-down menu with the arrow keys, use the spacebar to toggle checkboxes, and press Enter to confirm selections.

5. **Excel hides rows that don't match your selections, leaving only the rows with January, February, and March visible.**

6. **Use the filter button in D1 (see Step 3) and type** A **in the Search field to filter the list for months containing the letter** *a*. **Then enter** p **to narrow the list to April.**

7. **Turn on the Add Current Selection to Filter checkbox, and then click OK.**

   Your visible rows now include January through April. While you could have just enabled the April checkbox, the Add Current Selection to Filter checkbox allows for building complex filtering selections.

8. **Use the filter button in D1, select Filter by Color, and choose an option.**

   Filter by Color allows only one selection per column, unlike other filter settings.

This should give you a solid running start with filtering. From here, the possibilities are endless, and your data stays in focus.

REMEMBER

Hidden rows within filtered ranges remain protected during edits, letting you safely delete, format, or overwrite visible rows.

Clearing filters

Clear the decks — or rather, the filters! Excel's Clear Filters command removes all filtering from your data, restoring visibility to all rows while keeping the filter buttons intact — no mutiny required. Compare this to turning off the Filter feature entirely:

1. **Select any cell within a filtered list.**

2. **To clear filters, choose Data ➪ Clear or Home ➪ Sort & Filter ➪ Clear.**

   All rows become visible, but filter buttons remain.

WARNING

   Don't confuse this with the Home ➪ Clear drop-down, which offers options to reset everything (Clear All), remove styles (Clear Formatting), erase data (Clear Contents), remove commentary (Clear Notes and Comments), or get rid of links (Clear Hyperlinks).

3. **Alternatively, to disable filters, choose Data ➪ Filter or Home ➪ Sort & Filter ➪ Filter or press Ctrl+Shift+L (Windows) or Cmd+Shift+L (macOS).**

   This action removes all filter buttons and restores your data to its unfiltered state.

Reapplying filters

Reapplying sunscreen keeps you protected at the beach — and reapplying filters in Excel is just as vital when your data changes. The Reapply refreshes your filters, no SPF required! It stays disabled in the ribbon until at least one column is filtered. Here's how to give it a whirl (slide whistle optional, but encouraged):

1. **Filter the list in cells A1:D20 for January, February, and March**

2. **Select the first three months in column D, type** December, **and then press Ctrl+Enter.**

All three cells are overwritten simultaneously.

3. **Choose Data ⇨ Reapply or Home ⇨ Sort & Filter ⇨ Reapply.**

The rows containing the edited data (e.g., December) are now hidden because they no longer match the active filter criteria.

REMEMBER

The Reapply command works with all filter types, including colors and cell icons. It's perfect for managing exception lists — adjust colors as items are cleared, and then use Reapply to reveal what's left to tackle.

CROSS REFERENCE

Generate self-updating filter results with the FILTER function, focused on in Chapter 9.

Calculating with SUBTOTAL

Cue the infomercial announcer: "Are you tired of your formulas ignoring hidden rows and spilling the beans on everything? Enter the SUBTOTAL function — a multitasking marvel that knows when to keep a secret!" Seriously, whether you're filtering data or doing math on visible cells only, SUBTOTAL is your go-to for precise, tailored calculations.

Unlike most worksheet functions that act on all referenced cells, SUBTOTAL gives you the power to choose: include or exclude hidden rows. But wait, there's more! It can perform 11 different types of calculations. While there are 255 arguments, you'll typically only use the first two:

>> **function_num:** A code specifying the calculation type. One- or two-digit codes include hidden rows; three-digit codes ignore them. Here are your options:

- **AVERAGE:** Calculates the average of the referenced cells (1 or 101).

- **COUNT:** Counts the number of numeric cells (2 or 102).

- **COUNTA:** Counts all nonblank cells (3 or 103).

- **MAX:** Finds the highest value (4 or 104).

- **MIN:** Finds the lowest value (5 or 105).

- **PRODUCT:** Multiplies all values together (6 or 106).

- **STDEV.S:** Calculates the standard deviation for a sample (7 or 107).

TECHNICAL STUFF

  Standard deviation measures how much values differ from the average — not which relative causes the most family drama!

- **STDEV.P:** Calculates the standard deviation for an entire population (8 or 108).

- **SUM:** Adds up all values (9 or 109).

- **VAR.S:** Computes variance for a sample (10 or 110).

  Variance measures the average distance from the mean, squaring the differences to highlight bigger gaps.

- **VAR.P:** Computes variance for an entire population (11 or 111).

TECHNICAL STUFF

TIP

  Don't worry — typing the opening parenthesis brings up the function_num options, so no need to memorize the list.

» **ref1...ref254:** Up to 254 named ranges or ranges of cells.

Pairing SUBTOTAL with filters

Here's how to use SUBTOTAL with a filtered list:

1. **Clear any existing filters (refer to the "Clearing filters" section earlier in this chapter) or enable filter buttons if needed.**

2. **Enter formulas:**

   a) Enter =SUM(A2:A20) in cell A22.

   b) Enter =SUBTOTAL(9,A2:A20) in cell A23.

   Both formulas return the same amount.

3. **Use the filter button in C1 to display only rows that contain TRUE.**

   The SUM function in cell A22 remains unchanged, while the SUBTOTAL function in cell A23 calculates the total for visible rows in the range A2:A20.

Now bear with me a second — you might be thinking, "Wait, isn't 9 supposed to *exclude* hidden rows?" Rest assured; everything is explained shortly!

Differentiating SUBTOTAL

Unlike most worksheet functions, the SUBTOTAL function adapts to your data's context, taking several factors into account:

>> **Filtered datasets:** With filtered data, SUBTOTAL calculates values only in visible rows, regardless of using one-digit, two-digit, or three-digit function codes. For example:

  ● =SUBTOTAL(9, A2:20) and =SUBTOTAL(109, A2:A20) produces the same result when applied to filtered lists.

>> **Manually hidden rows:** For manually hidden rows (those hidden without filters), use the appropriate function code to include or exclude them. For example, if rows 2 through 5 are manually hidden:

  ● =SUBTOTAL(9, A2:A20) includes *all rows*, hidden and visible, meaning cells A2:A5 are included in the result.

  ● =SUBTOTAL(109, A2:A20) tallies *only visible rows*, excluding those manually hidden, so amounts in cells A2:A5 are not included in the result.

>> **Nonfiltered data:** The SUBTOTAL function in nonfiltered data sets automatically ignores nested SUBTOTAL and AGGREGATE functions, preventing double-counting data — a common pitfall in complex workbooks. For visual clarity, Figure 4-7, demonstrates how the SUBTOTAL function in cell F12 excludes the SUBTOTAL functions in cells F5 and F10.

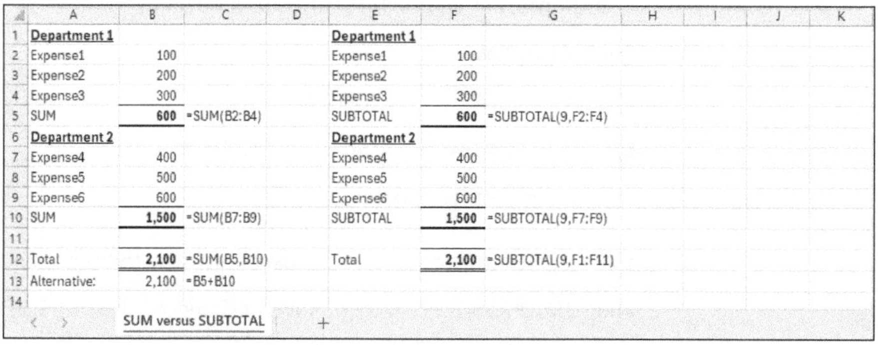

FIGURE 4-7:
The SUM
function versus
the SUBTOTAL
function.

REMEMBER

The SUBTOTAL function guards against formula errors. In Figure 4-7, if B5 excludes B2, both cells B5 and B12 return incorrect results. However, if F5 excludes F2, only F5 is wrong, but while F12 remains accurate — minimizing the impact of errors.

Using the AGGREGATE Function

If you're impressed by SUBTOTAL, "You ain't seen nothin' yet." The AGGREGATE function includes all 11 operations from SUBTOTAL and adds eight more, bringing the total to 19. Here's a breakdown of AGGREGATE's additional capabilities:

>> **MEDIAN:** Returns the middle value in a range or the average of the two middle values for an even number of rows (12).

>> **MODE.SNGL:** Finds the most frequently occurring value in a range (13).

>> **LARGE:** Allows you to specify the k-th largest value in a range (e.g., the 2nd largest) (14).

>> **SMALL:** Returns the k-th smallest value, acting as a counterpoint to LARGE (15).

>> **PERCENTILE.INC:** Calculates the k-th percentile of a range, including the minimum and maximum values (16).

>> **QUARTILE.INC:** Returns the quartile of a dataset, using inclusive percentiles (17).

>> **PERCENTILE.EXC:** Focuses on percentiles between the minimum and maximum, excluding both extremes (18).

>> **QUARTILE.EXC:** Excludes the minimum and maximum values to calculate quartiles (19).

The arguments for the AGGREGATE function depend upon the form that you wish to use. Here are the arguments if you use the Reference form, which references up to 253 ranges of cells:

>> **function_num:** Specifies the operation (1-19).

REMEMBER

As with SUBTOTAL, an onscreen drop-down menu lists the calculation types when you type the opening parenthesis.

» **options:** A single digit number that determines which values to ignore:

- **0 or omitted:** Ignore nested SUBTOTAL and AGGREGATE functions, which means include both hidden and visible rows.

- **1:** Ignore hidden rows, nested SUBTOTAL and AGGREGATE functions.

- **2:** Ignore error values, nested SUBTOTAL and AGGREGATE functions, which also means include both hidden and visible rows.

- **3:** Ignore hidden rows, error values, nested SUBTOTAL and AGGREGATE functions, basically the whole enchilada.

- **4:** Ignore nothing, which means nested SUBTOTAL and AGGREGATE functions are included in the result.

- **5:** Ignore hidden rows, which means only include visible rows.

- **6:** Ignore error values, which means that those pesky #N/A signs won't cause a cascade effect.

- **7:** Ignore hidden rows and error values, meaning visible rows are considered, but error values like #DIV/0! are not.

REMEMBER

A second drop-down menu appears after completing the function_num argument, allowing you to select which values to exclude, if any, for the calculation.

- **ref1. . .ref253:** Up to 253 named ranges or ranges of cells.

Here are the arguments if you use the Array form, which allows you to reference a single range or array, but includes an optional argument used with certain functions:

» **function_num:** Specifies the function to use (1-19).

- **options:** Determines exclusions (0-7).

- **array:** The range or array of data to evaluate.

- **k:** Required for functions like LARGE, SMALL, and percentiles, specifying the rank or position, sometimes referred to as ref2.

By way of example, the formula =AGGREGATE(9,3,A2:A20) sums the values in A2:A20, excluding hidden rows, error values, and nested SUBTOTAL or AGGREGATE functions. AGGREGATE gives you control: sidestep error values, choose to include hidden rows, or calculate percentiles on the fly.

Summarizing Lists with the Subtotal Feature

How often have you manually added subtotals to a list and then calculated the grand total yourself? What if you never had to do that again? Meet the Subtotal feature — an efficient solution for handling totals though it comes with some rough edges in formatting and removing subtotals. With Subtotal, you can:

>> Create an interactive outline for your data.

>> Insert up to eight levels of subtotals within a list.

>> Add page breaks after each subtotal for easier organization.

>> Choose any operation covered in the "Calculating with SUBTOTAL" section.

Alrighty, folks, grab your favorite wrestling trunks — ding, ding, ding . . . *Let's get ready to Suuuuubtooootaaaal!*:

1. **Prepare your data for subtotalling:**

   • Turn off any existing filter buttons in A1:A20 (see the "Clearing filters" section earlier in this chapter) to ensure the data is outlined.

   • Sort column D by month, either alphabetically or logically (see "Creating custom sorts" earlier in this chapter).

2. **Choose Data ⇨ Subtotal.**

   The Subtotal dialog box opens.

3. **Configure subtotal settings:**

   a) **Select Month from the At Each Change In field.**

      Use this drop-down to choose the field you want to subtotal.

   b) **Select Sum from the Use Function field.**

      This defaults to Sum if the last column contains numbers; otherwise, it defaults to Count.

   c) **Check Random and uncheck Month within the Add Subtotal To list.**

      The last column is selected by default.

4. **Adjust options:**

   a) **Leave Replace Current Subtotals on unless adding multiple levels of subtotals.**

   b) **Turn on Page Break Between Groups to insert a page break after each grouping (e.g. Month).**

   c) **Turn off Summary Below Data to place subtotals at the top of each group.**

      By default, subtotals and the grand total appear below each group and the list.

5. **Click OK to apply the subtotals.**

If no filter buttons are present, outline controls now appear on the left-hand side of the screen. Use the + or – buttons to expand or collapse sections or use the subtotal level buttons at the top to manage all sections. Choose Data ⇨ Ungroup Outline ⇨ Clear Outline to remove the outline.

Formatting subtotals

Formatting subtotal rows can take a twist. Unlike the Filter feature, which protects hidden rows, formatting outlined rows affects both hidden and visible rows. But you don't need to format each subtotal row individually. Instead:

» **Option 1:** Filter the list on rows ending with "Total", select and format the subtotal rows, and then clear the filter. Don't worry if subtotal amounts temporarily show as zeros — this happens when detail rows are hidden. The subtotals will reappear when the filter is removed.

» **Option 2:** Collapse the list to show only subtotals, select the amounts, and use the Go To Special command to isolate visible cells:

   1. **Choose Home ⇨ Find & Select ⇨ Go To Special ⇨ Visible Cells Only ⇨ OK.**

      If you're quick on the keys, press Alt+; (Windows) or Cmd+Shift+Z (macOS).

   2. **Apply your formatting as desired, and then click any other cell to finish.**

Both approaches work equally well — pick your favorite!

Removing subtotals

Alas, all good things must come to an end. If you decide to thank your subtotals for their service, and say fare thee well, well, just a couple of clicks are necessary:

1. **Select any cell within the subtotalled list.**

2. **Choose Data ⇨ Subtotal.**

   The Subtotal dialog box opens.

3. **Click Remove All to clear the subtotals from the list.**

WARNING

Brace yourself — we're entering Dr. Jekyll and Mr. Hyde territory. Subtotal starts off as helpful and cheerful, offering to handle your totals, but its darker side emerges when you remove them. This action is irreversible and disables undo for prior actions, so plan carefully.

Jumpstarting Insights with Quick Analysis

"Hey driver, follow that Excel feature — fast!" All car chase scenes aside, the Quick Analysis feature provides a smooth entry point into several powerful analytical tools across Excel:

>> **Conditional formatting:** This feature is so nice I'd love to gush about it twice, but my editor insists I point you to Chapter 13 instead.

>> **Charts:** Detecting a pattern? Yep, Chapter 12 — because, you guessed it, editor's orders.

>> **Totals:** Quick Analysis lets you add sums, averages, and counts, running totals or percentages to your list.

>> **Tables:** "Da rules are da rules," and my editor sets them — for this book at least. For all things tables, see Chapter 5.

>> **Sparklines:** Tiny charts that fit in worksheet cells are covered in in Chapter 12.

Here's a speedy survey of the Quick Analysis feature:

1. **Select two or more cells and then click the Quick Analysis button or press Ctrl+Q.**

   The Quick Analysis Tool appears.

2. **Hover over any option to see a preview of the formatting or command or be bold and make a selection.**

To dismiss the Quick Analysis tool, click any worksheet cell or press Escape.

TIP

If the Quick Analysis button distracts you, choose File ➪ Options, uncheck Show Quick Analysis Options on Selection in the General section, and click OK.

IN THIS CHAPTER

» **Contrasting data ranges and Excel tables**

» **Transforming data ranges to tables**

» **Customizing table styles and formatting**

» **Optimizing formulas and features**

» **Exploring table peculiarities**

» **Reverting tables back to standard ranges**

Chapter **5**

Tackling Tables

T his is the point in the book where the tables are going to turn — literally. If that feels ominous, have no fear; turning your data into Excel tables is almost always an upgrade. While there's one pesky quirk that can crimp your style in certain situations, Excel tables generally automate repetitive tasks, improve spreadsheet integrity, and streamline navigation. Who could ask for anything more?

You likely have a list of data to transform into an Excel table, but if not, here's how to create a reference to use throughout this chapter:

1. **Add headers:**

   a) **In cell A1, type** Month.

   b) **In cell B1, type** Quantity.

2. **Create a list of months:**

   a) **Type** January **into cell A2.**

   b) **Drag the Fill Handle in cell A2 down to cell A13 to autofill the remaining months.**

3. **Generate a series of amounts:**

   a) **Type** 100 **into cell B2.**

   b) **Type** 200 **into cell B3.**

   c) **Select cells B2:B3, then double-click the Fill Handle in cell B3 to automatically fill the series, completing it from 100 to 1200.**

   Excel requires only two cells to identify and replicate a pattern.

TIP

Comparing Data Ranges to Excel Tables

Nonblank areas of Excel worksheets are often referred to as *normal ranges* of cells or data ranges. In this era of "smart" everything, data in normal ranges could be considered "dumb," while data within Excel tables earns the "smart" label. Here's why:

» Formulas or features referencing normal ranges need manual updates when data is added.

» Standard cell references require navigation between sheets and result in unintelligible references that complicate auditing or revising.

» Column headings in normal ranges scroll offscreen unless you use the Freeze Panes feature to lock rows in place (see Chapter 4).

» In normal ranges, updating formulas requires manually copying changes up or down, risking skipped rows and errors.

» Navigating to a normal range of cells often requires switching tabs and scrolling within the sheet to find the desired data.

With just a few mouse clicks — or even faster keyboard shortcuts — you can tackle repetitive tasks and improve data integrity. Excel tables also bring much-needed structure to spreadsheets. Before converting data into a table, ensure it meets these requirements:

» A single row of unique and static column headings (headers in Excel) — formulas are not permitted here.

» Contiguous data with no blank rows, columns, totals or subtotals.

   Data rows within the table can include text, numbers, or formulas.

TIP

REMEMBER

Excel tables can include only a header row, data rows, and optionally a total row. For subtotals, use the PivotTable feature (Chapter 12) or the Subtotal feature with a normal range of cells (Chapter 4).

Creating Excel Tables

Before we go further, I have a question for you: What do you call a table with no legs? A spreadsheet! Rim shot. Don't worry, folks — I'm here for a couple hundred more pages. All jokes aside, here's the process for creating an Excel table:

1. **Click any cell within a normal range of data, such as cell A1.**

2. **Choose Insert ➪ Table from the ribbon or press Ctrl+T (Windows) or Cmd+T (macOS).**

   The Create Table dialog box opens, as shown in Figure 5-1.

3. **If the first row of your data consists of column headings, ensure the My Table Has Headers checkbox is selected.**

REMEMBER

   If My Table Has Headers is left unchecked, Excel adds generic headers like Column1, Column2, etc. For multiple header rows, Excel treats only the first row as column headings; others are part of the data.

4. **Click OK to transform the data range into an Excel table.**

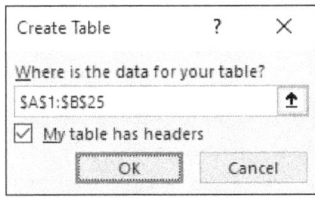

FIGURE 5-1:
The Create Table
dialog box.

When the conversion is complete, several things happen:

» The contextual Table Design (Windows) or Table (macOS) tab appears on the ribbon when your cursor is within the table but may require manual activation.

» A default table style with row banding is automatically applied — see the "Setting default table styles" section later in this chapter to customize it.

>> Filter buttons (Chapter 4) appear in the header row.

>> Column headers and filter buttons replace column letters in the worksheet frame when the header row scrolls offscreen and the active cell is within the table.

Resizing tables

When drafting the initial outline for this chapter, resizing Excel tables didn't make the cut — and with good reason. In most cases, Excel tables automatically expand to include new data added immediately to the right or below:

1. **Click on cell A13 then drag the Fill Handle down to cell A25.**

2. **Select cells B12:B13, then double-click the Fill Handle in cell B13 to automatically fill the series, extending it from 1200 to 2400.**

REMEMBER

Tables do not expand automatically if you bring ranges closer together by deleting rows or columns between them.

If you need to resize a table manually, use one of these methods:

>> **Resizing handle:** Click any cell within the table to reveal a small blue triangle in the bottom-right corner. Drag this handle to adjust the table's size as needed.

>> **Resize Table Command (Windows only):** Choose Table Design ⇨ Resize Table to open the Resize Table dialog box. Enter a new range in the field and click OK. While you cannot change the starting range of the table, you can adjust the ending cell reference.

REMEMBER

There's no need to turn the total row for a table off before resizing — Excel automatically repositions it to follow the new ending cell reference. For more about total rows, see the "Adding Total Rows" section later in this chapter.

Naming tables

What's in a name? Quite a lot — especially for tables. The first field in the Table Design tab, Table Name, contains a generic name, such as Table1. While functional, these generic names quickly blend together, much like Sheet1 and Sheet2. Renaming tables keeps things clear. Table names must follow these rules:

- » Names can include letters, numbers, underscores, and backslashes.

- » The first character must be a letter, underscore, or backslash.

- » Table names cannot conflict with existing names in the workbook. For example:

  - A table name cannot match an existing named range.

  - A table name cannot be a valid cell reference. For instance:

    - TAX2026 is not a valid table name (it resembles a cell reference).

    - TAX_2026 is valid and follows the rules.

- » Table names can be a single letter, underscore, or backslash, but cannot be C or R, as these are shortcuts for selecting the column or row of the active cell in the Name Box.

Here's how to rename a table:

1. **Select any cell within an Excel table; for example, cell A1.**

   The first row of an Excel table is called the Header Row.

2. **Use the Table Name field to assign a name. For example, enter the word `Sales` to name the table.**

You can also rename tables by choosing Formulas ➪ Name Manager. In the Name Manager dialog box, select the name of a table and then click Edit to open the Edit Name dialog box.

Navigating to and from tables

"Beam me to the table, Scotty!" For those unfamiliar, this is a playful nod to *Star Trek*, where characters would use a transporter to "beam" instantly to their destination. Similarly, Excel offers two quick ways to jump directly to your tables without scrolling endlessly through your data:

1. **Click on any cell that is not within a table; for example, cell J10.**

2. **Use one of these methods to navigate to a table:**

   - **Name Box:** Click the Name Box drop-down (above the worksheet grid) and select a table name from the list, such as Sales.

   - **Go To command:** Choose Home ➪ Find & Select ➪ Go To or press F5 or Ctrl+G (Windows) or Cmd+G (MacOS). Then select a table name from the Go To list and click OK.

If the worksheet containing the table is visible, Excel activates and selects the table's range of cells.

Windows users can double-click a table name to save a step.

The Name Box displays names assigned to worksheet cells first (in alphabetical order), followed by table names in a second alphabetical sequence. This quirk arises only in workbooks that use both types of names.

3. **To return to your previous location, choose Home ⇨ Find & Select ⇨ Go To, press F5, or Ctrl+G (Windows) or Cmd+G (MacOS).**

The Go To dialog box opens, as shown in Figure 5-2.

4. **Click OK or even better, press Enter.**

The Reference field contains the address of the cell location where you started, such as J10, letting you teleport back to your original position in the workbook with ease. This technique is particularly powerful and helpful in large workbooks.

FIGURE 5-2: The Go To dialog box.

Controlling table formatting

One aspect of Excel tables that often sends Excel users scrambling for Undo is banded row formatting. While intended to highlight table areas and help track rows, it may just not be your aesthetic. Fortunately, you have options.

Adjusting table formatting manually

Follow these steps to remove or adjust the style of a single table:

1. **Select any cell within the table; for example, cell A1.**

   The Table Design (Windows) or Table (macOS) tab appears within Excel's ribbon.

2. **Change or remove the style:**

   a) **Click the Table Styles drop-down.**

   b) **Choose a new style or select None (top-left) or Clear (bottom) to remove the formatting entirely.**

You can also adjust a table's style by toggling these options on the Table Design (Windows) or Table (macOS) tab:

» **Header Row:** Enabled by default, displays column titles for the table.

» **Total Row:** Initially sums or counts the last column of the table and is covered in more detail in the "Adding Total Rows" section later in this chapter.

» **Banded Rows:** Enabled by default, shades every other row.

» **First Column:** Bolds the contents of the first column.

» **Last Column:** Bolds the contents of the last column.

» **Banded Columns:** Shades every other column.

» **Filter Buttons:** Enabled by default, toggles Filter Buttons (covered in Chapter 4) on or off.

Establishing custom table styles

You cannot alter the built-in table styles, but you can use any existing style as a starting point:

1. **Choose Table Design ➪ Table Styles drop-down (Windows) or Table ➪ Table Styles drop-down (macOS).**

2. **Right-click on any existing style and choose Duplicate.**

3. **The Modify Table Style dialog box opens, as shown in Figure 5-3.**

4. **Use the Name field to rename your new style.**

5. **Select a table element from the list and click Format.**

   An abbreviated version of the Format Cells dialog box opens.

   The Column Stripe and Row Stripe options enable you to choose a stripe size between 1 and 9.

TIP

6. **Customize the font, borders, and fill color for the selected table element, and then click OK.**

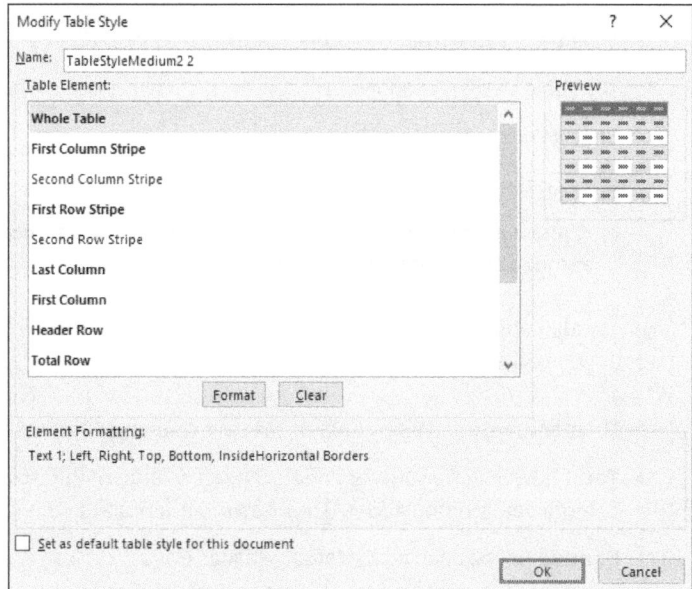

FIGURE 5-3:
The Modify Table
Style dialog box.

7. **Repeat steps 5 and 6 as needed to customize additional table elements.**

8. **Click OK to close the Modify Table Style dialog box.**

   Going forward, the custom style appears at the top of the Table Styles drop-down.

9. **Choose the new custom style from the Table Styles drop-down if you wish to apply it to the active table.**

REMEMBER

Custom styles apply only to the active workbook. When transferring a table with a custom style to a new workbook — by moving or copying — Excel creates a new style in the destination, though formatting, such as fill colors, may differ.

TIP

As any fashionista knows, styles come and go. Thankfully, in Excel, you can right-click on unwanted styles in the Table Styles drop-down and choose Delete. If only decluttering our closets were that easy!

Setting default table styles

You might be wondering why I didn't mention the Set as Default Table Style for This Document checkbox in the previous section. Sometimes, I like to test how closely my readers are paying attention — just one of my quirks. On a serious note, this checkbox allows you to define the default style for future tables in the current workbook. Follow these steps to customize the table style for new tables in the active workbook:

1. **Choose Table Design ⇨ Table Styles drop-down (Windows) or Table ⇨ Table Styles drop-down (macOS).**

2. **Right-click on a style and choose Set as Default.**

   If you prefer a no-frills approach, the first style listed in the Light section, labeled None in its ScreenTip, applies no formatting.

TIP

From now on, any tables you create in the active workbook reflect your own sense of style. However, custom table style defaults apply only to the active workbook, so you must repeat these steps in each workbook.

Automating Formulas and Features

The ease-of-use features discussed in the "Creating Excel Tables" section earlier in this chapter — such as headings and filter buttons that integrate seamlessly into the worksheet frame and the intuitive navigation techniques — already make tables well worth the small price of admission. But these benefits are just the tip of the iceberg.

Adding Total Rows

Many of your Excel tables can be elevated by adding a Total Row. But hold on — before you reach for the equal sign or AutoSum command, manual formulas aren't necessary. Here's how to add and customize a total row within an Excel table:

1. **Select any cell within a table; for example, cell A1.**

   The Table Design tab appears within Excel's ribbon.

2. **Turn on the Total Row option from the Table Design (Windows) or Table (macOS) tab.**

   A new row appears below the table, with the word Total in the first column and one of these amounts in the last column:

   - **Numeric total:** If it contains numbers, Excel automatically calculates the sum.

   - **Row count:** If it contains text or dates, Excel displays the count of non-blank cells.

3. **Adjust the total row as needed:**

- **Remove column total:** Click on the unwanted tally in the Total Row, select the AutoCalculate drop-down, and choose None.

- **Add column total:** Select a cell in the Total Row, click the AutoCalculate drop-down, and choose a mathematical operation (e.g., Average, Max, Min).

TIP

The AutoCalculate drop-down relies on the SUBTOTAL function (see Chapter 4), which excludes hidden rows. Selecting More Functions opens the Insert Function dialog box, where most functions (unlike SUBTOTAL) include hidden rows in calculations.

Some Excel features seem to suffer from amnesia — turn them off and back on, and it's like starting from scratch. Not the Total Row, though — it remembers your choices. To add more data, turn the Total Row off on the Table Design tab, append your data, and turn it back on. If life were this simple . . ..

Crafting calculated columns

What comes to mind when you hear "steely-eyed, cold, and calculated"? Maybe Gordon Gekko from *Wall Street*? Columns of formulas within a table don't need to be steely-eyed (though they might come across as a bit cold). But calculated? Absolutely — and that's precisely what makes them so powerful. Here's how to add a calculated column to a table:

1. Type Price in cell C1.

The table expands by one column. Alternatively, you can insert a new column within the table and then type the header name.

2. Type a formula into the first data row of the new column; for example, =ROW( ) in cell C2.

Notice how the formula is copied automatically through the last data row — this is a calculated column. In a normal range, you must copy the formula manually.

TECHNICAL
STUFF

The ROW() function returns the row number of a current row when the reference argument is omitted; otherwise, it returns the row number of the cell being referenced.

3. Make a change to the formula in any other row of the table, so that a different amount is returned; for example, change cell C10 to =ROW( )*10.

The change to the formula in cell C10 is applied to the rows above and below cell C10.

Leveraging structured references

In the movie *Groundhog Day*, a weatherman finds himself trapped in a time loop, reliving the same day over and over again until he learns to break free through personal growth. Similarly, many Excel users find themselves stuck in a loop of repetitive actions when using standard cell references, unaware of the efficiency structured references can bring.

Structured reference formulas within Excel tables save time and enhance usability. Unlike standard cell references, they use table and column names. For instance, within the same table, formulas reference only column names, while references from outside the table include both table and column names. Here are some key benefits of using structured references:

>> **Automatic column references:** Column names inherently reference all data rows in a column, improving data integrity.

>> **Dynamic range adjustments:** Formula references reflect changes when rows are added or removed.

>> **Enhanced readability:** Table and column names clearly describe the data directly, making formulas easier to read and maintain.

Structured references include one or more of the following components:

>> **Table name:** Identifies the table, such as Sales.

>> **Column name:** The name of a specific column within the table, such as [Quantity].

>> **Implicit intersection operator (@):** References the current row's value in a column, such as [@Price] or sometimes [@[Price]].

>> **Item specifiers:** Define specific sections of a table:

- **[#All]:** Includes headers row, data, and totals.

- **[#Headers]:** Refers to the header row.

- **[#Data]:** Refers to the data rows (default for column references).

- **[#Totals]:** Refers to the total row.

Structured references combine adaptability and ease of use, making them ideal for maintaining and auditing formulas. Here's a quick example:

1. **Type** Total **in cell D1.**

2. **In cell D2, type an equal sign, select cell B1, type an asterisk, select cell C1, and then press Enter.**

   The formula =[@Quantity]*[@Price] is equivalent to =B2*C2 but easier to interpret. The implicit intersection operator (@) tells Excel to use the value for the current row in each column.

Here's how to dig deeper with dynamic arrays and structured references:

1. **Carry out the following steps in cell F1:**

   a) **Type** =UNIQUE(.

   The UNIQUE function, covered in Chapter 9, lists distinct values.

   b) **Type** Sales **and then [to display the Formula AutoComplete list, as shown in Figure 5-4.**

   c) **Type [to display the Formula AutoComplete list, as shown in Figure 5-4.**

   The list shows options related to writing structured reference formulas, including column names in the Sales table, but does not appear if the table name is incorrect.

   d) **Use the arrow keys to select Month, then press Tab.**

   e) **Type] to close the column name reference and press Enter.**

   Excel automatically adds the closing parenthesis for UNIQUE.

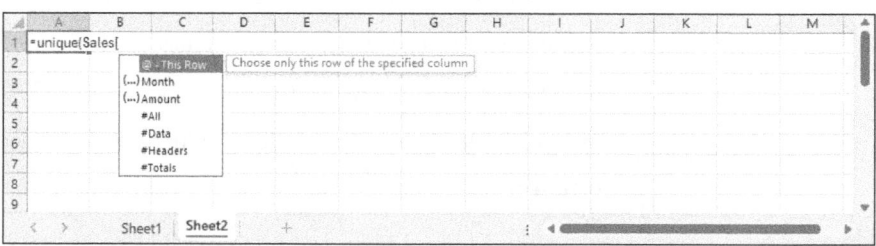

FIGURE 5-4: The structured reference version of the Formula AutoComplete list.

2. **Carry out the following steps in cell G1:**

   a) **Type** =SUMIF(.

   The SUMIF function, covered in Chapter 6, adds values based on matching criteria in a list.

   b) **Type the table name** Sales.

   c) **Type [to display the Formula AutoComplete list.**

   d) **Use the arrow keys to select Month, then press Tab.**

   e) **Type] to close the column name reference.**

   f) **Type a comma, then enter** F1#.

   The Spilled Range Operator (#), covered in Chapter 9, enables you to reference the results of a dynamic array function, such as UNIQUE.

   g) **Type a comma, then enter the table name** Sales **again.**

   h) **Type [to display the Formula AutoComplete List.**

   i) **Use the arrow keys to select Amount, and then press Tab.**

   j) **Type] to close the column reference, and then press Enter.**

Notice there's no need to leave cell F1 while writing this formula. Formula AutoComplete simplifies selecting table columns, while the Spilled Range Operator eliminates copying the formula down to F12. While not required in structured reference formulas, it's a touch of elegance — icing on the Excel formula-writing cake.

Disabling structured references

To avoid structured references within Excel tables, type cell addresses directly within formulas or disable the feature entirely by following these steps:

1. **Choose File ⇨ Options ⇨ Formulas. (Windows) or Excel ⇨ Preferences ⇨ Tables & Filters (macOS).**

2. **Clear the checkbox for Use Table Names in Formulas.**

3. **Click OK to close the dialog box.**

   This setting disables structured references, allowing you to use standard cell references exclusively.

Crafting self-expanding formulas

Structured references are the cat's meow for writing new formulas efficiently but offer little help for existing formulas with standard cell references. Fortunately, converting a normal range of data into an Excel table often improves the integrity of these older formulas.

Before you start popping corks, note that this technique works only when formulas reference all rows — excluding column headers — before the range is converted into a table.

This demonstration highlights the integrity of formulas referencing normal ranges to those referencing Excel tables:

1. **Create two additional sets of reference data:**

    a) **Select cells B1:B4, then choose Home ⇨ Copy or press Ctrl+C (Windows) or Cmd+C (macOS).**

    b) **Select cell I1, then choose Home ⇨ Paste or press Ctrl+V (Windows) or Cmd+V (macOS).**

    A copy of cells B1:B4 appears in cells I1:I4, including the banded row formatting.

    c) **Click the Paste Options button and select Values or choose Home ⇨ Clear ⇨ Clear Formats.**

    Using Paste Special Values provides an alternative to steps b and c.

    d) **Copy and paste cells I1:I4 to cell K1.**

2. **Add labels and formulas that reference both ranges:**

    a) **Type** Normal Range **into cell M1 and** Excel Table **into cell M2.**

    b) **Type the formula** =SUM(I2:I4) **into cell N1 and** =SUM(K2:K4) **into cell N2.**

    Both formulas return 600.

3. **Convert cells K1:K4 into an Excel table.**

    Refer to the "Creating Excel Tables" section earlier in this chapter for a refresher if needed.

4. **Add new data by typing** 400 **in cells I5 and K5.**

    The formula in N2, referencing an Excel table, dynamically updates to 400. In contrast, the formula in P1, which references a normal range, remains stuck at 300, as it requires manual editing to include the additional data.

Creating self-expanding charts

Repetitive tasks are truly the bane of my existence — and perhaps yours, too. In the early 1990s, as a bookkeeper, I often forgot to expand chart ranges to include the latest data until after printing reports. If only I had known about the List feature, now called the Table feature! This example compares static charts using normal ranges with self-expanding charts based on Excel tables:

1. **Create the first chart:**

   a) Select cell I1.

   b) Choose Insert ➪ Insert Column or Bar Chart ➪ Clustered Column (Windows) or Insert ➪ Column ➪ Clustered Column (macOS).

      As shown in Figure 5-5, a bar chart should appear on screen.

   c) Click on the title for the chart and type `Manual Update`.

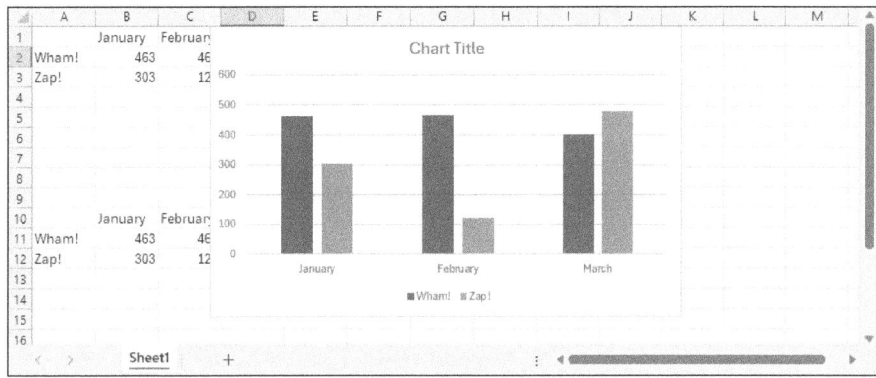

FIGURE 5-5:
A Clustered Column bar chart.

2. **Create the second chart:**

   a) Click on cell K1 and then choose Insert ➪ Insert Column or Bar Chart ➪ Clustered Column (Windows) or Insert ➪ Column ➪ Clustered Column (macOS).

   b) Change the title of the second chart to `Self-Updating`.

3. **Reposition the charts.**

   Use your mouse to select the Chart Area of each chart — that blank area outside of the Plot Area — to move the charts around so that you can see both charts at once.

4. **Expand the data sets by typing 500 in cells I6 and K6.**

5. **The chart titled Manual Update stands by stoically — patiently waiting for a manual resize of its data range, while the chart titled Self-Updating now displays a fifth column.**

Excel tables are a versatile tool that automate a wide range of Excel features. Beyond formulas and charts, they integrate seamlessly with Sparklines, PivotTables, PivotCharts (all covered in Chapter 12), and slicers.

Sifting data with slicers

While there's no cake or pizza involved, slicers offer a delightful and interactive way to filter data in tables, PivotTables, PivotCharts, and data models. These visual tools display clickable buttons, acting as a user-friendly remote control for filtering data (covered in Chapter 4). Slicers offer multiple benefits:

>> **Bird's-eye view of data:** Slicers show a distinct list of items for the column they are based on.

>> **Clear visualization:** Slicers make it easy to see which data is displayed and what is hidden.

>> **Customization:** The Slicer tab on the ribbon allows you to style slicers, modify headings, and adjust the number of columns in a slicer.

Here's how to sharpen your Excel skills with the Slicer feature:

1. **Select any cell within an Excel table, such as cell A1.**

   The Table Design (Windows) or Table (macOS) tab appears in the ribbon.

REMEMBER

   Slicers appear near the cursor's position when created. To avoid frustration, place your cursor in the table's header row before creating a slicer. Slicers created near the bottom of a table may shift far down the worksheet, making them difficult to track down.

TIP

   The Navigation task pane, discussed in Chapter 11, provides an easy way to track down wayward slicers that have drifted into Never Never Land.

2. **Choose Table Design ⇨ Insert Slicer (Windows) or Table ⇨ Insert Slicer (macOS).**

   The Insert Slicers dialog box opens.

3. **Select one or more fields, such as Month, and then click OK.**

   The slicer(s) appear on the worksheet.

REMEMBER

   Although you can select numeric columns from your table, slicers work best with text-based columns.

4. **Click any item within the slicer, such as January.**

   The table filters to show only rows that contain January, and total row amounts reflect only the visible rows.

5. **Hold down Ctrl (Windows) or Cmd (macOS) and select a second item in the slicer, such as February.**

   The table now displays activity for both January and February. In the slicer, selected items like January and February are shaded, while unselected items remain unshaded.

6. **To reset a slicer, click the Clear Filter button or choose Data ⇨ Clear.**

   Any rows hidden by the slicer's filter settings become visible.

Customizing slicers

You can stick with the basic slicer that Excel creates or personalize it to fit your style. When you click on a slicer, the Slicer tab appears in the ribbon, offering various customization options:

>> **Caption:** Use the Slicer Caption field to set a custom caption with no character restrictions.

>> **Slicer Settings:** Open the Slicer Settings dialog box to:

   • Control slicer item sort order.

   • Hide items with no data.

   • Enable sorting with Custom Lists (see Chapter 4).

>> **Slicer Style:** Choose prebuilt formats from the Slicer Styles drop-down or duplicate and customize styles, similar to table style customization.

>> **Columns:** By default, slicers display a single column. Adjust the columns as needed — limited only by what fits comfortably onscreen.

>> **Dimensions:** Adjust the slicer's height and width via the resizing handles or the Height and Width fields.

Removing slicers

When a slicer is no longer needed, you can remove it in two simple ways:

>> Right-click on the slicer, then choose Remove.

>> Click once on the slicer, and then press Delete on your keyboard.

If you change your mind after removing a slicer, you can undo the action by clicking Undo on the Quick Access Toolbar or pressing Ctrl+Z (Windows) or Cmd+Z (macOS).

REMEMBER

Active filters from slicers remain after its removal, leaving some rows hidden. Converting a table back to a data range removes slicers and clears filters — see the "Converting a Table to a Data Range" section later in this chapter.

Unpacking Table Quirks

Excel giveth, and Excel taketh away — mostly the former, but the latter can leave you questioning your sanity. Here's a quick rundown of some common Excel commands that behave differently — or become unavailable — when working within a table:

- » **Keyboard shortcuts:** Certain keyboard shortcuts behave differently within normal ranges of cells versus within tables:

  - **Ctrl+Plus (Windows) or Cmd+Shift+Plus (macOS):** In a normal range of cells, this keyboard shortcut opens the Insert dialog box. Within a data row of a table, it inserts a new row, even if only a single cell is selected. It does not function in the header row of a table but inserts a new column when used in the total row.

  - **Ctrl+Minus (Windows) or Cmd+Minus (macOS):** This keyboard combination deletes rows or columns, following the same behavior and nuances as the previous shortcut.

  - **Ctrl+A (Windows) or Cmd+A (macOS):** In a normal range of cells: selects the current region (the contiguous block of cells surrounding the active cell, whereas within a table:

    - **Header or total row:** Selects the entire table, including the header row and table row (if present).

    - **Data row:** Selects only the data rows. Pressing the shortcut a second time includes the header and total rows in the selection.

  - **Ctrl+Space:** In a normal range of cells, selects the entire worksheet column. Within a table, selects all data rows in the current column; press the shortcut again to include the header and total rows.

  - **Shift+Space:** In a normal range of cells, selects the entire worksheet row. Within a table, selects only the table row(s) for the current selection.

- » **Disabled commands:** The following commands may be unavailable based upon context:

  - **Home ⇨ Insert:** You cannot insert rows or columns within the header row of a table. However, this command works in any data or total row, where the Insert menu displays two additional options: Insert Table Rows Above and Insert Table Columns to the Left.

- **Home ➪ Delete:** You cannot delete the header row or any columns while the active cell is in the header row of a table. This command is available within data or total rows, where the Delete menu includes these additional choices: Delete Table Rows and Delete Table Columns.

- **Home ➪ Merge & Center:** The Merge & Center command is disabled within an Excel table, preventing you from merging cells in the table.

- **Insert ➪ Table:** The Table command is disabled when the active cell is within a table, as inserting one table within another is not allowed.

- **Data ➪ Subtotal:** The Subtotal feature (covered in Chapter 4) cannot be used in tables. Use the Total Row functionality instead, which dynamically adjusts to filtered data for similar results.

- **View ➪ Custom Views:** The Custom Views feature is entirely disabled in workbooks containing any Excel tables. Existing custom views remain intact but enter a "deep freeze," becoming accessible again once all tables are converted back to regular ranges of cells.

>> **Mouse clicks:** In a normal range of cells or data row of a table, double-clicking the bottom edge of a cell moves the active cell selection to the last non-blank cell in that column. In contrast, selecting a single header cell and then double-clicking on its bottom edge selects the entire column of the table.

Troubleshooting Tables

As noted in the "Resizing tables" section earlier in this chapter, tables should automatically expand to include new data. However, it's possible to accidentally turn off this in Excel for Windows. Here's how it might happen:

1. **Click any cell within the table to display the Table Design (Windows) or Table (macOS) tab.**

2. **Turn off the Total Row for the table by clearing the Total Row option, if necessary.**

3. **Enter data into the first blank cell below the table, such as** January **in cell A26.**

4. **Click the AutoCorrect Options button drop-down and notice — but do not click on — Stop Automatically Expanding Tables.**

WARNING

Selecting this option disables automatic table expansion across all your workbooks, leaving you with the chore of manually resizing tables from then on.

To ensure your tables expand automatically, verify the following Windows:

1. **Choose File ⇨ Options ⇨ Proofing ⇨ AutoCorrect Options.**

2. **Activate the AutoFormat As You Type tab.**

3. **Confirm that Include New Rows and Columns in Table is enabled.**

4. **While you're there, make sure Fill Formulas in Tables to Create Calculated Columns is also turned on.**

5. **Click OK twice to save your settings and close the dialog boxes.**

Mac users can choose Excel ⇨ Preferences ⇨ Tables & Filters to confirm or adjust their settings. By double-checking these options, you can ensure tables continue to automate their expansion and calculated columns without interruption.

Converting a Table to a Data Range

The phrase "all good things must pass," often attributed to the poet Chaucer in 1374, reminds us that the utility of even the most helpful features can sometimes come to an end. While Excel tables offer numerous benefits, there may be occasions where you need to revert them to normal ranges of cells. Here's how:

1. **Select a cell within the table.**

   The Table Design (Windows) or Table (macOS) tab appears within Excel's ribbon.

2. **Remove the formatting by expanding the Table Styles drop-down, and then choosing None at the top or Clear at the bottom.**

   Both options remove table-specific formatting.

3. **Choose Table Design ⇨ Convert to Range, and then click Yes to confirm.**

   If you have a change of heart, click Undo or press Ctrl+Z (Windows) or Cmd+Z (macOS) to restore the Table feature.

WARNING

Always remove styling from a table before converting it to a normal range. This prevents confusion and ensures that you or other users don't mistakenly assume table automation features are still active.

2

Mastering Formulas and Functions

Retrieve data with lookup functions.

Clean and manipulate text.

Write decision-making formulas with logic functions.

Use dynamic array functions for complex calculations.

Trace and debug Excel formulas.

IN THIS CHAPTER

» **Retrieving data vertically and tackling its constraints**

» **Working with horizontal lookups and their applications**

» **Combining functions for precise, flexible lookups**

» **Leveraging XLOOKUP for dynamic and powerful searches**

» **Addressing errors and overcoming common challenges**

Chapter **6**

Leveraging Lookup Formulas

I n the world of Excel, finding the right data can feel like searching for buried treasure. That's where lookup functions come into play. Think of VLOOKUP as the trusty map from *Treasure Island* — a tool that points you in the right direction but comes with limitations. Like Long John Silver, you might find yourself hobbling along with a metaphorical wooden leg when your data shifts or expands. You could jump ship to the more flexible MATCH/INDEX combination, but for a truly deep dive, nothing compares to XLOOKUP. This modern lookup function is like the submarine *Nautilus* from *20,000 Leagues Under the Sea*. With its advanced capabilities, your data exploration will know no bounds, gliding effortlessly across rows and columns, even through the trickiest scenarios. Let's delve into these functions and others to uncover their strengths — and where they might leave you marooned.

Lookup functions are powerful tools for retrieving information from lists in Excel, helping you strike gold without having to manually reference individual cells. If your own records are buried at the moment, you can use a prebuilt template instead:

» **Windows:** Choose File ⇨ New, type Check Register in the search bar, press Enter, select the Check Register with Chart template, and click Create.

» **macOS:** Download the Chapter 6 Check Register with Chart workbook from `www.dummies.com/go/excelfd` and open it in Excel.

You're now ready to start exploring your newfound treasure trove.

Navigating with VLOOKUP

Robert Louis Stevenson first published a serialized story, "The Sea Cook: A Story for Boys," in the magazine *Young Folks* between 1881 and 1882. The story was later published as *Treasure Island* in 1883. Once in book form, *Treasure Island* became a bestseller and remains a perennial classic. Similarly, VLOOKUP was historically the third most frequently used function in Excel (behind SUM and AVERAGE). Given its ubiquity, even if you've personally put VLOOKUP out to sea, you're likely to encounter it in spreadsheets created by others, making it important to understand its quirks.

The VLOOKUP function is both valuable and vexing. It simplifies data retrieval by eliminating the need for individual cell references within a list. The "V" stands for vertical, as VLOOKUP searches down a column to find a match and returns a value from a corresponding column to the right. Its arguments are:

» **lookup_value:** the text, numeric value, or formula that determines what to look for — in effect, a signpost leading the way to the treasure you're seeking.

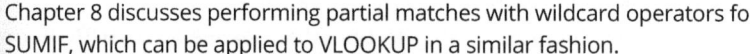

Chapter 8 discusses performing partial matches with wildcard operators for SUMIF, which can be applied to VLOOKUP in a similar fashion.

CROSS
REFERENCE

» **table_array:** a range of cells, typically spanning two or more columns — meaning this is where to plant your spade.

TIP

For smooth sailing, reference an Excel table for the table_array argument, as discussed in Chapter 5. Excel tables provide structured data that strengthens formula reliability and automatically incorporates new entries in the list.

» **col_index_num:** col_index_num: the column number in the table_array from which VLOOKUP retrieves your treasure — meaning the matching value. This match is based on the first column of the table_array.

>> **range_lookup:** FALSE or 0 (give me an exact match and nothing else will do), or TRUE or 1 (default) for an approximate match, meaning "meh, close enough."

Approximate matches work much like a pirate crew plundering the nearest booty: They settle for the closest value to the lookup_value without overshooting it.

Let's deploy VLOOKUP so you don't feel unmoored:

1. **Enter** `Coffee Shop` **in cell D26.**

    After all, pirates need caffeine too!

2. **Enter** `=VLOOKUP(D26,$E$12:$F$22,2,FALSE)` **in cell E26.**

    The formula returns Other, because the amount of coffee you drink is a closely guarded secret.

    Absolute references, such as $E$12:$F$22, are a best practice with VLOOKUP, compared to relative references like E12:F22. The differences between these reference types are explained in Chapter 2.

3. **Enter the following values:**

    - **Cell D27:** Cash with a trailing space, i.e., "Cash "
    - **Cell D28:** Credit Cards
    - **Cell D29:** Venmo

    The pirates want you to show them the money!

4. **Select cell E26 and then double-click the Fill Handle to copy the formula down through E29.**

    Shiver me timbers! All three cells return the #N/A error for different reasons:

    - **Trailing spaces:** Like barnacles on a ship, trailing spaces often go unnoticed until you look for them.
    - **Different spelling:** Cell E28 contains Credit Cards (plural), while the data in the table_array contains Credit Card (singular). Even the smallest details can scuttle your ship.
    - **Missing data:** Venmo isn't in the table_array — it seems our spreadsheet is a bit ahead of the pirates' time.

5. **Resolve the errors:**

    - **Trailing spaces:** Before you go overboard, select cell D27 and then click in the blank area of the formula bar to the right of the formula. The blinking cursor should perch snugly against the last character, like a loyal parrot on your shoulder. If there's even the slightest gap, press Backspace until everything is shipshape and tidy, and then press Enter. The data was revised, not the formula, so this should state "Based upon this revision, the formula in cell E27 returns Other."

- **Different spelling:** Select cell D28, press F2 (Windows) or Ctrl+U (macOS), tap Backspace once, and then press Enter to send that extraneous "s" over the fantail.

- **Missing data:** #N/A error values can feel like cannon blasts reverberating through your spreadsheet, especially if other formulas encounter it. You can patch the hull with the IFNA function (covered in Chapter 8):

    a) Edit cell E26 to use the formula =IFNA(VLOOKUP(D26,$E$12:$F$22, 2,FALSE),"Arrr!").

    b) Select cells E26:E28 then press Ctrl+D (Windows) or Cmd+D (macOS) to copy the formula down.

    Cells E26 and E27 return Other and Credit Card, respectively, while E28 boldly declares Arrr!

REMEMBER

Always use IFNA to handle #N/A errors instead of IFERROR, which can inadvertently swab away other error types, such as #REF!.

Steering clear of VLOOKUP's pitfalls

Despite its utility, VLOOKUP has limitations that might leave you feeling stranded on a deserted island:

- **Returns only a single match:** There may be more treasure hidden in your list, but you'll have to settle for one and done.

- **Error values to handle:** A #N/A error value is returned if no match is found — kind of like an unprintable word Long John Silver might mutter when the treasure isn't where it's supposed to be.

- **Inflexibility:** The lookup_value must be in the first column of the table_array, which might suit those accustomed to following strict rules but doesn't work for those seeking the freedom of the open seas.

- **Rigidity:** Cannot search to the left of the lookup column, meaning you're stuck following the map and can't venture off the grid.

- **Easily discombobulated:** The col_index_num is prone to errors when recorded as a static number: adding or removing columns in the table_array can cause data from the wrong column to be returned or result in a #REF! error value. It's a choice between fool's gold and walking the plank.

You can avoid the ire of a mutinous crew by using a dynamic function like MATCH (covered later in this chapter) to calculate the position of the col_index_num. Think of MATCH as a sextant guiding you with precision, rather than relying on the uncertainty of dead reckoning.

Avoiding shipwrecks with VLOOKUP

Now, let's explore how easily you can put VLOOKUP on a collision course with disaster:

1. **Edit the formula in cell E26 to change the col_index_num from 2 to 3, so the formula becomes:** `=IFNA(VLOOKUP(D26,$E$12:$F$22,3,FALSE), "Arrr!")`.

    The goal is to return the withdrawal amount, but #REF! appears because VLOOKUP is asking for column three in a two-column table_array. You just can't get there from here.

2. **Edit the formula in cell E26 to change the table_array $E12:$G22, so the formula becomes:** `=IFNA(VLOOKUP(D26,$E$12:$G$22,3,FALSE), "Arrr!")`.

    The formula now returns 3.65, because you scored a great deal on that cup of coffee.

3. **Double-click the Fill Handle in cell E26 to copy the formula down to cell E29.**

4. **To trigger another set of error values, select column F and choose Home ⇨ Delete or press Ctrl+- (Windows) or Cmd+- (macOS).**

    Removing column F resets the table_array to $E$12:$F$22, but the col_index_num is still 3. As a result, cells E26:E28 return #REF! — VLOOKUP found matches but couldn't return values. E29 returns Arrr! because VLOOKUP couldn't find Venmo, triggering #N/A, which IFNA intercepted, while letting #REF! error values through.

5. **Choose Undo on the Quick Access Toolbar or press Ctrl+Z (Windows) or Cmd+Z (macOS) to restore column F.**

    Anchors aweigh! Disaster dodged! The withdrawal amounts now appear in cells E26:E28, while E29 continues to proclaim Arrr!

6. **Select column F and then choose Home ⇨ Insert or press Ctrl++ (Windows) or Cmd++ (macOS).**

Blow me down! The table_array is reset to $E$12:$H$22 but col_index_num is still 3, so cells E26:E28 return the category names instead of withdrawal amounts. If we were to keep the new column in place, we'd need to change the col_index_num to 4 in E26, and then copy the formula down again.

7. **Choose Undo on the Quick Access Toolbar or press Ctrl+Z (Windows) or Cmd+Z (macOS) to remove the new column.**

    The withdrawal amounts reappear in cells E26:E28, while E29 continues to proclaim Arrr!

TIP

I've covered how table_array and col_index_num mishaps can lead to errors or incorrect results, but they're not the only hazards lurking beneath the surface. Numbers-stored-as-text can also send your lookup adrift — but I'll navigate that reef in the "Troubleshooting Lookup Formulas" section later in this chapter.

At this point, you hopefully have a sense of how to be victorious with VLOOKUP — or perhaps immensely grateful for vanquishing it to Davy Jones's locker.

Hoisting HLOOKUP

Let's duck into one of Excel's secluded coves for a quick review of the HLOOKUP function. As you might have guessed, the V in VLOOKUP stands for vexing — oops, I mean vertical, as in searching vertically down a column — while the H in HLOOKUP stands for horizontal, as in searching across a row. Its arguments are nearly identical to those of VLOOKUP:

>> **lookup_value:** the text, numeric value, or formula that determines what to look for, in effect a wayfinding mark that confirms our direction.

>> **table_array:** a range of cells, typically spanning two or more rows, comprising the murky waters that you wish to search.

>> **row_index_num:** the row number in the table_array from which HLOOKUP retrieves your prize, meaning the matching value. This match is based on the first row of the table_array.

>> **range_lookup:** FALSE or 0 (zero): exact match, TRUE or 1: (default) for an approximate match.

HLOOKUP encounters all the same challenges as VLOOKUP, including its inflexibility and susceptibility to errors when data structures change — leaving you adrift without a compass if your data doesn't align perfectly.

Exploring MATCH and INDEX

Historically, Excel users frustrated with VLOOKUP often jumped ship to the MATCH and INDEX functions, which work together like an anchor and chain:

» **MATCH:** Grounds your search, pinpointing an exact position in the data.

» **INDEX:** Acts as the chain, connecting to the anchor (MATCH) and retrieving the value you're looking for.

Unlike VLOOKUP, which can feel like a ship with its rudder stuck, steering you only to the right, the MATCH/INDEX combo gives you the freedom to navigate anywhere you decide to go.

Anchoring with MATCH

While most lookup functions deliver your request on a silver platter, MATCH provides what might feel like a coded signal — it returns the position of the data you're looking for, representing a row or column number. The MATCH function has the following arguments:

» **lookup_value:** The text, numeric value, or formula that represents your quest, including partial matches with wildcard operators (covered in Chapter 8).

» **lookup_array:** A range spanning all or part of a single column or row — like peering at your data through a telescope, focused and precise, instead of scanning with wide-angle binoculars.

» **match_type (optional):** Three options are available:

  ● **1 (default):** An approximate match less than or equal to the lookup_value. The values in the lookup_array must be placed in ascending order, like arranging the crew from shortest to tallest.

  ● **0:** An exact match. The values in the lookup_array can be in any order, meaning "all hands on deck."

  ● **-1:** The smallest value greater than or equal to the lookup_value. The values in the lookup_array must be in ascending order, for when you want to sail past the horizon.

TECHNICAL STUFF

The XMATCH function starts with the same three arguments but adds a fourth one, search, which lets you look from the bottom of a list to the top — replacing Excel's former top-down-only approach.

Let's set sail with MATCH:

1. **Enter this formula in cell F26: =MATCH(D26,E12:E22,0).**

   The formula returns 4 because Coffee Shop appears on the fourth row of the range E12:E22.

2. **Double-click the Fill Handle in cell F26 to copy the formula down through cell F29.**

   Avast! F27 and F28 both return 5, though Cash is on row six and Credit Card is on row seven — E12:E22 in E26 is a relative reference. #N/A appears in F29 because Venmo isn't in the lookup_array.

3. **Update the formula in cell F26 to =MATCH(D26,$E$12:$E$22,0) and then copy it down through cell F29.**

   Ahoy there! Fair winds and following seas — at least for the first three rows, thanks to the absolute reference. Since we're bringing in the INDEX function, it's too soon to tackle #N/A, but we'll square it away.

TIP

Sharpen your VLOOKUP cutlass by using MATCH to chart a course through the first row of your table_array, dynamically setting the col_index_num for smoother sailing and avoiding some of the errors we encountered earlier.

Connecting with INDEX

The INDEX function returns a result based on coordinates you specify, much like navigating to a specific longitude, latitude, or both at once. Users typically commission the MATCH function to return the positions. In this context, INDEX has three arguments:

TECHNICAL STUFF

» **array:** a range of cells, like the coordinates on a map charting the course for your data, or an array constant.

An array constant in Excel is a comma-separated sequence of text or numbers enclosed in curly brackets. Semicolons can designate row breaks when necessary.

» **row_num:** Specifies the row in the array from which to retrieve data. This argument is required unless column_num is provided, and it can be a static number or dynamically determined, much like setting the heading of your vessel based on the tides.

» **column_num (optional):** Specifies the column in the array from which to retrieve data, and can be static or dynamic, like choosing between locking the wheel in a fixed position or putting your ship on autopilot.

Let's see how fast we can go by navigating with INDEX and MATCH together to a single vertical coordinate:

1. **Update the formula in cell F26 to:** `=INDEX($G$12:$G$22,MATCH(D26,$E$12:$E$22,0))`.

   The formula returns 3.65, just the same as IFNA/VLOOKUP cell E26.

2. **Copy the formula down through cell F29.**

   Cells F27 and F28 return 50 and 936.48, while F29 causes our parrot to shriek with the #N/A error value.

3. **Update the formula in cell F26 to:** `=IFNA(INDEX($G$12:$G$22,MATCH(D26,$E$12:$E$22,0)),"Arrr!")` **then copy it down to cell F29.**

   Now that we've cleared the decks, withdrawal amounts appear in cells F26:F28 and Arrr! appears in F29 instead of #N/A.

Now, let's set up a sailing duel between VLOOKUP and INDEX/MATCH:

1. **Select column F and then choose Home ⇨ Insert or press Ctrl++ (Windows) or Cmd++ (macOS).**

   Oh no! VLOOKUP hit a reef, as evidenced by category names in cells E26:E27, while INDEX/MATCH sails on smoothly, displaying withdrawal amounts. And now you see why longtime seafarers — er, Excel users — prefer to navigate the oceans of data with INDEX/MATCH.

2. **Choose Undo on the Quick Access Toolbar or press Ctrl+Z (Windows) or Cmd+Z (macOS) to remove the new column.**

   This puts VLOOKUP back on course for additional comparisons down the line.

Plotting two coordinates with INDEX

Now that we've navigated the waters with a single MATCH guiding us through the data, it's time to set our course for deeper waters. To truly appreciate the power of INDEX, we need to chart two matches — one for the row and one for the column. There's no navigating by the stars here, you'll be locking in your lookups with GPS precision with the Function Arguments dialog box:

1. **Enter** Category **into cell G25.**

   This serves as the lookup value for a second MATCH function, which we'll use to populate the column_num in the INDEX function.

TIP

Chapter 14 demonstrates how to use Data Validation to create a drop-down list within a cell, preventing users from tying themselves in knots with slight typos in inputs that serve as lookup values.

2. Click on cell H26.

3. Click the Insert Function button on Excel's Formula bar or choose Formulas ⇨ Insert Function.

The Insert Function dialog box opens.

4. Type INDEX in the Search for a Function field, and then click Go.

The Select a Function list updates with possible matches.

5. Select INDEX from the Select a Function list, and then click Go.

The Select Arguments dialog box rarely appears, but does for functions like INDEX with multiple argument lists.

6. Click OK to accept the default set of arguments, in this case array, row_num, column_num.

7. Fill in the fields within the Function Arguments dialog box, as shown in Figure 6-1:

a) Enter $C$12:$G$22 in the Array field or select cells C12:G22 and then press F4 (Windows) or Cmd+T (macOS).

This represents a range of data, basically where we plan to go fishing.

b) Enter MATCH($D26,$E$12:$E$22,0) in the Row_num field.

This returns 4. The relative reference $D26 acts as a sea anchor, keeping MATCH fixed on column D when copied across the row, while allowing row numbers to roam when copied down.

c) Enter MATCH($G$25,$C$10:$G$10,0) in the Column_num field.

This also returns 4 because Category appears in the fourth column of C10:G10. The absolute reference $G$25 anchors the column heading input.

Required arguments appear in bold in the Functions Arguments dialog box.

REMEMBER

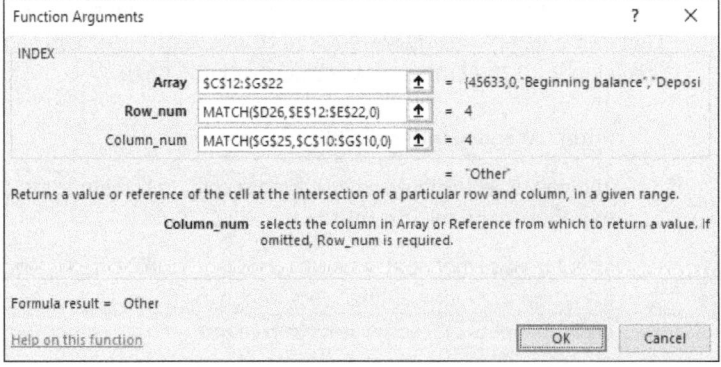

FIGURE 6-1:
The Function Arguments dialog box.

8. **Click OK to write the formula to the cell.**

   The formula =INDEX($C$12:$G$22,MATCH($D26,$E$12:$E$22,0),MATCH ($G$25,$C$10:$G$10,0)) appears in the cell and returns Other.

   fx

   Use the Function Arguments dialog box to deconstruct existing formulas. Click within a function's parentheses in the Formula Bar, even for nested functions, and then click Insert Function to break down its arguments.

9. **Double-click the Fill Handle in cell G26 to copy the formula down to cell G29.**

   The pesky #N/A error surfaces once more in cell G29, like a sea monster emerging from the depths.

10. **To perfect your formula, update cell G26 to: =IFNA(INDEX($C$12:$G$22, MATCH($D26,$E$12:E$22,0),MATCH($G$25,$C$10:$I$10,0)),"Arrr!") and then copy the formula down to G29.**

    The INDEX/MATCH/MATCH crew populates the value argument, while "Arrr!" stands by in the value_if_na position, functioning as a life preserver if no match is found.

11. **Update cell G25 to Check #.**

    Cells G26:G28 display results from column C of the array, illustrating that, unlike VLOOKUP, the INDEX function can return data from any direction.

12. **Update cell D29 to Paycheck.**

    Cell G29 returns 0 because the matching cell in column D is blank.

Hiding zero values

Excel functions that reference blank cells typically return 0. Although logic functions (see Chapter 8) are commonly used to display alternate results, these formulas can quickly feel like you've been caught in a cyclone — requiring the calculation that sometimes returns zero to be listed twice in the formula that hides the zeros. The LET function (see Chapter 4) can simplify this by assigning a name to the calculation, but you can also achieve the same result with a custom number format:

1. **Select cells G26:G29.**

2. **Choose Home ➪ Format ➪ Format Cells or press Ctrl+1 (Windows) or Cmd+1 (macOS).**

   The Format Cells dialog box opens.

3. **Choose Custom on the Number tab.**

4. **Enter #;#; in the Type field, as shown in Figure 6-2.**

   The format breaks down as follows:

   - The first # displays text and positive numbers.

   - The second # displays negative numbers.

   - The omitted third segment causes blank cells to appear blank.

   You can also include custom text in the third segment. For example: #;#;"Not Found" causes the words Not Found to appear instead of 0, but only for display purposes. The cell still evaluates to 0 in calculations.

5. **Click OK to close the Format Cells dialog box.**

   Cell G29 appears blank due to the custom number format, which suppresses zeros in the third segment.

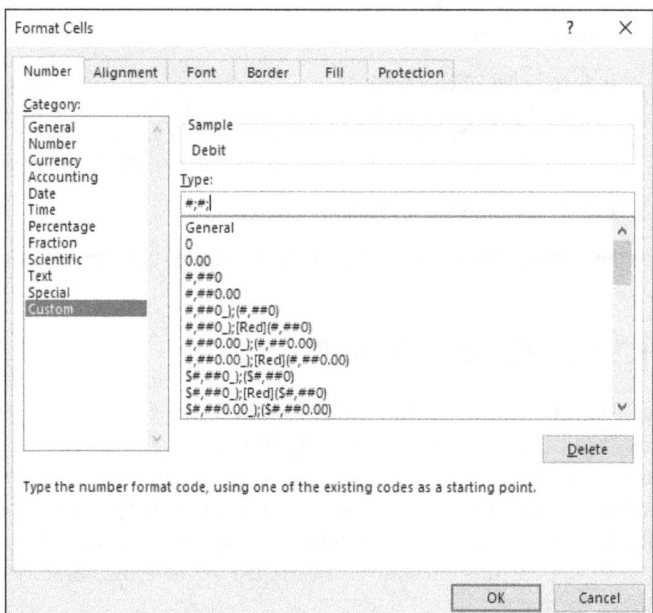

FIGURE 6-2:
The Custom category Number tab in the Format Cells dialog box.

Cruising with XLOOKUP

Similar to *Treasure Island*, Jules Verne's wildly forward-thinking *20,000 Leagues Under the Sea* first appeared in serial form in the French magazine *Magasin d'Éducation et de Récréation* before being published as a complete novel in 1870.

The story follows an expedition that sets out to find a sea monster, only to discover an advanced submarine commanded by the enigmatic Captain Nemo. The *Nautilus* carries its passengers to unfathomable depths, including the lost city of Atlantis — just as XLOOKUP empowers you to uncover submerged wonders in your spreadsheets.

Jules Verne wasn't one to rest on his laurels. His earlier works include *Journey to the Center of the Earth* (1864), *From the Earth to the Moon* (1865), and *Around the World in Eighty Days* (1872). Similarly, XLOOKUP formulas in this section use structured references, as detailed in Chapter 5, instead of traditional cell references. While XLOOKUP accepts either approach, advanced functions in Excel are most effective when paired with robust formula-writing techniques.

Let's embark on a deep-sea expedition with XLOOKUP by first taking a surface look at its arguments. As we dive deeper into this section, more treasures are revealed:

>> **lookup_value (required):** The text, numeric value, or formula that establishes your bearing — just like VLOOKUP and MATCH — but with the added flexibility to specify multiple values."

>> Unlike VLOOKUP and MATCH, which accept wildcard operators without qualification, XLOOKUP requires you to specify the match_mode argument if the lookup_value includes one or more wildcards. Think of VLOOKUP and MATCH as carefree swimmers proclaiming, "Come on in, the water's fine!" while XLOOKUP insists you strap on a life vest first.

>> **lookup_array (required):** The stretch of water you're searching, whether row- or column-based, similar to MATCH, and adaptable to the number of lookup values you specify.

>> **return_array (required):** The waters where you'll retrieve your catch — adaptable to multiple rows or columns, but it must match the type of range specified in lookup_array.

>> **if_not_found (optional):** The lifeboat that can save the day when a match can't be found, replacing #N/A with something more helpful.

>> **match_mode (optional):**

- **0 (default):** Exact match. If no match is found, #N/A appears unless an alternative is provided in if_not_found.

- **-1:** Exact match or next smaller item. If no match is found, the next smaller item is returned. The lookup_array column must contain numeric values but doesn't need to be sorted — letting the crew come as they are.

- **1:** Exact match or next larger item. If no match is found, the next larger item is returned, assuming that lookup_array contains numeric values — some sensibilities must be maintained, after all.

- **2:** Partial match, based on a wildcard system where question marks (?), asterisks (*), and tildes (~) enable flexible matching, as discussed in Chapter 8.

TIP

See this blog's cheat sheet (available at www.dummies.com/go/excelfd) to catch the scoop on the regular expressions option sneaking its way into XLOOKUP — too late for the print edition, but not too late for you.

>> **search_mode (optional):** XLOOKUP defaults to standard searches, which don't require the lookup_array to be sorted. Binary searches, on the other hand, are faster — like a corsair skimming across the waves — but they require your data to be meticulously sorted. Even a single untucked shirttail in the lookup_array can cause binary searches to return #N/A. Both types of searches can be conducted from the top down (imagine diving from the surface to the seabed) or from the bottom up (ascending from the sea floor to the surface). Here's how to set your preference:

- **1 (default):** Perform a standard search starting at the first item.

- **-1:** Perform a reverse standard search starting at the last item.

- **2:** Perform a binary search, assuming that the lookup_array is sorted in ascending order.

- **-2:** Perform a binary search, assuming that the lookup_array is sorted in descending order.

TECHNICAL STUFF

Binary searches work only on sorted data and quickly narrow down results by splitting the search range in half, instead of checking each item one by one.

STRUCTURED REFERENCES

Structured references let you refer to table data (see Chapter 5) using names instead of cell coordinates, making formulas easier to write, read, and update. When working with tables:

- Column names replace traditional A1-style references (for example, TBL_Transactions[Description] instead of E12:E22).

- Formulas auto-expand when new data is added to the table.

- Formulas stay readable, even when structure changes — no more guessing what D12:D22 refers to.

Let's get our sea legs with XLOOKUP and explore the basics with a twist: the formula will use structured references instead of normal cell references (see the sidebar for a definition of structured references).

1. **Ensure that the following inputs exist:**

   - **Cell D26:** Coffee Shop

   - **Cell D27:** Cash

   - **Cell D28:** Credit Card

   - **Cell D29:** Venmo (change this back from Paycheck if needed)

2. **Click on cell C10, go to the Table Design in the ribbon, and then note the TBL_Transactions in Table Name field.**

   Table names (see Chapter 5) enable you to reference an Excel table by its name rather than cell coordinates.

3. **Use the following steps to build a formula with structured references:**

   a) **Type** =XLOOKUP(D26, **into cell H26.**

      This populates the lookup_value argument.

   b) **Type** TBL **and then press the Tab key to add the TBL_Transactions table name to the lookup_array argument.**

   c) **Type [to display a list of column headings from the table.**

   d) **Select Description with your mouse, or arrow down to Description and press Tab.**

   e) **Type] to close the lookup_array argument and then type a comma.**

      At this point the formula bar should contain =XLOOOKUP(D26,TBL_Transactions],

   f) **Type** TBL **and then press the Tab key to add the TBL_Transactions table name to the return_array argument.**

   g) **Type [to display a list of column headings from the table.**

   h) **Select Category with your mouse, or arrow down to Category and then press Tab.**

   i) **Type] to close the return_array argument.**

   j) **Finish out the formula by typing) and then press Enter.**

      The formula =XLOOKUP(D26,TBL_Transactions[Description],TBL_Transactions [Category]) should return Other, just as it does with VLOOKUP and INDEX/MATCH.

4. **Drag the Fill Handle from cell H26 down through cell H29.**

   Cells H26:H27 correctly return Other, H28 returns Credit Card, and H29 returns #N/A, because Venmo does not appear in the data.

5. **Update the formula to handle #N/A errors:**

   a) **Select cell H26.**

   b) **Click Insert Function.**

   c) **Enter** `Arr!` **in the If_not_found field.**

TIP

   Be sure to include double quotes around text in the if_not_found argument when editing XLOOKUP in the Formula Bar. However, the Function Arguments dialog box automatically adds the double quotes when you close it.

   d) **Click OK.**

   The formula =XLOOKUP(D26,TBL_Transactions[Description],TBL_Transactions[Category],"Arrr!") in H29 should now return Arrr! instead of #N/A.

6. **Add a new transaction to the register:**

   a) **Type** `Venmo` **in cell E23.**

   b) **Choose Other from the Data Validation list in cell E23.**

   c) **Type** `40` **in cell G23 as a nod to Jimmy Buffet's song "A Pirate Looks at Forty."**

   Cell H29 returns Other, while cells E29:G29 all return Arrr! This illustrates how structured references within formulas improve integrity, as covered in more detail in Chapter 5.

Switching fields in XLOOKUP

Now that we've found our footing on calm seas, it's time to venture into deeper waters and uncover the true power of XLOOKUP. Let's begin by retrieving data from any column within an Excel table or data range. To keep things straightforward, we'll build on the formula introduced in the previous section:

1. **Select cell H26.**

2. **Click in the formula bar just to the right of the second [.**

3. **Press Alt+Down Arrow (Windows) or Ctrl+Option+Down Arrow (macOS) to display the AutoComplete list, shown in Figure 6-3.**

FIGURE 6-3:
The
AutoComplete
list for structured
reference
formulas.

Formula bar: `=XLOOKUP(D26,TBL_Transactions[Description],TBL_Transactions[Category], "Arrr!")`

`XLOOKUP(lookup_value, lookup_array, return_array, [if_not_found], [match_mode], [search_mode])`

AutoComplete list:
- (...) Date
- (...) Check #
- (...) Description
- (...) Category
- (...) Withdrawal
- (...) Deposit
- (...) Balance
- #All
- #Data
- #Headers
- #Totals

4. **Select Check # from the AutoComplete list then press Tab to swap out the field name.**

A single quote appears before the # symbol in the Check # heading to distinguish it as text rather than the spilled range operator (see Chapter 9). Excel adds it automatically when selecting from AutoComplete ([), but you must remember to include it when typing field names manually.

5. **Press Enter to apply the change to the formula.**

6. **Copy the formula down through cell H29.**

Cells H26:H28 return entries from the Check # column. Cell H29 returns 0 because the Venmo transaction does not have a check number reference. For ways to handle zero values, refer to the "Hiding zero values" sidebar earlier in this chapter.

This demonstrates that XLOOKUP can return values to the left of the lookup_array when needed, while structured references simplify reviewing and editing formulas. By default, this formula starts searches at the top of the lookup_array. Let's make a few adjustments to set the stage for a demonstration of searching a list from the bottom up in the following section:

1. **Select cell H26.**

2. **Click inside the (in the formula bar or press F2, then use the arrow keys to navigate to that position.**

A ScreenTip displays XLOOKUP's arguments.

3. **Click lookup_value within the ScreenTip to select that portion of the formula.**

Alternatively, hold down the Shift key and use the arrow keys to select that part of the formula.

4. **Select cell G26, or type G26 into the formula.**

5. **Click or navigate to the right of the first [.**

6. **Press Alt+Down Arrow (Windows) or Ctrl+Option+Down Arrow (macOS) to display the AutoComplete list.**

7. Select Category from the AutoComplete list, then press Tab to swap out the field name.

8. Click or navigate to the right of the second [.

9. Press Alt+Down Arrow (Windows) or Ctrl+Option+Down Arrow (macOS) to display the AutoComplete list.

10. Select Balance from the AutoComplete list then press Tab to swap out the field name.

11. Press Enter to apply the change to the formula.

The formula =XLOOKUP(E26,TBL_Transactions[Category],TBL_Transactions[Balance],"Arrr!") returns 1745.7, the balance for the first instance of Other in the Category column, as XLOOKUP defaults to searching from the top of the list downward.

Ascending through your data with XLOOKUP

Now, let's instruct XLOOKUP to change course by searching from the bottom up:

1. Select cell H26.

2. Click to the left of) in the formula bar or press F2 and then use the arrow keys to navigate to that position.

3. Type two commas to make the search_mode argument available.

Skipping over match_mode confirms the default option of 0, which specifies an exact match.

4. Type –1 to populate the search_mode argument, and then press Enter to apply the change.

The formula =XLOOKUP(E26,TBL_Transactions[Category],TBL_Transactions[Balance],"Arrr!",,-1) should now return 2655.64, which is the balance for the last Other transaction list — or 1550.37, if the Venmo transaction wasn't added earlier.

5. Optional: Copy the formula in cell H26 down to H29.

Cell H27 returns 2655.54 because cells E26:E27 contain Other. Cell H28 returns 613.89 by matching on Credit Card, while H29 returns Arrr! (in lieu of #N/A) because cell E29 contains Arrr!

The revised formula in cell H26 demonstrates that while lookup_value, lookup_array, and return_array are required, you can omit the if_not_found and match_mode arguments if their default values meet your needs.

Exploring wildcard matches with XLOOKUP

XLOOKUP is often exacting, but you can enable it to loosen up a little by using wildcard operators, which allow you to perform partial matches:

1. **Enter** Shop **and** Store **into cells D32:D33, respectively.**

2. **Enter this formula into cell E32:**
   =XLOOKUP("*"&D32,TBL_Transactions[Description],TBL_Transactions[Description]).

   You're not seeing double — the formula searches and returns data from the same column. It returns #N/A because a wildcard wasn't explicitly specified.

3. **Edit the formula in cell E32 to add** ,,2 **before**).

   The formula =XLOOKUP("*"&D32,TBL_Transactions[Description],TBL_Transactions[Description],,2) now returns Coffee Shop.

   To search for Shop appearing anywhere within a column, use "*"&D32&"*" — this allows extra characters before or after, like Shopper. To account for trailing spaces, use D32&"*", which matches Shop followed by anything, including spaces.

4. **Double-click the Fill Handle in cell D32 to copy the formula down to D33.**

   The formula in cell D33 returns Grocery Store.

Partial matches can retrieve results from any column. In this case, I had XLOOKUP look up and return data from the same column to highlight its partial match capabilities.

Wildcard operators are covered in more detail in Chapter 8.

Steering XLOOKUP to use multiple criteria

Another previously unfathomable capability that XLOOKUP offers is the ability to search on two or more criteria simultaneously. Such formulas can get a bit complex, so let's build it step by step:

1. **Enter** ATM **and** Other **into cells D35:E35, respectively.**

2. **Type** =XLOOKUP(D35&E35, **into cell F36.**

Multiple lookup_value criteria in XLOOKUP are combined with the concatenation operator (&).

3. **Type** `TBL` **and then press the Tab key to add TBL_Transactions to the formula.**

4. **Type** `[C`, **press Tab, and then type** `]` **to add the Check # field to the lookup_array.**

   Typing a letter narrows the choices in the AutoComplete list.

   At this point =XLOOKUP(D35&E35,TBL_Transactions[Check '#] should appear in the formula bar.

5. **Type** `&TBL` **and then press Tab to add TBL_Transactions to the formula.**

6. **Type** `[Ca`, **press Tab, and then type** `]` **to add the Category field to the lookup_array.**

7. **At this point =XLOOKUP(D35&E35,TBL_Transactions[Check '#]&TBL_Transactions[Category] should appear in the formula bar.**

   Multiple lookup_array ranges are joined together using the & operator.

8. **Type** `,TBL` **and then press Tab to add tbl_Transactions to the formula.**

9. **Type** `[De`, **press Tab and then type** `]` **to add the Description field to the return_array.**

10. **Finish out the formula with** `)` **and then press Enter.**

    The completed formula =XLOOKUP(D35&E35,TBL_Transactions[Check '#]&TBL_Transactions[Category],TBL_Transactions[Description]) returns Cash.

You can specify as many criteria as needed using this convention, making XLOOKUP a powerful tool for multi-criteria searches.

Reeling in multiple results with XLOOKUP

Just as the *Nautilus* could traverse any part of the ocean, XLOOKUP similarly has few boundaries. Let's use XLOOKUP to return multiple results in two ways, first across multiple columns, and then within the SUM function to return the total of multiple values:

1. **Set up a set of sample data:**

   a) **Enter** January **into cell B1 of a blank worksheet.**

   b) **Drag the Fill Handle in cell B1 across to cell M1 to create a twelve-month series.**

c) Enter `Turtle Soup` and `Hake Surprise` into cells A2:A3, respectively — a nod to the exotic and unexpected dishes served aboard Captain Nemo's *Nautilus*.

After all, when you're dining under the sea, why not keep things adventurous?

d) Enter this formula into cell B2: `=ROW()+COLUMN()`.

This formula calculates the sum of the current row and column numbers.

e) Copy the formula across to cell M2 and down to cell M3.

f) Type `Total` in cell N1.

g) Select cells N2:N3, then click Home ⇨ AutoSum or press Alt+= (Windows) or Cmd+Shift+T (macOS).

2. Use XLOOKUP to return multiple results:

a) Enter this formula into cell B6: `=XLOOKUP(A6,$A$1:$A$3,$B$1:$M$3)`.

Even though cell A6 is blank, the formula returns January through December, demonstrating XLOOKUP's ability to:

- Match on blank cells, unlike most lookup functions.
- Spill results across multiple cells in dynamic arrays (Chapter 9).

b) Type `Hake Surprise` and `Turtle Soup` into cells A7:A8.

c) Select cells B6:B8 and then press Ctrl+D (Windows) or Cmd+D (macOS) to copy the XLOOKUP formula down.

Twelve monthly results appear in rows 7 and 8.

3. Use XLOOKUP with the SUM function:

a) Click on cell B6 and then press Delete to clear the months.

b) Edit the formula in cell B7 to =SUM(XLOOKUP(A7,$A$1:$A$3, $B$1:$M$3)).

The formula returns 126, matching the total in cell N3, and demonstrating how XLOOKUP can seamlessly return cell references when used within other functions.

c) Copy the formula in cell B7 down to cell B8.

The formula in cell B8 returns 114, matching the total in N2.

4. **Transition the formula to structured references:**

a) **Enter** Entree **in cell A1.**

Excel's AutoCorrect feature may change this to Entrée. Is that a dark cloud gathering on the horizon, hinting at trouble ahead?

REMEMBER

In Excel, Entrée and Entree are treated as two different words, meaning they won't match directly in formulas. For this demonstration, leave Entrée as is. If you want to undo an unwanted AutoCorrection, click the Undo command on the Quick Access Toolbar or press Ctrl+Z (Windows) or Cmd+Z (macOS). Then type Entree again — Excel leaves it unchanged.

TIP

To remove pet peeve AutoCorrections (like Entrée), go to File ➪ Options ➪ Proofing. Click AutoCorrect Options, select the row containing the unwanted correction, and click Remove. Click OK twice to close the dialog boxes.

b) **Assuming that your cursor is now in cell A2, choose Insert ➪ Table.**

The Create Table dialog box opens.

c) **Click OK to convert the data into an Excel table (see Chapter 5).**

d) **Enter** Dining **into the Table Name field on the Table Design Tab.**

e) **Enter this formula into cell C7:** =XLOOKUP(A7,Dining[Entrée], Dining[January]:Dining[December]).

The formula should return 12 monthly results.

WARNING

If you type Entree without the accented "e," an error occurs. Use the AutoComplete list to select field names, as demonstrated earlier in this chapter.

With XLOOKUP's ability to return multiple results, you're no longer limited to one piece of treasure at a time — you can haul in an entire bounty of data, all with a single, dynamic formula.

Troubleshooting Lookup Formulas

Lookup formulas have a knack for driving even the calmest sailors to mutter some salty language. While I've sprinkled some of the nuances throughout this chapter, let's navigate through the most common frustrations that can arise with lookup formulas and steer toward smooth waters:

» **Trailing spaces:** I'll never forget the first time I encountered this. To date myself, it was back in the days of Lotus 1-2-3, and I had just mastered VLOOKUP. It worked flawlessly — except for one maddening #N/A that refused to cooperate. After what felt like hours of head-scratching, I finally uncovered the culprit: a sneaky trailing space at the end of the word VLOOKUP was trying to match. Let's just say it was a hard-won lesson in paying attention to the smallest details! See the "Navigating with VLOOKUP" section earlier in this chapter for a demonstration.

TIP

Chapter 7 explains how to use the TRIM function to eliminate trailing spaces effectively. Alternatively, wildcard operators, covered in the "Exploring wildcard matches with XLOOKUP" section of this chapter, can help address similar issues in certain scenarios.

» **#VALUE! error:** This error typically arises when there are mismatched ranges in a lookup formula. For instance, in XLOOKUP, if the lookup_array spans 10 cells while the return_array spans only 8, the formula results in a #VALUE! error. To avoid this issue, ensure that both arrays cover the same number of cells.

» **Misspelled or missing values:** As shown in the "Navigating with VLOOKUP" section, mismatches can arise when singular values appear in one part of a spreadsheet and plurals in another. Additionally, data may be missing entirely. VLOOKUP and MATCH return #N/A when the cell referenced by the lookup_value argument is blank, while XLOOKUP has the unique ability to match on blank cells, as discussed in the "Reeling in multiple results with XLOOKUP" section.

REMEMBER

The IFNA function (see Chapter 8) allows you to provide alternatives to the #N/A error value when using older lookup functions like VLOOKUP or MATCH. Newer functions like XLOOKUP simplify this process with the built-in if_not_found argument, eliminating the need for an additional function.

» **Numbers stored as text:** Numbers that you type into a spreadsheet are stored as numeric values by default, unless you convert them to text by typing a single quote (') before the number or applying the Text number format. Trying to match a numeric value in a criterion cell to a number stored as text in a data range can lead to unexpected mismatches and make you question your Excel abilities.

Let's walk through a quick scenario to unravel the common issue of numbers stored as text:

1. **Type '1 in cell A1 of a blank worksheet.**

   If a green triangle appears in cell A1, Excel is flagging a potential issue — text-based numbers can cause mismatches in formulas like VLOOKUP or XLOOKUP. However, Excel isn't always consistent about displaying this indicator, so don't rely solely on its presence.

TIP

   Chapter 8 covers the ISNUMBER and ISTEXT functions, which can help you distinguish whether your numbers are the real deal or just fool's gold.

2. **Drag the Fill Handle in cell A1 down to cell A26 to create a series of text-based numbers.**

3. **Enter this formula into cell B1: =CHAR(64+ROW()).**

   The letter A appears in the cell.

TECHNICAL STUFF

   The CHAR function in Excel returns a specific character based on a numeric code from the ASCII character set. For example, =CHAR(64+ROW()) in cell B1 returns the letter A because 65 is its corresponding ASCII code. It's also useful for inserting special characters, such as line breaks (=CHAR(10)) or symbols, into text.

4. **Double-click the Fill Handle in cell B1 to copy the formula down to cell B26.**

5. **Type 15 in cell D1 — a nod to the famous line "Fifteen men on the dead man's chest — Yo-ho-ho, and a bottle of rum!" in *Treasure Island*.**

6. **Enter this formula in cell E1: =XLOOKUP(D1,A:A,B:B).**

   The formula returns #N/A, even though you can clearly see the number 15 in cell A15.

TIP

   The formula uses entire column references, a future-proofing technique to ensure your lookup formula remains functional even as the data expands. While Excel tables are the best way to maintain lookup formula integrity, this approach serves as a reliable alternative when converting data to an Excel table isn't feasible.

7. **To resolve the issue of mismatched text-based numbers and numeric values, try one of these solutions:**

   - **Convert the lookup value to text:** Add a single quote before the number 15 in cell D1.

   - **Use the TEXT function:** Update the formula in cell E1 to: =XLOOKUP(TEXT(D1,0),A:A,B:B).

- **Convert text-based numbers in column A:** Instead of using the VALUE function, try this simple method:

  a) **Select column A.**

  b) **Choose Data ⇨ Text to Columns.**

  The Text to Columns wizard opens.

  c) **Click Finish.**

  Excel transforms the text-based numbers in column A into numeric values. Text to Columns forces Excel to evaluate the data type in each cell, converting text-based numbers into numeric values while leaving nonnumeric cells unchanged.

By keeping these troubleshooting tips in mind, you'll master lookup formulas and steer clear of the common pitfalls that can disrupt smooth sailing in Excel.

IN THIS CHAPTER

» **Adjusting text case effortlessly**

» **Eliminating extraneous spaces**

» **Combining text seamlessly**

» **Dividing or extracting text**

» **Exchanging text and formulas**

Chapter **7**

Transforming Text and Numbers

This chapter is all about the classic good-versus-evil battle between the Autobots and the Decepticons on the planet Cybertron . . . cue the record scratch. Okay, not those Transformers. The formulas and features covered here are also transformers — just without the capital T. Data often lands on desks in formats that could generously be described as "suboptimal." For instance, someone (no names mentioned, but their title is a four-letter word that starts with "b" and ends with "s") may have left the CAPS LOCK key on while entering data. A truly devilish challenge in Excel involves dealing with cells riddled with extraneous spaces — ask me how I learned that one the hard way. Thankfully, in Excel, knowledge is indeed power.

Other scenarios that trip people up include combining text from two or more cells. Retyping it isn't necessary — Excel handles it with ease. And, of course, anything painstakingly stitched together inevitably ends up being pulled apart later by someone else. Luckily, Excel provides tools for that too. The chapter closes with techniques for pulling the classic switcheroo, swapping out text or even parts of formulas on the fly — and most importantly, without breaking a sweat (or retyping).

Reworking Text without Retyping

I know this is an Excel book, but I need to step outside my domain for a moment to bemoan a keyboard shortcut that Excel's software siblings — namely Outlook, PowerPoint, and Word — offer but Excel unfortunately doesn't: Shift+F3. This nifty shortcut toggles text through the following case options:

>> **Uppercase:** ALL LETTERS ARE CAPITALIZED. AND NO, I AM NOT SHOUTING.

>> **Lowercase:** e.e. cummings fans, rejoice, as all letters are changed to lowercase.

>> **Proper case:** The First Letter Of Each Word Is Capitalized.

Excel doesn't provide a shortcut for toggling text cases in this fashion, but it does offer a collection of worksheet functions to handle case changes. So, while you can't rely on Shift+F3 here, you're still covered — just in a slightly less glamorous way.

Before we get this party started, let me clarify that this is a BYOB (bring your own beverage) event, not a BYOT (bring your own text) situation. I can't help you with what's in your cup, but if you're feeling parched for text, I've got you covered:

1. Type January **into cell A1 of a blank worksheet.**

2. **Click on cell A1 and drag the Fill Handle down through cell A12.**

You now have a full series of 12 months to work with — just be sure not to place your drink behind your laptop. That never ends well for me.

Capitalizing with UPPER

The UPPER function converts text to ALL CAPS and has a single argument:

> **text:** A cell reference (A1), formula (=CONCAT("Month: ",A1)), or characters enclosed within double quotes ("January") that you wish to convert to ALL CAPS

There are two ways to use UPPER to capitalize text. You can experiment with your own data or follow along with my sample data:

>> **Single cell formula:** Use UPPER to reference a single cell and copy the formula down as needed:

   1. Enter =UPPER(A1) **in cell B1.**

2. **Click on cell B1 and either double-click the Fill Handle to copy the formula down through cell B12, or take the scenic route and drag the Fill Handle from B1 down through B12.**

>> **Spilled range formula:** You can also transform multiple cells to upper-case at once, with a single formula:

1. **Type** =UPPER(**in cell C1.**

2. **Select cells A1:A12.**

3. **Type**) **and then press Enter.**

   Cells C1:C12 will be instantly filled with month names in ALL CAPS.

TIP

   If you're thinking, "I don't remember being able to do this in Excel before," you're spot on. This functionality goes by terms like spilled ranges or dynamic arrays — and Chapter 9 dives into all the nitty-gritty details.

How exciting! Your data is now SCREAMING OFF THE SCREEN! With your results safely in columns B and C, you might be tempted to get rid of that pesky original text in column A:

1. **Click on column A, then choose Home ⇨ Delete, or press Ctrl+Minus (Windows) or Cmd+Hyphen (macOS).**

2. **Ruh-roh! Disaster strikes — our revamped text is gone, replaced by #REF! error values.**

   This "situation," as they call it on the street, happens because the formulas in columns B and C reference the data in column A, which is now deleted. But don't panic; the next section walks you through an easy fix.

3. **Click Undo on the Quick Access Toolbar or press Ctrl+Z (Windows) or Cmd+Z (macOS).**

   The original text is back, and all is right in the spreadsheet world once more.

Pasting values only

Rest assured, this section isn't about imposing your morals on others. Instead, it's about a special way of pasting data so that the receiving cells contain static values instead of formulas. It's so nice, we'll do it twice — not because I enjoy double work, but so I can highlight an important nuance:

>> **Single-cell formulas:** Converting formulas to values is straightforward:

1. **Select the cells that contain a formula, e.g., cells B1:B12.**

2. **Choose Home ⇨ Copy or press Ctrl+C (Windows) or Cmd+C (macOS).**

3. **Choose Home ⇨ Paste drop-down ⇨ Values or press Ctrl+Shift+V in Windows to overwrite the existing formulas.**

4. **Column A can now be safely deleted without affecting your results.**

» **Spilled range formulas:** There's a bit of nuance to this approach:

1. **Select the cell that contains the spilled range formula, e.g., C1.**

2. **Choose Home ⇨ Copy or press Ctrl+C (Windows) or Cmd+C (macOS).**

3. **Choose Home ⇨ Paste drop-down ⇨ Values or press Ctrl+Shift+V in Windows to overwrite the existing formulas.**

4. **Dagnabbit! — a #SPILL! error value appears in C1.**

The issue arises because spilled range formulas generate results across multiple cells, even though you entered a single formula. To convert these results to values, you must copy all the output cells, e.g., C1:C12, and follow the steps for single-cell formulas instead.

Converting with LOWER

The LOWER function converts text to all lowercase and as you might expect, has a single argument:

text: A cell reference or characters enclosed within double quotes that you wish to convert to all lowercase

Everything mentioned about the UPPER function applies equally to the LOWER function. Both functions are straightforward to use because they convert all characters in the specified text without exceptions.

Formalizing with PROPER

The PROPER function converts text to proper case, meaning the first letter of each word is capitalized, while most other letters are in lowercase. Unlike UPPER and LOWER, the results returned by PROPER can be a bit unpredictable. First, let's confirm that PROPER has a single argument:

text: A cell reference or characters enclosed in double quotes that you want to convert to proper case

Everything mentioned about the UPPER function applies to the PROPER function as well. But here's the nuance: any characters appearing after apostrophes also get capitalized, and other letters you expect to remain capitalized may be unexpectedly altered. Let's pull the handle on PROPER and see what pops out:

1. Enter McDonald's TV Service in cell F1.

2. Enter =PROPER(F1) into cell G1.

   The results of the formula will be Mcdonald'S Tv Service.

There's no way to finesse the results, other than perhaps using the SUBSTITUTE function that is covered later in this chapter, or you can use the Replace command, which is covered in Chapter 11. In this instance, you'll need to make at least three replacements:

» Mcd with McD

» 'S with 's

» Tv with TV

Alas, sometimes in Excel solving one problem causes one or more new problems.

Converting text-based numbers and dates

One of the most mind-bending moments for Excel users comes when numeric data looks like a number, smells like a number, and feels like a number — but it's all an illusion, stored as text instead. While Chapter 2 explores how basic arithmetic functions can handle numbers stored as text, most worksheet functions treat text-based numbers as zeros. To convert text-based numbers or dates into true numeric values, use one of these functions:

» **VALUE:** Converts text-based numbers or dates — whether in a cell or returned by a formula — into numeric values.

» **DATEVALUE:** Extracts the numeric value from a date stored as text in a cell or produced by a formula.

Here's the catch: while VALUE handles both text-based numbers and dates, DATEVALUE is limited to text-based dates and throws a #VALUE! error if applied to text-based numbers. The nuance is worth noting — but there's a bonus: using VALUE not only simplifies your work by reducing the characters you need to type but also frees up mental real estate for yet another Excel function! Below, you can take these functions for a spin:

1. **Give Excel a little love by typing** `'February 14, 2027` **into cell A1 of a blank worksheet.**

REMEMBER

   Always include a single quote at the start of fully spelled-out dates; otherwise, Excel may try to be "helpful" and convert your input into a numeric date value, formatting it as dd-mmm-yy.

2. **Enter** `=VALUE(A1)` **or** `=DATEVALUE(A1)` **into cell C1.**

   Both formulas return 46432, the date serial number for 2/14/2027.

3. **Select cell C1 and then choose Home ⇨ Number Format drop-down ⇨ Short Date.**

   Alternatively, select Home ⇨ Format ⇨ Format Cells, or press Ctrl+1 (Windows) or Cmd+1 (macOS) to open the Format Cells dialog box and make a selection from the Date category on the Number tab.

4. **Enter** `'1000` **into cell A2, using a single quote to ensure the number is treated as text.**

5. **Enter** `=VALUE(A2)` **in cell B2.**

   The formula result is 1000, now stored as a numeric value.

6. **Enter** `=DATEVALUE(A2)` **into cell C2.**

   The formula result is #VALUE! because DATEVALUE cannot convert numeric values.

CROSS REFERENCE

   Chapter 9 covers IS functions, like ISNUMBER and ISTEXT, which help identify the exact state of a cell's contents.

Removing extraneous spaces

One of the toughest spreadsheet lessons I've learned — and that I've seen others learn — is that extraneous spaces sometimes lurk at the end of cell contents. Sometimes it's a careless tap of the space bar when typing into a cell, and sometimes it's extra spaces hitching a ride on data imported from elsewhere, like an accounting report or a list of transactions from your bank. These spaces are like crocodiles, resting motionless in the swampy areas of your spreadsheet. Their trap springs when you try to reference data with certain worksheet functions (see Chapter 6 for the lowdown on lookups and Chapter 8 for the iffiness of logic functions).

Here's the kicker: onscreen, "bamboozle" without a trailing space looks identical to "bamboozle " with one. But the latter will absolutely leave you feeling bamboozled when your formulas or lookups fail unexpectedly. One way to check for trailing spaces is to double-click on a suspect cell and look closely at the formula bar to see if the cursor blinks right next to the last character. If there's a gap, you've got one or more spaces hitching a ride. Sure, you can use the Backspace key to exterminate these critters, but I'm betting you don't want to do that for more than a cell or two. Fortunately, there's a formula for that.

Cleaning up text with TRIM

Think of TRIM as a weight-loss method for your cells — it sheds those pesky extra spaces while keeping exactly one space between words. Of course, there's a nuance I need to share with you, but first, here's the argument:

> **text:** A cell reference, a text string enclosed in double quotes, or a formula result from which to remove extraneous spaces

At the risk of sounding like a broken record (ask your dad; he remembers), you'll use the TRIM function in the same way as the UPPER function. Now, here's the catch with TRIM: punctuation is treated as a word. Put it to the test:

TIP

1. **Enter the following text into cell I1 of a blank worksheet** `Excel is fun !` `But extra spaces are not.`

   Hint: Hit the space bar twice between each word and the punctuation.

2. **Enter this formula into cell I2:** `=TRIM(I1)`.

Only one space appears between each word, but an extra space lingers before the exclamation mark and the period. As with PROPER, there's no direct way to finesse this. Your best options are the trusty Replace command (see Chapter 11) or the SUBSTITUTE function. Fortunately, unless someone is feeling particularly diabolical, most users won't intentionally put a space before punctuation.

TECHNICAL
STUFF

If you encounter spaces that TRIM won't touch, welcome to the world of nonbreaking spaces, which I discuss later in this chapter in the "Managing nonbreaking spaces" section.

Merging text together

Welcome to the part of the book where we explore merging — not freeway zipper merges, though I almost went there! Starting fresh, this section celebrates the union of data from two or more cells into a single cohesive unit. Forget the wedding bells; this process, known as concatenation, is easier to do than it is to pronounce (and no, saying it three times fast isn't required). This chapter covers traditional methods of combining text. Chapter 15 expands on this with artificial intelligence, letting Excel merge text for you — no formulas required!

You can use formulas in Excel to combine the following types of data:

REMEMBER

>> **Cell contents:** Any data within a worksheet cell can be combined.

Numeric values in worksheet cells appear in their raw format when referenced. For example, referencing a cell containing 7/1/2026 displays 46204 (the date's serial number) in the merged text, not the formatted date. See the section on the TEXT function later in this chapter for a solution.

>> **Numbers:** Combine numbers with other numbers, with standalone text, or with cell contents.

>> **Text:** Any nonnumeric values not within a worksheet cell must be enclosed in double quotes.

Before we get into the nitty gritty of combining text like a high-powered deal-maker, allow me to first make sure that you have some sample data to work with. If you're thinking, "Data? I don't need no stinkin' data," just hang with me for a second so that I can help you steer clear of some extreme overhelpfulness on Excel's part:

1. **Enter the data from the following table into cells A1:C3 of a blank worksheet.**

City	State	ZIP
Funkytown	CA	90210
West Quoddy Head	ME	04652

TIP

Funkytown can be anywhere that you let the music play, while West Quoddy Head is a real geographic landmark and, ironically, the easternmost point in the continental United States.

If you end up with 4652 in cell C3, it's not your eyes playing tricks on you, Excel really despises leading zeros with a passion. I have two solutions for you:

2. **Convert the number to text:**

   a) Type '04652 into cell C3 and then press Enter.

   This prevents Excel from gobbling up the leading zero like Cookie Monster but may cause Excel to throw a flag on the play.

b) **If a green error checking triangle appears in cell C3, click on the cell and hit the Error Checking Options button, and then choose Ignore Error.**

Take that, Excel!

3. **Or, apply the ZIP Code number format:**

a) **Choose Home ⇨ Format ⇨ Format Cells, press Ctrl+1 (Windows) or Cmd+1 (macOS), or use my go-to technique: clicking the Number Settings button in the lower-right corner of the Number section on Excel's Home tab.**

The Format Cells dialog box opens.

b) **Choose Special from the Numbers tab.**

c) **Choose ZIP Code and then click OK.**

You're now protected from having the Elvis song "Return to Sender" play out in real life.

Appending with the ampersand

We're about to create a combo here but hold the jazz and fast food. The ampersand (&) operator lets you combine text and numbers as seamlessly as adding numbers together:

1. **Enter this formula into cell D2: =A2&B2&C2.**

The formula returns FunkytownCA90210, which is funky, indeed.

2. **Enter this formula into cell F2: =A2&", "&B2&" "&C2.**

Get down! This formula returns Funkytown, CA 90210.

3. **Now that we're cooking with gas, copy the formula from cell F2 down to cell F3.**

Immediate buzzkill: The formula returns West Quoddy Head, ME 4652. Once again, the leading zero in the ZIP code gets gobbled up — the postmaster general is not going to be amused.

Formatting numbers with TEXT

You've probably noticed that leading zeros are treated like dangerous sharp objects to be avoided at all costs. In this situation, Excel has the brain of a Labrador retriever: instead of "must chase ball," it's "must do math with numbers." Hey! Excel! Leave them digits alone!

Fortunately, you can bend Excel to your will by using the TEXT function, which takes two arguments:

>> **value:** A cell, formula result, or numeric value that you want to convert to text

>> **format_code:** A text string defining the formatting you wish to apply

I could write a whole chapter on structuring format codes, but I'm sorry, Alice — I just don't have time to go through the looking glass with you today. Instead, let me show you how to find a list of cheat codes:

1. **Click on cell C3.**

2. **Choose Home ⇨ Format ⇨ Format Cells, press Ctrl+1 (Windows) or Cmd+1 (macOS).**

   The Format Cells dialog box opens.

3. **Choose Custom from the Categories list under the Numbers tab.**

4. **Verify that the format code for ZIP Code (00000) appears in the Type field.**

   If it does not, Choose Special from the Categories list, select ZIP Code, and then return to the Custom category.

   Format codes can be a mix of zeros, commas, hash signs, @ symbols, parentheses, minus signs, colons, slashes, and even AM/PM for time formatting.

TECHNICAL STUFF

5. **Double-click on the format code in the Type field or manually select the entire field.**

6. **Press Ctrl+C (Windows) or Cmd+C (macOS) or right-click and choose Copy.**

7. **Press Escape or click Cancel to close the Format Cells dialog box.**

8. **Revise the formula in cell C3 to: =A3&", "&B3&" "&TEXT(C3,"00000").**

   Note: The format code must be enclosed in double quotes. You can type it manually, but since it's already on your clipboard, pasting is easier.

You should now have a perfectly formatted formula result of West Quoddy Head, ME 04562. I don't know about you, but restoring the leading zero makes me feel groovy!

TECHNICAL STUFF

Once you get the hang of number format codes, you can confidently type them directly into the TEXT function. It's also worth experimenting with different format codes in the Custom field to format worksheet cells creatively. One of my favorite examples is the format code 0" Years". This handy code lets me display the word Years alongside a number in a single cell. For instance, if a cell contains a number representing years, I don't need to type "Years" in an adjacent cell to label it — it's built right into the display!

Combining with CONCAT

Once upon a time there was a worksheet function named CONCATENATE that was commonly used to concoct combinations of text. That function took a walk in the woods one fine day, did some self-improvement work, and returned as the leaner, trimmer CONCAT function. All fairy tales aside, the CONCATENATE function exists in Excel for compatibility purposes. So, let's get down to business with CONCAT, which has up to 255 arguments:

>> **text1:** A cell reference, range, text, number, or formula to combine

>> **text2. . .text255:** Additional references, ranges, text, numbers, or formulas to combine

Unlike CONCATENATE, which only supported single cell references, CONCAT allows ranges. Here's how it works:

1. **Type the number 1 into cell F1 of a blank worksheet.**

2. **Click F1 and drag the Fill Handle down to F9 while holding Ctrl (Windows) or Option (macOS).**

   The numbers 1 through 9 should fill the range. If every cell shows 1, click AutoFill Options and select Fill Series.

3. **In any blank cell, enter =CONCAT(F1:F9).**

   The formula result should be 123456789.

4. **For a delimited result, enter =CONCAT(F1,",",F2,",",F3).**

   The result should be 1,2,3.

Any text not in a cell must be enclosed in double quotes, just like with the ampersand operator.

Delimited refers to the separation of data elements using a specific character, such as a comma, space, or semicolon. In Excel, delimiters are commonly used to format text strings or organize data in a consistent, structured way.

Teaming up with TEXTJOIN

An immutable truth of Excel is that many users end up doing things the hard way, whether due to lack of knowledge or lack of time — thinking, "I'm too busy to stop and figure out how to work smarter." While the ampersand and CONCAT functions are major improvements over manually retyping text, there's always room for growth. I'm not one to rest on my laurels, so let's level up our text combinations with TEXTJOIN, which offers the following arguments:

>> **delimiter:** Specifies the separator between text values. This can be an empty text string (""), one or more characters enclosed in double quotes (e.g., ", "), or a cell reference containing a valid text string.

>> **ignore_empty:** Set to TRUE to ignore empty cells or FALSE to include them.

Choosing FALSE adds a delimiter for each blank cell, while TRUE ensures delimiters are only added between nonblank cells.

>> **text1:** The first text element to combine, which can be a cell reference, range, text, number, or formula.

>> **text2. . .text252:** Additional elements to combine, with the same flexibility as text1.

Let's now put TEXTJOIN to the test:

1. **Type 1 into cell A1 of a blank worksheet, 3, into cell A3, and 5 into cell A5.**

2. **Type =TEXTJOIN(", ",TRUE,A1:A5) into cell B1.**

   The formula result should be 1, 3, 5. Delimiters only appear after the actual data.

3. **Type =TEXTJOIN(", ",FALSE,A1:A5) into cell B2.**

   The formula result should be 1, , 3, , 5.

TEXTJOIN is ideal for situations where you need to insert a character, such as a space or comma between the contents of two or more cells, such as combining first and last names and adding a space in the middle.

Extracting or Splitting Text

In this section, breaking down pristine walls of text into tiny, sortable pieces takes center stage, transforming long strings into manageable bits for better organization and analysis. Say goodbye to retyping text — Excel's tools let you cut through it like a hot knife through butter. Speaking of which, anyone else craving toast? Excuse me for a moment while I find the bread.

Breaking up data with Text to Columns

Apologies to Neil Sedaka but breaking up is anything but hard to do in Excel. With the Text to Columns feature, you can slice and dice data from a single column into two or more columns with ease. Think of it as the chainsaw of data transformation — powerful, precise, and oddly satisfying to use. If you need some sample data to work with, enter this text into a blank worksheet:

>> **A1:** Funkytown, CA 90210

>> **A2:** West Quoddy Head, ME 04652

Now, let's break some . . . stuff (this is a family-friendly book, after all):

1. **Select data within a single column, e.g., cells A1:A2.**

   WARNING

   Ensure you have enough blank columns to the right of your data to avoid overwriting anything important.

2. **Choose Data ⇨ Text to Columns.**

   The Convert Text to Columns wizard opens. The first step asks you to choose the file type that best describes your data:

   - **Delimited:** Use this if your data contains separators like commas, spaces, tabs, or any single character.

     TIP

     You can use TEXTSPLIT, TEXTBEFORE, and TEXTAFTER to specify multi-character delimiters, as covered later in this chapter.

   - **Fixed width:** Use this if your data is aligned in neat columns, with each field in a given column occupying the same width, even if the entries themselves vary in length.

3. **Accept the default selection of Delimited and click Next.**

4. **Choose Comma and Space.**

   Notice in the Data Preview window, shown in Figure 7-1, that the sample data splits into five columns due to the spaces in "West Quoddy Head."

5. **Clear the checkbox for Space to reduce the split to two columns (city in one column, state and ZIP code in the other) and choose an option:**

   - **Next >:** Continue to Step 3 to refine text separation settings.

   - **Finish:** End the wizard here if the current split meets your needs.

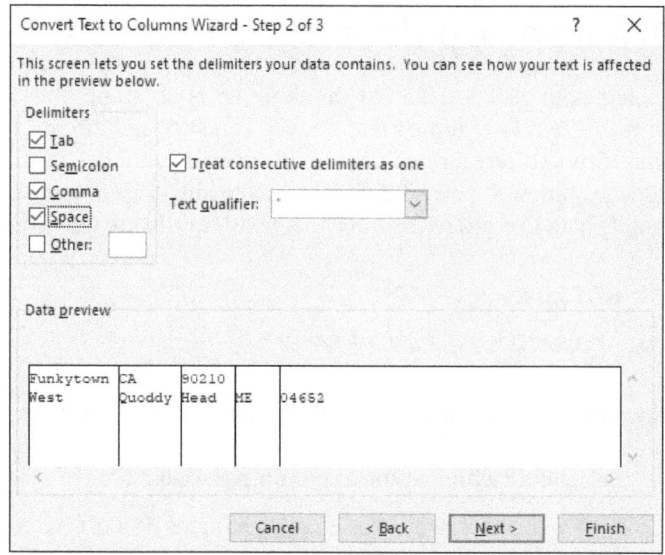

FIGURE 7-1:
The delimited
version of Step 2
of the Text to
Columns wizard
gone awry.

6. **If needed, select data from a second range that you wish to divide up, such as cells B1:B2.**

7. **Choose Data ⇨ Text to Columns.**

   The Convert Text to Columns Wizard opens.

TIP

8. **Choose Fixed Width and then click Next >.**

   In Excel for Windows, double-click Fixed Width to jump to Step 2 of 3.

9. **Adjust column breaks in the Data Preview window, as shown in Figure 7-2:**

   ● **Create a column break:** Click a position on the ruler or Data Preview to add a break line.

   ● **Delete a column break:** Double-click an existing break line to remove it.

   ● **Move a column break:** Drag a break line to adjust its position.

REMEMBER

   Scroll through the Data Preview window to review all rows, as Excel only displays breaks for visible rows.

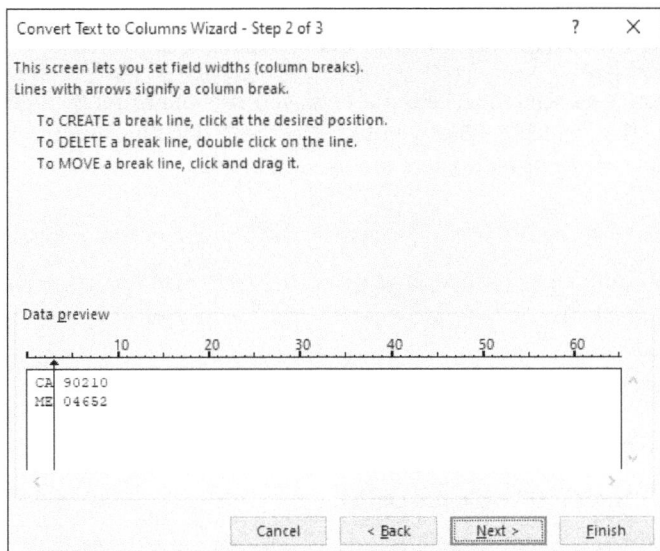

Convert Text to Columns Wizard - Step 2 of 3   ? ✕

This screen lets you set field widths (column breaks).
Lines with arrows signify a column break.

    To CREATE a break line, click at the desired position.
    To DELETE a break line, double click on the line.
    To MOVE a break line, click and drag it.

Data preview

        10   20   30   40   50   60

CA 90210
ME 04652

Cancel   < Back   Next >   Finish

FIGURE 7-2:
The fixed-width version of Step 2 of the Text to Columns wizard.

10. This time around, click Next > to advance to step 3, as opposed to Finish.

If you're working with the sample data, clicking Finish at this point causes the ZIP code to be treated as numeric values, which drops the leading zero in 04562.

11. Select the ZIP code column and choose Text to prevent leading zeros from being dropped. Other options include:

- **General:** Converts numeric values to numbers, dates to date format, and everything else to text

- **Date:** Specifies the date format of the original data

- **Do not import (skip):** Exclude a column entirely

12. To specify a different location, use the Destination field to place the split data in a different location.

13. Click Finish to close the Text to Columns wizard.

If the unbundled data causes you umbrage, click Undo.

REMEMBER

TIP

One of my favorite tricks with Text to Columns is converting text-based numbers into actual values. Simply select a single-column range containing numbers stored as text, then choose Data ⇨ Text to Columns ⇨ Finish. Voilà!

Leveraging LEFT to extract text

There's no need to feel left out here; you're about to get the lowdown on the LEFT function, which enables you to extract text starting from the left-hand side of a cell or string of text. There are two arguments:

>> **text (required):** A cell reference, range, text, number, or formula

>> **num_chars (optional):** Number of characters to extract, defaults to 1 if omitted

Let's give LEFT a try:

1. **Type Text Triathlon in cell A1 of a blank worksheet.**

2. **Enter =LEFT(A1) into cell B1.**

   The formula extracts the first character, returning T by default.

3. **Enter =LEFT(A1,4) into cell B2.**

   The formula extracts the first four characters, returning Text, starting from the left.

Finding characters within cells

You might have noticed that the LEFT function works similarly to the Fixed Width option in the Text to Columns wizard, as covered in the previous section. However, there are situations where you might want to extract text dynamically — say, up to the first instance of a space. Sure, newer functions introduced later in this chapter make this task a breeze, but for old times' sake, let's revisit the classic pairing of LEFT and FIND for dynamic text extraction.

The FIND function has three arguments:

>> **find_text (required):** The character(s) you wish to search for, which can be entered directly, referenced from a cell, or returned by a formula

REMEMBER

   FIND is case-sensitive and does not support wildcard searches, meaning it only looks for exact matches. For case-insensitive or wildcard searches, use the SEARCH function, which supports characters like * or ? to find partial matches.

>> **within_text (required):** A cell reference, range, text, number, or formula where you want to search

>> **start_num (optional):** The starting character position for the search, defaults to 1 if omitted

REMEMBER

FIND returns #VALUE! if the specified character isn't found or if the start_num argument is invalid, such as less than 1 or greater than the number of characters in within_text.

Combining LEFT and FIND

Here's how to use FIND as the num_chars argument for the LEFT function:

1. **Assuming cell A1 contains the words** Text Triathlon, **enter** =FIND(" ",A1) **in cell B3 — making sure to type a space between the quotation marks.**

   The formula returns 5, indicating the space is in the fifth position.

2. **Update the formula in cell B3 to become:** =LEFT(A1,FIND(" ",A1)-1).

   The result is Text. Without subtracting 1, the result would include a trailing space, as FIND returns the position of the space itself.

This approach showcases how the classic duo of FIND and LEFT can be used to dynamically extract text, even before diving into the newer functions that simplify this process further.

Slicing text with MID

Let's say you want to jump right into the middle of some text and extract a specific portion. Enter the MID function, galloping to the rescue! This function comes with three straightforward arguments:

>> **text:** A cell reference, range, text, number, or formula containing the text you want to extract from.

>> **start_num:** The starting character position for extraction, which is a required argument.

>> **num_chars:** The number of characters to extract. This required argument can exceed the length of the text, and MID will simply return whatever remains, starting from the specified position.

REMEMBER

The MID function returns #VALUE! if you omit the start_num or num_chars arguments. If num_chars is set to zero, the result is an empty value.

Maybe you'd like to see MID in action? Let's dive in:

1. **Enter =MID(A1,6,3) into cell B4.**

   This formula extracts Tri because the formula is returning three letters starting from the sixth position.

2. **Update the formula in B4 to =MID(A1,6,50).**

   The formula now extracts Triathlon, returning up to 50 characters starting from the sixth position. This demonstrates that you can specify any number greater than or equal to zero without causing an error — 0 returns an empty string instead.

Pulling characters with RIGHT

In *Raising Arizona*, Holly Hunter's character Ed famously says, "Turn to the right" during the iconic mugshot scene. Now it's your turn to do the same — both literally and functionally. The RIGHT function comes to the rescue when you need to snag text from the tail end of a string.

Think of the RIGHT function as the yang to the LEFT function's yin, offering identical arguments:

» **text (required):** A cell reference, range, text, number, or formula

» **num_chars (optional):** Number of characters to extract, defaults to 1 if omitted

Let's take RIGHT for a run around the block:

1. **Enter =RIGHT(A1) into cell B5.**

   The formula extracts the last character, returning n by default.

2. **Enter =RIGHT(A1,9) into cell B6.**

   The formula extracts the last nine characters, returning Triathlon, working from the right-hand side.

COUNTING CHARACTERS WITH LEN

By this point you may have realized that it can sometimes be helpful to count the number of characters in a worksheet cell. As you might expect, there's a function for that: LEN, which is short for length. The single text argument enables you to specify a cell reference, range, text, number, or formula for which LEN returns the character count.

Divvying with TEXTSPLIT

If you frequently break text into smaller segments, you'll likely go bananas over TEXTSPLIT. Just a heads-up — you'll need to bring your own ice cream and chocolate sauce. I'm fresh out, courtesy of two ravenous teenagers. TEXTSPLIT takes things up a notch compared to the earlier functions we've explored — it's a bit more mind-bending, as it can split text into both columns and rows simultaneously.

TIP

TEXTSPLIT is a dynamic array (or spilled range) function, part of a family of similar functions covered in Chapter 9. These functions bring flexibility and power to data manipulation, making it easier to work with structured outputs and dynamic calculations.

This powerhouse function comes with six flexible arguments:

>> **text (required):** A cell reference, range, text, number, or formula.

>> **col_delimiter (optional):** One or more characters that define where to split text into columns.

>> **row_delimiter (optional):** One or more characters that define where to split text into rows.

>> **ignore_empty (optional):** Defaults to TRUE, which skips over consecutive delimiters. Use FALSE to create empty cells where delimiters occur back-to-back.

>> **match_mode (optional):** Defaults to 0 for a case-sensitive delimiter search. Use 1 for a case-insensitive search.

>> **pad_with (optional):** Defaults to the #N/A error unless you specify a value to fill gaps caused by uneven splits.

TEXTSPLIT brings plenty of flexibility to your data-cleaning toolbox — even if it can't fix a teenager's midnight snack raid! Let's divide the illustrations of TEXTSPLIT into two segments. The first will involve a sentence:

1. **Type** To be, or not to be, that is the question. **into cell A1 of a blank worksheet.**

2. **Enter** =TEXTSPLIT(A1,",") **into cell A2.**

   The formula uses the text and col_delimiter arguments. As shown in Figure 7-3, the results populate across A3:C3.

3. **Type** =TEXTSPLIT(A1,,",") **into cell A6.**

   This formula uses the text and row_delimiter arguments, while omitting col_delimiter. As shown in Figure 7-3, the results populate down A6:A9.

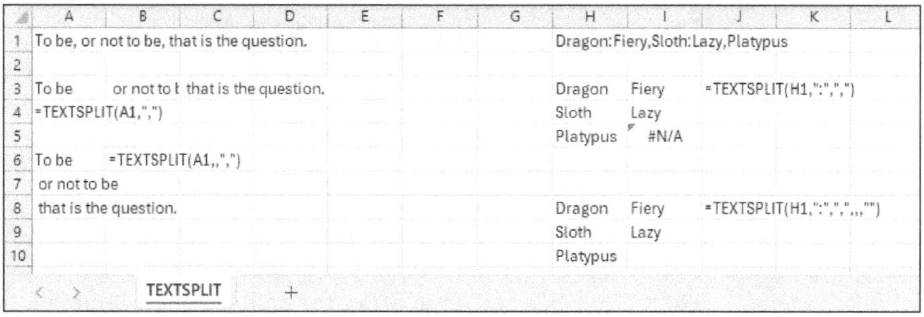

Figure table (TEXTSPLIT spreadsheet):

	A	B	C	D	E	F	G	H	I	J	K	L
1	To be, or not to be, that is the question.							Dragon:Fiery,Sloth:Lazy,Platypus				
2												
3	To be	or not to t	that is the question.					Dragon	Fiery	=TEXTSPLIT(H1,":",",")		
4	=TEXTSPLIT(A1,",")							Sloth	Lazy			
5								Platypus	#N/A			
6	To be	=TEXTSPLIT(A1,,",")										
7	or not to be											
8	that is the question.							Dragon	Fiery	=TEXTSPLIT(H1,":",",",,,"")		
9								Sloth	Lazy			
10								Platypus				

TEXTSPLIT   +

FIGURE 7-3:
Examples of
TEXTSPLIT
in action.

Now, we'll take it up a notch by including two delimiters:

1. **Type** Dragon:Fiery,Sloth:Lazy,Platypus **into cell H1.**

2. **Enter** =TEXTSPLIT(H1,":",",") **into cell H3.**

   This formula uses a colon as the col_delimiter and a comma as the row_delim-iter. As shown in Figure 7-3, the results span H3:I5. Cell H5 displays #N/A because Platypus doesn't have a value — some things in life, like the platypus, simply defy explanation.

3. **Enter** =TEXTSPLIT(H1,":",",",,,"") **into cell H8.**

   This formula adds an empty string ("") for the pad_with argument, replacing #N/A with blank cells. As shown in Figure 7-3, the results span H8:I10, with I10 appearing blank. In this case, the ignore_empty and match_mode arguments are omitted.

REMEMBER

You can skip optional arguments in Excel by typing a comma to move to the next argument in the sequence. This flexibility allows you to use only the arguments you need.

Tinkering with TEXTBEFORE and TEXTAFTER

Much like Joni Mitchell's "Both Sides Now," TEXTBEFORE and TEXTAFTER let you view your data from two perspectives — what comes before and what follows after — making text extraction effortless. These functions are a modern alterna-tive to the classic LEFT/FIND combination covered earlier in this chapter. This time, it's a BOGO deal (buy one, get one free), because both functions share the same arguments; they simply approach the task from opposite directions.

TEXTBEFORE and TEXTAFTER have the following arguments:

- **» text (required):** A cell reference, range, text string, number, or formula from which to extract information.

- **» delimiter (required):** One or more characters that indicate where to split the text. The function uses this delimiter to identify what comes before or after it.

- **» instance_num (optional):** Specifies the instance of the delimiter to use as the starting point. Defaults to the first occurrence if not specified.

- **» match_mode (optional):** Determines whether the delimiter search is case-sensitive. Defaults to 0 (case-sensitive). Set to 1 for a case-insensitive search.

- **» match_end (optional):** Indicates whether the end of the text should be treated as a delimiter. Defaults to 1 (match the delimiter at the end). Set to 0 to exclude matching the delimiter at the text's end.

- **» if_not_found (optional):** Specifies a value to return if the delimiter is not found at the specified position. Defaults to the #N/A error value if no value is provided.

These arguments allow for intricate text extractions, though writing out detailed examples could lead to a tangle of 0s and 1s that might blur together. Instead, I'll keep things simple with a practical example:

1. **Enter your first and last name into cell A1 of a blank worksheet.**

   For this example, I'm typing David Ringstrom.

2. **Type =TEXTBEFORE(A1," ") into cell A2 (don't forget to include a space between the quotation marks).**

   My formula returns David. How about yours?

3. **Type =TEXTAFTER(A1," ") into cell A3 (don't forget to include a space between the quotation marks).**

   The formula returns Ringstrom for me. How about yours?

These are just the basics — rest assured, there's so much more you can achieve with TEXTBEFORE and TEXTAFTER. Once you've mastered these essentials, you'll find them indispensable for advanced text manipulations!

Swapping out Text and Formulas

Working with data can feel a bit like playing with paper dolls — swapping out outfits until everything looks just right. SUBSTITUTE and REPLACE act as the ultimate wardrobe changers for your spreadsheet, helping you trade outdated text for something that fits perfectly. Meanwhile, the LET function takes things up a notch, cutting down repetition by assigning names to inputs or formula chunks, making your formulas not only sharp but delightfully svelte.

Switching out text with SUBSTITUTE

SUBSTITUTE may not sing like The Who, but it sure knows how to hit the right note — letting you swap out old text for something that fits your data better, no pinball wizardry required. The function has the following arguments:

>> **text (required):** The cell reference, range, text string, number, or formula containing the text you want to modify.

>> **old_text (required):** One or more characters you want to search for within the text argument.

>> **new_text (required):** One or more characters to replace the old_text with, or two quotation marks ("") to replace the old text with nothing.

>> **instance_num (optional):** By default, SUBSTITUTE replaces every instance of old_text. If you specify instance_num, only that specific occurrence is replaced.

Rest assured, SUBSTITUTE only works its magic when it finds a match for the old_text argument — if no match is found, the original text remains intact. Now, slide your way into some substitution:

1. **Enter sample data:**

   - **In cell A1, type:** GA–University of GA.

   - **In cell A2, type:** FL–University of FL.

   TIP
   The annual gridiron showdown between the University of Georgia and the University of Florida is affectionately known as the "World's Largest Outdoor Cocktail Party," a celebration as spirited as the rivalry itself.

2. **Choose your fighter: in cell B1, enter either of the following formulas:**

   - =SUBSTITUTE(A1,"GA","Georgia")

   - =SUBSTITUTE(A1,"FL","Florida")

3. **Copy the formula to B2 by dragging the Fill Handle from cell B1 to cell B2 or else click on cell B2 and use either of these keyboard shortcuts:**

- **Ctrl+' (Windows) or Cmd+' (macOS):** Copies the contents of the cell directly above the active cell but does not copy formatting.

- **Ctrl+D (Windows) or Cmd+D (macOS):** Copies the contents and formatting from the cell above into the selected cell(s) and can be applied to multiple rows at once.

Depending on the formula you chose, one cell shows the original value from column A, and the other displays either Georgia-University of Georgia or Florida-University of Florida. Notice that both instances of GA or FL are replaced.

4. **Now let's replace only the second instance. Select cells E1:E2, type either of the following formulas, and then press Ctrl+Enter.**

- `=SUBSTITUTE(A1,"GA","Georgia",2)`

- `=SUBSTITUTE(A1,"FL","Florida",2)`

Depending upon the formula you chose, you see the value from column A for one cell and either GA-University of Georgia or FL-University of Florida in the other cell. This time only the second instance of GA or FL was replaced.

Managing nonbreaking spaces

Hey there, I see your eyes rolling, thinking, "Why do I need to know about non-breaking spaces?" Maybe you don't — unless, of course, you're someone who copies and pastes data from web pages into Excel. I mean, who would ever do that these days?

Nonbreaking spaces are special space characters used on web pages to keep text aligned. They look and feel just like regular spaces — until you try to remove them. That's when the fun begins because TRIM won't cut it alone. You'll need a combo of SUBSTITUTE and CHAR.

The CHAR function takes one input:

number: A value between 1 and 255 that represents the character you want to return — like a secret code, where each number unlocks a different symbol, letter, or space

Now let's banish those sneaky extra spaces:

1. **Go to www.davidringstrom.com/nonbreaking and copy this sentence to the clipboard: Here's a text string with three nonbreaking spaces between each word.**

2. **Select cell A1 of a blank worksheet, and then choose Home ⇨ Paste drop-down ⇨ Match Destination Formatting or press Ctrl+Shift+V (Windows only).**

3. **Type =TRIM(A1) into cell B2.**

   Notice that none of the extra spaces are removed.

4. **Type =SUBSTITUTE(A1,CHAR(160)," ") into cell A3.**

   Excel replaces the nonbreaking spaces with regular spaces, but the change is imperceptible because both look identical.

5. **Type =TRIM(SUBSTITUTE(A1,CHAR(160)," ")) into cell A4.**

   Oh sweet relief! The extra spaces are gone!

TECHNICAL STUFF

If the SUBSTITUTE/CHAR combination doesn't work for you, try this =TRIM(CLEAN(A1)). The CLEAN function removes nonprintable characters, which can free up TRIM to do its job.

Overwriting characters with REPLACE

Sometimes a quick swap just won't cut it — it's a true case of out with the old and in with the new. That's where the REPLACE function shines, surgically removing part of your text and seamlessly dropping in its replacement:

> **old_text:** The cell reference, range, text string, number, or formula containing the text you want to modify.

REMEMBER

Don't overthink this one — despite being called old_text, it's really just the equivalent of the text argument used in most functions covered in this chapter.

>> **start_num:** The position within the old_text where the replacement begins.

>> **num_chars:** The number of characters in old_text you want to replace.

>> **new_text:** The character(s) to insert in place of the removed text. Use two quotation marks ("") for an empty string.

I already gave my Social Security Number to a silver-tongued gentleman on the phone today, so I figure in for a penny, in for a pound — let's share it with you for this next example:

1. **Type** 123–45–6789 **into cell A1 of a blank worksheet.**

2. **Type** =REPLACE(A1,1,7,"***-**-") **into cell B1.**

   The formula returns ***-**-6789. Phew, now my digits are safe at last — better late than never!

Defining variables with LET

OK, hang on while I flip through my vinyl collection to set the tone for this next section. "Let It Go"? Too chilly. "Let It Be"? A bit too passive. Ah, found it — when it comes to cleaning up your formulas, the LET function lets you simplify, streamline, and take control, like a rock star at the top of their game.

With LET you can assign names to inputs and intermediate results within a formula. These names only apply to the formula itself and can store values or calculations, improving both clarity and performance. By calculating intermediate results once, LET eliminates redundancy, which makes your formulas faster and easier to edit.

Within LET, you must define at least one name-value pair and a final calculation. You can include up to 126 name-value pairs, and you're not required to use all defined names in the final calculation. A key benefit of LET is that repetitive calculations only need to be listed once — so future edits become easier, since changes only need to be made in one place.

Here's a sense of LET's arguments:

>> **name1:** A name that you wish to assign to an input or portion of a formula.

>> **name_value1:** The input, value, or intermediate calculation assigned to name1.

>> **calculation_or_name_2:** If you're only defining one name-value pair, enter the final calculation here. Otherwise, use this to define another name.

>> **name_value2:** If calculation_or_name2 contains a name, enter the associated input or intermediate calculation. Otherwise, omit this argument.

This pattern can continue with additional name-value pairs, up to 126 pairs in total, with the final argument serving as the calculation that uses one or more of the defined names.

Documenting formula inputs

And now for the lowdown on the LET function regarding naming inputs:

1. **Enter the following sample data into a blank worksheet:**

   - **A1:** `Quantity` | **B1:** `Price` | **C1:** `Tax`

   - **A2:** `10` | **B2:** `50` | **C2:** `7%`

2. **Let's now carry out a simple price calculation two ways:**

   - **Without LET:** Enter this into cell A4: `=A2*B2*(1+C2)`

     This formula calculates the total (535), but offers no clarity about what each value represents.

   - **With LET:** Enter this into cell A5: `=LET(qty,A2,price,B2,tax,C2,qty*price*(1+tax))`

     This formula also returns 535 but is far clearer. By assigning names to inputs, you're leaving a roadmap for anyone reviewing the formula.

3. **LET evaluates names from left to right, so defining names in the proper order is critical:**

   - **Incorrect order:** Enter this formula into cell A6: `=LET(qty,A2,price,B2*(1+tax),tax,C2,qty*price)`

     This formula returns the #NAME? error value because tax is referenced in the name_value2 argument before it has been defined.

   - **Correct order:** Enter this formula into cell A7: `=LET(qty,A2,tax,c2,price,B2*(1+tax),qty*price)`

     The formula returns 535 because tax is now defined before using it in the price calculation.

Naming repetitive calculations

The LET function truly shines when formulas contain repetitive calculations. Not only does it simplify complex formulas, but it also reduces editing effort. Let's demonstrate with a simple error-handling example:

1. **Enter some sample data into a blank worksheet:**

   - **A1:** `100`

   - **B1:** `0`

2. **Enter this formula into cell C1:** `=A1/B1`.

   The formula returns #DIV/0! because Excel doesn't allow numbers to be divided by zero.

3. **Enter this old-school formula in cell C2:** `=IF(ISERROR(A1/B1),0,A1/B1)`

   This returns 0 because ISERROR handles the division by zero error. However, the calculation A1/B1 appears twice, meaning edits require double the effort.

REMEMBER

   While I used the classic IF/ISERROR combo here for illustration, the modern, streamlined approach is IFERROR. For example: =IFERROR(A1/B1, 0). Chapter 8 dives deeper into logic functions like these.

4. **And now LET enters the chat in cell C3:** `=LET(calc,A1/B1,IF(ISERROR(calc),0,calc))`.

   LET assigns A1/B1 to calc, so the calculation appears once. This approach is cleaner, better documented, and easier to edit.

The LET function is a powerful tool for creating clean, efficient formulas. Whether you're naming inputs or simplifying repetitive calculations, LET helps you take control of your formulas — like a true spreadsheet celebrity.

IN THIS CHAPTER

» **Understanding information functions**

» **Calculating with decision-making functions**

» **Controlling error values returned by formulas**

» **Analyzing data based upon conditions**

» **Mastering complex formula logic**

Chapter **8**

Harnessing Logic Functions

D ecisions, decisions. Every day we're faced with choices, from what to eat for breakfast to whether to hit the snooze button just one more time. In Excel, logic functions let you automate those decisions, guiding your data down the path it needs to follow. But as in life, decisions have consequences. Poorly thought-out choices — especially those prefaced with "Y'all watch this" — can lead to disastrous outcomes. Similarly, hastily crafted logic functions can wreak havoc on your spreadsheet, often with results that are equally catastrophic.

Making Basic Formulaic Decisions

Logic functions are driven by logical tests that use logical operators such as =, <, >, <=, or >=, as well as information functions, often referred to as IS functions. Each IS function evaluates a single value or reference against a specific condition, as indicated by its name, and returns TRUE or FALSE.

Exploring information functions

Here's a quick overview of the information functions that Excel provides:

>> **ISBLANK:** Returns TRUE if a cell is blank or FALSE if the cell is not blank. For instance, =ISBLANK(A1) returns TRUE if cell A1 is blank, or FALSE if not. =A1="" is a common alternative.

>> **ISERR:** Returns TRUE if the value returns any error value except #N/A.

>> **ISERROR:** Returns TRUE if the value returns any error value, including #N/A.

CROSS REFERENCE

Excel's error values are explored in depth in the bonus chapter "Ten Frustrating Prompts" (available at www.dummies.com/go/excelfd).

>> **ISLOGICAL:** Returns TRUE if the value is a logical value (TRUE or FALSE).

>> **ISNA:** Returns TRUE if the value is the #N/A error value.

>> **ISNONTEXT:** Returns TRUE if the value is not text, including blank cells.

>> **ISNUMBER:** Returns TRUE if the value is a numeric value (including dates) and FALSE if the value is text, even if it appears to be a number. Text-based numbers may be preceded by a single quote (') or formatted using the Text number format.

>> **ISREF:** Returns TRUE if the value is a valid cell reference.

>> **ISTEXT:** Returns TRUE if the value is text.

These IS functions are highly useful for error-checking, validating data, and building robust, condition-driven formulas in Excel. They ensure your logic flows smoothly, even in the most complex spreadsheets.

Deciding with IF

The IF function is like a lesson from the classic children's book *The Poky Little Puppy*: If you get home in time, then you get rice pudding; otherwise, it's straight to bed! In Excel, IF evaluates your condition and decides whether you're enjoying a calorie-free virtual dessert or missing out!

The IF function has the following arguments:

>> **logical_test:** A calculation that evaluates to TRUE or FALSE

>> **value_if_true:** The calculation, text, or number to return when the logical test evaluates to TRUE

>> **value_if_false:** The calculation, text, or number to return when the logical test evaluates to FALSE

Assume the Poky Little Puppy's mother wants him home by 6:00 p.m. He'll get rice pudding if he's on time; otherwise, he'll have to go straight to bed. Here's how to structure the formula:

1. **Enter** 5:59 PM **into cell A1 of a blank worksheet, making sure to include the PM designation.**

   Excel assumes times in the 12-hour format are AM unless specified as PM. For example, entering 6:00 is interpreted as 6:00 AM, while entering 18:00 (24-hour format) is always interpreted as 6:00 PM. However, 6 p is also interpreted as 6:00 PM — just make sure there's a space between the 6 and the p.

2. **Enter this formula into cell B1:** =IF(A1<TIMEVALUE("6:00 PM"),"Rice pudding","Straight to bed").

   The formula returns Rice pudding because 5:59 PM is earlier than 6:00 PM.

   The TIMEVALUE function converts a text-based time into a numeric value that Excel can evaluate.

3. **Update cell A1 to** 6:00 PM **(ensure that you include PM).**

   The formula now returns Straight to bed because 6:00 PM is not less than TIMEVALUE("6:00 PM"). Poor puppy — penalized by our formula error!

4. **Modify the formula in B1 to:** =IF(A1<=TIMEVALUE("6:00 PM"),"Rice pudding","Straight to bed").

   This update changes < to <=, allowing 6:00 PM to return Rice pudding. The puppy is vindicated!

Always test IF functions under various conditions. Even a small error, like using < instead of <=, can cause valid results to be treated as invalid.

Nesting IF functions

If only decision-making in life were always so black and white. More often than not, you may find yourself needing to make multiple decisions at once — let alone within a single cell. In Excel, one way to handle such situations is by nesting one IF function within another, placing it inside the value_if_true or value_if_false arguments. Excel even allows up to 64 levels of nested IF functions.

Up through Excel 2003 we were limited to nesting up to eight levels of IF functions. I always found that to be a perfectly acceptable constraint, because in general, any time I start stacking IF functions together, if I step back, I can generally find some better alternatives, as you see as this chapter rolls on.

Extend the Poky Little Puppy example by introducing an additional condition:

>> **Home by 4:00 PM: The puppy gets his favorite dessert — chocolate custard.**

>> **Home by 6:00 PM: He gets rice pudding — it'll do.**

>> **Otherwise: He'll go straight to bed without dessert. Yikes!**

Here are the steps:

1. **Update cell A1 to** `3:59 PM`.

2. **Modify the formula in cell B1 to** `=IF(A1<=TIMEVALUE("4:00 PM"), "Chocolate custard",IF(A1<=TIMEVALUE("6:00 PM"),"Rice pudding", "Straight to bed"))`.

   The formula returns `Chocolate custard` because 3:59 PM, when the puppy screeched in, is earlier than 4:00 PM.

3. **Update cell A1 to** `5:55 PM`.

   The formula returns `Rice pudding` because the puppy made it back under the fence after 4:00 PM but before 6:00 PM.

4. **Update cell A1 to** `6:01 PM`.

   The formula returns `Straight to bed` because the puppy missed both deadlines, and his mother is a stickler for punctuality.

Nesting IF functions is a powerful yet risky endeavor because each additional IF increases the complexity and the need for thorough testing of all possible conditions.

Managing multiple conditions with IFS

Nested IF functions can quickly devolve into multi-row formula bar concoctions that even Rube Goldberg might admire. Fortunately, the IFS function simplifies complex decision-making. It evaluates up to 127 conditions and returns a value corresponding to the first condition that evaluates to TRUE. While IFS eliminates the need for nesting, it still requires careful sequencing of conditions, because they are evaluated in order.

The IFS function has the following arguments:

>> **logical_test1:** A required condition that evaluates to TRUE or FALSE

>> **value_if_true1:** The result returned if logical_test1 is TRUE

- » **logical_test2..127:** Optional additional conditions to evaluate

- » **value_if_true2..127:** Results corresponding to the additional conditions

Each test must be followed by its corresponding result, alternating as test2, result2, test3, result3, and so on. Improperly structured IFS functions can return these errors:

- » **#VALUE!:** Appears when a logical test does not evaluate to TRUE or FALSE

- » **#N/A:** Appears when no conditions evaluate to TRUE

Restructure the Poky Little Puppy's dessert schedule using IFS, with an additional condition:

- » **Home by 2:00 PM:** He enjoys strawberry shortcake (my favorite!).

- » **Home by 4:00 PM:** He gets chocolate custard (his favorite!).

- » **Home by 6:00 PM:** He gets rice pudding.

- » **Otherwise:** He goes straight to bed without dessert.

Here are the steps:

1. **Update cell A1 to** `2:00 PM`.

2. **Enter the following formula in cell B2:**

   a) **Type** `=IFS(A1<=TIMEVALUE("2:00 PM"),"Strawberry shortcake",` **and then press Alt+Enter (Windows) or Ctrl+Option+Return (macOS) to create a line break within the formula bar.**

   TIP

   Line breaks make long formulas easier to read. If you later decide you're fine with the normal text wrap, use the Delete key to remove these invisible characters.

   b) **Type** `A1<=TIMEVALUE("4:00 PM"),"Chocolate custard"`, **and then add a line break.**

   c) **Type** `A1<=TIMEVALUE("6:00 PM"),"Rice pudding"`, **and then add a line break.**

   d) **Type** `TRUE,"Straight to bed")`, **and then press Enter.**

   The formula returns `Strawberry shortcake`. What a good boy the Poky Little Puppy is!

3. **Update cell A1 to** `4:00 PM.`

The formula returns `Chocolate custard`. He made it in by a whisker!

4. **Update cell A1 to** `6:00 PM.`

The formula returns `Rice pudding`. The puppy pants in relief.

5. **Update cell A1 to** `6:06 PM.`

The formula returns `Straight to bed`. The TRUE condition serves as a catch-all default value. Try again tomorrow, puppy!

The IFS function offers a cleaner alternative to nesting multiple IF functions but still demands strict attention to sequencing and detail to avoid logical errors.

Alternating outcomes with SWITCH

The SWITCH function works like a linear version of XLOOKUP (covered in Chapter 6), with lookup values embedded directly within the formula. It lets you test multiple cases efficiently and provides up to 126 result/value pairs, plus a default value if none match. SWITCH eliminates the need for cumbersome nested IF functions and offers more flexibility than IFS because its value arguments don't need to follow any specific order.

The SWITCH function has the following arguments:

» **expression:** The value, text, formula, or cell reference to test

» **value1:** The first instance to compare against expression

» **result1:** The result, meaning value, text, formula, or cell reference to return if expression matches value1

» **default_or_value2..126:** Either an optional default value (if no matches are found) or up to 126 additional values to test

» **result2..126:** The corresponding results to return when expression matches the respective value

The default value is always placed after the final set of value/result pairs. If no default is provided and there's no match, SWITCH returns the #N/A error.

SWITCH is case-insensitive, so "adrian", "Adrian", and "ADRIAN" all count as a match. The SWITCH function is perfect for replacing both numeric and text-based values. Here are two practical examples:

>> **Fiscal quarter (year starts October):**

1. **Enter 4 into cell D1.**

2. **Enter this formula into cell E1:** =SWITCH(D1,1,"Q2",2,"Q2",3,"Q2",4, "Q3",5,"Q3",6,"Q3",7,"Q4",8,"Q4",9,"Q4",10,"Q1",11,"Q1 ",12,"Q1").

The formula returns Q3, because 4 corresponds to the third quarter in this fiscal year.

The SWITCH function returns #N/A if the expression is blank or does not match any specified values.

>> **Iconic rivalries:**

1. **Enter Tom into cell A1 of a blank worksheet.**

2. **Enter this formula into cell B1:** =SWITCH(A1,"Tom","Jerry","Harry"," Voldemort","Woody","Buzz").

The formula returns Jerry since Tom is matched to Jerry.

3. **Update cell A1 to Woody.**

The formula now returns Buzz.

4. **Update cell A1 to Rocky.**

The formula returns #N/A because there isn't a match on Rocky and no default value was provided.

5. **Modify the formula in B1 to include a default value:** =SWITCH(A1,"Tom", "Jerry","Harry","Voldemort","Woody","Buzz","Namless Nemesis").

The formula now returns Namless Nemesis because Rocky does not match any of the specified values.

With SWITCH, you can efficiently manage complex logic and avoid the headaches of nested IFs or rigid ordering of cases.

VLOOKUP can be configured to mimic the functionality of SWITCH by using an array constant. For example:

```
=VLOOKUP(A1,{"Tom","Jerry";"Harry","Voldemort";"Woody","Buzz"},2,0)
```

If B1 contains "Tom", the formula returns "Jerry", and similarly for other pairs. The array constant functions as an inline lookup table, where each row specifies a lookup value and its corresponding result.

Selecting options with CHOOSE

"Choosy mothers choose . . ." Um, anyone else suddenly craving peanut butter? The CHOOSE function lets you pick from a list of values based on a given index. Here's how it works:

>> **index_num (required):** A number between 1 and 254 that determines which value from the list CHOOSE returns.

If index_num is less than 1 or greater than the number of provided values, CHOOSE returns the #VALUE! error value.

>> **value1 (required):** The value required first. This can be text, a number, a formula, or a cell reference to return when index_num equals 1.

>> **value2..value254 (optional):** Additional values for CHOOSE to select from.

Here are two ways to use CHOOSE — neither sticks to the roof of your mouth:

>> **Returning a value:**

1. **Enter** 3 **into cell A3.**

2. **Enter this formula into cell B1:** =CHOOSE(A3,"Lions","Tigers", "Bears","Oh, my!").

   The formula returns Bears since it is the third value in the list.

3. **Change the value in A3 to** 5.

   The formula now returns #VALUE! because there is no fifth value in the list.

The #VALUE! error returned by CHOOSE offers valuable feedback that IF cannot provide. For example, the formula =IF(A3=1,"Lions",IF(A3=2, "Tigers",IF(A3=3,"Bears","Oh, my!"))) returns Oh, my! when cell A3 contains any number other than 1, 2, or 3 — failing to flag an invalid input. Oh, my, indeed.

>> **Returning a cell reference**

1. **Enter** 10 **into cell G1 and then drag the Fill Handle down to cell G5.**

   Cells G1:G5 should all contain 10.

2. **Enter the number** 5 **into cell I1.**

3. **Type this formula into cell I2:** =SUM(G1:CHOOSE(I1,G1,G2,G3,G4,G5)).

   The formula sums the range G1:G5, returning 50.

4. **Enter the number** 1 **into cell I1.**

   The formula in I2 now returns 10, summing only G1:G1.

With CHOOSE, you can streamline decision-making in your formulas, making them easier to read and manage without the complexity of nested logic.

Handling Error Values

Alexander Pope rarely receives credit for coining the phrase "To err is human, to forgive divine" in his 1711 poem *An Essay on Criticism*. Spreadsheet errors, however, are so prevalent that Dr. Raymond Panko, professor emeritus at the University of Hawai'i's Shidler College of Business, built his career as a leading authority on the subject. While the bonus chapter "Ten Frustrating Prompts" (available at `www.dummies.com/go/excelfd`) delves into error values in detail, this chapter focuses on managing those responses formulaically.

CROSS
REFERENCE

Chapter 10 explores techniques for testing formulas to handle tricky responses, while Chapter 14 focuses on user-proofing your spreadsheets to prevent formula errors before they occur.

Handling missing data with IFNA

The IFNA function gracefully handles #N/A errors by returning an alternate value when a formula results in #N/A. If no error occurs, the formula's result is returned. Classic lookup functions like VLOOKUP, HLOOKUP, and MATCH often return #N/A — short for "not available" — when the lookup_value isn't found. Rest assured, Excel isn't being insouciant and saying "Nah!" Modern replacements like XLOOKUP and XMATCH simplify error handling with their built-in if_not_found argument, reducing the need for nested functions.

CROSS
REFERENCE

Lookup functions are covered in detail in Chapter 6.

The IFNA function has two required arguments:

TECHNICAL
STUFF

>> **value:** A calculation that could potentially return the #N/A error

   Use the NA function if you need to force a formula to return #N/A, such as =IF(A1="Excel","Nice!",NA()).

>> **value_if_na:** Alternate text, numbers, formula or cell reference to return when value returns #N/A

The IFNA function is often paired with VLOOKUP to handle missing matches. Follow these steps to practice using it:

1. **Create a sample workbook:**

   - **Windows:** Choose File ➪ New, type Streaming Show in the search bar, press Enter, select the Streaming Show List template, and click Create.

   - **macOS:** Download the Chapter 8 Streaming Show List workbook from `www.dummies.com/go/excelfd` and open it in Excel.

2. **Employ VLOOKUP:**

   a) **Type** `Fiends` **in cell B1.**

   b) **Enter** `=VLOOKUP(B1,C4:G7,4,FALSE)` **in cell C1.**

   The formula returns `Comedy, Romance` from column G, the fifth column in the table_array of C4:G7 because the value in cell B1 was found in the first column.

3. **Trigger the #N/A error value by updating cell B1 to** `Lawns of Attraction`**.**

   The formula in cell C1 returns #N/A because that show does not appear in column C.

4. **Incorporate IFNA by modifying the formula in cell C1 to** `=IFNA(VLOOKUP(B1,C4:G7,5,0),"Unknown Genre")`**.**

   The formula returns `Unknown Genre`.

5. **Test IFNA by updating cell B1 to** `Fame of Gnomes`**.**

   The formula in C1 returns `Adventure, Drama, Fantasy`.

6. **To trigger a different error value, right-click on column E and then choose Delete.**

   The formula in C1 now returns #REF! because VLOOKUP is referencing a nonexistent fifth column in the updated table_array (which is now only holds four columns).

The IFNA function is effective for handling #N/A errors but does not manage other error values (e.g., #REF!, #VALUE!, #DIV/0!). For those, additional error-handling techniques are required.

REMEMBER

Use IFNA instead of IFERROR when the #N/A error is the most likely invalid response to arise. This targeted approach ensures you handle the specific error without masking unexpected issues, like #REF! or #DIV/0! As discussed in the next section, the broad scope of IFERROR can sometimes make debugging more challenging by suppressing errors you didn't anticipate.

Identifying MIA data with ISNA

As discussed in the "Making Basic Formulaic Decisions" section earlier in this chapter, the ISNA function is an information function that determines whether a calculation returns #N/A. It returns TRUE if the result is #N/A, or FALSE otherwise. Historically, ISNA was used to handle #N/A errors, but it came with a drawback — the formula portion that might return #N/A often needed to be repeated. Reference the Streaming Show List workbook from the previous section to illustrate:

1. **Type the following formula into cell D1:** `=ISNA(VLOOKUP(B1,C4:D7, 2,FALSE))`.

   If B1 is set to Fame of Gnomes, the formula returns FALSE because a match is found.

2. **Update cell B1 to** `Rats and Recreation`.

   The formula in D1 now returns TRUE because Rats and Recreation does not appear in the range C4:C7.

3. **Modify the formula in cell D1 to:** `=IF(ISNA(VLOOKUP(B1,C4:D7,2,FALSE)), "Unknown Rating", VLOOKUP(B1,C4:D7,2,FALSE))`.

   If B1 contains Rats and Recreation, the formula now returns Unknown Rating.

4. **Update cell B1 to** `Mouse With Cards`.

   The formula in D1 returns the three-star rating because ISNA evaluates to FALSE as VLOOKUP finds a match for the show name.

REMEMBER

This valid but dated error-handling approach successfully manages #N/A errors, but it introduces a new challenge: going forward, the VLOOKUP formula must be edited in two places instead of one. This can complicate formula maintenance and is why more modern functions like IFNA or XLOOKUP are preferred for handling errors more efficiently. A cleaner approach is `=IFNA (VLOOKUP(B1,C4:D7,2,FALSE),"Unknown Rating")`.

CROSS REFERENCE

Chapter 7 explores how to use the LET function to eliminate repetitive calculations within formulas by assigning names to portions of formulas that are used multiple times.

Managing error values with IFERROR

The IFERROR function acts as a course correction for wayward Excel formulas that return an error value for any reason. Unmanaged error values — such as #REF!, #DIV/0!, and #NAME? — can cause a cascade effect, where other functions that reference the error also display it. The IFERROR function serves as a catchall, replacing any error value with an alternate result specified by the user.

The function has two required arguments:

>> **value:** A calculation that might return an error value

>> **value_if_error:** The alternate text, number, formula, or cell reference to return when an error occurs

Follow these steps to see how IFERROR can resolve division by zero errors:

1. **Type 100 in cell A1 of a blank worksheet.**

2. **Type 0 in cell B1.**

3. **Add this formula to cell C1: =A1/B1.**

   The formula returns #DIV/0! because Excel does not allow division by zero.

4. **Modify the formula to =IFERROR(A10/B10,"-").**

   The formula now returns - (a dash) instead of #DIV/0!

5. **Update cell B10 to 90.**

   The formula in C10 recalculates and returns 1.11111.

REMEMBER

While IFERROR is a versatile tool for handling errors, its broad scope can sometimes mask unexpected issues. For instance, it may suppress a #REF! error caused by deleted cell references, making it harder to identify and address the root cause. Use it thoughtfully to balance error management with transparency.

Counting errors with ISERR and ISERROR

Given the rise of artificial intelligence and public surveillance, the thought of a running log of our mistakes being counted might feel unsettling. Fortunately, in Excel, keeping a tally of errors in critical workbooks is a practical and much less intrusive task. You can achieve this using the SUM function in combination with either ISERROR or ISERR.

As covered earlier in the chapter:

>> **ISERROR:** Returns TRUE if a referenced cell contains any error value.

>> **ISERR:** Returns TRUE if a referenced cell contains any error value except #N/A.

Here's a comparison of the functions:

1. **Generate error values:**

   a) **Type** =1/0 **into cell D1 to generate a #DIV/0! error.**

   b) **Type** =NA() **into cell D2 to generate #N/A.**

   c) **Type** =David **(or any name without quotation marks) into cell D3 to generate #NAME?**

   d) **Type** 100 **into cell D4.**

2. **Test for error values with ISERR by entering this formula into cell E1:**
   =ISERROR(D1:D4).

   A dynamic array fills cells E1:E4, displaying TRUE for error cells D1:D3 and FALSE for D4.

3. **Convert the error values to numeric values by modifying the formula in cell E1 to:** =ISERROR(D1:D4)*1.

   A dynamic array fills cells E1:E4, showing 1 for error cells D1:D3 and 0 for D4. Multiplying by 1 converts TRUE to 1 and FALSE to 0.

4. **Count the error values by modifying the formula in cell E1 to:**
   =SUM(ISERROR(D1:D4)*1).

   The formula returns 3, the count of error values in D1:D4.

5. **Count non-#N/A error values by swapping out ISERROR with ISERR in cell E10 to:** =SUM(ISERR(D10:D13)*1).

   The formula now returns 2, because ISERR excludes #N/A.

TIP

Chapter 13 demonstrates how to use conditional formatting to color-code cells based on their values. This can help quickly identify and address error indicators in your data.

Evaluating Data Based upon Criteria

This section is all about breaking through analysis paralysis — that overwhelming dread that strikes when the boss asks, "Hey, what's the total sales of Soft Kitty Sweaters?" or "How many Roommate Agreement Notebooks have sold?" Or worse, "What's the average sales price of Fun with Flags Decor in Bazinga Valley?" Don't panic! Summing, counting, and averaging with ease is on the horizon, whether it's based on a single criterion or, if you're feeling quantum, up to 127.

While there might indeed be a big bang if Excel offered a template related to string theory, we can aim for a more down-to-earth alternative instead:

1. **Create a sample workbook:**

   - **Windows:** Choose File ➪ New, type Diet and Exercise in the search bar, press Enter, select the Diet and Exercise Journal template, and click Create.

   - **macOS:** Download the Chapter 8 Diet and Exercise Journal workbook from www.dummies.com/go/excelfd and open it in Excel.

2. **Activate the EXERCISE worksheet.**

Summing selectively with SUMIF

SUMIF adds values in a specified range based on given criteria. If no match is found, it returns 0. The function has three arguments:

- >> **range (required):** the cells in a single column or row to evaluate for the specified criteria.

- >> **criteria (required):** the condition that determines which cells to sum. This can be a number, formula, cell reference, text, or function.

- >> **sum_range (optional):** the cells to add if different from range.

Summing a criterion without spilled ranges

SUMIF is straightforward but can cause issues for unsuspecting users. This example of sums values for four individual criteria:

1. **Select cells E4:E20, press Ctrl+C (Windows) or Cmd+C (macOS), or choose Home ➪ Copy.**

2. **Select cell G4, then press Ctrl+Shift+V (Windows) or choose Home ⇨ Paste Special ⇨ Values.**

3. **Choose Data ⇨ Remove Duplicates.**

The Remove Duplicates dialog box opens.

4. **Click OK twice, once to close the Remove Duplicates dialog box, and a second time to close the results prompt.**

Four workouts should appear in cells G4:G7.

5. **Type** Burpees **into cell G8.**

6. **Choose Data ⇨ Sort A to Z.**

The workouts should now appear alphabetically.

7. **In cell H4, enter:** =SUMIF(E4:E20,G4,C4:C20).

Don't panic — the formula returns 0 because, honestly, who would *want* to do burpees?

TECHNICAL STUFF

The list in the sample data is formatted as an Excel table, so if you navigate to the cells in question while writing the formula, you might end up with =SUMIF(Exercise[NOTES], G4, Exercise[DURATION (MIN)]). This is known as a structured reference. Chapter 5 extols all the virtues of this method of formula writing.

8. **Double-click the Fill Handle in H4 to copy the formula through H8.**

Totals appear for each workout — except for burpees. But hold up before you take that celebratory swig of Gatorade!

9. **It's time to check our work:**

a) **Click on column H to display the sum of the amounts in Excel's Status Bar — 485 should appear.**

If you don't see statistics in the Status Bar after selecting two or more nonblank cells, right-click on the Status Bar and turn on Sum, Average, and Count at a minimum.

TIP

b) **Click on column C — 605 should appear.**

Uh oh, trouble in paradise — based on column C Excel thinks you logged 605 minutes of exercise, while the sum of column H insists it's only 485. You might just have to do those burpees after all.

Troubleshooting SUMIF

The issue stems from the formula using relative references. By the time the formula in H4 is copied down to H8, it auto-adjusts to reference E8:E24 and C8:C24, excluding two instances of Treadmill Exercise from the range, as well as the single instance of Low Impact Aerobics. Fortunately, there's an easy fix:

1. **Update the formula in H4 to** `=SUMIF($E$4:$E$20,G4,$C$4:$C$20)` **or** `=SUM IF(E$4:E$20,G4,C$4:C$20)`.

    The formula now incorporates absolute or mixed references that freeze the row positions in place.

    In this context, there are no dollar signs around G4 because we want to freeze the range and sum_range arguments while letting the criteria fly free as a bird. Otherwise, we'd see the total for burpees on every row — and that just won't do.

    REMEMBER

2. **Double-click the Fill Handle in H4 to copy the formula down to H8.**

    The workout totals now tally up to 605.

This demonstrates how even small missteps in cell references can lead to significant discrepancies.

CROSS REFERENCE

The differences between relative, mixed, and absolute cell references, along with the keyboard shortcut for toggling between them, are covered in Chapter 1.

WARNING

Always ensure that the criteria_range and sum_range arguments are equally sized. SUMIF does not return an error when the ranges have differing sizes; instead, it attempts to calculate a result, which is most likely incorrect due to the discrepancy.

There is, however, a situation where SUMIF (and SUMIFS) bewilderingly returns #VALUE!, making you think a previously functioning formula is suddenly possessed. This occurs when either function references data in another workbook — a concept known as a workbook link. Unlike most Excel functions, which don't differentiate whether the referenced workbook is open or closed, SUMIF and SUMIFS care deeply.

Fortunately, the error is easy to resolve: simply open the referenced workbook and leave it open in the background. If managing the workbook repeatedly becomes tedious, consider using the SUMPRODUCT function as a hidden workaround. An equivalent formula built with SUMPRODUCT won't care one whit about whether the referenced workbook is open or closed. The scoop is just around the corner in the "Computing with SUMPRODUCT" section.

Summing criteria with spilled ranges

The spilled range operator (#), discussed in more detail in Chapter 9, elevates SUMIF to a new level when criteria reference the results of a dynamic array, also known as a spilled range:

1. **In cell G10 enter** =UNIQUE(E4:E20).

   Four workouts appear in cells G10:G13.

2. **Enter the formula** =SUMIF(E4:E20,G10#,C4:C20) **into cell H10.**

   Totals for each workout populate dynamically in H10:H13, and no workouts are omitted.

The spilled range operator eliminates the need for absolute or mixed references. While the results may spill into multiple cells, the formula itself resides in just a single cell.

Although SUMIF predates Excel's dynamic array functionality by decades, this example highlights how older functions can seamlessly integrate with modern features, delivering powerful and efficient results.

Using wildcard operators

If someone in your life is described as a wildcard, you probably never know what to expect from them next. In Excel, though, wildcards are much more predictable — and highly useful — allowing you to perform partial-match searches with ease. Excel supports three wildcard characters:

>> **Asterisk (*):** Think of this as the "go big or go home" operator, representing any number of characters, including none at all. For example, *boom matches thunderboom, babyboom, or just boom. It's also Marvin the Martian's favorite way of figuring out where the kaboom went.

>> **Question mark (?):** You won't be crying "96 Tears" with this wildcard. Representing a single character, it helps you find matches like b?m for bim and bam, but not boom. A shoutout to Question Mark and the Mysterians for this one.

>> **Tilde (~):** Sometimes you need to search for an actual asterisk (*) or question mark (?). Adding a tilde before either character tells Excel to treat it as plain text. For example, ~*boom matches the literal text *boom — and it's not a fuse after all.

Only certain worksheet functions in Excel support wildcard matching. Common examples include the functions covered in this section, as well as VLOOKUP, SEARCH, and XLOOKUP. However, logical comparisons like =A1="ka*" do not support wildcards, because these are evaluated strictly as literal comparisons. Sorry, Marvin — keep searching.

It's time for an explosive wildcard example:

1. **Type** Workout **into cell G15.**

2. **Enter this formula into cell H15:** =SUMIF(E4:E20,"*"&G15,C4:C20)

In this case, the asterisk is enclosed in double quotes and joined to the contents of cell G15 with an ampersand (&). The formula returns 230, which is the sum of the durations in column C where the corresponding entries in column E end with the word "workout."

Wildcard matches are case-insensitive, so "*workout" matches Workout or workout but not work out. Sorry, John and Paul — Excel just can't work it out.

Aggregating with SUMIFS

SUMIF only scratches the surface when it comes to adding values based on your chosen criteria — SUMIFS takes it to the next level by letting you sum values using up to 127 criteria pairs. Like SUMIF, it returns 0 if no matches are found. However, unlike SUMIF, SUMIFS requires you to specify the sum_range as the first argument, giving you plenty of runway to add as many criteria as needed.

The SUMIFS function has the following arguments:

» **sum_range (required):** Cells within a single column or row to sum.

» **criteria_range1 (required):** Cells within a single column or row to test against a criterion.

» **criteria1 (required):** Criterion that can be text, numbers, or a formula defining the condition to match. Operators like >, >=, <, and <= can be used but must be enclosed in quotes (e.g., ">=300" or ">="&A1).

» **criteria_range2..127 (optional):** Additional ranges for criteria.

» **criteria2 (optional):** Additional criteria to evaluate.

Many users opt to kick SUMIF to the curb in favor of SUMIFS exclusively, avoiding the hassle of remembering to specify the criteria_range and sum_range arguments in the correct order.

And now for a quick run through with SUMIFS:

1. **Enter 300 into cell I3.**

2. **Enter this formula into cell I4:** =SUMIFS(C$4:C$20,E$4:E$20,G4,D$4:D$20, ">="&I$3)

    This formula sums the duration (minutes) from column C, based on two conditions:

    - A match for the workout type in column E.

    - Calories burned in column D must be greater than or equal to the value in I3 (currently 300). The absolute reference ensures the formula always refers back to I3 instead of adjusting when copied.

3. **Double-click the Fill Handle in cell I4 to copy the formula down through cell I8.**

    The formula results should match what appears in Figure 8-1.

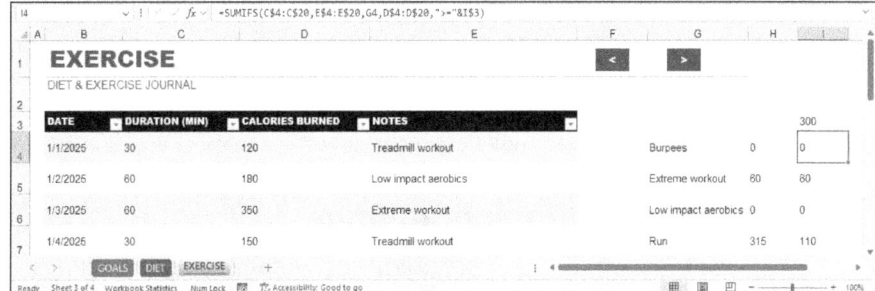

FIGURE 8-1: SUMIFS formula results based upon two criteria.

And here's the tale of the tape:

>> Burpees returns 0 because the workout does not appear within the criteria range.

>> Low Impact Aerobics also returns 0 because the single workout burned only 180 calories, falling below the 300-calorie threshold.

>> The totals for Run and Treadmill Workout are less than what SUMIF returned in column H because the results are now limited to workouts that burned over 300 calories.

REMEMBER

In case you missed the earlier "Troubleshooting SUMIF" section, SUMIFS returns #VALUE! when referencing data in a workbook that isn't open. While this doesn't apply here, it's a common stumbling block for many Excel users.

Computing with SUMPRODUCT

SUMPRODUCT is a worksheet function with a split personality, think Jekyll and Hyde, but without downsides:

>> **Multiplying values, then summing the results:** SUMPRODUCT multiplies the values in two or more columns and then sums the results of those multiplications.

>> **Adding up matching amounts based on criteria:** SUMPRODUCT can seamlessly replace both SUMIF and SUMIFS, effortlessly handling references to data in workbooks that aren't currently open in Excel.

The SUMPRODUCT has the following arguments:

>> **array1:** The first array to multiply and add, or to search for a specific criterion

>> **array2..255:** Additional arrays to multiply, add, search for criteria, or sum based on specified conditions

The SUMPRODUCT function lives up to its name, combining the power of multiplication and summation in one formula. What makes this function truly remarkable, though, is its versatility. Whether you need to perform straightforward calculations or tally data based on criteria, SUMPRODUCT has you covered.

Multiplying and summing

The standard use of SUMPRODUCT multiplies corresponding values across arrays and then summing the results. This functionality shines in scenarios where you need to calculate weighted averages, aggregate costs, or handle other operations that combine multiplication and addition:

1. **Create some sample data by entering the following formula into cell L3:** =RANDARRAY(5,2,1,10,TRUE).

This formula breaks down as follows:

- **rows:** 5 specifies the number of rows of random numbers to return.

- **columns:** 2 specifies the number of columns of random numbers to return.

- **min:** 1 specifies the smallest random number to return.

- **max:** 10 specifies the largest random number to return.

- **integer:** TRUE specifies that the random numbers should be whole numbers.

    RANDARRAY is a volatile worksheet function, meaning it recalculates whenever you make any edits within the worksheet grid. To freeze the numbers in place, select cells L1:M5, choose Home ⇨ Copy, and then go to Home ⇨ Paste ⇨ Values. This replaces the formulas with their current values, preventing further recalculations.

2. **Multiply the results and add up the sum by using standard formulas:**

    a) **Enter this formula in cell N3:** =L3*M3.

    b) **Double-click to copy the Fill Handle in cell N3 to copy the formula down to cell N7.**

    c) **Click on cell N8 and press Alt+= (Windows) or Cmd+Shift+T (macOS) to use the AutoSum feature to add up the values in cells N3:N7.**

    If keyboard shortcuts aren't your thing, choose Home ⇨ AutoSum.

3. **To accomplish the same results with one formula instead of multiple steps, enter the following formula into cell O8:**
    =SUMPRODUCT(L3:L7,M3:M7)

    Each column of values you wish to multiply must be referenced individually, as shown. While the formula =SUMPRODUCT(L3:M7) might seem more efficient, it produces incorrect results because it multiplies and sums values across the combined range rather than treating columns independently.

Calculating totals by criteria

SUMPRODUCT's alter ego is its ability to act as a stand-in for SUMIF and SUMIFS. By adding up values that meet specific criteria, SUMPRODUCT offers a more flexible alternative that even handles data in closed workbooks without breaking a sweat:

1. **Enter this formula into cell J4:** =SUMPRODUCT(($D$4:$D$20>=$H$4)*($E$4:$E$20=G4)*$C$4:$C$20)

    This formula uses a single array argument that breaks down as follows:

    - **($D$4:$D$20>=$H$4):** This acts like the criteria_range1/criteria1 arguments in SUMIFS. Unlike SUMIF or SUMIFS, the >= operator is not enclosed in double quotes. Always enclose search parameters within SUMPRODUCT in parentheses. The $H$4 absolute reference ensures the formula always refers to the correct input.

- **($E$4:$E$20=G4):** Think of this as criteria_range2/criteria2. Again, no double quotes around the operator, and keep the reference to G4 limber, loose, and relative.

- **$C$4:$C$20:** This is the equivalent of the sum_range argument in SUMIFS.

2. **Double-click to copy the Fill Handle in cell J3 to copy the formula down to cell J8.**

   In essence, SUMPRODUCT evaluates each row in the specified ranges, assigning a 1 for matches and a 0 for non-matches in column D, and another 1 or 0 for matches or non-matches in column E. It then multiplies the results for each row by the corresponding values in column C and adds up the total.

TECHNICAL STUFF

If the Exercise worksheet resided in a workbook named Journal.xlsx, the formula would look like this: =SUMPRODUCT(([Journal.xlsx]Exercise! $D$4:$D$20>=H$4)*([Journal.xlsx]Exercise! $E$4:$E$20=G4)* [Journal.xlsx] Exercise!$C$4:$C$20).

Troubleshooting SUMPRODUCT

Here are a couple of situations that can result in SUMPRODUCT returning error values:

>> **#REF!:** This error value arises if you attempt to use the spilled range operator (#) with SUMPRODUCT, or if you delete a column or row that SUMPRODUCT is referencing.

>> **#VALUE!:** This error value arises if any of your search criteria are numeric but your criteria range equivalents include one or more cells that contain text.

>> **#N/A:** This error value arises when your criteria_range or sum_range equivalents are not all sized the same.

Counting with COUNTIF

COUNTIF is like Count von Count from Sesame Street, clipboard in hand, keeping track of exactly what you ask for — complete with that unmistakable Dracula voice. "One apple, two apples, three apples that meet my criterion! Ah-ah-ah!" And just like the Count, every time COUNTIF works its magic, you might find yourself imagining thunder and lightning booming in celebration of your success.

The COUNTIF function has two arguments, but who's counting?

>> **range:** A set of cells within a single column or row that you want to search

>> **criteria:** A text string, number, or formula that evaluates to a specific value, determining which instances to count.

Here's how to avoid putting fingerprints on your monitor by using COUNTIF:

1. **Enter this formula into cell K4:** =COUNTIF($E$4:$E$20,G4).

2. **Double-click the Fill Handle in cell K4.**

The formulas are copied down through cell K8 and return the number of instances of each workout.

REMEMBER

COUNTIF is case-insensitive, so it doesn't differentiate between "Workout" and "workout." However, leading or trailing spaces in your criteria can impact results — Excel doesn't cull extraneous spaces for you! You can work it out, though, with wildcards; for instance, =COUNTIF($E$4:$E$20,"*workout*") causes Excel to match "workout" anywhere within the text, whether it's at the beginning, middle, or end of the cell's contents.

3. **To create a dynamic array version, enter this formula into cell I11:** =COUNTIF(E4:E20,G4#).

Birds of a feather flock together, which means that COUNTIF also requires any linked workbooks to remain open in the background. Fortunately, you can use SUMPRODUCT as a stand-in for both COUNTIF and COUNTIFS, as shown here:

1. **Enter this formula into cell J10:** =SUMPRODUCT(($E$4:E$20=G10)*1).

The formula returns 0 if you omit the *1 at the end. In this context, SUMPRODUCT needs something to multiply the matching rows by; otherwise, there's nothing for it to add up.

2. **Double-click the Fill Handle in cell J9.**

REMEMBER

Unlike most Excel functions, SUMPRODUCT does not support the spilled range operator (#).

TECHNICAL STUFF

You can use COUNTIF to tally specific error values within a range. For instance, =COUNTIF(A1:H4,"#VALUE!") returns the number of instances of #VALUE!. However, you cannot use wildcards to count errors, even though wildcards are allowed for other types of searches.

Tallying multiple conditions with COUNTIFS

You don't have to be Raymond Babbitt from *Rain Man* to appreciate this next function, which enables you to count items based on as many as 127 criteria — though he might remind you that Wapner comes on at 5 o'clock today. The COUNTIFS function has the following arguments:

» **criteria_range1:** A required range of cells within a single column or row to test against a criterion.

» **criteria1:** A required criterion that can be text, numbers, or a formula defining the condition to match. As with SUMIF and SUMIFS, operators like >, >=, <, and <= can be used but must be enclosed in quotes (e.g., "*workout" or ">="&A1).

» **criteria_range2..127:** Optional additional ranges for criteria.

» **criteria2..127:** Optional additional criteria to evaluate.

Say we want to count the number of 40-minute runs we've completed — or perhaps that Forrest Gump has completed:

1. **Enter the word** Run **in cell G17.**

2. **Type** 40 **into cell H17.**

3. **Enter this formula into cell I17:** =COUNTIFS($E$4:$E20,G17,$C$4:$C$20,H17).

   The formula returns 4. Replacing H17 with ">="&H17 increases the result to 5, as it then includes the 45-minute run.

Calculating conditional averages

When is an average not so average? When it comes with conditions! The AVERAGEIF function lets you calculate an average for values that meet a single condition and includes the following arguments:

» **range (required):** Two or more cells to average — because, face it, the average of a single cell would just be the value of that cell.

» **criteria (required):** Specifies which cells are averaged. This can be text, like "apples"; numbers, like 42 (or "42" if you enjoy typing extra characters); or comparison operators, like ">42" (in which case, the double quotes are required).

>> **average_range (optional:** Cells to average if different from range.

You're barking up the wrong tree if you try to use AVERAGEIF to create a weighted average. That lowdown is covered in Chapter 2.

Here's a quick rundown:

1. **Enter the words** Treadmill Workout **into cell G18.**

2. **Add this formula into cell H18:** =AVERAGEIF($E$4:$E20,G18,$C$4:$C20).

   The formula returns 28.3333, a reminder of how long we tend to run in place — metaphorically, if nothing else.

   Cue the drug company announcer: "AVERAGEIF is a powerful tool for calculating conditional averages, but side effects may include returning #VALUE! errors when referencing data in a closed workbook. Consult your workbook's status before proceeding."

Creating other conditional calculations

Hmmm, there's definitely a pattern here. It's like when Charlie from *It's Always Sunny in Philadelphia* connects all the red string on the conspiracy board — except this time, the pattern actually makes sense. That's why I'm not going to spell out the arguments for AVERAGEIFS. To quote the Talking Heads' song "Once in a Lifetime": "Same as it ever was!"

Hypothetical scenario: You want to use AVERAGEIF or AVERAGEIFS to reference data in another workbook. Rather than wrangling workbooks, you can use one SUMPRODUCT to sum the total of what you want to average and divide that by a second SUMPRODUCT that counts the number of instances. Where there's a will, there's a way — well, most of the time.

For the sake of completeness, allow me to give a couple of quick shoutouts to similar functions:

>> **MINIF/MINIFS:** Returns the smallest number based on one or more criteria

>> **MAXIF/MAXIFS:** Returns the largest number based on one or more criteria

You're on your own if you're referencing other workbooks with these functions, because there's no way to cajole SUMPRODUCT into finding the smallest or largest value. Instead, let the #VALUE! error values that pop up serve as a friendly reminder to keep that source workbook open in the background.

Refining Advanced Formulaic Decisions

You know the drill — sometimes, making multiple decisions at once can leave you feeling pulled like Stretch Armstrong. Thankfully, in Excel, you don't have to stretch yourself thin to test for multiple conditions. The first two functions in this section simplify complex decision-making, while the third adds a twist with reverse logic when needed.

Combining conditions with AND

The AND function allows you to evaluate up to 255 logical tests, returning TRUE if all tests are TRUE, or FALSE if even one test is FALSE. The AND function has the following arguments:

>> **logical1:** A calculation that evaluates to TRUE or FALSE.

>> **logical2..255:** Optional additional calculations that evaluate to TRUE or FALSE.

Now, to revisit the Poky Little Puppy example from the "Deciding with IF" section earlier in this chapter. The clever puppy has figured out that staying out past midnight resets the dessert determinator, making him eligible for rice pudding. To counter this, his mother has decided to simplify her dessert calculator:

>> **Home after 9:00 AM and before 6:00 PM:** Rice pudding

>> **Otherwise:** Extra responsibilities

Now, you can use the AND function within the IF function to handle this logic:

1. **Enter** `12:00 PM` **into cell A1 of a blank worksheet or revisit your earlier work if the workbook is still open.**

2. **Add this formula to cell A2:** `=AND(A1>=TIMEVALUE("9:00 AM"),A1<=TIMEVALUE("6:00 PM"))`.

   The formula returns TRUE because 12:00 PM is greater than or equal to 9:00 AM and less than or equal to 6:00 PM.

3. **Update cell A1 to** `8:59 AM`.

   The formula in A2 now returns FALSE because 8:59 AM is earlier than 9:00 AM.

4. **Modify cell A2 to:** `=IF(AND(A1>=TIMEVALUE("9:00 AM"),A1<=TIMEVALUE("6:00 PM")),"Rice pudding","Extra responsibilities")`

   The formula returns Extra responsibilities because the AND function evaluates to FALSE.

In short, the AND function enables you to streamline decision-making by ensuring all conditions are met, creating precise and reliable logic in your formulas.

Expanding criteria with OR

The OR function allows you to evaluate up to 255 logical tests, returning TRUE if at least one test evaluates to TRUE, or FALSE if none of the tests evaluate to TRUE. The OR function has the following arguments:

>> **logical1:** A calculation that evaluates to TRUE or FALSE.

>> **logical2..255:** Optional additional calculations that evaluate to TRUE or FALSE.

The Poky Little Puppy's mother could have used the OR function instead of AND as part of her dessert calculator:

>> **Home before 9:00 AM or after 6:00 PM:** The puppy gets extra responsibilities because he's breaking the schedule.

>> **Otherwise:** Rice pudding.

Now, you can use the OR function within the IF function to handle this logic:

1. **Type** `3:00 AM` **or** `3 A` **into cell A1.**

2. **Add this formula to cell A3:** `=OR(A1<TIMEVALUE("9:00 AM"),A1>TIMEVALUE("6:00 PM"))`.

   The formula returns TRUE because, although 3:00 AM is earlier than 9:00 AM (TRUE), it is not considered later than 6:00 PM (FALSE) — no matter what the puppy's mother thinks.

3. **Update cell A1 to** `5:00 PM` **or** `5 P`.

   The formula in A3 now returns FALSE because 5:00 PM is not earlier than 9:00 AM nor later than 6:00 PM. What a perfect puppy!

4. **Modify cell A3 to:** `=IF(OR(A1<TIMEVALUE("9:00 AM"),A1>TIMEVALUE("6:00 PM")),"Extra responsibilities","Rice pudding")`

   The formula returns `Rice pudding` because the OR function evaluates to TRUE.

To summarize, the OR function simplifies complex scenarios by checking if any condition is true, making your formulas more adaptable and flexible.

TECHNICAL STUFF

The specialized XOR function performs an exclusive OR operation, returning TRUE only when an odd number of logical tests evaluate to TRUE. If an even number of tests are TRUE, or all are FALSE, the function returns FALSE.

Negating conditions with NOT

It's time to channel your inner Valley Girl . . . not! Seriously, the NOT function is like a switch that flips TRUE values to FALSE and FALSE values to TRUE. The NOT function has a single argument:

>> **logical:** A calculation that evaluates to TRUE or FALSE.

The NOT function is often used to create reverse logic. Here are some practical examples:

>> **Identifying values that don't meet specific criteria:** =NOT(A1=10) returns TRUE when A1 is equal to anything other than 10.

>> **Creating opposite conditions in an IF statement:** =IF(NOT(A2="Completed"), "Hold your horses!","Done and dusted!")

>> **Identifying nonblank cells:** =NOT(ISBLANK(A1)) returns TRUE if cell A1 is not empty.

>> **Excluding values:** =NOT(AND(A1>=10,A1<=20)) returns TRUE if A1 contains a value less than 10 or greater than 20.

Chapter **9**

Carving Data with Dynamic Arrays

S everal million years ago, the Colorado River began carving and shaping what we now know as the Grand Canyon in northern Arizona. Spanning 277 miles in length, up to 18 miles wide, and over a mile deep (about the size of some of your data sets, amirite?), the canyon is uniquely illuminated at dawn, when horizontal rays of the sun reveal its stunning natural wonders — a rare spectacle on Earth.

The Colorado River tirelessly reshapes the canyon, much like dynamic array functions reshape your data — breaking free from single-cell constraints and allowing your data to flow and transform effortlessly. Once you see what these new functions can automate, you might feel like you've been manually repeating tasks for millions of years. Joining the free Microsoft 365 Insider program can grant you early access when new worksheet functions are added to Excel, provided using a beta version of Excel and its Office companions isn't a dealbreaker for you — or your employer.

Sifting Through Data Dynamically

Dynamic array functions can transform your data much like the forces that shaped the Grand Canyon:

>> **Spilling results:** Automatically populate adjacent cells with as many results as needed.

>> **Automating traditionally manual tasks:**

  • **Removing duplicates:** The UNIQUE function is like a butte, isolating distinct values from a range and standing alone after the surrounding material erodes.

  • **Sorting:** The SORT and SORTBY functions mirror the strata of the canyon, ordering data into meaningful layers, like terraces, creating stepped sequences for easier analysis.

  • **Filtering lists:** The FILTER function works like a mesa, retaining a flat, useful expanse of relevant data while clearing away the excess — keeping only what's meaningful based on your criteria.

Since dynamic arrays are formula-based, changes to your data are reflected immediately. However, just like the Colorado River, they need room to roam, often requiring a broad expanse of blank cells to perform their magic. If existing data blocks the flow, a #SPILL! error value signals the issue. No mop and bucket are needed — simply move the obstructing data or relocate the formula, and you're back in action.

Dynamic arrays mark a significant evolution in Excel's functionality, providing more powerful and flexible tools for data analysis. This chapter explores various ways to leverage these functions, offering a solid foothold for understanding and utilizing dynamic arrays effectively.

Let's dig up an Excel template to use as source data:

1. **Create a sample workbook:**

  • **Windows:** Choose File ➪ New, type Diet and Exercise Journal in the search bar, press Enter, select the Diet and Exercise template, and click Create.

  • **macOS:** Download the Chapter 9 Diet and Exercise workbook from www.dummies.com/go/excelfd and open it in Excel.

2. **Activate the DIET worksheet, which has an Excel table named Diet.**

When you click a cell within an Excel table, such as B3 in this example, the Table Design (Windows) or Table (macOS) tab appears in Excel's ribbon, as shown in Figure 9-1. On the left side of this ribbon tab, the Table Name field displays either a generic name, like Table1, or a custom name, such as Diet. This tab also provides tools for formatting, filtering, summarizing, and exporting the table.

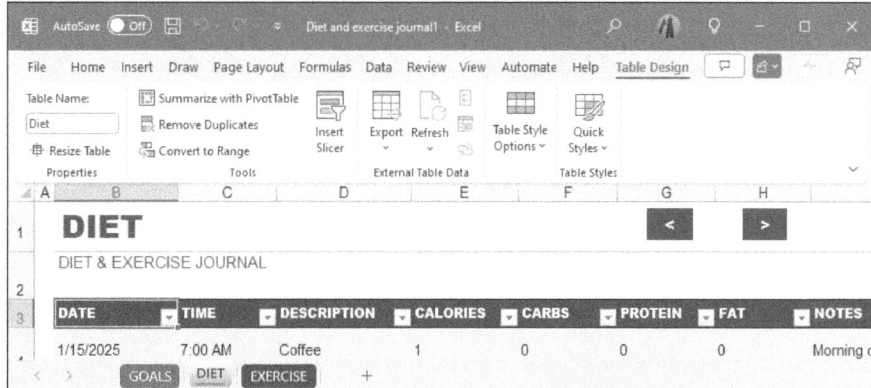

FIGURE 9-1:
The Table Design
tab and Table
Name field.

You're now ready to start excavating your data with dynamic array functions. While all the functions in this chapter can operate with standard cell references (like D4:D19), I primarily use structured references to demonstrate the formulas referring to data formatted as an Excel table (like Diet[Description] — see Chapter 5). After all, who wants to rely on Stone Age techniques when working with modern worksheet functions?

REMEMBER

Structured reference formulas offer better data integrity and largely eliminate the need for absolute or mixed references (as discussed in Chapter 1). This makes formulas more robust and reduces the likelihood of errors when adjusting or copying them across your worksheet.

Removing duplicates with UNIQUE

A butte is an isolated hill or small mountain with steep, often vertical sides and a relatively flat top. This geological formation typically forms when harder rock layers cap a softer rock base, which erodes away more quickly over time. The UNIQUE function works similarly, isolating distinct values from your data and leaving behind a clean, streamlined result.

The UNIQUE function includes three arguments:

>> **array (required):** The range of cells, Excel table, or dynamic array from which you want to carve out unique values — much like the Colorado River carved the Grand Canyon out of Arizona. Examples include D4:D19, Diet[DESCRIPTION], or the output of a function like FILTER.

>> **by_col (optional):** Determines whether to evaluate uniqueness across rows or columns, akin to examining the stratification of the canyon walls:

● **TRUE:** Analyzes by columns, like observing horizontal rock layers (e.g., A1:Z1).

● **FALSE (default):** Analyzes by rows, like tracing vertical paths through the canyon (e.g., A1:A26).

>> **exactly_once (optional):** Defines how uniqueness is evaluated, mirroring how erosion reveals different formations:

● **TRUE:** Returns items that appear exactly once, like geological formations that exist only in one location within a landscape. If no such formations exist, a #CALC! error signals that there are no uniquely singular items in the range.

When set to TRUE, the UNIQUE function applies the database definition of uniqueness: it returns only those items that appear exactly once in the specified range. Items that occur more than once are excluded entirely from the results.

● **FALSE (default):** Returns one of each distinct item, much like cataloging one example of each type of formation in a canyon, regardless of how often they appear throughout the landscape.

Here's how to create a structured reference formula to demonstrate a basic use of the UNIQUE function:

1. In cell C23, type =UNIQUE(Diet to begin the formula.

2. Type [to display the AutoComplete list, shown in Figure 9-2, which shows the column headings for the Diet table.

3. Select DESCRIPTION using your mouse or arrow keys, then press Tab to add the field name to the formula.

4. Type]) and then press Enter to complete the formula.

The formula returns five unique values.

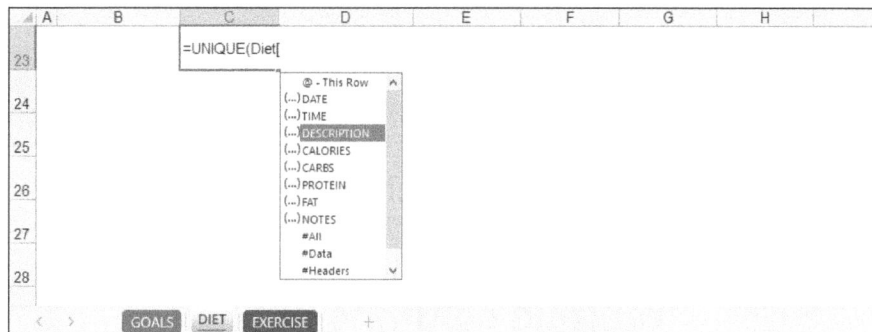

FIGURE 9-2:
The
AutoComplete list
for a structured
reference
formula.

Now, let's edit the formula to apply the database definition of unique:

1. **Select cell C23 and click before the) or press F2, and then use the arrow keys to navigate to that position in the formula.**

2. **Type a comma to close the array argument, followed by a second comma to skip the optional by_col argument.**

   Skipping an argument in this way instructs Excel to use the default value — FALSE — indicating analysis by row.

3. **Type TRUE and then press Enter to apply the edits.**

   The formula =UNIQUE(Diet[DESCRIPTION],,TRUE) now returns #CALC! because every item in the DESCRIPTION column appears more than once.

4. **Next, let's swap the DESCRIPTION field for the CALORIES field:**

   a) **Click after the [or press F2 and navigate to that position.**

   b) **Press Alt+Down (Windows) or Ctrl+Option+Down Arrow (macOS) to display the AutoComplete list, as shown in Figure 9-1.**

   c) **Choose CALORIES, press Tab, and then press Enter to apply the change.**

   The formula now returns eight unique items, excluding 1, 10, and 477, as these values appear in the CALORIES column more than once.

5. **Enter this formula into cell D23: =UNIQUE(Diet[Calories]).**

   The formula returns eleven unique items, including 1, 10, and 477 and illustrates some of the nuances that can arise when sifting through data ranges.

TIP

   This formula could be written as =UNIQUE(E4:E19) when using standard references to exclude the header row, or as =UNIQUE(E3:E19) if you want to include the header row in the results.

REMEMBER

A key benefit of dynamic array functions over manual processes is that they always reference the original copy of the data, leaving it intact. In contrast, manual processes often modify the original data directly, potentially leading to unintended changes or loss of information. This makes dynamic array functions a safer and more efficient option for organizing and analyzing data.

Removing duplicates from multiple columns

Let's add a level of complexity to the UNIQUE function by removing duplicates from two columns at once. Much like combining two geological strata to study their combined impact, this formula merges values from two fields:

1. **Start the formula by typing this into cell F23:** `=UNIQUE(Diet[De`, **and then press Tab, and type** `]` **to add the Description field to the array argument.**

2. **Type** `&": "&` **to add a colon and a space between the two columns.**

3. **Type** `Diet[N`, **press Tab, and then type** `]` **to add the Notes field to the formula.**

4. **Type** `)`, **then press Enter to complete the formula.**

   The formula provides a two-for-one option by identifying unique Description/Notes pairs, and then inserting a colon and a space between each result.

TIP

If the list is not formatted as an Excel table, use this standard reference formula: `=UNIQUE(D4:D19&": "&I4:I19)`.

Organizing with SORT

After you've eliminated duplicates from a list, you may want to sort the results — much like organizing a rock collection based upon size or other characteristics. The SORT function helps you organize data from a range or dynamic array in ascending or descending order. It includes four arguments:

>> **array (required):** The range of cells, Excel table, or dynamic array you want to reorganize.

>> **sort_index (optional):** The position of the column (or row) within the array to base the sort on. Defaults to 1 if omitted.

>> **sort_order (optional):** The order in which to sort the data:

   • **1 (default):** Sort in ascending order (e.g., A to Z).

   • **−1:** Sort in descending order (e.g., Z to A).

>> **by_col (optional):** Determines whether to sort by columns or rows.

- **TRUE:** Sort by column, horizontally.
- **FALSE (default):** Sort vertically, by row.

Let's dig into the SORT function by rearranging the output of the UNIQUE function:

TIP

1. **Update the formula in cell D23 to:** `=SORT(UNIQUE(Diet[CALORIES]))`.

   The results in cells D23:D33 now appear in ascending order, from 1 to 500.

   This formula could be written as =SORT(UNIQUE(E4:E19))

2. **Now let's reverse the order of the dynamic array that starts in cell D23:**

   a) **Click in the formula bar just before the final), or press F2 and use the arrow keys to navigate to that position.**

   b) **Type a comma to close the sort_index argument (or type 1 since the array contains only one column), then type a second comma followed by –1 to indicate sorting in descending order.**

   c) **Press Enter to apply the changes to the formula.**

   The updated formula: =SORT(UNIQUE(Diet[CALORIES])),,-1) displays the unique listing of calories sorted from largest to smallest.

TIP

   If the list is not formatted as an Excel table, use this standard reference formula: =SORT(UNIQUE(E4:E19),,-1).

REMEMBER

   You can only edit a dynamic array formula from its starting cell. Clicking any other cell within the array shows the formula grayed out in the formula bar, like smoke, and it disappears — again like smoke — when you click inside the formula bar.

   SORT returns #VALUE! if -1 for the sort_order is inadvertently entered into the sort_index argument.

WARNING

3. **Update cell E6 to change 283 to 750.**

   The SORT/UNIQUE combination in cell D23 now returns results to cells D23:D33, ranked in descending order from 750 to 1. Much like layers of sedimentary rock forming over time, dynamic array functions organize and refine data effortlessly. It's like discarding your shovel in favor of a precision water drill — dynamic arrays automate what would otherwise involve the manual use of Remove Duplicates and Sort, both covered in Chapter 4.

WARNING

The SORT function can introduce a potential data integrity risk when referencing multi-column ranges. If the sort_index argument is set to a static number, changes to the structure of the array — such as adding or removing a column — can cause the function to sort based on the wrong column. To mitigate this risk, consider using dynamic methods, such as MATCH (covered in Chapter 6), to calculate the column position based on a header value, ensuring the correct column is always referenced, even if the array structure changes.

Ordering multiple columns with SORTBY

The SORT function is like using a pickaxe to chip away at a specific layer of rock — it requires you to define a single sort_index, making it effective but less adaptable if the structure of your "rock face" (data) changes. While you can sort by multiple columns by nesting SORT functions, it can quickly become challenging to manage the hierarchy.

SORTBY, on the other hand, is like using a stone sorter in a quarry to let multiple layers of material naturally fall into place based on criteria you define. With SORTBY, you can dynamically specify multiple sorting criteria (arrays), providing more precision and adaptability — just as a stone sorter automatically organizes raw materials into ordered groups.

>> **array (required):** The range of cells, Excel table, or dynamic array you want to reorganize.

>> **by_array1 (required):** The address of the first range of cells that you wish to organize.

>> **sort_order1 (optional):** The order in which to sort the data:

- **1 (default):** Sort in ascending order (e.g., A to Z).

- **-1:** Sort in descending order (e.g., Z to A).

>> **by_array2..64 (optional):** Optional additional ranges for sorting.

>> **sort_order2..64 (optional):** Optional additional sort orders.

Let's get down and dirty and rearrange the diet list. We'll organize it in ascending order by description and then descending order by calories:

1. **Start building the formula by entering** =SORTBY(Diet, **into cell L23.**

This tells Excel to sort the entire contents of the Excel table named Diet and closes the array argument.

2. **Type** Diet[Des, **press Tab to add the DESCRIPTION field to the formula, and then type**] **,.**

The comma closes the by_array1 argument. At this point, the partial formula should be =SORTBY(Diet,Diet[Description],.

3. **Type** 1, **to indicate that the DESCRIPTION field should be sorted in ascending order.**

The comma closes the sort_order1 argument, resulting in the partial formula of =SORTBY(Diet,Diet[Description],1,.

4. **Type** Diet[Cal, **press Tab to add the CALORIES field to the formula, and then type**] **,.**

The comma closes the by_array2 argument. At this stage, the formula looks like this: =SORTBY(Diet,Diet[Description],1,Diet[CALORIES],.

5. **Type** –1) **and then press Enter.**

This closes the sort_order2 argument and completes the formula of =SORTBY (Diet,Diet[Description],1,Diet[CALORIES],1-1).

TIP

If the list is not formatted as an Excel table, use this standard reference formula: =SORTBY(B4:I19,D4:D19,1,E4:E19,-1).

As shown in Figure 9-3, dynamic array functions retrieve data but not formatting. Column L comprises date serial numbers, while column M contains time serial numbers. You must still manually format dynamic array results.

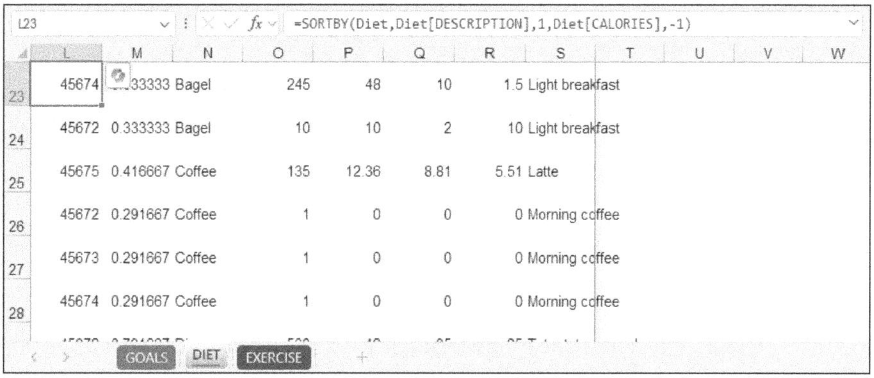

L23			fx	=SORTBY(Diet,Diet[DESCRIPTION],1,Diet[CALORIES],-1)							
	L	M	N	O	P	Q	R	S	T	U	V	W
23	45674	.33333	Bagel	245	48	10		1.5 Light breakfast				
24	45672	0.333333	Bagel	10	10	2		10 Light breakfast				
25	45675	0.416667	Coffee	135	12.36	8.81		5.51 Latte				
26	45672	0.291667	Coffee	1	0	0		0 Morning coffee				
27	45673	0.291667	Coffee	1	0	0		0 Morning coffee				
28	45674	0.291667	Coffee	1	0	0		0 Morning coffee				

GOALS   DIET   EXERCISE   +

FIGURE 9-3:
Dynamic array functions and formulas return unformatted cell contents.

Finding specific data with FILTER

You could think of the FILTER function as a soil sifter, allowing the data you want to keep to pass through while leaving behind the records you don't need. It's a simple yet powerful tool for separating the useful from the irrelevant, much like how a sifter separates fine soil from rocks and debris. The difference? This isn't a manual hand sieve like the Filter feature. The FILTER function is fully automatic, dynamically updating to display new, relevant results whenever you change an input. It's like having a high-tech sifting machine at your fingertips!

The FILTER function has the following three arguments:

>> **array (required):** The range of cells, Excel table, or dynamic array you want to reorganize.

>> **include (required):** Tells Excel which rows or columns to keep. It must be a list of TRUE or FALSE values that matches either:

- The number of rows, to filter rows.

- The number of columns, to filter columns.

Examples include:

- **Structured Reference:** Diet[Description]="Bagel" or Diet[Description]=B40 (where B40 contains the word "Bagel") returns rows from the array where the description is "Bagel."

- **Standard Cell Reference:** D4:D14="Bagel" or D4:D14=D40 (where D40 contains the word "Bagel") filters the rows in the array where cells D4:D14 are equal to "Bagel."

WARNING

- The FILTER function returns #VALUE! if the include argument doesn't match the shape of the data. Structured references help avoid this issue by automatically adjusting to the table's size, making formulas more reliable and easier to use.

>> **if_empty (optional):** A value to return when no matches are found. If omitted and there are no matches, FILTER returns a #CALC! error value. For example, you could display "No Matches Found" instead.

Let's figure out how to FILTER specific rows from a list:

1. **Enter the word** Coffee **into cell B40.**

2. **Enter the following formula into cell B41:** =FILTER(Diet,Diet[DESCRIPT ION]=B40).

   This instructs Excel to return all rows from the Diet table where the DESCRIPTION column matches the contents of cell B40 and returns four rows.

REMEMBER

   The FILTER function returns only data, so values like dates and times may appear as serial numbers if not properly formatted.

TIP

If the list is not formatted as an Excel table, use this standard reference formula: =FILTER(B3:I19,D3:D19=B40).

3. **To filter for a different item, such as Toast, update cell B40 to contain the word** Toast.

The formula in cell B41 automatically updates to return the two rows where Toast appears in the DESCRIPTION column.

Filtering for multiple criteria

The Include argument acts like a sieve in a geologic dig, allowing you to filter data based on two or more sets of criteria. The number of results returned depends on your choice of operator, much like how the mesh size determines the size of arti-facts that pass through:

» **Asterisk (*):** Acts as an "and" operator. For example: =FILTER(Diet,(Diet [DESCRIPTION]="Dinner")*(Diet[CALORIES]>400)) returns rows where the DESCRIPTION field equals Dinner and the CALORIES field is greater than 400.

» **Plus (+):** Acts as an "or" operator. For example, =FILTER(Diet,(Diet[DESCRIPTIO N]="Lunch") + (Diet[DESCRIPTION]="Dinner")) returns rows where the DESCRIPTION field contains either Lunch or Dinner.

REMEMBER

Always enclose multiple criteria in parentheses to ensure that Excel evaluates the Boolean arrays correctly. This prevents ambiguity and ensures the intended logic is applied to your FILTER formula.

As noted earlier, the include argument uses Boolean arrays — effectively convert-ing criteria into a series of TRUE or FALSE values, which are equivalent to 1 or 0, respectively. The operator you choose determines how these Boolean values com-bine to filter records.

Be careful to use the "or" operator (+) only when filtering for two or more criteria within the same column. Using it across different columns can lead to unex-pected results:

» **=FILTER(Diet,(Diet[DESCRIPTION]="Coffee")+(Diet[NOTES]="Morning Coffee")):** The include argument breaks down as follows:

• The first condition, (Diet[DESCRIPTION]="Coffee"), selects all rows where "Coffee" appears in the DESCRIPTION column.

• The second condition, +(Diet[NOTES]="Morning Coffee"), selects rows where "Morning Coffee" appears in the NOTES column.

REMEMBER

These conditions are evaluated independently, so rows satisfying either condition are returned, even if the values are in different columns.

Let's break it down further:

>> **Result of the "or" operator (+):** The formula =FILTER(Diet, (Diet[DESCRIPTION]="Coffee") + (Diet[NOTES]="Morning Coffee")) returns rows with "Morning Coffee" but also includes one row with "Latte." This happens because "Latte" satisfies the NOTES condition independently of the DESCRIPTION condition.

>> **Using the "and" operator (*):** The formula =FILTER(Diet, (Diet[DESCRIPTION]= "Coffee") * (Diet[NOTES]="Morning Coffee")) would return only the three "Morning Coffee" rows and exclude the "Latte" row. This is because both conditions must be met simultaneously for a row to be included.

Managing Spilled Ranges

Dynamic array functions have the unique ability to spill results into as many additional cells as needed — provided no obstacles stand in their way. When a dynamic array encounters an impediment, the #SPILL! error values appears, signaling that it needs more room to roam — much like a claustrophobic herd of bison. This error value can also occur if a user overwrites any part of a spilled range, which, intentionally or not, can help manage those who attempt to impose their will over the data.

Let's create a #SPILL! error value — don't worry, no aisle announcements are required for the cleanup:

1. **Type 1 in to cell A1 of a blank worksheet.**

2. **Hold down the Ctrl key and drag the Fill Handle in cell A1 down to cell A10, creating a series of numbers from 1 to 10.**

3. **Enter this formula in cell C1: =A1 : A10.**

   The numbers 1 through 10 fill cells C1:C10.

4. **Select cell C5 and then press Delete.**

   The dynamic array is unaffected, as pressing Delete on any cell other than the first cell in the spilled range has no effect.

5. **Type the number 8 in cell C5.**

   The dynamic array results disappear, replaced by the #SPILL! error value in cell C1.

6. **Click on cell C1.**

   Excel highlights the theoretical range the dynamic array requires to display its results.

7. **Erase cell C5.**

   The dynamic results reappear in cells C1:C10.

This sequence demonstrates how dynamic arrays interact with obstacles and how the #SPILL! error value can help identify and resolve conflicts.

Creating self-adjusting amortization tables

You may be surprised to learn that most worksheet functions, even those dating back to Excel 1.0, now support dynamic arrays, much like the basic cell reference example in the previous section. A great way to showcase the potential of dynamic arrays in Excel is by creating a dynamic amortization schedule, which breaks down the interest and principal for a loan on a period-by-period basis.

Here's how to create the loan amortization table on a blank worksheet:

1. **Type in the loan parameters:**
   - **Cell A1:** Interest Rate
   - **Cell B1:** 7.0%
   - **Cell A2:** Term (years)
   - **Cell B2:** 30
   - **Cell A3:** Loan Amount
   - **Cell B3:** $500,000
   - **Cell A4:** Payment
   - **Cell B4:** =PMT(B1/12,B2*12,-B3)

   The PMT function has three required arguments (and two optional arguments that I'm omitting):
   - **rate:** The monthly interest rate, calculated as the annual rate in cell B1 divided by 12.
   - **nper:** The total number of payment periods, calculated as the term in years (cell B2) multiplied by 12 months per year.
   - **pv:** The present value of the loan amount, entered as -B3 to reflect cash outflow.

The formula =PMT(B1/12, B2*12, -B3) computes the monthly loan payment as $3,326.51. This value represents the fixed monthly payment required to fully amortize a $500,000 loan over 30 years at an annual interest rate of 7.0%.

- **Cell A5:** `Start Date`
- **Cell B5:** `1/1/2027`

2. **Enter in the column headings:**

   - **Cell A7:** `Period`
   - **Cell B7:** `Date`
   - **Cell C7:** `Interest`
   - **Cell D7:** `Principal`
   - **Cell E7:** `Balance`

3. **To number the loan periods, enter `=SEQUENCE(B2*12)` into cell A8.**

   A series of numbers from 1 to 360 appears in cells A8:A367. SEQUENCE is a dynamic array function with the following arguments:

   - **rows (required):** Specifies the number of rows to fill, calculated as B2*12 (30 years × 12 months).
   - **columns (optional):** Defaults to 1, creating a single column.
   - **start (optional):** Defaults to 1, so the sequence begins at 1.
   - **step (optional):** Defaults to 1, incrementing each number by 1.

4. **To calculate the date for each period in the loan, enter the formula `=EOMONTH(B5,A8#-2)+1` into cell B8.**

   This formula generates a series of loan payment dates, starting with 1/1/2027, based on the loan start date in cell B5. The EOMONTH function calculates the last day of a month and has two arguments:

   - **start_date:** The base date, which is the loan start date in cell B5.
   - **months:** The number of months to adjust:
     - **A8#:** The spilled range referencing period numbers (1 through 360).
     - **-2:** Moves the calculation back two months to compute the last day of the prior period's month.

   Adding 1 to the result of EOMONTH shifts the date to the first day of the current loan period.

Dates in Excel are stored as serial numbers representing the number of days since December 31, 1899. To quickly format the date column, select cell B8, press Ctrl+Shift+Down Arrow (Windows) or Cmd+Shift+Down Arrow (macOS) to highlight all relevant cells, then click the Number Format field on the Home tab, type S (for Short Date), and press Enter.

If the formula in cell B8 returns #VALUE!, verify that the date in cell B5 is a numeric value. Ensure it doesn't contain any leading or trailing spaces, as these can cause the formula to fail.

5. **To compute the interest portion of each monthly payment, enter this formula in cell C8:** `=IPMT(B1/12,A8#,B2*12,-B3)`.

The formula returns $2,916.67 for the first loan period. The IPMT function breaks down the interest payment for each period with the following arguments:

- **rate:** The monthly interest rate, calculated as the annual rate in cell B1 divided by 12.

- **per:** The loan period for which the interest is calculated, using the spilled range operator A8# to reference periods 1 through 360.

- **nper:** The total number of payment periods, calculated as the term in years (cell B2) multiplied by 12 months per year.

- **pv:** The present value of the loan amount, entered as -B3 to reflect cash outflow.

6. **To compute the principal portion of each monthly payment, enter this formula in cell D8:** `=PPMT(B1/12,A8#,B2*12,-B3)`.

This formula computes the principal payment for each loan period, returning $409.85 for the first period. The PPMT function uses the same arguments as IPMT.

The IPMT and PPMT functions only apply the Currency format to the first cell of a dynamic array, leaving the remaining cells unformatted. To apply the Currency format to the entire range, select the spilled range, go to the Home tab, and choose Currency from the Number Format drop-down.

The $ symbol on Excel's Home tab applies the Accounting Number format, which aligns the currency symbol and digits for cleaner columnar presentation, differing from the Currency number format, which places the symbol next to the number.

7. **To compute the ending balance for each period of the loan, enter the formula** `=SUMIF(A8#,">"&A8#, D8#)` **into cell E8.**

The formula returns 499590.2 as an unformatted amount for the first loan period. The SUMIF function is covered in Chapter 6, but here's a quick breakdown:

- **range:** A8# references the spilled range for loan periods (e.g., 1 to 360).

- **criteria:** ">"&A8#: Creates a condition to sum the principal amounts (D8#) for all periods greater than each period in A8#.

- **sum_range:** D8# references the spilled range containing the principal portion of each payment.

8. **To see the dynamic array formulas in action, change cell B2 to 1 instead of 30.**

This adjustment updates the loan term from 30 years to 1 year, as shown in Figure 9-4, dynamically recalculating all spilled ranges and formulas — including payment amounts, interest, principal, and ending balances — across the worksheet. This demonstrates the power of dynamic arrays to adapt instantly to changes in input values.

	A	B	C	D	E	F	G	H	I	J	K	L
1	Interest Rate	7.00%										
2	Term (years)	1										
3	Loan Amount	500,000										
4	Payment	$43,263.37										
5	Start Date:	1/1/2027										
6												
7	Period		Date	Interest	Principal	Balance						
8		1	1/1/2027	2,916.67	40,346.71	459,653.29						
9		2	2/1/2027	2,681.31	40,582.06	419,071.23						
10		3	3/1/2027	2,444.58	40,818.79	378,252.44						
11		4	4/1/2027	2,206.47	41,056.90	337,195.54						
12		5	5/1/2027	1,966.97	41,296.40	295,899.14						
13		6	6/1/2027	1,726.08	41,537.29	254,361.85						
14		7	7/1/2027	1,483.78	41,779.60	212,582.25						
15		8	8/1/2027	1,240.06	42,023.31	170,558.94						
16		9	9/1/2027	994.93	42,268.45	128,290.49						
17		10	10/1/2027	748.36	42,515.01	85,775.48						
18		11	11/1/2027	500.36	42,763.02	43,012.47						
19		12	12/1/2027	250.91	43,012.47	-						
20												

Dynamic Amortization Table

FIGURE 9-4: Dynamic array amortization table adjusted to show one year.

Reshaping your data

Historically in Excel, reshaping data often involved retyping, manual copy-pasting, crafting complex formulas, or relying on macros (see Chapter 16). With Excel's newer range-shaping functions, these labor-intensive approaches are largely obsolete. The formulas in this section build on the Diet and Exercise Journal workbook created at the start of this chapter.

Appending data with VSTACK and HSTACK

The VSTACK and HSTACK functions enable you to combine up to 127 ranges vertically or horizontally, respectively, into a single unified dataset. Both functions share the same arguments:

» **array1 (required):** The first range or array that you wish to combine.

» **array2..127 (optional):** Additional ranges or arrays to include.

Earlier, the FILTER function returned only the matching rows, but it did not include the column headers. To keep headers in the filtered results, use VSTACK, which stacks arrays vertically:

1. **Enter** =VSTACK(**in cell L41 to start the formula.**

2. **Type** Diet[#Headers], **to include the header row.**

3. **Type** FILTER(Diet,Diet[Description]=B40) **to filter the data rows.**

4. **Type**) **to close the VSTACK function, then press Enter.**

TIP

VSTACK and HSTACK accept cell addresses, table names, and spilled ranges. For example, the formula =VSTACK(B3:I3, B41#) combines the headings from row 3 with the filtered results spilling from cell B41, creating a unified dataset in the range where the formula is entered. This flexibility allows you to seamlessly integrate static headers and dynamic results into a single output.

By stacking the header row above the filtered results, VSTACK allows you to create a cohesive and readable output, combining both structure and data seamlessly. HSTACK works in a similar fashion to merge sets of columns together.

Selecting and refining rows and columns

Sometimes, you may want to return a subset of data and/or reorder columns — such as extracting just the Notes and Calories columns from the Diet list. The CHOOSECOLS function allows you to selectively extract up to 126 columns from a range or array. It has the following arguments:

» **array:** The range, table, or array from which you want to selectively return or reorder columns.

» **col_num1 (required):** The position of the first column in array that you want to return.

» **col_num2..126 (optional):** Additional column positions to return.

The formula =CHOOSECOLS(Diet,8,4) extracts the CALORIES and NOTES columns from the Diet table and then swaps their positions. NOTES is the eighth column in the table, while CALORIES is the fourth column.

REMEMBER

Using static position numbers, such as 8 and 4, can introduce data integrity risks if the structure of the array changes in the future. To avoid this, consider using dynamic position calculations, such as the MATCH function (Chapter 6), to ensure your formula adapts to structural changes.

TIP

The CHOOSEROWS function works similarly to CHOOSECOLS, but instead of specifying column positions with col_num, you use row_num arguments to selectively return and/or reorder rows from a range or array.

Conversely, the TAKE and DROP functions allow you to extract or remove rows or columns from a range, table, or array. Both functions share the following arguments:

>> **array (required):** Specifies the number of rows to keep or remove.

>> **rows (optional):** Specifies the number of rows to keep or remove.

   • **TAKE:** Enter a positive number to extract the specified number of rows starting at the top of the array, or a negative number to extract rows from the bottom.

   • **DROP:** Enter a positive number to exclude the specified number of rows starting at the top, or a negative number to exclude rows from the bottom.

>> **columns (optional):** Specifies the number of columns to keep or remove:

   • Enter a positive number to work from the left-hand side of the array.

   • Enter a negative number to work from the right-hand side of the array.

Although the rows and columns arguments are both listed as optional, you must specify at least one. For example:

>> **=TAKE(Diet[#All],5):** Returns the first five rows from the Diet table, starting with the header row.

>> **=TAKE(Diet,,2):** Returns the last two columns of the Diet table, excluding the header row.

Wrapping data across rows or columns

The WRAPROWS and WRAPCOLS functions allow you to coil your data into rows or columns, much like a rattlesnake resting in the sun. These functions reshape your data into a structured arrangement, making it easier to analyze and present. Both functions have the same arguments:

>> **vector:** Data arranged in a single row or column (also known as a one-dimensional array).

>> **wrap_count:** The maximum number of values before wrapping:

- **WRAPROWS:** Specifies the number of columns across each row that the data should fill before wrapping to the next row.

- **WRAPCOLS:** Specifies the number of cells down each column that the data should fill before wrapping to the next column.

>> **pad_with:** The value used to fill empty cells instead of #N/A. For example, use "" to leave the cells blank.

Here's how to wrap your head around the functions:

1. **Type** January **in cell A1 of a blank worksheet.**

2. **Drag the Fill Handle in cell A1 down to cell A12 to create a list of months.**

3. **Enter this formula in cell D1:** =WRAPROWS(A1:A12,7).

   Cells D1:J1 display January through July, while cells D2:H2 display August through December. Cells I2:J2 display #N/A, since there are only 12 months, and no pad_with argument was provided.

4. **Enter this formula in cell C4:** =WRAPCOLS(A1:A12,7,"").

   Cells D4:D10 display January through July, while cells E4:E8 display August through December. Cells E9:E10 appear blank because the pad_with argument replaces #N/A with "".

These examples highlight how these functions can structure and display data, making long lists easier to interpret.

TIP

The EXPAND function creates a dynamic array with a specified number of rows and columns, filling any additional space with a custom value or leaving it blank.

Transposing arrays into rows or columns

In Excel, transpose refers to the process of flipping the orientation of data in a range, array, or table — like flipping sedimentary rock layers to reveal hidden fossils. Rows become columns, and columns become rows, often to reorganize data for better readability or analysis. A longstanding technique involves using the TRANSPOSE function, which has a single array argument. While reliable, it might feel as ancient as the rocks themselves compared to the newer dynamic array functions TOROW and TOCOL.

1. **Enter this formula into cell B1:** =ROW().

2. **Double-click the Fill Handle in cell B1 to copy the formula down to cell B12.**

3. **Enter the following formula into cell D12:** =TRANSPOSE(A1:B14).

   The names January through December appear in cells D12:O12, and the numbers 1 through 12 appear in cells D13:O13, transposed from a vertical column into a horizontal row. Cells P12:Q13 contain zero because cells A13:B14 are blank.

   Wrap the LEFT function (Chapter 7) around TRANSPOSE to hide zeros in blank cells, e.g., =LEFT(TRANSPOSE(A1:B14),50). Note that the LEFT function converts numeric values to text.

TECHNICAL STUFF

4. **Enter the following formula into cell D15:** =TRANSPOSE(D12#).

   This formula uses the spilled range operator (#) to dynamically reference the spilled range from D12:O13 and flips the month names and numbers into D15:E26, converting them from rows into columns.

This sequence demonstrates how TRANSPOSE switches data orientations across multiple rows or columns. Conversely, the TOROW and TOCOL functions transform ranges or arrays into a single row or column. Both functions have the same arguments:

>> **array (required):** The range of cells, Excel table, or dynamic array to be transformed into a single row or column.

>> **ignore (optional):** Determines which values to exclude:

   - **0 (default):** Keeps all values.
   - **1:** Ignores blank cells.
   - **2:** Ignores errors (e.g., #N/A, #DIV/0!, #CALC!).
   - **3:** Ignores blanks and errors.

>> **scan by column:** Sets the scanning direction:

   - **TRUE:** Scans by column, row by row.
   - **FALSE (default):** Scans by row, column by column.

TOROW or TOCOL pair effectively with the UNIQUE function to create a unique list from multidimensional arrays, flattening rows and columns into a single dimension. They also work as data cleanup tools, removing blanks and errors with ease.

IN THIS CHAPTER

» **Tracing formula links**

» **Breaking formulas down**

» **Displaying formulas onscreen**

» **Identifying and resolving formula errors**

» **Controlling when formulas calculate**

Chapter **10**

Tracing and Debugging Formulas

ormulas are often the backbone of Excel spreadsheets, but working with them can sometimes feel like navigating a hedge maze while blindfolded — frustrating, disorienting, and occasionally leading to the digital equivalent of walking into a wall. This chapter arms you with these essential skills for managing and troubleshooting formulas, so that you can find your way out with confidence:

» **Visually tracing formula links between cells,** revealing how different parts of your workbook connect

» **Breaking formulas down in slow motion,** stepping through each calculation like a forensic investigator

» **Displaying formulas directly onscreen,** making it easier to audit a worksheet or create documentation

» **Walking through Excel's Error Checking prompts and feature,** which flag some (but not all) formula mishaps before they trip you up

» **Controlling when formulas calculate,** ensuring your data stays fresh without bogging down massive workbooks with unnecessary recalculations

Chapter 1 covers how to execute commands across multiple worksheets at once by creating a group. However, most formula auditing commands — except for Show Formulas — are disabled when worksheets are grouped.

Before we can troubleshoot formulas, we need some formulas to troubleshoot — it's a bit of a chicken-and-egg situation. To get you started, here's how to access a ready-made workbook:

>> **Windows:** Choose File ⇨ New, type Loan Comparison Calculator in the search bar, press Enter, select the Loan Comparison Calculator template, and click Create.

>> **macOS:** Download the Chapter 10 Loan Comparison Calculator from www.dummies.com/go/excelfd and open it in Excel.

Tracking Precedent and Dependent Cells

The Trace Precedents and Trace Dependents commands create a breadcrumb trail of a formula's dependencies — because numbers don't just appear out of thin air (even if it can feel that way). Here's what the features do:

>> **Trace Precedents:** Identifies which cells feed values or formulas into the selected cell.

>> **Trace Dependents:** Shows which cells rely on the selected cell for their calculations.

>> The Trace Precedents and Trace Dependents features only act on one cell at a time. You can trace multiple cells, but you must trace each cell individually — no shortcuts, no bulk tracing, just a test of patience.

Precedent and dependents can be:

>> **Direct:** Values or formulas that feed directly into or from the selected cell.

>> **Indirect:** Cells containing intermediary calculations that influence the selected cell or that indirectly rely on it, meaning you might have to follow the daisy-chain a few steps back to see the full picture.

To help visualize these connections, Excel uses tracer arrows:

>> **Solid blue arrow(s):** Mark connections to other cells on the current worksheet.

>> **Dashed black arrow(s) with a worksheet icon:** Indicate connections to cells on other worksheets or in different workbooks.

Tracing precedent cells in formulas

Here's how to use the Trace Precedents feature to develop a schematic of the cells a formula relies on:

1. **Select cell C11 on the Payment Comparison tab.**

2. **Choose Formulas ⇨ Trace Precedents.**

   Like a detective's red string board, Excel draws tracer arrows to reveal direct connections to cells B4 and B10 ⇨ no baritone narrative required.

WARNING

   Manually saving your workbook via File ⇨ Save, the Save command on the Quick Access Toolbar, or Ctrl+S (Windows) or Cmd+S (macOS) erases all tracer arrows — without warning or confirmation.

3. **Double-click the tracer arrow that links cells B4 and B11.**

   B4 becomes the active cell, allowing you to inspect its contents and see how it contributes to the dependent formula.

4. **Double-click the tracer arrow that links cells B4 and B11 again.**

   B11 is reactivated, bringing you back to the dependent cell so you can continue analyzing its relationship to other cells.

5. **Choose Formulas ⇨ Trace Precedents a second time.**

   Additional tracer arrows reveal the first level of indirect connections to cell B11 — such as C8:C9 — as well as the fact that cell B4 feeds into C10 — because oh, what a tangled web we weave in Excel.

6. **Choose Formulas ⇨ Trace Precedents a third time.**

   The second level of indirect connections is revealed, as shown in Figure 10-1. Cells C5:C7 influence cell B11, while dashed tracer arrows pointing to cells C8 and C9 indicate that cells located in another worksheet or workbook play a role in shaping B11 — because sometimes, it takes a village.

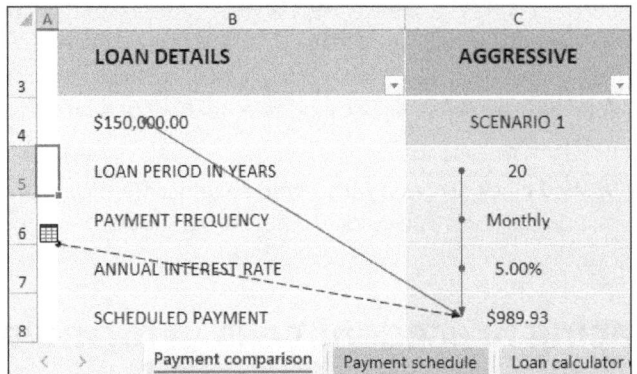

FIGURE 10-1:
Tracer
arrows identify
precedent cells.

REMEMBER

Excel won't explicitly tell you when you've reached the end of the dependency chain. The only clue? New arrows stop appearing. If you click Trace Precedents again and nothing changes, you've mapped all the precedents Excel is willing to reveal.

7. **Double-click the dashed tracer arrow that points to cell C8.**

The Go To dialog box opens.

8. **In the Go To list, double-click a cell reference or select an entry, and then click OK.**

One of two things can happen:

- **The precedent cell(s) are activated.** In this case, B5:F8 on the Loan Calculator Data worksheet become the active cells, allowing you to examine their role in the formula.

- **The "Reference is not valid" message appears.** You won't run into this prompt in this workbook, but it shows up when trying to navigate to a cell in a workbook that isn't open. Click OK on the prompt, open the linked workbook, and then try again — because Excel expects you to share the load.

9. **Choose Home ⇨ Find & Select ⇨ Go To, press Ctrl+G (Windows) or Cmd+G (macOS), or F5.**

The Go To dialog box opens, and the dependent cell's address appears in the Reference field.

10. **Click OK or press Enter.**

You instantly return to cell C8 on the Payment Comparison worksheet — no going over the river and through the woods this time!

Identifying dependent cells

The Trace Dependents command works in reverse, visually identifying cells in any open workbooks that refer to a selected cell:

1. **Select cell E3 on the Payment Schedule worksheet.**

2. **Choose Formulas ⇨ Trace Dependents.**

   Tracer arrows appear on the screen, showing that the formulas in cells E9:11 directly reference cell E3.

3. **Choose Formulas ⇨ Trace Dependents a second time.**

   A dizzying array of tracer arrows appear as the first level of indirect cell dependencies is revealed — Excel's way of showing just how interconnected your data really is.

4. **Select cell A1 and then choose Formulas ⇨ Trace Dependents.**

   The prompt shown in Figure 10-2 indicates that no dependent cells were found — proving that, at least in this case, A1 isn't pulling any strings behind the scenes.

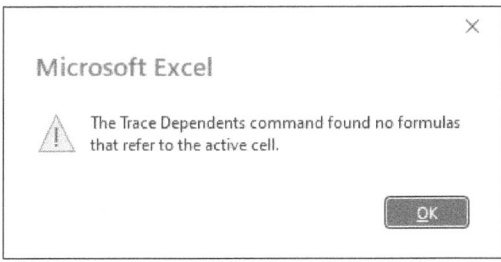

FIGURE 10-2:
An indication that no cells refer to the currently selected cell.

Navigate between dependent cells by double-clicking the tracer arrows, just as you would for precedent cells.

Removing tracer arrows

You can remove the tracer arrows, but Excel doesn't let you clear them for individual cells — it's all or nothing at the worksheet level. Use one of the following techniques:

>> **All arrows:** Choose Formulas ⇨ Remove Arrows to clear all precedent and dependent arrows from the worksheet in one go.

>> **Precedent arrows:** Choose Formulas ⇨ Remove Arrows drop-down ⇨ Remove Precedent Arrows to clear only the precedent tracer arrows from the worksheet.

>> **Dependent arrows:** Choose Formulas ⇨ Remove Arrows drop-down ⇨ Remove Dependent Arrows to clear all dependent tracer arrows from the worksheet.

Selecting precedent and dependent cells

You can wrangle all precedent or dependent cells at once using Go To Special — because manually tracing every arrow is a one-way ticket to frustration:

1. **Select cells C11:E11 on the Payment Comparison worksheet.**

2. **Choose Home ⇨ Find & Select ⇨ Go To Special.**

   The Go To Special dialog box opens, as shown in Figure 10-3.

3. **Choose Precedents, and then click OK to accept the default Direct Only option.**

   Cells C10:E10 are selected — navigate through them by pressing Tab or highlight them using Home ⇨ Fill Color if you want to leave your mark.

REMEMBER

   Select Precedents or Dependents to enable the Direct Only and All Levels options.

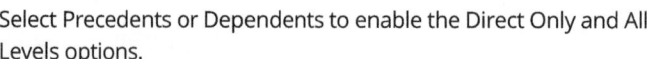

FIGURE 10-3:
The Go To Special dialog box.

4. **Choose Home ⇨ Find & Select ⇨ Go To Special again.**

5. **Choose Precedents, then All Levels, and click OK.**

    Cells B4 and C5:E10 are selected, revealing the full dependency web.

6. **Select cell A1.**

7. **Choose Home ⇨ Find & Select ⇨ Go To Special ⇨ Dependents and then click OK.**

    A No cells were found message appears — turns out, A1 is all alone, with no dependents to call its own. The same prompt appears when no precedents can be identified.

If you'd rather keep your hands on the keyboard, use these shortcuts in Windows or macOS:

- » **Ctrl+[:** Select direct precedents

- » **Ctrl+Shift+{:** Select all precedents

- » **Ctrl+]:** Select direct dependents

- » **Ctrl+Shift+}:** Select all dependents

REMEMBER

Go To Special identifies only cells on the active worksheet, so if you're chasing links across multiple sheets, you may still need to use Trace Precedents or Trace Dependents to follow the trail.

Evaluating Formulas

The Evaluate Formula feature is a handy tool for breaking down complex formulas, allowing you to step through each part of the calculation process at your own pace. Follow these steps to see a formula unfold in slow motion:

1. **Select cell C11 on the Payment Comparison worksheet.**

2. **Choose Formulas ⇨ Evaluate Formula.**

    The Evaluate Formula dialog box opens, and the cell contents appear within the Evaluate field, as shown in Figure 10-4.

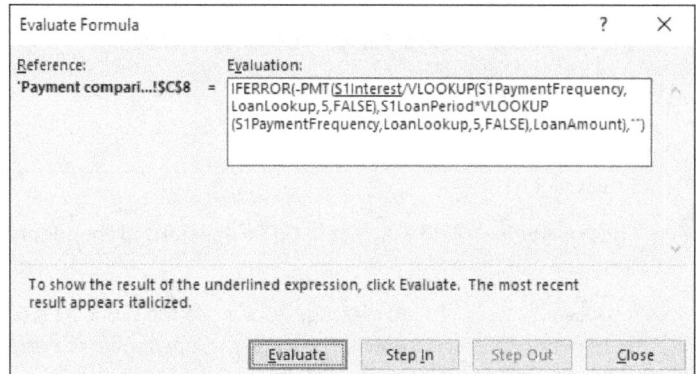

FIGURE 10-4:
The Evaluate
Formula
dialog box.

Evaluate Formula

Reference: Evaluation:
'Payment compari...!$C$8   =   IFERROR(-PMT(<u>S1Interest</u>/VLOOKUP(S1PaymentFrequency,
                                 LoanLookup,5,FALSE),S1LoanPeriod*VLOOKUP
                                 (S1PaymentFrequency,LoanLookup,5,FALSE),LoanAmount),"")

To show the result of the underlined expression, click Evaluate. The most recent result appears italicized.

Evaluate   Step In   Step Out   Close

3. **Use one of these actions to step through the calculation:**

   - Click Evaluate to convert the underlined portion of the formula to its corresponding value.

   - Click Step In to navigate to a referenced cell, and then click Step Out to replace the reference with its actual value.

     If the referenced cell isn't currently visible, Excel activates it so you can follow along.

4. **Keep clicking Evaluate or Step In/Out until the final formula result appears or exit the process by clicking Close.**

REMEMBER

You can't edit formulas in the Evaluate Formula dialog box, which prevents accidental changes. However, if you do need to edit the formula, you must close the dialog box and edit the formula in the cell or Formula Bar.

Revealing Formula Underpinnings

Your typical view of a worksheet displays formula results, meaning if you want to see what's really going on, you're stuck peeking inside one cell at a time — either by editing it or squinting at the Formula Bar. But Excel has your back with two ways to lift the veil:

>> **Show Formulas:** Instantly flips all formulas on a worksheet into view.

>> **FORMULATEXT:** Nope, this isn't how Kelly Rowland texted "WHERE YOU AT?" to Nelly in *Dilemma* — how she pulled that off in Excel remains a mystery. Instead, the FORMULATEXT function exposes formulas hiding in other worksheet cells.

Displaying all formulas

Instead of playing "guess the formula" one cell at a time, you can display all formulas on a worksheet by way of the Show Formulas feature, which enables you to toggle formula view on or off — letting you see inside all the cells at once. Here's how:

1. **Activate the Payment Comparison worksheet and then choose Formulas ⇨ Show Formulas or press Ctrl+` (Windows) or Cmd+` (macOS).**

   The worksheet switches to formula view, displaying all formulas in their respective cells instead of their calculated results.

TIP

   Formulas are often longer than their results, so some columns may need to be widened for readability. Drag column borders or use Home ⇨ Format ⇨ AutoFit Column Width to adjust as needed. If you don't want to alter your live worksheet, consider making a copy first.

2. **To print all formulas on a worksheet while ensuring clarity, follow these steps:**

   a) **Turn on the View ⇨ Gridlines and View ⇨ Headings checkboxes.**

      The Gridlines option adds cell boundaries to the printout, making formulas easier to read, while the Headers option displays row numbers and column letters.

   b) **Choose File ⇨ Print to print the worksheet.**

   c) **Turn off the Gridlines and Headings options unless you want to keep those settings in place.**

TIP

   If you are printing formulas for documentation purposes, in Chapter 3, I discuss adding headers and footers to worksheets that can include the date and/or time of the printout, workbook name and path, and worksheet name.

Extracting formulas with FORMULATEXT

FORMULATEXT has a single argument:

> **reference:** A single cell (A1) or a range (A1:A10) if you want to expose multiple formulas at once — no SMS plan required.

Here's how to put it to use:

1. **Type =FORMULATEXT(C4:C11) in cell G4 of the Payment Comparison worksheet (don't forget to toggle Show Formulas off if needed).**

Cells G4:G7 return #N/A because no formulas exist in C4:C7, while G8:G11 display the formulas from C8:C11 — lifting the curtain on what's really driving those values.

2. **Revise the formula in cell G4 to this**: `=IFNA(FORMULATEXT(C4:C11), C4:C11)`.

Now, cells G4:G11 display either the formulas from cells C4:C11 (where applicable) or the actual cell values if no formula exists.

I discuss the IFNA function in Chapter 8, but in short, it provides an alternate result when a formula returns #N/A — in this case, displaying the original cell value instead of an error.

TIP

Investigating Issues with Error Checking

Excel tries it's best to catch spreadsheet errors, helping you avoid embarrassing miscalculations and questionable data. But the fact remains — it's not a mind reader. It won't catch mistakes where what you *meant* to do and what you *actually* told Excel to do are two very different things.

To stay ahead of errors, it helps to understand what Excel can flag and how to interpret its warnings. When Excel detects a potential issue, it provides built-in tools to help you track down and resolve the problem — sometimes just spotting mistakes is half the battle. Don't worry, though — Excel does its best to help you clean up the mess.

Using background error checking

Excel automatically flags potential issues by placing a green triangle in the upper left-hand corner of affected cells. When needed, click on a flagged cell to display the Error Checking Options button, and then open the drop-down menu to identify the issue and choose whether to fix or ignore it.

Here's an example:

1. **Type** `'1/1/26` **in cell E6 of the Payment Schedule worksheet, and then press Enter, making sure to include the single quote at the start.**

Flag on the play! Excel throws up a green triangle, signaling a violation of the "years represented as two digits" rule. This causes issues only when dates are formatted or stored as text.

2. **Select cell E6 and then click on the Error Checking Options button to display the menu shown in Figure 10-5.**

The first item on the drop-down menu is inactive, serving as Excel's way of saying "Look, I found something suspicious." Depending on the error, you might see options to fix it, ignore it, edit the cell in the formula bar, or tweak Excel's error checking settings — sometimes Excel just loves to be extra (see the upcoming "Fine-tuning error checking rules" section).

3. **Choose Convert XX to 19XX.**

The data remains text-based, but Excel swaps the two-digit year for a four-digit one — poof! The error-checking triangle disappears, and Excel lets you carry on without further judgment.

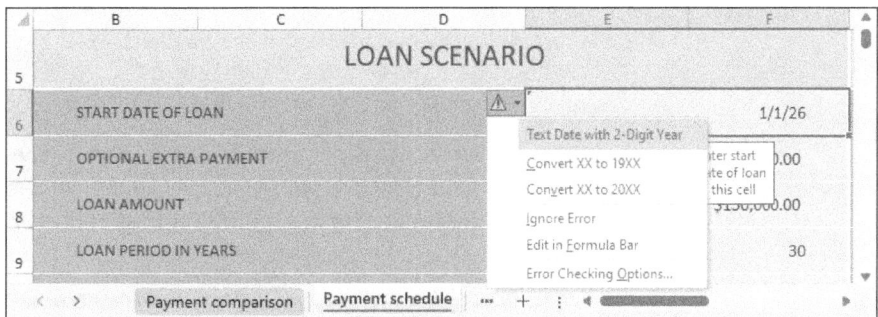

FIGURE 10-5:
Error Checking
Options menu.

Ignoring background checking errors

If you disagree with Excel's contention that a cell contains an error, you can choose Ignore Error from the Error Checking Options drop-down menu. You can ignore errors on a cell-by-cell basis, or ignore an error in multiple cells at once:

1. **Select cell B15 to ignore a single error, or cells B15:F733 to ignore multiple errors in one go.**

TIP

To select a block of contiguous cells within a column, click on the first cell, and then press Ctrl+Shift+Down Arrow (Windows) or Cmd+Shift+Down Arrow (macOS).

2. **Click the Error Checking Options button, and then choose Ignore Error from the drop-down menu.**

The error indicator vanishes for the selected cell(s).

To reset all ignored errors within a workbook, choose File ⇨ Options ⇨ Formulas and then, in the Error Checking section, click Reset Ignored Errors.

TIP

Decoding Excel's error checking rules

Excel uses a set of rules for flagging potential spreadsheet blunders — though it doesn't always get things right. Here's what it considers suspicious:

CROSS REFERENCE

>> **Cells containing formulas that result in an error:** As covered in the bonus chapter "Ten Frustrating Prompts" (available at www.dummies.com/go/excelfd), Excel throws out error values like #N/A and #VALUE! when it hits a calculation roadblock. Think of this as Excel shaking its head and saying, "Tsk, tsk."

CROSS REFERENCE

>> **Inconsistent calculated column formula in tables:** As mentioned in Chapter 5, Excel tables are supposed to keep formulas uniform across columns — unless you override them. If you introduce an inconsistency, Excel glares at you via an error flag.

>> **Cells containing years represented as two digits:** Excel isn't here for the Y2K-era nostalgia. If you enter a two-digit year as text, Excel flags it as a potential error to avoid any "Wait, is that 1926 or 2026?" confusion.

>> **Numbers formatted as text or preceded by an apostrophe:** If you've ever wondered why Excel refuses to sum a column of numbers, check if they're masquerading as text. Excel sees numbers stored as text as suspicious because they don't play nice in calculations.

>> **Formulas inconsistent with other formulas in the region:** If Excel notices that most formulas in a block follow one pattern, but a rogue formula breaks the mold, it assumes you might have made a mistake (or that you're up to something).

>> **Formulas that omit cells in a region:** Ever try to sum a column but accidentally leave out the last row? Excel flags formulas that exclude adjacent cells from a range, suspecting an oversight.

WARNING

Excel doesn't always catch these omissions, so whenever you add new data, double-check that all relevant cells are included in your formulas. Otherwise, you might end up with a calculation that's almost right — but not quite. Close only counts in horseshoes and hand grenades.

CROSS REFERENCE

>> **Unlocked cells containing formulas:** As covered in Chapter 14, Excel marks all cells as locked by default, which allows users to protect cells formulas from accidental edits when worksheet protection is enabled. Formulas in unlocked cells are flagged as a security risk.

>> **Formulas referring to empty cells:** Excel assumes that you might be referencing an empty cell by mistake, but there are many valid reasons for doing so — like when working with a template that hasn't yet been filled in.

TIP

>> **Data entered in a table is invalid:** If you're working with an Excel table linked to SharePoint data, Excel flags any entry that doesn't match the expected data type — because SharePoint plays by strict rules.

See Chapter 14 for how to use Data Validation to restrict the type of data that can be entered into specific cells.

>> **Misleading number formats:** If cell A1 is formatted as currency but cell B1 (which contains =A1) is formatted as a date, Excel assumes something sketchy is happening and flags it.

>> **Cells containing data types that couldn't refresh:** Excel's data types — currency, geography, and stocks — pull in near real-time updates from external sources. If your internet connection drops, Excel throws up an error, politely informing you that your data is now frozen in time.

>> **Cells containing stale values:** When a formula hasn't recalculated after dependent cells change, Excel strikes through the value to warn you that it's out of date. If only Excel could do the same for expired milk.

Fine-tuning error checking rules

If it feels like Excel is constantly crying wolf, you can fine-tune its error-checking options to cut down on the noise. While you can turn off background error checking entirely (choose File ⇨ Options ⇨ Formulas (Windows) or Excel ⇨ Preferences ⇨ Error Checking (macOS) clear the Background Error Checking option, and then click OK), it's usually better to disable only specific rules. That way, you minimize false positives without completely tuning out Excel's error indicators — because when Excel does flag a *real* issue, you don't want to miss it.

1. **Choose File ⇨ Options ⇨ Formulas (Windows) or Excel ⇨ Preferences ⇨ Error Checking (macOS) or choose Error Checking Options from the Error Checking Options button drop-down menu.**

2. **Uncheck the boxes for any errors that you'd rather not have Excel flag.**

   Sometimes, Excel's idea of a problem isn't your idea of a problem. I typically disable "Numbers formatted as text" and "Formulas referring to empty cells" since they tend to generate more noise than actual issues.

3. **Click OK to confirm your choices.**

REMEMBER

Changes to the error checking rules apply globally to all Excel workbooks — you can't customize them per workbook. If you only need to suppress error indicators in specific cases, use the Ignore Error command instead.

Exploring the error checking feature

Background error checking is like taking the express train — you see error indicators whiz by as Excel flags them in real time, but it's up to you whether to stop and investigate. The Error Checking command, on the other hand, is the local train, making you pause at every detected issue along the way. It scans the active worksheet for cells flagged with green triangles, stopping at each one so that you can review and address the problem.

Here's how to hop on board:

1. **Activate the Payment Comparison worksheet and then choose Formulas ⇨ Error Checking.**

   A message states The error check is complete for the entire sheet because no cells are flagged.

2. **Activate the Payment Schedule worksheet and then choose Formulas ⇨ Error Checking.**

   The Error Checking dialog box opens, as shown in Figure 10-6.

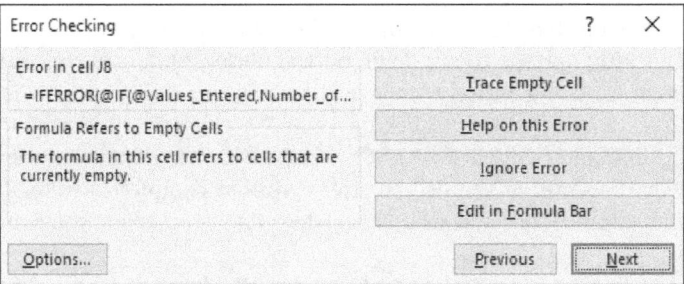

FIGURE 10-6:
The Error
Checking
dialog box.

3. **Within the dialog box, choose a command that corresponds to one of these options:**

   - Correct the error.
   - Display help documentation on the error.
   - Ignore the error.
   - Edit the cell in the Formula Bar.
   - Navigate through other cells with errors.

TIP

The Options button opens a dialog box where you can enable or disable error checking rules before proceeding with the error check.

4. **After the error check is complete, click OK on the confirmation prompt.**

   You don't have to resolve all errors in one session; you can return to the Error Checking feature at any time.

Cleaning Up Circular References

A *circular reference* in Excel is a formula that refers to itself — much like a snake eating its own tail. The formula's result feeds back into itself, creating an endless loop. 'Round and 'round it goes (100 times, to be exact), until Excel throws up its hands and displays a circular reference message.

Here's how to purposefully create a circular reference:

1. **Enter 100 and 200 into cells A1 and A2 of a blank worksheet.**

2. **Type =SUM(A1:A2) into cell A3.**

   The formula correctly returns 300.

3. **Update the formula in cell A3 to =SUM(A1:A3) and then press Enter.**

   Oh, snap! Excel throws up the warning shown in Figure 10-7.

4. **Click OK to dismiss the error prompt.**

   The formula in cell A3 returns 0 because Excel refuses to chase its own tail.

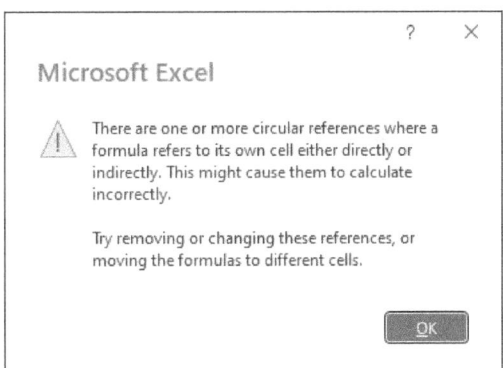

FIGURE 10-7:
Circular reference warning prompt.

TECHNICAL STUFF

In rare cases, you might actually want Excel to work through circular references in your workbooks instead of shutting it down. To allow this, choose File ⇨ Options ⇨ Formulas (Windows) or Excel ⇨ Preferences ⇨ Calculation (macOS) and turn on the Enable Iterative Calculations checkbox. With this setting on, Excel no longer displays circular reference warnings in any of your workbooks.

The Maximum Iterations field controls how many times Excel attempts to resolve the circular reference before giving up. The Maximum Change field determines the smallest value difference Excel accepts before considering the calculation "close enough."

There are two ways to track down circular references:

>> **Status Bar message:** If a circular reference exists on the active worksheet, Excel's status bar displays Circular References along with the cell address. Unfortunately, this message isn't clickable — so no shortcuts here — but at least it tells you exactly where to look. However, if Enable Iterative Calculations is turned on, this message disappears — but Calculate remains in the status bar if circular references exist.

>> **Circular References command:** If the Status Bar reports "Circular References" but doesn't show a cell address, the culprit is hiding in another worksheet or open workbook. Use these steps to track it down:

1. **Choose Formulas ⇨ Error Checking drop-down ⇨ Circular References, and then select a cell reference.**

   The cell containing the circular reference formula is activated.

   The Circular References command is disabled if none of the currently open workbooks contain circular references or if the Enable Iterative Calculations setting is turned on.

REMEMBER

2. **Revise the formula in cell A3 to** =SUM(A1:A2).

   The Circular Reference indicator vanishes from the status bar.

Monitoring Changes via the Watch Window

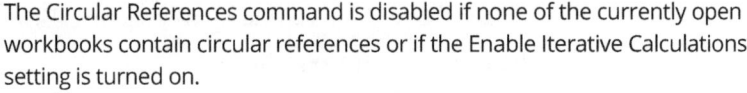

The Watch Window features one of Excel's most underappreciated tools, letting you keep an eye on key cells across multiple worksheets — or even workbooks — without the hassle of jumping from cell to cell. It tracks several useful details, including:

>> **Book:** The workbook containing the watched cell

>> **Sheet:** The worksheet name

TIP

» **Name:** The name assigned to a watched cell (if applicable)

Choose Formulas ⇨ Define Name to name a worksheet cell or range.

» **Cell:** The address of the watched cell

» **Value:** The current value in the cell

» **Formula:** The formula (if any) inside the cell

Think of the Watch Window as a real-time dashboard for your most important numbers — no more endless scrolling or flipping between sheets just to check a value. And if you need to jump to a watched cell, just double-click its row in the Watch Window to teleport straight to it.

Here's how to put the Watch Window to work:

1. **Select cells J73:K73 on the Payment Schedule worksheet.**

   Preselecting cells often speeds things up when using Excel features that reference specific cells, saving you a few extra clicks.

2. **Choose Formulas ⇨ Watch Window.**

   The Watch Window dialog box opens.

3. **Click Add Watch.**

   The Add Watch dialog box opens. The next steps vary:

   - **Windows:**

     a) **Click Add Watch**

     b) **Adjust the cells to watch, if needed.**

     c) **Click Add to start tracking the specified cells.**

   - **macOS: The selected cells appear in the Watch Window automatically.**

   To watch additional cells, select a range then click +.

   As shown in Figure 10-8, information about the cells appears in the Watch Window.

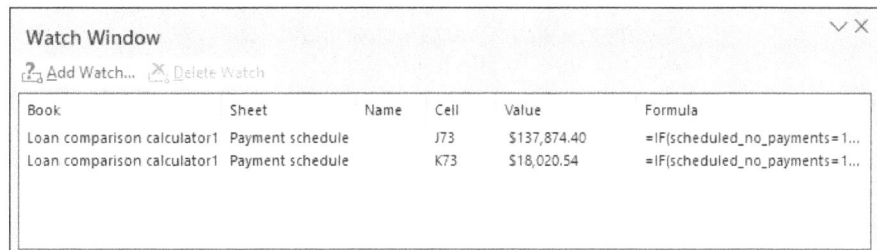

FIGURE 10-8:
The Watch
Window
dialog box.

4. **To test it out, change the interest rate in cell D7 of the Payment Comparison worksheet to 7%.**

   The value for cell J73 should update from 137,874.40 to 139,250.63, and for K73, from $18,020.54 to $25,368.51 in the Watch Window.

5. **To navigate to a watched cell, double-click a cell reference within the Watch Window.**

   This action activates the corresponding cell.

6. **Click the Close (X) button.**

   The Watch Window dialog box closes. You can reopen it at any time to continue monitoring key cells.

Docking the Watch Window

As shown in Figure 10-9, you can dock the Watch Window along any edge of the worksheet. To dock it, drag the title bar to the desired edge, like the right-hand side of the screen. Adjust the size of the columns as necessary to hide any irrelevant columns, making it easier to monitor and navigate to important cells. If you prefer a floating window, drag the Watch Window away from the edges and position it anywhere on your screen(s) for easy monitoring.

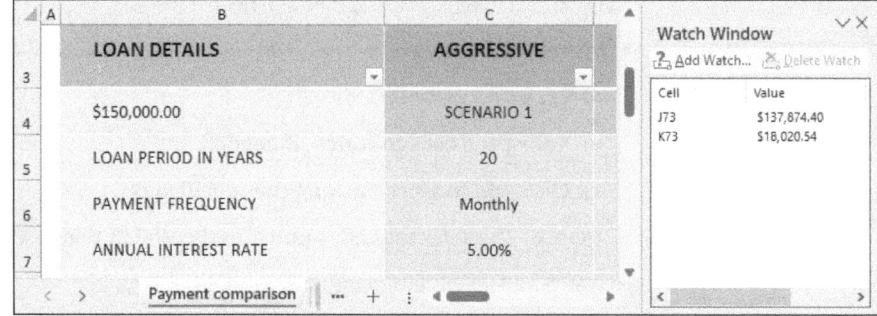

FIGURE 10-9: Docked version of the Watch Window dialog box.

Removing watches

To remove a watch, click on the cell reference and choose Delete Watch (Windows) or - (macOS). To eliminate multiple watches, click the top watch, hold the Shift key, click the last one, and then delete. Alternatively, hold the Ctrl (Windows) or Cmd (macOS) key and select multiple watches individually, then delete.

The Delete Watch command doesn't ask for confirmation and cannot be undone. Think twice before deleting any watches.

Controlling When Excel Calculates

Excel formulas recalculate automatically by default, instantly updating whenever you make changes — no extra effort required. For example, if you change cell C6 of the Payment Comparison tab from Bi-Monthly to Annually, the loan cost in cell C11 changes automatically — before you can even blink. Most Excel users never give calculation settings a second thought but knowing your recalculation options can come in handy, especially when working with massive workbooks that make Excel feel like it's moving in slow motion.

Adjusting calculation options

To view or modify the workbook calculation method, choose Formulas ⇨ Calculation Options, and then select an option:

>> **Automatic:** Excel formulas recalculate instantly whenever a referenced cell changes.

>> **Partial:** This option tells Excel to calculate formulas automatically — except for those inside Data Tables and Python results. Since both features can cause sluggish recalculations, Excel can exclude them to keep things running smoothly.

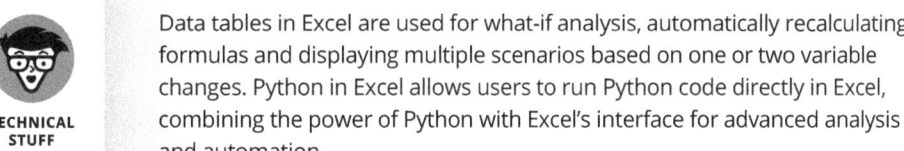

Data tables in Excel are used for what-if analysis, automatically recalculating formulas and displaying multiple scenarios based on one or two variable changes. Python in Excel allows users to run Python code directly in Excel, combining the power of Python with Excel's interface for advanced analysis and automation.

>> **Manual:** Excel doesn't recalculate formulas unless you manually trigger it. If uncalculated formulas are lurking in your worksheet, Calculate appears in the Status Bar as a not-so-subtle reminder.

Sometimes, Excel may switch to Manual calculation mode unexpectedly.

When you set the calculation mode to Manual, Excel recalculates a workbook each time it is saved. To disable this in Windows (but not macOS), go to File ⇨ Options ⇨ Formulas, uncheck the Recalculate Workbook Before Saving option, and click OK. This affects all workbooks globally.

If a workbook is set to Manual calculation, Windows users can choose Formulas ⇨ Calculation Options ⇨ Format Stale Values to have Excel visually indicate uncalculated amounts with a strikethrough — a subtle nudge that your numbers might be out of date.

Recalculating Excel workbooks

This section is relevant only if you use Partial or Manual calculation modes — because sometimes, Excel needs a little nudge to do the math. To recalculate an entire Excel workbook, try one of the following methods:

>> Click the word Calculate on Excel's Status Bar.

>> Choose Formulas ⇨ Calculate Now.

>> Press F9, or Fn+F9 if your keyboard requires it.

To recalculate only a single worksheet:

>> Choose Formulas ⇨ Calculate Sheet.

>> Press Shift+F9, or Shift+ Fn+F9 if necessary.

3

Expanding Beyond the Basics

Chapter **11**

Navigating Through Worksheets and Workbooks

This chapter dives into ironing out the wrinkles in navigating worksheets and workbooks. Folding a fitted sheet remains beyond my expertise (and perhaps anyone's), but I provide guidance for leaping confidently from one spot in a spreadsheet to another. Taming unruly worksheets and workbooks becomes manageable with the Custom Views feature, which applies a buffet of settings in one fell swoop. Consider this your Magellan-worthy recipe for conquering spreadsheet navigation.

Finding and Replacing Data within Cells

As much as I'd like to, I'm afraid I can't help you track down where you last left your car keys. True story — I once stashed my own keys in such a clever spot that I almost had to call an Uber so that I could pick up my kids from school. Finding your data, though, is a whole different ball game. The Find and Replace features in Excel reside on separate tabs within the Find and Replace dialog box, shown in Figure 11-1. This handy tool lets you search for data across worksheets and replace all or part of a cell's contents. Use one of the following methods to open the corresponding tab:

>> **Find tab:** Choose Home ⇨ Find & Select ⇨ Find or press Ctrl+F (Windows) or Cmd+F (macOS).

>> **Replace Tab:** Choose Home ⇨ Find & Select ⇨ Replace or Ctrl+H (Windows) or Cmd+H (macOS).

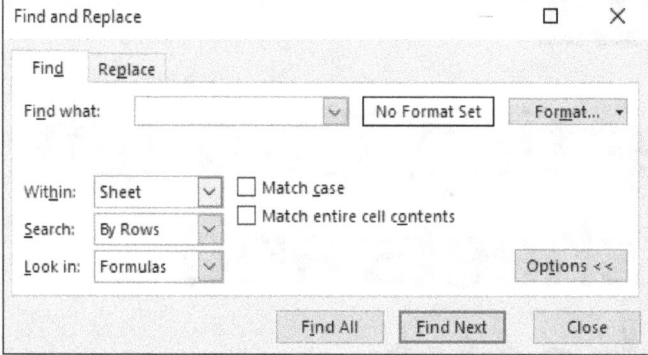

FIGURE 11-1:
The Find and Replace dialog box.

Searching within worksheet cells

Before diving in, why not appreciate that Excel cells, unlike biological cells, don't come with nuclei or mitochondria. But they do have their own vital functions — like holding data and formulas.

The key to clear communication is specificity — the more direct you are about what you want, the better your chances of getting it. The same holds true when searching your worksheets. Be vague in your search, and Excel essentially shrugs with a "Dunno?" Here's how to ask the Find tab for exactly what you want:

TIP

>> **Find What:**  No need to stumble around in the dark (mode) here — this field lets you specify the text or numbers you want to search for. 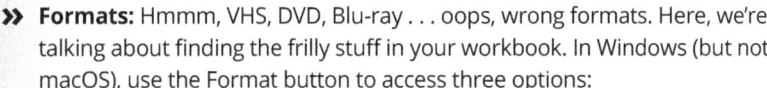 It even includes a drop-down menu of recent search criteria for quick access. Leave it blank if you're searching solely by formatting or combine search criteria with formatting for a more targeted approach.

If the Find What field is the only option visible, click Options to reveal additional search choices.

>> **Formats:** Hmmm, VHS, DVD, Blu-ray . . . oops, wrong formats. Here, we're talking about finding the frilly stuff in your workbook. In Windows (but not macOS), use the Format button to access three options:

- **Format:** Click here to erase the contents of your hard drive . . . just kidding! I'm just seeing if you're paying attention. This command opens the Format Cells dialog box, where you can define one or more formatting criteria for your search.

- **Choose Format from Cell:** Select a worksheet cell to use as a template for finding other cells with the same formatting. Think of it as rounding up birds of a feather in your spreadsheet flock.

- **Clear Find Format:** If this option seems a bit foggy, it's because it starts off disabled. It activates after selecting one of the first two options, allowing you to clear any formatting criteria and start fresh.

>> **Within:** Choose Sheet to search the current worksheet or Workbook to search the entire workbook. It's like deciding whether to search just your room for the TV remote or tearing apart the whole house — your call!

>> **Search:** Select By Rows or By Columns to steer the search direction within the worksheet. It's like choosing whether to stroll through the grocery store aisles or scan each shelf up and down.

>> **Look in:** Refine your search, much like deciding which flavor of Neapolitan ice cream to dig your spoon into first:

- **Formulas:** Unfortunately, it's unlikely that you can uncover the secret ingredients in Coca-Cola, but you can track down your own special calculation mix by searching formulas for specific cell references, function names, or other inputs.

- **Values:** This concept might come up in a philosophy class if you're pondering the meaning of life, but in Excel, it's all about what's in the cell — whether it's the raw contents or the calculated results.

- **Comments:** Personally, I steer clear of online comments — they're often a breeding ground for chaos. Thankfully, your spreadsheets should be free of divisive debates. Search comments (marked by a purple indicator in the upper-right corner of a cell) for @ mentions or specific content.

- **Notes:** It's been ages since I've seen anyone with a ribbon tied to their finger as a reminder, but Notes are the digital equivalent. Search notes (marked with a red triangle in the upper-right corner of a cell) for specific words or numbers — no strings attached.

>> **Match Case:** Think of this as the tennis equivalent of calling out "fault!" — Excel pays close attention to whether it's uppercase or lowercase, ensuring your search hits only the exact match.

>> **Match Entire Cell Contents:** Includes only cells that match the exact contents of the Find What field. Basically, it's you telling Excel, "Read my lips: I want this specific data." When this option is on, partial matches are not allowed, so searching for Pay won't find Payroll.

REMEMBER

If you still haven't found what you're looking for (cue U2 — the band, not the cell), keep in mind that the Match Case and Match Entire Cell Contents options are sticky, often staying enabled until you turn them off. If you run into the "We couldn't find what you were looking for" prompt, double-check that these settings aren't stealthily sabotaging your search.

It's your party, and you can search if you want to. Once you lock in your search criteria, Excel gives you a couple of options:

>> **Find Next:** Takes you directly to the first cell that matches your criteria — like being the first guest to show up at the party. On macOS, a Previous button also appears, allowing you to navigate back to the prior search result.

>> **Find All:** All for one, and one for all! Displays a list of all matching cells, complete with clickable links for easy navigation. The list serves up details like the workbook, worksheet, cell name (if assigned), cell address, cell value, and formula (if applicable).

Replacing text within worksheet cells

The Replace tab is like swapping out decaf for regular coffee — same general setup, but with a bit more buzz. It keeps most of the options from the Find tab, with a few key twists:

- >> **Replace With:** Enables you to pull a classic switcheroo by specifying what to replace in the Find What field.

- >> **Replace Format button:** While it's not explicitly labeled, this second instance of the Format button lets you specify alternate formatting to apply to cells matching the criteria — think of it as transferring your old Gilad Janklowicz workout tapes to DVD. Don't worry, your secret is safe with me.

- >> **Look in:** This field allows you to choose only Formulas, which implicitly includes values — a bit of a two-for-one deal.

REMEMBER

You cannot replace text in comments or notes, only within worksheet cells.

If you prefer to play it safe, use the Find Next button to navigate to the first cell with a match, and then click Replace to make changes one at a time. But if you're feeling bold and a little rebellious, let a sinister laugh escape your lips as you devilishly hit Replace All, unleashing your changes across the entire worksheet or workbook in one dramatic swoop.

REMEMBER

There's a middle ground: to limit where replacements happen, select two or more cells before opening the Find & Replace dialog box. If instant regret strikes because you replaced more than you intended, no worries — just click Undo on the Quick Access Toolbar or press Ctrl+Z (Windows) or Cmd+Z (macOS).

Exploring with the Navigation Task Pane

In a way, Find & Replace feels like hand-to-hand combat — intimate, cell-by-cell interactions. On the other hand, the Navigation task pane provides a space-age satellite view of your workbook and worksheets. Originally introduced by Microsoft as an accessibility feature to help users with assistive technologies navigate more effectively, it turns out this tool makes all of us more efficient navigators in the Excel universe.

As shown in Figure 11-2, the Navigation task pane provides a complete list of all worksheets, including both hidden and visible ones. To display this task pane, choose View ⇨ Navigation. Powered by AI, this feature does require an internet connection — without it, you're left out in the cold, navigating within your workbook the old-school way.

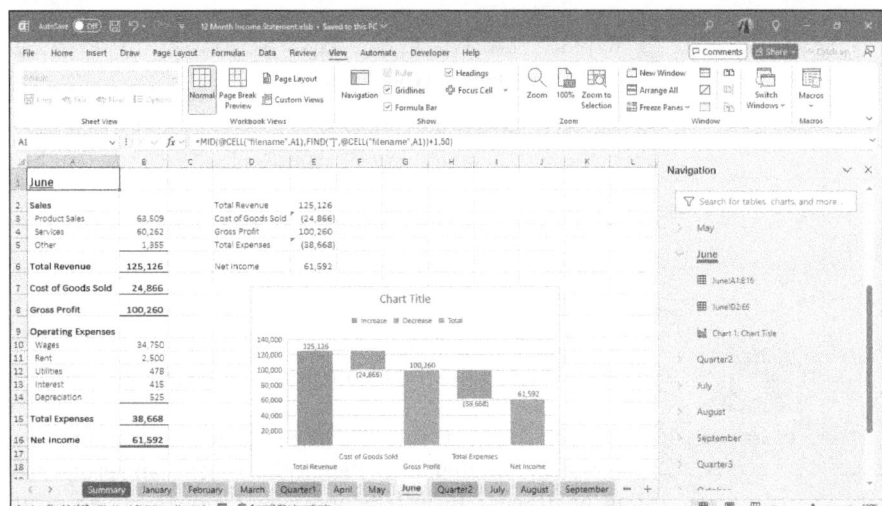

FIGURE 11-2:
The Navigation
task pane.

The Navigation task pane provides the following information for every sheet in a workbook:

>> **Locations of non-blank cells:** Think of this as your eye-in-the-sky — a bird's-eye view of every cell or block of cells that isn't empty. Click any range address to jump straight there.

>> **Names of worksheet objects:** This lists noncell elements on the worksheet, making them easy to navigate to with a simple click. This includes images, PivotTables, Charts, Slicers, Text Boxes — anything that functions as an object rather than standard cell content. And yes, while PivotTables technically reside within worksheet cells, Excel still treats them as distinct objects.

To activate a worksheet, left-click on its name, or right-click the name to bring up a context menu with the following options:

>> **Rename:** Pick a fresh nom-de-plume for the worksheet in question.

>> **Delete:** Brings up a confirmation prompt asking if you're sure about removing the worksheet from the workbook — no take-backs after this!

>> **Hide (or Show):** Tuck a visible worksheet out of sight or bring a hidden one back into the limelight.

Jumping to Locations with Go To

Well, you can't collect $200, but you can jump to cell JAI1 if you like. There's no need to roll any dice here; the Go To command enables you to navigate to specific locations within a workbook:

1. **Choose Home ⇨ Find & Select ⇨ Go To, or if you're fast with your fingers, press F5, Ctrl+G (Windows) or Cmd+G (macOS).**

   The Go To dialog box appears.

2. **Enter cell address, range name, or table name within the Reference field, or select from the Go To list.**

3. **Click OK, or press Enter to close the dialog box and get on with things.**

REMEMBER

The Go To dialog box lets you navigate to specific cell locations but doesn't extend its reach to objects like charts, images, or PivotTables.

Targeting Specific Cells with Go To Special

Alrighty, I'm about to go full Monty on you . . . pick a card, any card. Actually, I mean pick a cell — any type — using the Go To Special commands. Here's how:

1. **Choose Home ⇨ Find & Select ⇨ Go To Special.**

   The Go To Special dialog box shown in Figure 11-3 opens.

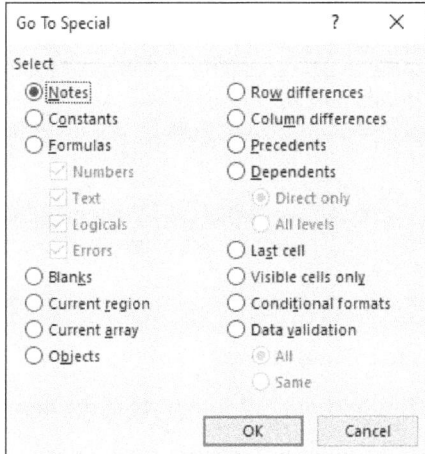

FIGURE 11-3:
The Go To Special
dialog box.

2. **Choose any of the following options:**

- **Notes:** Selects cells containing notes. Perfect for tracking down those little sticky-note reminders anchored by red triangles sprinkled across your spreadsheet.

REMEMBER

  You cannot select cell comments — anchored with purple indicators — using Go To Special.

- **Constants:** Selects cells with non-formula data, such as text, numbers, or dates. Unlike the mysteries of the universe, these constants are straightforward — no PhD or telescope required!

- **Formulas:** Selects cells containing formulas — anything that kicks off with an equal sign, like Excel's way of saying, "Time for some math!"

TIP

  You can refine the constants or formulas options by specific types, such as numbers, text, logical values (TRUE/FALSE), or errors.

- **Blanks:** Selects all blank cells within the selected range. Handy for spotting gaps in your data — like finding the potholes in your spreadsheet road.

- **Current Region:** Selects the block of contiguous data surrounding the active cell — basically a group hug for your data. This option shines when you're wrangling tables or data ranges.

TIP

  Those with nimble fingers can press Ctrl+A (Windows) or Cmd+A (macOS) to instantly select the current region on the fly.

- **Current Array:** Don't cry over spilled milk — er, data! This option makes it easy as pie to select the output of an array formula, whether from modern dynamic array ranges or old-school Ctrl+Shift+Enter legacy array formulas.

CROSS REFERENCE

  As demonstrated in Chapter 9, dynamic array functions — also called spilled range functions — automatically populate results across as many cells as needed.

- **Objects:** To feel as free as a bird, use this option to select all graphical objects — shapes, charts, images, or text boxes — that gracefully float above the worksheet. Perfect for hassle-free bulk formatting or quick deletions.

- **Row Differences:** Viva la difference! Selects cells in rows that differ from the first cell in the selection. Here's a quick example of how to compare data horizontally, row by row:

  1. **Type** =ROW( ) **into cell A1 of a blank worksheet, and then copy the formula across to column M.**

  2. **Overwrite the formula into cell G1 by typing the number 1 and pressing Enter.**

3. **Select cells A1:M1, and then choose Home ⇨ Find & Select ⇨ Go To Special ⇨ Row Differences ⇨ OK.**

4. **Cell G1 is selected because it differs from cells A1:F1 and H1:M1.**

   If you hadn't overwritten cell G1, Excel would have reported, "No cells were found" because all the cells would have contained consistent formulas.

- **Column Differences:** Selects cells in columns that differ from the first cell in the selection. Use this to quickly search vertically down columns for inconsistencies — and live life in the fast lane!

- **Precedents:** Selects cells referenced by the active cell's formula. Perfect for tracing the origins of a calculation — like following breadcrumbs back to the source.

- **Dependents:** Selects cells that rely on the active cell for their formulas. Useful for pinpointing where a cell's value influences other calculations — like mapping a ripple effect through your spreadsheet.

TIP

   You can refine the Precedents and Dependents options by specifying Direct or Indirect relationships between cells.

- **Last Cell:** Selects the last cell in the worksheet that contains data or formatting. Handy for quickly identifying the boundaries of your worksheet content.

- **Visible Cells Only:** Selects just the visible cells within a range, ignoring hidden rows or columns. This helps prevent accidental edits or deletions of hidden data — because out of sight shouldn't mean out of control.

- **Conditional Formats:** Selects cells with conditional formatting applied, making it easy to spot where rules are driving the formatting in your worksheet. After all, rules are rules!

CROSS REFERENCE

   Chapter 13 covers conditional formatting in detail.

- **Data Validation:** Selects cells with data validation rules applied, making it handy for auditing drop-downs or other data entry restrictions. Because every spreadsheet needs a little quality control.

CROSS REFERENCE

   Chapter 14 explores user-proofing techniques, such as using Data Validation to enforce rules and maintain data integrity.

3. **Click OK or press Enter to confirm your selection.**

   One of two things occurs:

- Excel selects the corresponding cells or objects based on your choice.

- The "No cells were found" prompt appears if there's nothing matching your criteria.

THE GHOST OF DATA PAST

Excel identifies the Last Cell as the furthest cell down and to the right that has ever been edited since the file was opened, even if it's now blank. This explains why selecting Last Cell might land you in an empty spot — t's not just about where data was but also where Excel thinks data might still be. The last cell also affects the size of the horizontal and vertical scrollbars.

To reset it, simply erasing the content won't suffice — you need to delete the rows and columns beyond your data, then save the workbook. This restores proper synchronization between your scrollbars and your data, so scrolling no longer drags you off into the boonies. You can use the Navigation task pane discussed earlier to identify the actual confines of your data, say A1:Z382. To reset your scrollbars and the last cell, select cell AA1 and then press Ctrl+Shift+Right Arrow (Windows) or Cmd+Shift+Right Arrow (macOS). Right-click on any column and then choose Delete. Next click on cell A383 and then press Ctrl+Shift+Down (Windows) or Cmd+Shift+Down (macOS). Right-click on any row and then choose Delete. Choose File ➪ Save or press Ctrl +S (Windows) or Cmd+S (macOS) to save your workbook, and both your scroll bars, and the last cell of the worksheet will be reset.

Navigating with the Name Box

The Name Box is the field located to the left of the Formula Bar. Most Excel users assume its sole purpose is to display the address of the active cell, but I could easily list two dozen different actions you can perform with it. Don't worry — there are no geeky details here, just a couple of highlights:

REMEMBER

>> **Navigating to a specific cell:** Type any cell address and press Enter to jump directly to a specific cell in the worksheet. For bonus points, type a cell range, such as A1 : B10, to select a block of cells.

Any misspelled cell references typed into the Name Box may unintentionally become names in your workbook. To clean them up, go to Formulas ➪ Name Manager and remove them.

>> **Navigating to objects:** Type the name of an object that floats above the worksheet, such as Text Box 1 or Chart 1, to navigate to it.

>> **Navigating to ranges or tables:** Click the Name Box drop-down to display a list of named ranges and tables — select any name to go straight to its location.

Activating Worksheets

Two sheet navigation arrows appear at the bottom left-hand corner of the Excel window, and offer a couple of options:

>> **Shifting worksheet tabs:** If your workbook contains more worksheet tabs than can be displayed on screen, click the left or right arrows to move the tabs in the corresponding direction.

>> **Display the Activate dialog box:** Right-click on either navigation arrow to open the Activate dialog box, from which you can choose any visible worksheet, and then click OK.

>> **Activate the first or last worksheet:** Hold Ctrl (Windows) or Options (macOS) and left-click the left navigation arrow to jump to the first worksheet in the workbook, or left-click the right navigation arrow to jump to the last worksheet.

TIP

For those who prefer the keyboard over the mouse, press Ctrl+Page Up (Windows) or Fn+Cmd+Up Arrow (macOS) to activate the worksheet to the left, or Ctrl+Page Down (Windows) or Fn+Cmd+Down Arrow (macOS) to move to the right. On some Windows keyboards, the Fn key may be required (for example, Fn+Ctrl+Page Up).

Reordering Worksheets

The easiest way to reposition a worksheet is to use your left mouse button to drag and drop the worksheet tab into a new position. In Excel for Windows, you can also drag worksheets between workbooks — hold down the Ctrl key while you do so if you want to move a copy of a worksheet. Think of it like rearranging furniture — except this time, you won't throw out your back. If you do have heavier lifting to do, you can use these steps instead:

1. **Activate the first worksheet that you wish to move or copy. To include additional worksheets:**

   - Hold Shift and click the last worksheet tab in the group for contiguous selections.

   - Hold Ctrl and click individual tabs for noncontiguous selections.

2. **Choose Home ⇨ Format ⇨ Move or Copy Sheet or right-click on one of the selected sheet tabs and choose Move or Copy.**

   The Move or Copy dialog box opens.

3. **Select the destination workbook from the To Book list if needed:**

   - Choose a specific workbook currently open in Excel.

   - Select (new book) to move the sheets into a new, blank workbook.

4. **From the Before Sheet list, select where to place the worksheet(s) within the tab sequence.**

   The default is the beginning unless specified otherwise.

5. **Check Create a Copy if you want to duplicate the worksheet(s) rather than move them.**

   WARNING

   Tread carefully here; if you inadvertently skip over the Create a Copy checkbox, then you could end up moving worksheets from one workbook to another instead of copying. Given that the receiving workbook is automatically activated, it's then very easy to overlook the fact that the worksheets are no longer present in the original workbook.

6. **Click OK to complete the move or copy. If you need more time to decide, click Cancel to take a breather.**

Splitting Worksheet Windows

Viva Las Vegas! Splitting panes in Excel is a lot like splitting aces at the blackjack table — it doubles your chances to win by letting you view two or four areas of your worksheet at once. Think of it as instant pane (heh, pain) relief. Here's how to split a worksheet window:

1. **Position your cursor where you want the split to occur:**

   - **Two horizontal panes:** Select any cell in the first visible row.

   - **Two vertical panes:** Select any cell in the first visible column.

   - **Four panes:** Select any cell in the middle of the worksheet grid.

2. **Choose View ⇨ Split.**

   Depending upon your choices, one or two split bars appears.

   TIP

   If your screen resolution cuts off the word Split, note that this command is located to the right of New Window.

You can now scroll the panes independently, reducing navigation time and increasing efficiency. To remove the split, double-click a split bar or choose View ⇨ Split again to turn off the feature.

WARNING

The Freeze Panes and Split features are like the feuding Earps and Clantons of the American Old West — you can't use both at the same time. If Freeze Panes is enabled, the Split command replaces the frozen pane with a split. Conversely, enabling Freeze Panes while a split is active uses the split position for freezing panes.

Viewing Two or More Worksheets at Once

In the movie *Multiplicity*, Michael Keaton learns how to clone himself to be in multiple places at once — with less than ideal results. Fortunately, in Excel, you can (and should) be in two or more places at once within your workbooks, thanks to the New Window command:

1. Open or activate a workbook that contains at least two worksheets.

Or go rogue and stick with a workbook that only has one worksheet — this technique can serve as an alternative to the Split feature covered earlier.

2. Choose View ⇨ New Window.

The new window subtly opens on top of the original, which might mislead you into thinking that nothing has happened.

3. Arrange the windows:

- **Separate Monitors:** To arrange the windows on separate monitors:

   1. **Click Restore Down (Windows) or Zoom Out (macOS, represented by the yellow Minimize/Zoom button in the traffic light-style controls).**

   2. **Drag the window's title bar to the desired monitor.**

   3. **Click Maximize (Windows) or the yellow button again (macOS).**

- **Single Monitor:** You can also arrange windows on a single screen:

   1. **Choose View ⇨ Arrange All.**

      The Arrange Windows dialog box opens.

   2. **Select an arrangement option:**

- **Tiled:** Divides all windows into tiles on one monitor.

- **Horizontal:** Stacks windows side-by-side on screen, ideal for viewing rows.

- **Vertical:** Arranges windows top-to-bottom on screen, helpful for viewing columns.

- **Cascade:** Stacks the windows with visible title bars, allowing quick access to a window with a single mouse click.

4. **To arrange only the windows of the active workbook, click Windows of Active Workbook.**

   By default, Excel arranges all open windows — except for any windows that you have minimized.

5. **Click OK to finalize the arrangement.**

REMEMBER

Creating additional windows doesn't mean you've opened the workbook multiple times. It simply allows you to view and work on different parts of the same workbook simultaneously. If only we could pull this off without consequence in real life!

Applying Custom Views

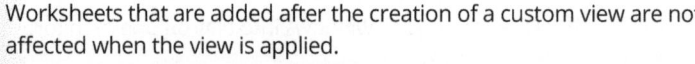

Rumor has it that in the early days of Starbucks, Howard Schultz was vibing with Excel's Custom Views feature when he had an aha moment: "What if everyone could customize their coffee orders the way I'm customizing my views?" Well, that's what I read on the internet, so it must be true.

Custom Views is one of Excel's often-overlooked gems, an automation feature that lets you carry out any combination of tasks across an entire workbook. To clarify, Custom Views doesn't alter your data but instead stores a snapshot of settings — kind of like a preset filter, and so much more, for your workbook — that you can apply with a single click. These settings can include any combination of the following:

>> **Hiding or unhiding worksheets:** The hidden or visible status of all worksheets at the time a view is created is saved. When you select the view, Excel applies these settings, allowing you to hide or unhide multiple worksheets in one fell swoop. (And exactly what is a fell swoop? It means doing something suddenly or all at once — Shakespeare's Macbeth coined the term.)

REMEMBER

Worksheets that are added after the creation of a custom view are not affected when the view is applied.

>> **Hiding or unhiding rows and columns:** Each custom view saves and reapplies the hidden or visible status of every row and column in the workbook. It's like having an instant ticket to the micro-level details of a worksheet, so that you can focus, with the macro view just a couple of clicks away.

>> **Adjusting the Zoom level:** Each custom view saves the Zoom level of a worksheet, letting you toggle how much data is displayed onscreen. (Nope, we're not talking online meetings — this is all about seeing more or less of your data at a glance.) Check out the upcoming "Zooming In and Out" section for some zesty zingers!

>> **Applying page layout settings:** Each custom view saves the page layout settings for every worksheet. For instance, you can toggle between printing a worksheet in portrait for one scenario and landscape for another. This flexibility lets you cater to your boss's preference for wide margins (to allow for commentary) while you keep margins near zero for your own printouts — because, face it, you've got work to do.

>> **Applying filters:** Custom views capture the status of the filter buttons (meaning on or off) as well as any filters applied to any columns within the worksheet. Filtering is a fantastic way to zero in on important data, but as covered in Chapter 4, it can become a tad tedious when done manually.

>> **Activating a cell:** Custom views save the location of the active cell when the view is created and return you to that cell when the view is applied. Think of it as black car service in Excel — apply the view, and you're dropped right at the front door of the cell you need, ready to get down to business.

>> **Sizing and positioning the active window:** Custom views store and apply the position of the active window within a workbook but only affect the first window. For most users, this feels less like a feature and more like Excel punking you by resizing a maximized window whenever a view is applied. Be mindful of the active window's state when creating a view to avoid surprises.

>> **Selecting cells:** Like an elephant, Custom Views remember a remarkable amount of information about your workbook, including the currently selected range of cells. This can be both a blessing and a curse. If you clicked the Select All button to unhide rows and columns before creating a view and left the cells selected, every cell will be selected each time you apply the view. On the flip side, if you frequently copy a specific block of cells, Custom Views are an excellent way to have Excel tee up your data, ready for a quick copy and paste.

WARNING

Alrighty, I don't want you to think I've pulled a bait-and-switch — but you can't use the Custom Views feature if your workbook contains an Excel table, as covered in Chapter 5. Back in the day, these features coexisted peacefully in Excel for Mac, but that harmony is no longer the case on macOS or Windows. If, like me, you think these features go together like peanut butter and jelly, head to File ⇨ Feedback ⇨ Make a Suggestion (Windows) or Help ⇨ Feedback ⇨ Make a Suggestion (macOS) and tell Microsoft to resolve this impasse, pronto!

Another caveat to keep in mind: Custom Views cannot override worksheet or workbook protection, as covered in Chapter 14 on securing worksheets and workbooks. This means you cannot use Custom Views to hide or unhide rows or columns on protected worksheets. If you try, Excel prompts you with "Some view settings could not be applied." Similarly, when workbook protection is enabled, Custom Views cannot hide or unhide worksheets — and in this case, Excel offers no feedback. It's like screaming into the void.

Creating custom views

OK, now that we've covered the good news/bad news, it's time to create some custom views to hide and unhide worksheets:

1. **Open a workbook that has two or more worksheets within it.**

   Need inspiration? Press Ctrl+N (Windows) or Cmd+N (macOS) to create a new blank workbook, then click the New Sheet button a couple of times to create three worksheets.

2. **Check for hidden worksheets by choosing Home ⇨ Format ⇨ Hide & Unhide or right-click any worksheet tab and confirm that Unhide Sheet or Unhide is disabled.**

3. **If the Unhide Sheet or Unhide is enabled, choose the command to open the Unhide dialog box, select all worksheets, and then click OK.**

4. **Move to the cell you'd like activated when the custom view is applied.**

5. **Choose View ⇨ Custom Views.**

   The Custom Views dialog box opens.

REMEMBER

   If the Custom Views command is disabled, it means your workbook contains an Excel table. You can either forgo using Custom Views or convert the tables back to ranges (see Chapter 5).

6. **Click Add (Windows) or + (macOS).**

   The Add View dialog box opens.

7. **Assign a name, such as All Worksheets, to the view. Optionally, turn off Print Settings and/or Hidden Rows, Columns, and Filter Settings if you want to exclude them.**

REMEMBER

   Any other aspects that Custom Views captures — such as cell selection, window position, hidden or visible sheets, and so on — are automatically captured and applied, with no option to disable them.

8. **Click OK to create the view.**

9. **Hide at least one worksheet within the workbook.**

   Feel free to adjust other settings captured by Custom Views.

TIP

   Need a refresher on hiding sheets? Right-click the worksheet tab and choose Hide, or go the scenic route: Home ⇨ Format ⇨ Hide & Unhide ⇨ Hide Sheet.

10. **Choose View ⇨ Custom Views.**

11. **Choose View ⇨ Custom Views, click Add (Windows) or + (macOS), and create a second view (for example, VIP Worksheets Only).**

12. **Choose View ⇨ Custom Views.**

13. **Select the first view that you created and then click Show.**

REMEMBER

   Applying a Custom View restores settings as they were at the time the view was saved, but it doesn't restrict how you use your workbook. You can freely switch between the views as needed while continuing to work.

Using the Custom Views Quick Access Toolbar shortcut

I think that my biggest complaint about Custom Views — apart from not being able to use them with tables — is that it's so easy to forget about the clever solutions that I've implemented to make my life easier. It's not like we're all just hanging out on the View tab of Excel's ribbon all day. Fortunately, in Excel for

Windows, you can elevate your experience with Custom Views by adding a drop-down list to your Quick Access Toolbar:

1. **Choose File ⇨ Options ⇨ Quick Access Toolbar.**

   The Quick Access Toolbar section of the Excel Options dialog box appears.

2. **From the Customize Quick Access Toolbar drop-down, select the current workbook.**

   By default, changes to the toolbar apply to all workbooks. Selecting a specific workbook lets you create a toolbar that appears only when that workbook is open — and travels with the file, so your colleagues that use Excel for Windows can benefit from your handiwork.

3. **Choose Commands Not in the Ribbon from the Choose Commands From list.**

4. **Scroll down and select Custom Views.**

TIP

   To jump directly to the Custom Views command, click once on the list and type D. This highlights the first command starting with D and ensures Custom Views appears on screen.

5. **Click Add or double-click Custom Views.**

   Custom Views appears on the list on the right.

6. **Click OK to confirm.**

Going forward, you can select a custom view directly from your Quick Access Toolbar, bypassing View ⇨ Custom Views. A bonus: the drop-down always shows the most recently applied view — something the Custom Views dialog box doesn't provide.

Zooming In and Out

Don't snooze on the Zoom feature — it zips you into the perfect view of your worksheet, whether you're zipping out to see the big picture or zooming in to scrutinize the smallest details. When's the last time you spotted six Z's in a single sentence? All word play aside, the Zoom section of the View tab of Excel's ribbon sports three commands:

>> **Zoom:** Opens the Zoom dialog box, where you can choose preset zoom options or use a custom field to adjust the zoom to as high as 400% or as low as 10%.

REMEMBER

No, you don't necessarily need to get your eyes checked — Excel's Page Break Preview command automatically adjusts the zoom level of a worksheet to 60%. Conversely, Page Layout changes the zoom level to 100%, overriding any custom zoom level you may have applied. Rest assured, switching back to Normal view restores the zoom to your specified level, or 100% if you haven't set one.

TECHNICAL STUFF

Excel begins displaying range names directly on the worksheet at 39% zoom or lower. At this zoom level, instead of showing cell content, Excel replaces it with the defined range names, making it easier to identify and navigate named ranges in your worksheet.

>> **100%:** This isn't Excel's way of glad-handing you — instead this resets the zoom level to the default, bringing your worksheet back to standard proportions.

>> **Zoom to Selection:** Oh man, if only suitcases had this feature! When you're dealing with offscreen columns or rows, select the cells you want always visible and choose View ➪ Zoom to Selection. Excel adjusts the zoom level (up or down) so your selected range fits perfectly onscreen.

TIP

A Zoom Slider control appears on the right-hand side of Excel's status bar, showing the current worksheet zoom level. In Windows, click the number to open the Zoom dialog box, or use the slider to refine your zoom level. Personally, I always right-click the status bar and turn off the Zoom slider — I just can't seem to avoid accidentally hitting it while scrolling through worksheets, which inevitably leads to me saying words I'd rather my mother not hear.

Chapter **12**

Visualizing and Summarizing Data

Walking into the toothpaste aisle at the grocery store feels like stepping into chaos. There are endless options — whitening, tartar control, fluoride, sensitive teeth, charcoal, gel, paste, mint, and cinnamon. All you wanted was something to clean your teeth! Similarly, Excel offers a staggering array of tools for visualizing and summarizing data. The options can feel overwhelming when all you really want are clean, healthy insights.

This chapter serves as a guide through Excel's version of the toothpaste aisle. From PivotTables and PivotCharts to classic charts, the tools for distilling raw data into digestible summaries or creating visuals to communicate trends and patterns take center stage here. The focus stays on cutting through the noise and getting straight to sparkling, well-polished results — leaving you confident in navigating Excel's endless options and making your data shine — just like a good toothpaste leaves you with a dazzling smile.

Introducing Excel charts

Excel charts are visual representations of worksheet data, designed to spotlight trends, patterns, and comparisons. These versatile tools come in many flavors, from trusty bar and line charts to specialized options like scatter plots. Seasoned users can craft their go-to favorites using commands on the Insert tab of Excel's ribbon, while the Recommended Charts feature acts as a helpful sidekick, suggesting the best way to graphically showcase your data when inspiration runs dry. And don't worry about buyers' remorse — switching to a different chart type is quick and easy, especially when your boss takes one look and says, "Huh?"

This exploration of charts riffs off one of the most data-driven sports in America: baseball. Much like every pitch, swing, and hit is analyzed to uncover patterns and trends, Excel charts allow you to visualize and break down your data with the precision of a seasoned statistician.

TECHNICAL
STUFF

Excel charts are referred to as objects, meaning they float above the worksheet — much like a blimp lazily drifting over a stadium. This design makes charts easy to move around, but keep in mind they can obscure any data sitting beneath them.

Creating a chart from scratch

There's a bit of chicken-versus-egg involved with charts — you need some data first. Equally important is using the right tool for the job. Standard Excel charts shine when presenting summarized data, but trying to chart hundreds or thousands of rows of detail likely results in a jumbled mess, like sending your entire roster to bat at once. That's where two power hitters step up to the plate:

>> **Analyze Data:** Chapter 15 dives into this AI-powered utility, the analytics ace that turns even unwieldy datasets into easy-to-read charts. It's like having a coach call the perfect play — Excel generates suggestions on the fly, or you can ask natural language questions for tailored insights.

>> **PivotCharts:** The graphical counterpart to PivotTables, PivotCharts summarize data into categories and corresponding values. Think of them as the cleanup hitter, organizing your data into a format that's ready to drive in runs. Check out the "Participating with PivotCharts" section toward the end of this chapter for the full rundown.

With that said, you can take control of what feels like a runaway data horse — or, to stay on theme, a ballgame spiraling out of control — and get back on track. If you need a sample dataset before stepping into the batter's box, follow these steps to whip one up:

1. **Type** Inning 1 **into cell B1 of a blank worksheet.**

2. **Drag the Fill Handle for cell B1 across to cell D1.**

   The headers Inning 1, Inning 2, and Inning 3 appear in cells B1:D1.

3. **Type** `Fastball` **and** `Curveball` **into cells A2 and A3, respectively.**

4. **Enter** 3, 5, 7 **into cells B2:D2 and** 6, 8, 10 **into cells B3:D3.**

TIP

When entering data across rows, press Tab or Right Arrow instead of Enter to jump to the cell in the next column.

Batter up! You're now ready to step up to the plate.

Using Recommended Charts

Recommended Charts was one of Excel's earliest forays into artificial intelligence over a decade ago. Talk about a slow burn! Like a seasoned pitching coach reading the game, this feature helps you transform a dataset into a polished chart without breaking a sweat:

1. **Select any cell within your data set, e.g., cell A1.**

REMEMBER

By default, Excel charts use the contiguous block of cells surrounding the active cell as their data source. This means you can skip preselecting your data — unless there are blank rows or columns, which might lead to some awkward gaps in your chart. That's like calling for a pitch with no one on the mound — delay of game!

2. **Choose Insert ⇨ Recommended Charts.**

In Excel for Windows, the Recommended Charts tab of the Insert Chart dialog box opens, as shown in Figure 12-1. In macOS, an abbreviated drop-down menu offers a few suggestions.

3. **Take a quick detour to the All Charts tab (see Figure 12-2), your comprehensive playbook for exploring the 50-odd chart types Excel has to offer.**

It's like surveying the entire roster of players in the league, foreshadowing you calling your own plays.

4. **Activate the Recommended Charts tab, then click on any chart in the scrollable list on the left to display a larger preview of the chart, along with an explanation of the story it tells and when to use it.**

Think of this as Excel giving you a deep dive into a star player's stats, highlighting their strengths and when to put them in the lineup.

All charts in the Insert Chart dialog box are based on your data, giving you a chance to take some practice swings before connecting with the ball.

REMEMBER

5. **Click OK to confirm your choice and close the Insert Chart dialog box.**

A new chart now graces your worksheet, showcasing your data like a perfectly executed double play.

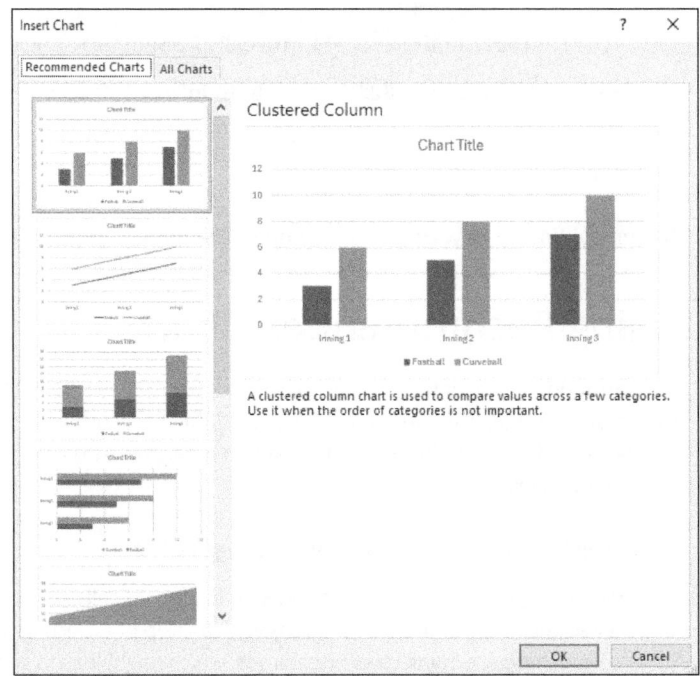

FIGURE 12-1:
The
Recommended
Charts tab of the
Insert Chart
dialog box.

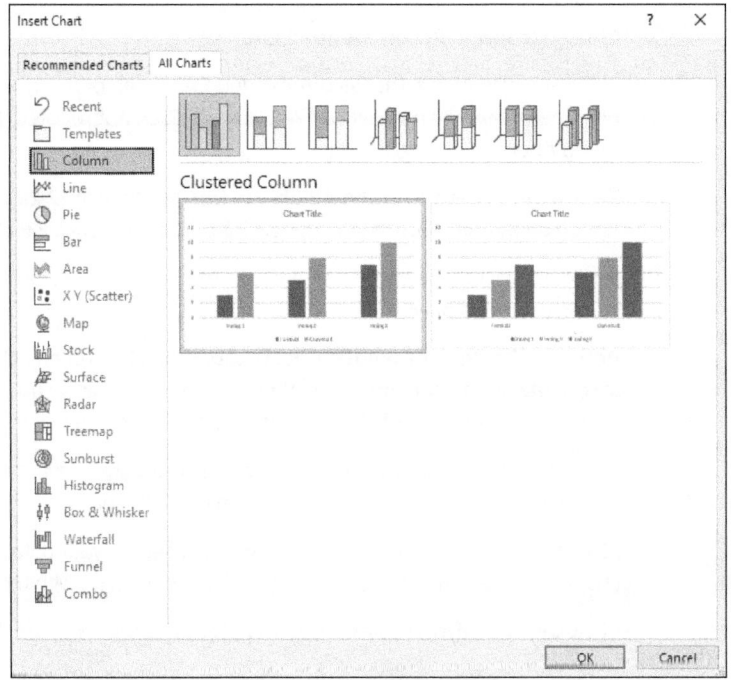

FIGURE 12-2:
The All Charts tab
of the Insert
Chart dialog box.

Building charts directly

As with any skill that we master, recommendations are often helpful at first, such as tips on how to best hold our bat, but once we've honed our skills, recommendations can feel stifling. You can use the earlier steps to choose a chart type directly from the All Charts tab, or hit a line drive at the chart type of your choice by way of the Insert tab on Excel's ribbon:

1. **Click any cell in your data range, like A1 — your leadoff hitter in this data lineup.**

2. **Activate the Insert tab of Excel's ribbon, and then choose a chart category drop-down (macOS users will see abbreviated versions of these screen tips):**

   - **Insert Column or Bar Chart:** TGIF! Oh wait, not that kind of bar — use these charts to visually compare values across a few categories.

     Steal a base by pressing Alt-F1 (Windows) or Fn+Option+F1 (macOS) to create a column chart on the fly in the active worksheet.

   - **Insert Line or Area Chart:** Perfect for showing trends over time or categories, like tracking runs scored inning by inning.

   - **Insert Pie or Doughnut Chart:** Mmmm, pie! Sadly, it's not edible — these round charts give you virtual slices of your data. If you're craving real pie, make a dash to a diner or coffee shop.

   - **Insert Hierarchy Chart:** Featuring Treemap and Sunburst charts. And no, these aren't quirky ballpark sodas — they're great for visualizing hierarchies, such as how data is organized into categories and subcategories, much like a team's roster divided by positions.

   - **Insert Statistic Chart:** Baseball geeks, rejoice! Here resides Histogram and Box and Whisker charts, ideal for analyzing performance metrics.

   - **Insert Scatter (X, Y) or Bubble Chart:** Show relationships between two sets of values, like comparing batting averages and on-base percentages.

   - **Insert Waterfall, Funnel, Stock, Surface, or Radar Chart:** This mouthful of a command name is a catch-all for specialized chart types that didn't make it onto any other teams.

   - **Insert Combo Chart:** There's no free lunch or smooth jazz here — just a chart that lets you display data using bar and line charts together.

   - **Maps:** This drop-down features a single Filled Map option, perfect for comparing values across geographic regions. But beware of the More Map Charts option — it's a trap! Excel just loops you back to the same Filled Map chart.

The chart lands on your worksheet, ready for you to jazz up with labels, colors, or whatever flair your heart desires. Play ball!

REMEMBER

Excel gives you a sneak peek at your chart, but if your screen resolution pulls a grounder and blocks part of the preview, don't sweat it. Just resize your window or grab a bigger monitor. Think of it as moving from the bleachers to box seats — better views all around.

Deconstructing and Customizing Charts

Depending on the chart you pick, a standard set of default elements rolls out like a rookie lineup (see Figure 12-3) — ready for you to tweak into an MVP performance:

» **Chart area:** The outer borders of your chart's world — like the outfield fence, it defines the boundaries while leaving space for the action in the middle.

» **Chart title:** The name of the stadium, setting the stage for what viewers can expect from the game — or chart.

» **Horizontal (Category) Axis:** Also known as the x-axis, this is the baseline that groups your data. Without it, you'd have a game with no field lines — a chaotic free-for-all.

» **Legend:** The chart's dugout lineup card, translating colors and symbols so fans (and you) can follow the game.

» **Plot area:** The infield of your chart — where the action happens. But beware: Erasing the underlying data means no game — just an empty diamond.

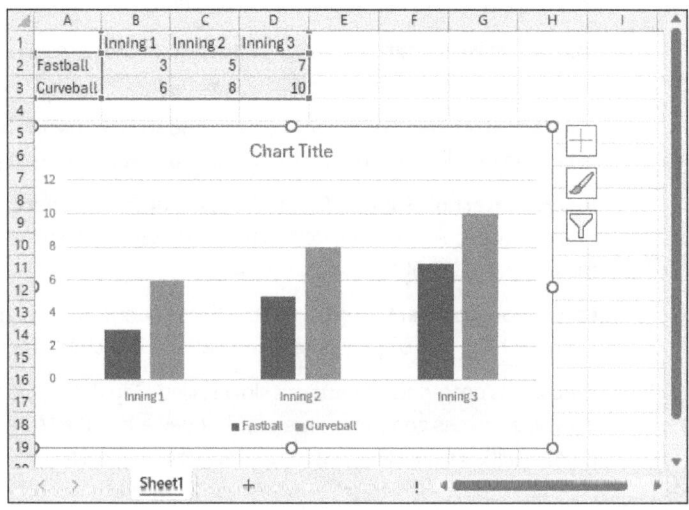

FIGURE 12-3:
A standard
Clustered
Columns chart.

Customizing charts

The Chart Design and Format tabs appear in Excel's ribbon whenever you click on a chart, accompanied by the three buttons, shown in Figure 12-3:

» **Chart Elements:** Think of the Chart Elements menu as your chart's coach, ready to swap players in and out of the lineup to create a winning combination. Whether you're fine-tuning your chart for the big leagues or just tinkering in the minors, this menu has you covered.

The first layer of the menu acts like a manager calling plays from the dugout — toggle features on or off with a simple click. Hover over a chart element, and you step into the batter's box of customization, with options to fine-tune each feature. If you're feeling ambitious, swing for the fences with the More Options choice, opening the Format task pane for all-star tweaking.

Here's the lineup of chart elements you can adjust using the Chart Elements button or Chart Design ⇨ Add Chart Element:

- **Axes:** The first and third base lines of your chart, keeping everything in play and defining the X-axis (horizontal, category labels) and Y-axis (vertical, value numbers). Enabled by default because even the best game needs boundaries.

- **Axis Titles:** Like adding a player's hometown under the scoreboard, these titles provide extra context for your axes. Optional, but they can be a game-changer for clarity.

- **Chart Title:** The stadium marquee that announces the game — use it to define your chart's purpose or leave it blank for the mystery game of the week.

- **Data Labels:** The play-by-play announcers of your chart, calling out exact numbers at each data point. Disabled by default, because sometimes less is more.

- **Data Table:** The box score for your chart, showing the raw numbers beneath the action. Ideal for when you want both the game highlights and the stat sheet.

- **Error Bars:** The ballpark range for your data points, showing the potential variation or uncertainty in the numbers. It's like saying, "The score could land anywhere within this range, depending on the play."

- **Gridlines:** The chalk lines of your chart, giving structure to the field. Horizontal lines appear by default, but you can go full groundskeeper and add vertical ones too.

- **Legend:** Your chart's playbook, decoding colors and shapes into understandable categories. A must-have for fans in the cheap seats.

- **Trendline:** The veteran player who sees where the game is headed, revealing patterns or overall direction in your data.

- **Up/Down Bars:** The instant replay of your line or stock charts, highlighting the highs and lows between two series over time.

>> **Chart Styles:** Think of these as your team uniforms — choose from various looks to give your chart a unique vibe. The Chart Styles button even lets you adjust color palettes for a cohesive theme, with more advanced options available through the Format menu for those ready to channel their inner graphic designer.

>> **Chart Filters:** The dugout of your chart, where you can manage the roster by picking and choosing players — specific data series or points. Much like the Filter feature in worksheets (see Chapter 4), just remember to click Apply to lock in your lineup.

REMEMBER

Hiding rows or columns in your worksheet can result in players — er, data points or series — vanishing from the field (or rather, the chart). Keep your data lineup visible to ensure everyone stays in the game.

With this roster of tools, charts go from rookie status to championship contenders. With these options at your disposal, striking out isn't even on the table!

Maintaining chart data

Data marches on, just like the accumulation of baseball statistics, which means you may need to periodically add more data to your charts. And just like plays at the plate, there are multiple ways to make it happen. Carry out these steps to build on the chart from the "Creating a chart from scratch" section earlier in this chapter:

1. **Enter Slider into cell A4.**

2. **Enter 5, 7, 9 into cells B4:D4.**

3. **Select cells A4:D4.**

4. **Choose Home ⇨ Copy or press Ctrl+C (Windows) or Cmd+C (macOS).**

5. **Click on the chart and then press Ctrl+V (Windows) or Cmd+V (macOS).**

   A new data series appears on the chart.

6. **Select cells C1:D4 and then drag the Fill Handle in cell D4 to E4.**

   A fourth inning appears within the data range but does not appear on the chart.

7. Click once on the chart and then drag the selector handle in cell D4 to cell E4.

The new data appears on the chart.

8. Select cells C1:E4 and then drag the Fill Handle from E4 to F4.

9. Click once on the chart to activate the object, then choose Chart Design ⇨ Select Data.

The Select Data Source dialog box opens, as shown in Figure 12-4.

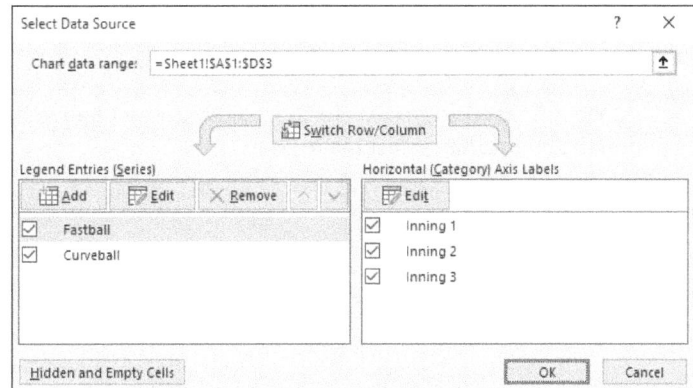

FIGURE 12-4:
The Select Data
Source
dialog box.

10. Select cells A1:F4 in the worksheet to update the chart's data range.

TIP

The Chart Data Range field is an example of a reference edit field in Excel. The bonus chapter "Ten Frustrating Prompts" (available at www.dummies.com/go/excelfd) explains how to use the F2 key to toggle such fields between Enter and Edit modes.

11. Click OK to close the Select Data Source dialog box.

REMEMBER

The Select Source Data dialog box also enables you to add or remove data series and control Horizontal (Category) Axis Labels.

The manual steps shown here are just one way to add data to charts. Chapter 5 explores the Table feature for creating self-expanding charts, while Chapter 9 dives into dynamic array functions, also known as spilled range functions. Both techniques can help you level up to all-star status when it comes to Excel charts.

Moving and resizing charts

Charts are a switch-hitter feature in Excel, typically floating above worksheet cells, but ready to transition into a Chart Sheet instead. Here's how to move charts to new locations.

To move a chart within a worksheet, follow these steps:

1. **Latch onto the chart by holding down your left mouse button anywhere in the chart area.**

2. **Drag the chart to a new location.**

   Alternatively, right-click on the chart, choose Cut, and then paste the chart into the desired location.

To move a chart to a chart sheet or another worksheet, do this:

1. **Click on the chart once to activate it as an object.**

2. **Choose Chart Design ➪ Move Chart or skip step 1 and right-click directly on the chart, then select Move Chart.**

   The Move Chart dialog box opens, as shown in Figure 12-5.

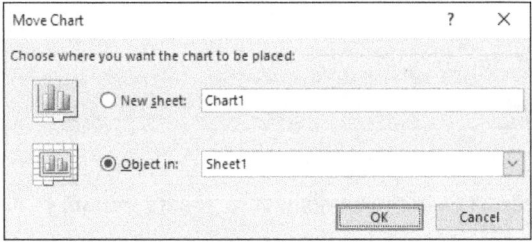

FIGURE 12-5:
The Move Chart
dialog box.

3. **Choose your desired location:**

   - **New Sheet:** Moves the chart to a chart sheet, a blank canvas with a worksheet-style tab but no grid of cells, much like a tarp covering the infield — clear, open, and ready for action. Chart sheets make charts more accessible compared to those embedded within worksheets.

   - **Object In:** Moves the chart to any existing worksheet within the current workbook, like runners advancing bases after a batter draws a walk.

4. **Click OK to close the dialog box and complete the move.**

   You cannot undo any prior actions, including moving a chart, after using the Move Chart dialog box. Now that's foul!

WARNING

Charts can be resized as well, letting you create Little League–sized graphs or go all out with full-size charts ready for the big leagues. To begin, click once on a chart to activate the object, and then use either technique:

>> **Resizing Handles:** Drag any of the eight resizing handles to change the size of the chart, like a pitcher trying to catch a runner off base.

Hold down Alt (Windows) or Options (macOS) while resizing to snap the chart to the worksheet grid — now that's a precision throw! To snap multiple charts, choose Page Layout ⇨ Align ⇨ Snap to Grid (Windows) or Shape Format ⇨ Arrange ⇨ Align ⇨ Snap to Grid (macOS). Going forward, charts automatically align to the underlying worksheet grid as you resize.

REMEMBER

Snap to Grid stays enabled as a permanent setting until you repeat the steps to turn it off, like a rain delay that just won't end.

>> **Shape Height/Width:** Update the Shape Height and Shape Width fields in the Size group of the Format tab to specify the chart's dimensions in inches, almost like measuring the distance of a home run ball. For more detailed adjustments, right-click the chart, choose Format Chart Area ⇨ Size & Properties ⇨ Size, and fine-tune the settings as needed.

TIP

To adjust the dimensions of two or more charts simultaneously, hold down Ctrl (Windows) or Cmd (macOS) while clicking on each chart. Then use the Shape Height and Shape Width fields on the Shape Format tab of the ribbon to set uniform dimensions — no baseball analogies this time.

Transferring chart formatting and elements

Except for certain celebrity players, it's easy to see players as interchangeable, which is often the case when teams make trades or call up players from the minor leagues. New faces regularly appear on the field, but each player's career statistics remain uniquely theirs. Similarly, most formatting and elements can be trans-ferred between charts, creating a uniform look. The technique is simple, but take your time — otherwise, you may bobble the ball, er, your chart:

1. **Click once on the chart area of the chart that has the desired formatting and elements.**

2. **Choose Home ⇨ Copy or right-click on the chart area, then choose Copy.**

3. **Click once on the chart area of the chart that you wish to update.**

4. **Choose Home ⇨ Paste drop-down ⇨ Paste Special.**

   An abbreviated version of the Paste Special dialog box opens, as shown in Figure 12-6.

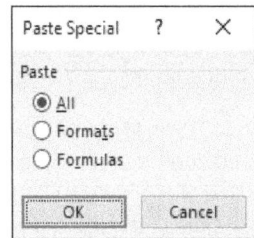

FIGURE 12-6:
The abbreviated
version of the
Paste Special
dialog box.

REMEMBER

WARNING

5. **Choose Formats and then click OK or skip a step by double-clicking on Formats in Excel for Windows.**

All formatting is applied from the first chart to the second and the mix of chart elements on the second chart is adjusted to match those of the first chart, meaning added or removed.

If you choose the Paste command instead of Paste Special, or select All or Formulas, you may paste more than you bargained for — merging the data from both charts together. Fortunately, you can erase your error from the record books by choosing Undo or pressing Ctrl+Z (Windows) or Cmd+Z (macOS).

Creating and applying chart templates

In Excel for Windows (but not macOS), chart templates are the pinch hitters of the game, ready to step in at a moment's notice. These templates bundle a chart type, chart elements, and formatting into a single package that can be applied with just a few mouse clicks. They ensure your charts keep a consistent look and feel — like an opening lineup where everyone's uniform is crisp, clean, and untouched by a stolen-base slide (at least for now).

Get your batting gloves on — you're about to knock chart formatting out of the park:

1. **Click once on a chart, such as the sample chart expanded on in the "Maintaining chart data" section earlier in the chapter.**

2. **Choose Chart Design ⇨ Chart Styles drop-down, then select a style from the gallery or customize the chart formatting to your liking.**

3. **Choose Chart Design ⇨ Add Chart Element ⇨ Data Table ⇨ With Legend Keys or click Chart Elements ⇨ Data Table ⇨ No Legend Keys.**

A data table appears on the chart.

TIP

The Data Table option isn't available for certain chart types, such as Pie or Waterfall Charts.

4. **Right-click on the chart area and then choose Save As Template.**

The Save Chart Template dialog box opens.

REMEMBER

Always distinguish between the chart area and a chart element, such as the plot area, because commands may not appear in the resulting context menu if the wrong part of the chart is selected — talk about a wild throw!

5. **Assign a name to the chart template file and then click Save.**

TECHNICAL STUFF

Chart template files have a .CRTX file extension that cannot be opened directly in Microsoft Excel. You can, however, update a template by saving over an existing copy.

6. **Click any cell within the source data for your existing chart.**

7. **Apply the template:**

- **Windows:** Choose Insert ⇨ Recommended Charts ⇨ All Charts ⇨ Templates, choose a template, then click OK.

- **macOS:** Start with any built-in chart, then choose Chart Design ⇨ Change Chart Type ⇨ Templates, then choose a template.

TIP

To apply a template to an existing chart in Excel for Windows, click once on the chart and then choose Chart Design ⇨ Change Chart Type. The Change Chart Type dialog box opens to the All Charts tab, from which you can make a selection from the Templates section.

Managing templates

You can mark a single chart template as the default template in Excel for Windows, and then start new charts by way of a keyboard shortcut:

1. **Choose Insert ⇨ Recommended Charts.**

2. **Choose Templates from the All Charts tab.**

3. **Right-click on your preferred template and then click Set as Default Chart.**

4. **Select any cell within a range of data that you wish to present in chart form, and then press Alt+F1.**

A chart using the default template settings appears in your worksheet.

In Windows, a Manage Templates button appears at the bottom of both the Insert Chart and Change Chart Type dialog boxes when you click Templates on the sidebar. This button opens a Windows Explorer window, allowing you to back up, copy, or remove templates as needed. In macOS, choose Chart Design ➪ Change Chart Type ➪ Manage Templates.

Spotlighting Trends with Sparklines

Sparklines are the Excel equivalent of "miniatures" in the candy aisle — think Hershey's Miniatures or Snickers Minis. These bite-sized charts fit snugly within individual worksheet cells, providing a compact, sweet solution for data visualization. Sparklines excel (pun intended) in situations where you're juggling multiple data sets or dealing with limited space, offering a quick and effective way to highlight patterns. These in-cell charts — available as line, column, or win-loss types — serve up just enough insight to satisfy your data-crunching cravings:

>> **Line and Column Sparklines:** Compact versions of line and bar charts, useful for comparing relative values within a dataset.

>> **Win-Loss Sparklines:** Binary bar charts that show positive or negative values above or below a central axis without reflecting scale.

To get started with Sparklines:

1. **Set up the data:**

   a. **Enter 25, 6, 2, 4 in cells A1:D1 of a blank workbook.**

   Fun fact: This is a subtle nod to the classic song by Chicago, "25 or 6 to 4." The title, as explained by its writer, Robert Lamm, refers to the time of day — 25 or 26 minutes to 4:00 AM — when the song was written.

   b. **Enter =A1*2 into cell A2 and then use the Fill Handle in cell A2 to copy the formula down to cell A5.**

   c. **Drag the Fill Handle in A5 across to cell D5.**

   Cells A1:D5 Rows now have values doubling row by row.

2. **Insert Sparklines:**

   a. **Select cells E1:E5.**

   b. **Choose Insert ➪ Line or Insert ➪ Sparklines ➪ Line.**

   The Create Sparklines dialog box opens, as shown in Figure 12-7.

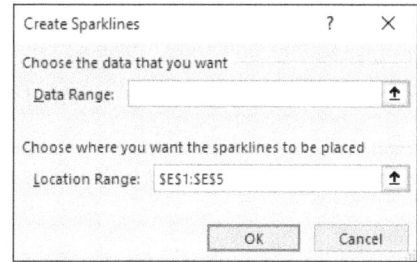

FIGURE 12-7:
The Create
Sparklines
dialog box.

c. **Use the Data Range field to specify cells A1:D5.**

d. **Click OK (or press Enter) to close the dialog box.**

REMEMBER

The Location Range must be on the active worksheet. Start by selecting target cells for Sparklines to avoid workflow interruptions. The Data Range can be located anywhere within the active workbook or a linked workbook.

3. **To adjust vertical scaling, choose Sparkline ⇨ Axis ⇨ Same For All Sparklines in the Vertical Axis Maximum Value Options group.**

   This adjustment enhances differentiation between Sparklines.

4. **To enhance Sparkline visibility:**

   a. **Select rows 1:5.**

   b. **Choose Home ⇨ Format ⇨ Row Height or skip step a by right-clicking one of the row numbers and choosing Row Height.**

   c. **Set height to 30 and then click OK.**

REMEMBER

Sparklines sizes are predicated on row height and column width. Adjust either or both settings to make Sparklines appear larger onscreen.

5. **To toggle the Sparklines to another type, choose Sparkline ⇨ Column.**

   Sparklines in E1:E5 now display as compact column charts.

Explore these options on the Sparkline tab for added functionality:

>> **Sparkline:** Click the Edit Data drop-down to reveal these commands:

   • **Edit Group Location & Data:** Change the data range or location for grouped Sparklines.

   • **Edit Single Sparkline's Data:** Change the data range or location for a single Sparkline.

   • **Hidden & Empty Cells:** Define how to manage empty cells (Gaps, Zero, or Connect Data Points) and data in hidden rows or columns.

>> **Type:** Toggle between Line, Column, and Win-Loss Sparklines.

>> **Show:** Highlight specific points (high, low, first, last, or negative values) within Sparklines.

>> **Style:** Apply built-in styles or customize colors with Sparkline Color and Marker Color.

>> **Axis:** Defines the reference line against which Sparkline data points are plotted.

- **Axis Type:** Sparklines default to General Axis Type for uniform intervals, but you can choose Data Axis Type for irregular time-based intervals.

- **Show Axis:** Enable Show Axis to display a horizontal axis line.

- **Plot Data Right-to-Left:** Flips the order that data appears within the Sparkline.

- **Vertical Axis options:** Adjust for consistent scaling across Sparklines or specify custom min/max values.

>> **Group/Ungroup:** Grouped Sparklines share formatting changes. Use Ungroup to format Sparklines independently.

>> **Clear:** Remove Sparklines using Sparkline ➪ Clear Selected Sparklines to remove a single Sparkline, or Sparkline ➪ Clear Selected Sparkline Groups to remove multiple.

Pressing Delete removes cell content layered over Sparklines but does not remove the Sparklines themselves. Use Clear instead.

REMEMBER

Unleashing the Magic of PivotTables

Creating PivotTables is almost as magical as conjuring order out of chaos — whether you imagine wrinkling your nose like Samantha from *Bewitched* or waving your hands like Wanda in *WandaVision*. Beyond the burgeoning AI features being added to Excel (see Chapter 15), PivotTables have historically offered a rare chance to say, "Excel, take the wheel," letting you step back from tedious number crunching.

In short, think of PivotTables as an automatic report writer within Excel. Despite their somewhat imposing name, no special skills are required to create PivotTables, as long as your data meets certain specifications:

>> **Data must be contiguous:** Ensure your data exists within a block of cells without blank rows or columns. Individual blank cells are allowed but appear as "(Blank)" in nonnumeric fields or are treated as zeros in numeric ranges.

>> **Unique headers are essential:** The first row of your data must have unique and descriptive titles. Rename vague or similar column headings to make building your PivotTable easier and more intuitive.

REMEMBER

Column headings, often referred to as "headers," are optional in many Excel features but are mandatory for PivotTables. For compatibility, Chapter 17 explores techniques to fit lengthy column labels into individual cells, ensuring they meet the requirements without compromising readability.

>> **Numeric columns must be clean:** Columns holding numeric values should avoid text-based entries (e.g., "n/a") in any rows other than the header. If such text entries exist, Excel treats the entire column as text, requiring you to clean or convert the data to display as numeric amounts.

By ensuring your dataset meets these simple conditions, you unlock the full power of PivotTables, making it as effortless as waving a wand — otherwise, you might find yourself wrinkling your nose in frustration.

Just as a house needs a foundation, PivotTables need data. Without data, there can be no PivotTables — so here's a solid base to build on:

>> **Windows:** Choose File ⇨ New, type Grocery List in the search bar, press Enter, select the Grocery List (With Category Totals) template, and click Create.

>> **macOS:** Download the Chapter 12 Grocery List workbook from www.dummies. com/go/excelfd and open it in Excel.

The Grocery List (With Category Totals) is an example of an ideal dataset thanks to its Item, Store, and Category columns, which can be used to group data effectively. Additionally, the grocery list is formatted as an Excel table (see Chapter 5), preventing data integrity issues when adding new data.

REMEMBER

If the data were not already formatted as an Excel table, the words Grocery List appearing next to the list could pose a problem by causing Excel to overlook the headers in the row below. Best practices recommend that PivotTable source data be bounded by the worksheet frame or separated by at least one blank row and column on all sides.

Refining Recommended PivotTables

If you've ever found yourself staring at a dataset, unsure of how to summarize it, think of Recommended PivotTables as the "phone a friend" option from *Who*

Wants to Be a Millionaire? Excel steps in to offer a lifeline, presenting a list of suggested PivotTables tailored to your data. With just a few clicks, you can select a readymade option and let Excel do the heavy lifting — no stress, no second-guessing. It's like having an expert on speed dial for your reporting needs!

Follow these simple steps to get started with Recommended PivotTables:

1. **Select a cell within your data set, such as B4 in the sample grocery list.**

2. **Choose Insert ➪ Recommended PivotTables.**

In Excel for Windows, the Recommended PivotTables task pane, shown in Figure 12-8, appears for some users, while others are greeted by the Recommended PivotTables dialog box.

- In the task pane, you can scroll to the bottom and click Show All Results, which displays the number of additional PivotTable options.

- In the dialog box, a list appears on the left, and selecting an option shows a preview — though it mirrors the list entry and may not add much value.

MacOS users won't see either — Excel simply drops a PivotTable on a new worksheet, swinging for the fences.

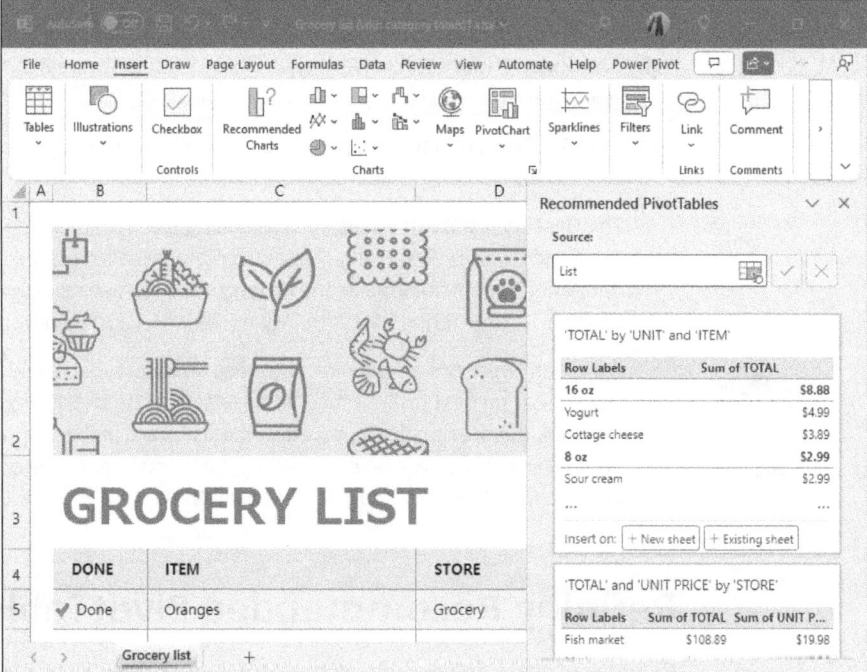

FIGURE 12-8:
The Recommended PivotTables task pane.

3. Select a template:

- **Task pane users:** Click New Sheet within the TOTAL by CATEGORY and STORE PivotTable.

  The PivotTable appears on a new worksheet, as shown in Figure 12-9.

- **Dialog box users:** Select Sum of TOTAL by CATEGORY, and then click OK.

  A simpler PivotTable appears on a new worksheet.

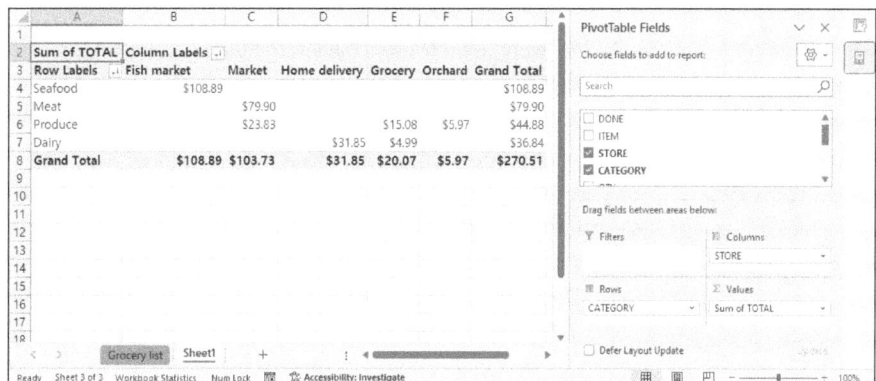

FIGURE 12-9:
A PivotTable and the PivotTable Fields task pane.

WARNING

Task pane users, be cautious when using the Existing Sheet button within the Recommended PivotTables task pane. PivotTables overwrite any cell contents in their placement area (though Excel provides a warning). A bigger issue arises when PivotTables are placed too close together — this can result in reports that cannot be updated as more rows or columns are added. One PivotTable cannot "push" another out of the way.

4. Click on any cell within the PivotTable.

The contextual PivotTable Analyze and Design tabs appear within Excel's ribbon, along with the PivotTable Fields task pane shown in Figure 12-9.

CROSS REFERENCE

Chapter 15 discusses the Home ⇨ Analyze Data command, a more powerful version of Recommended PivotTables that could eventually replace it.

Exploring the PivotTable Fields task pane

The PivotTable Fields task pane serves as the control center for building and changing PivotTable reports. It includes the following key areas:

≫ **Field List:** Displays headers from the source data, in the same order as the worksheet columns. Use the Search field to quickly find specific fields. Checked fields are included in the current PivotTable.

Excel for Windows users can choose Settings ⇨ Sort A to Z to reorder the field list alphabetically.

>> **Filters:** Fields placed here allow filtering at a higher level, outside the report itself.

>> **Columns:** Fields here display unique items as columns in the report.

>> **Rows:** Fields here display unique items as rows in the report.

>> **Values:** Numeric fields are summed by default, while nonnumeric fields are counted.

Click the drop-down for any field in the Values area, then select Field Settings to specify the type of calculation for summarizing the data, such as Count, Average, Max, or Min.

In Excel for Windows, the Defer Layout Update option, found at the bottom of the PivotTable Fields task pane, functions similarly to setting an Excel worksheet to manual calculation. It pauses PivotTable recalculations, which can significantly improve performance when working with large datasets or performing complex operations. This option lets you make multiple changes to the PivotTable layout before applying them all at once by clicking Update.

You may find it helpful to relate the areas of the PivotTable Fields task pane to the PivotTable created by Recommended PivotTables (your layout may vary based on Excel's recommendations). If your PivotTable doesn't match the layout shown in Figure 12-9, adjust the fields as follows:

>> **Columns:** Drag the STORE field to create a column for each store.

>> **Rows:** Drag the CATEGORY field here to create a row for each category.

>> **Values:** Drag the TOTAL field here so that the PivotTable calculates the sum of each category by store.

Once these adjustments are made, your PivotTable should be structured for the next steps.

Grand totals appear by default but can be toggled on or off for an individual PivotTable using the Design ⇨ Grand Totals command. For setting a permanent preference, Windows users can refer to the "Customizing PivotTable options" section later in this chapter.

This setup showcases why these reports are called PivotTables — some of the row-based data has been "pivoted" into columns. To fully grasp the concept of pivoting, some adjustments are in order:

1. **Drag the STORE field from the Columns area into the Rows area or click the STORE drop-down and select Move to Row Labels.**

   As shown in Figure 12-10, store names now appear beneath the category names. This can result in duplication, such as "Grocery" appearing under both Produce and Dairy sections.

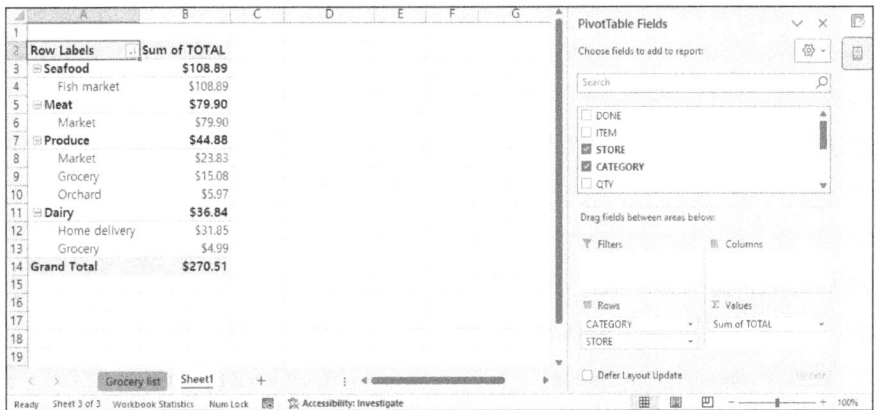

FIGURE 12-10:
An updated
PivotTable.

TIP

Subtotals appear at the top of each group by default but can be toggled or repositioned for an individual PivotTable using the Design ⇨ Subtotals command. Similar to grand totals, you can also modify an Excel option to set a permanent preference.

2. **Drag the STORE field above the CATEGORY field in the Rows area or click the STORE drop-down and select Move Up or Move to Beginning.**

   The report now lists stores alphabetically, with corresponding categories shown beneath each one. However, this causes categories like "Produce" to appear multiple times, under different stores.

3. **To solve the duplication, drag the CATEGORY field from the Rows area into the Columns area.**

   The report now shows one row per store and columns for each category, dropping duplication and making the report more concise.

This illustrates the power of PivotTables — often, just a few tweaks are enough to transform a report into a highly effective summary.

Rolling your own PivotTables

"Hold the pickle, hold the lettuce . . ." wait a minute, get out of my grocery list! I want what I want! You can truly have it your way with PivotTables by following these steps:

1. **Select any cell within a data range or Excel table, such as cell B4.**

   REMEMBER

   Converting data ranges to Excel tables, as explained in Chapter 5, is a best practice that ensures new data additions are automatically included and displayed accurately.

2. **Choose Insert ⇨ PivotTable or Table Design ⇨ Summarize with PivotTable (Windows) or Insert ⇨ Table ⇨ PivotTable (macOS).**

   The PivotTable from Table or Range (Windows) or Create PivotTable (macOS) dialog box opens.

   REMEMBER

   The contextual Table Design ribbon tab only appears when the active cell or selection is within an Excel table.

3. **Check the Table/Range field, which displays one of these options:**

   - **Table name:** Default names like Table1 or custom names like List show the source data is formatted as an Excel table.

   - **Data range:** Cell coordinates (e.g., $A$1:$D$50) show the source data is a normal range of cells.

   - **Empty field:** If the Table/Range field is as empty as the milk, bread, and egg racks in Atlanta grocery stores when snow is in the forecast, click Cancel and start over at Step 1. Proceeding without data means you must select a range manually. Additionally, unless you choose New Worksheet, the PivotTable lands in the cell specified in the Location field, possibly overwriting unrelated data in your worksheet.

4. **Click OK to close the dialog box and create your new PivotTable.**

   A blank PivotTable appears on a new worksheet (if you accepted the default) or the specified location if you decided to freestyle.

5. **Add fields to the report by dragging a field into the corresponding area or clicking its checkbox:**

   - **Nonnumeric fields:** Added to the Rows area

   - **Date and time hierarchies:** Added to the Columns area

   - **Numeric fields:** Added to the Values area, summing amounts by default

That's truly all there is to creating a PivotTable! Keep reading, though — PivotTables may need some added care and feeding. Luckily, it's far less demanding than a Tamagotchi!

Refreshing PivotTables

In the 1970s, TV viewers were urged to "Take the Nestea plunge," a campaign promising instant refreshment with a dramatic backward dive into swimming pools. Whether the tea delivered on its promise is debatable, but the ad certainly inspired countless teenagers to mimic the iconic trust-fall. Tepid tea may not suit everyone's taste, but there's no avoiding the plunge into the Refresh command when it comes to PivotTables. Whenever your data changes, the Refresh command ensures your PivotTable stays accurate and up to date.

Unlike formulas, which automatically recalculate whenever related cells are updated, PivotTables function more like a snapshot-in-time of your data. When you create a PivotTable, Excel stores a copy of the underlying data in a hidden PivotTable cache, which serves as an intermediary for generating and supporting your report. This design means any updates to the source data require a manual refresh to ensure your PivotTable reflects the latest changes — a reality that explains why Excel is rife with Refresh commands:

>> **PivotTable Analyze ⇨ Refresh:** Refreshes an individual PivotTable. Use the shortcut Alt+F5 (Windows) or Command+Option+R (macOS).

>> **Data ⇨ Refresh All:** Refreshes all PivotTables and Data Connections (see the bonus chapter "Automating Data Transformation with Power Query" available at www.dummies.com/go/excelfd). Use the shortcut Ctrl+Alt+F5 (Windows) or Command+Option+Control+R (macOS).

>> **Context menu:** Right-click on a PivotTable and choose Refresh from the menu.

Enabling refresh upon opening

In this age of self-empowerment, it's important to set yourself up for success, and Excel lets you do just that by enabling PivotTables to refresh automatically when their workbook is opened. This setting is a one-time adjustment for individual PivotTables, but don't miss the "Customizing PivotTable options" section later in this chapter if you'd prefer to streamline and automate this process for all your reports (as long as you're using Excel for Windows).

Here's the inside track:

1. **Click on any cell within a PivotTable.**

   The contextual PivotTable Analyze and Design tabs appear in Excel's ribbon.

   The PivotTable Analyze tab goes into a zombie-like state when you select rows intersecting a PivotTable. Fortunately, you won't need to hire a lab assistant named Igor or flip a massive power switch — simply click any cell within the PivotTable to resurrect the commands.

2. **Choose PivotTable Analyze ⇨ Options ⇨ Data.**

   The Data tab of the PivotTable Options dialog box opens.

3. **Turn the Refresh Data When Opening the File option on.**

   Adjusting the Number of Items to Retain Per Field setting to None prevents Excel from showing deleted items when filtering a PivotTable. Without this tweak, you might sometimes feel like your PivotTable is possessed, holding on to ghostly remnants of data long gone.

4. **Click OK to close the dialog box and apply the setting.**

   Going forward, this PivotTable refreshes itself every time you open the workbook. Now, if only you could get a cup of coffee to appear just as effortlessly. . . .

Changing PivotTable data sources

Although you can swap out a PivotTable's data source, it's more common to expand the data source to include new rows or columns added to a normal range of cells. Follow these steps to confirm that a PivotTable is capturing all relevant data:

1. **Click on any cell within the PivotTable.**

2. **Choose PivotTable Analyze ⇨ Change Data Source.**

   The Change PivotTable Data Source dialog box opens.

3. **Check the Table/Range field to figure out the current data source:**

   - **Table Name:** If the PivotTable is based on a table, it automatically includes new data, so resizing isn't necessary. However, refreshing the PivotTable is always needed.

   - **Cell Reference:** If the PivotTable is based on a range, Excel highlights the range with a dashed border. Scroll to ensure the border extends to the bottom of the data. If it doesn't, reselect the entire range to include the new data.

4. **Click OK to close the dialog box and apply any changes.**

Closing the dialog box also refreshes the PivotTable, giving you a convenient two-for-one when manually resizing the data source.

Sifting PivotTable data for clarity

Some folks are famous for having no filter — saying whatever comes to mind without hesitation. In Excel, however, filters are crucial, especially when working with PivotTables. Arranging fields in the PivotTable Fields task pane is only the first step in creating a meaningful report. You have four main ways to display subsets of data within your report:

» **Filter buttons:** Chapter 4 explores filtering data in worksheet cells, and those techniques apply equally to PivotTables. Depending on the context, you may see some combination of these options on PivotTable filter menus:

- **Label Filters:** Restrict rows or columns based on their content.

- **Value Filters:** Restrict rows or columns based on grand totals.

- **Date Filters:** Restrict rows or columns based on specified date criteria.

- **Select Field:** Specify which field you wish to filter when two or more fields appear in the Rows or Columns areas.

  Filtering a specific column within a PivotTable takes some finesse because the Filter commands on Excel's menus are disabled when a PivotTable cell is selected. To enable filtering, select a cell adjacent to the PivotTable, then choose Data ⇨ Filter.

TECHNICAL STUFF

» **Slicers:** Introduced in Chapter 5 for Excel tables, slicers provide a visual and interactive way to filter data. They work just as effectively with PivotTables, offering a user-friendly alternative to traditional drop-down filters.

1. **Choose PivotTable Analyze ⇨ Insert Slicer.**

   The Insert Slicers dialog box appears.

2. **Select one or more fields, then click OK.**

   The slicer(s) appear on the worksheet, displaying selectable items from the chosen field(s).

3. **To filter a single item in the PivotTable, click any item on the slicer.**

4. **Or, to filter multiple items, hold down Ctrl (Windows) or Cmd (macOS), and then select two or more items, or click and drag on the slicer with your left mouse button.**

   In either case, the PivotTable collapses to only show rows or columns related to the item(s) you selected.

5. **To reset a slicer, click Clear Filter.**

   The PivotTable expands to show all columns or rows related to the filtered field.

   To use a Slicer to filter two or more PivotTables that are based upon the same data set at once, right-click on the Slicer, choose Report Connections from the menu, and then select the PivotTables.

>> **Timelines:** Think of this feature as a Slicer's cooler, date-savvy cousin. It lets you specify a date range to filter your PivotTable dynamically. Just make sure your source data includes at least one column formatted as dates — Excel can't time travel without them. Choose PivotTable Analyze ⇨ Insert Timeline to get started.

>> **Report Filter:** The Filters area in the PivotTable Fields task pane enables you to filter an entire report based on one or more fields. You can even create individual worksheets for each filter criterion. The following steps build on the PivotTable created in the "Refining Recommended PivotTables" section:

1. **Select any cell within the PivotTable to activate the PivotTable Fields task pane.**

   If the PivotTable Fields task pane doesn't appear, choose PivotTable Analyze ⇨ Field List.

2. **Drag the STORE field into the Filters area.**

   A new field appears above the PivotTable, from which you can select one or more stores from the Filter menu.

3. **To create individual PivotTables for each criterion, choose PivotTable Analyze ⇨ Options ⇨ Show Report Filter Pages.**

   The Show Report Filter Pages dialog box opens.

   This command is disabled until at least one field is placed in the Filters area of the PivotTable Fields task pane.

4. **Select a field from the Show All Report Filter Pages Of if more than two fields are present.**

5. **Click OK to close the dialog box and create individual PivotTables.**

6. **To remove the resulting worksheets, select the first worksheet in the group.**

7. **Hold Shift and click the last worksheet in the group.**

8. **Right-click any tab in the group and choose Delete or go to Home ⇨ Delete drop-down ⇨ Delete Sheet.**

9. **Confirm the deletion.**

TIP

PivotTables allow sorting much like worksheet cells, but each row field is sorted independently, giving you precise control over the order of your data.

Customizing PivotTable options

Historically, PivotTables gave you a decent head start on report creation — like handing you a preassembled bike but leaving you to figure out the pedals, handle-bars, and seat adjustments. If your preferences for subtotals, grand totals, or other settings strayed from Excel's defaults, you'd be stuck making a series of tedious manual adjustments. Thankfully, Excel for Windows (but not macOS) lets you curb this madness with a few one-time tweaks in the Excel Options dialog box:

1. **Choose File ⇨ Options ⇨ Data.**

The Data section of the Excel Options dialog box opens, promising a world where PivotTables work the way you want them to.

2. **Click Edit Default Layout.**

The Edit Default Layout dialog box appears, ready to bend PivotTables to your will.

Here are the settings you can tweak to save yourself from future headaches:

» **Layout Import:** Found the perfect PivotTable setup? Select a cell in that masterpiece and click Import to immortalize those settings as your new defaults. Instant trendsetter.

» **Subtotals and Grand Totals:** Decide exactly where you want those pesky totals — no more playing Excel's default guessing game.

» **Report Layout:** Set the default layout for PivotTables:

• **Show in Compact Form:** All Rows area fields cram into the first column, cozy but possibly chaotic.

• **Show in Outline Form:** Fields spread out hierarchically with subtotals taking the spotlight.

• **Show in Tabular Form:** Each Rows area field gets its own column, like a proper Excel democracy.

>> **PivotTable Options:** Opens the PivotTable Options dialog box, where the Data tab hides two game-changing settings:

- **Refresh Data When Opening the File:** Start your work session off on the right foot with freshly updated PivotTables, ready to impress. Just remember, they're not mind readers — you need to manually refresh them later as needed.

- **Number of Items to Retain Per Field:** Set this to None to keep deleted items from haunting your Filter lists.

REMEMBER

Changes to Excel's options apply only to future workbooks you create. Any existing PivotTables or PivotCharts cling to their old ways, so you need to manually adjust them if they're stuck in the past. Even within the current workbook, new PivotTables and PivotCharts won't adopt the updated defaults — you must set those preferences separately.

Engaging with PivotCharts

PivotCharts are like the rockstars of Excel — bold, dynamic, and ready to steal the show when your worksheet data gets too unwieldy for standard charts to manage. While those basic charts we discussed earlier work just fine for smaller gigs, PivotCharts are built for the big stage, effortlessly turning complex data into eye-catching, interactive visuals. Want to create your own PivotChart masterpiece? Here's how:

1. **Select cell B4 of the grocery list template we've been raving about in this chapter. (Yes, grocery lists deserve PivotCharts, too.)**

2. **Choose Insert ⇨ PivotChart.**

   The Create PivotChart dialog box opens.

TIP

   In Windows, the Insert ⇨ PivotChart drop-down boldly suggests you can create a standalone PivotChart with its PivotChart and PivotChart & PivotTable options. Spoiler alert: it's all lies. No matter what you pick, Excel insists on creating an accompanying PivotTable. Luckily, you can then move the PivotChart wherever you like in your workbook — it won't hold a grudge.

3. **Populate the Table/Range field.**

   This is where you tell Excel what to chart, just like when you're "Rolling your own PivotTables" (earlier in this chapter).

4. **Click OK to create the PivotChart.**

   Voilà! A blank PivotChart appears, eagerly awaiting your direction — like a canvas craving its first brushstroke. All it needs now are the fields you want to include to start its data-driven dazzle.

5. **Build your PivotChart by dragging fields into these areas of the PivotChart Fields task pane:**

a. **Drag STORE to Filters.**

This allows you to filter the chart's data by store.

b. **Drag CATEGORY to Axis (Categories).**

This defines the horizontal axis (or vertical axis for bar charts) by displaying categories.

c. **Drag ITEM to Legend (Series).**

This divides data into series, adding color to distinguish different items.

d. **Drag TOTAL to Values.**

This determines the numbers displayed in the chart displays, calculating totals by category and item.

To wind up this section, here's a series of quick tips related to PivotCharts:

>> **Toggle Field Buttons:** Head to PivotChart Analyze ⇨ Field Buttons to show or hide those handy filter buttons on the chart. Think of it as tidying up your chart's outfit.

>> **Resizing and Refreshing:** When the data changes, your PivotChart needs a refresh or resize — no one likes a chart stuck in the past.

>> **Using Slicers and Timelines:** Bring some interactivity to the party with Slicers (see Chapter 5) and Timelines, just like you would for PivotTables.

>> **Formatting PivotCharts:** PivotCharts can be jazzed up just like standard charts. Go ahead, give it some flair — Excel won't judge.

TIP

Most of the techniques in the "Deconstructing and Customizing Charts" section earlier in this chapter also apply to PivotCharts.

IN THIS CHAPTER

» **Exploring conditional formatting options**

» **Highlighting cells based upon specific criteria**

» **Visualizing data with graphical cell formatting**

» **Ranking cells using color and formatting**

» **Designing custom formatting rules**

» **Managing and protecting conditional formatting**

Chapter **13**

Contemplating Conditional Formatting

C onditional formatting lets you add a dynamic layer of style to your cells that shifts as your data changes. Most rules are a breeze to set up — just fill in one or more blanks or select a prebuilt style, boom, instant flair. Feeling fancy? Stack multiple rules like colors, borders, data bars, color scales, and cell icons. And if you're the type who prefers full creative control, conditional formatting lets you create custom rules based on cell values or formulas, giving your spreadsheet a polished, responsive look.

Before you dive into this chapter, may I suggest some mood music, "Just Dropped In (To See What Condition My Condition Was In)" by Kenny Rogers and the First Edition, to get you through creating these sample data sets?

1. **Enter this formula in cell A1 of a blank worksheet:** =CHAR(ROW(A1:A26)+64).

   This fills cells A1:A26 with the entire alphabet.

TECHNICAL STUFF

The CHAR function in Excel returns a specific character based on the ASCII (or Unicode) value you provide. For instance, =CHAR(65) returns "A" because 65 corresponds to the uppercase letter "A" in the ASCII table, while =CHAR(97) returns lowercase "a". Similarly, =CHAR(ROW(A1:A26)+64) converts row numbers into their corresponding letters, uppercase letters, A through Z.

2. **Add the following labels in columns C1 through C5, which correspond to the arguments for the RANDARRAY function:**

   - **C1:** Rows
   - **C2:** Columns
   - **C3:** Min
   - **C4:** Max
   - **C5:** Integer

TIP

   RANDARRAY is an Excel function that generates an array of random numbers within a specified range, with options to define the number of rows, columns, minimum value, maximum value, and whether the values should be integers.

3. **Enter the following values in columns D1 through D5:**

   - **D1:** 11
   - **D2:** 7
   - **D3:** 100
   - **D4:** 1000
   - **D5:** TRUE

4. **Enter this formula into cell C10:** =SORT(RANDARRAY(D1,D2,D3,D4,D5)).

   This generates eleven rows and seven columns of random numbers between 100 and 1000, sorted in ascending order. As you progress through the chapter, adjust these inputs to create dynamic data sets that you can apply various conditional formatting rules to:

   - **D1:** Adjusts the number of rows.
   - **D2:** Adjusts the number of columns.
   - **D3:** Adjusts the lower range of the values (input a number or date in this cell).
   - **D4:** Adjusts the upper range of the values (input a number or date in this cell).

Dates initially appear in serial number form. Select the range and then choose Short Date from the Number Format list on the Home tab of Excel's ribbon to display them in a more readable date format.

- **D5:** TRUE causes RANDARRAY to return whole numbers; FALSE returns decimal numbers.

Enter FALSE in cell D5 to generate numbers with decimal values (or time values for dates).

5. **To generate different sets of numbers after applying conditional formatting, press F9 (Windows) or Fn+F9 (macOS), or choose Formulas ⇨ Calculate.**

RANDARRAY is a volatile worksheet function, so making any content changes (but not formatting) in the workbook also regenerates the numbers. If you prefer a static set, copy the range and use Home ⇨ Paste drop-down ⇨ Values to replace formulas with fixed numbers.

In Excel, volatile functions recalculate every time any cell value changes, even if the change is unrelated to the function, which can impact performance in large workbooks. Nonvolatile functions recalculate only when their referenced data changes. For example, RAND(), NOW(), TODAY(), and RANDARRAY() are volatile, while functions like SUM(), VLOOKUP(), and INDEX() are nonvolatile.

Formatting with Quick Analysis

When you select a range of cells in Excel for Windows, the Quick Analysis button pops up like an eager intern, ready to dazzle you with formatting, charts, and other analytical goodies. No need to go spelunking through the ribbon — just click the button at the bottom-right corner of your selection and let Excel do some of the heavy lifting. Charts or Sparklines? Right there (and in Chapter 12). Totals or Conditional formatting? Served up fresh. It's like a buffet of Excel wizardry, minus the questionable seafood.

If the Quick Analysis button feels like an overenthusiastic assistant, you can disable it by following these steps:

1. **Choose File ⇨ Options.**

   The Excel Options dialog box opens.

2. **Clear the Show Quick Analysis Options on Selection checkbox in the General section.**

3. **Click OK to save your settings.**

Once disabled, the Quick Analysis button no longer appears automatically — but you can still summon it anytime by pressing Ctrl+Q after selecting a range.

Here's a taste of what's possible with conditional formatting:

1. **Select a range, such as C10:C20, and then press Ctrl or click the Quick Analysis button.**

   The Quick Analysis tool opens, as shown in Figure 13-1.

TIP

   If the Quick Analysis tool obscures your data, scroll the worksheet to ensure at least 10 rows are visible beneath your selection.

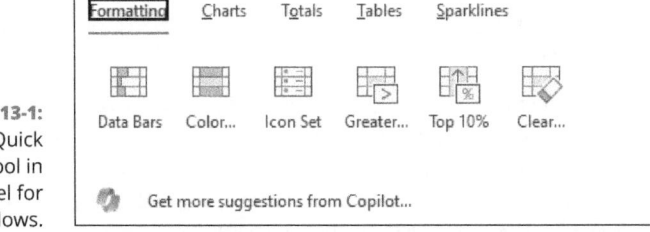

FIGURE 13-1:
The Quick
Analysis tool in
Excel for
Windows.

2. **Hover over an option on the Formatting tab to see a live preview of the conditional formatting — as much as is visible around the Quick Analysis tool — and then click an option to apply it:**

   - **Data Bars:** Displays a visual representation of each amount's contribution percentage toward the total sum of your selection.

   - **Color Scales:** Applies a three-color gradient, with green for the highest values, red for the lowest, and white for midpoint values.

   - **Icon Set:** Green arrows mark values equal to or above 67% of the total, yellow arrows mark values between 33% and 67%, and red arrows mark values below 33%.

   - **Greater Than:** Highlights cells with a light red fill and dark red text if their values exceed the midpoint. You can adjust the threshold and formatting in the Greater Than dialog box.

   - **Top 10%:** Highlights cells in the top 10% with light red fill and dark red text, making high values stand out.

   These options offer a fast, visual approach to data analysis by highlighting trends and outliers. There's no customization here — think of this as a small Whitman's Sampler, tempting you to explore the full box of chocolates, er, conditional formatting options.

3. **To remove conditional formatting via Quick Analysis:**

   a. **Select a range of cells that contain conditional formatting (e.g., C10:C20).**

   b. **Press Ctrl or click the Quick Analysis button.**

   c. **Click Clear . . . on the Formatting tab.**

Decoding Conditional Formatting Options

Conditional formatting offers, shall we say, a curated selection of settings from the Format Cells dialog box. This means you may end up gnashing your teeth when that one perfect format isn't available for conditional use. Let's break down what you can — and cannot — apply through conditional formatting:

>> **Number Formats:** All number formatting options are available.

>> **Font Styles and Effects:** You can apply the Regular, Italic, Bold, and Bold Italic font styles to cells, along with font colors, and the Strikethrough effect.

REMEMBER

You cannot use conditional formatting to apply fonts or font sizes to cells. You also cannot change the direction of text, nor apply the subscript or superscript effects.

>> **Borders:** You get a limited selection here — just some, not all, of the border options available in the full Format Cells dialog box. As shown in Figure 13-2, the Style list gives you about half the usual choices. Bottom line? You can change the color, but not the weight, and forget about inside or diagonal borders.

>> **Fill:** Here's where you can run amok, adding background colors, patterns, and fill effects to your heart's delight — conditional formatting doesn't hold you back in the fill department.

REMEMBER

You're out of luck if you want to dynamically tweak the Locked or Hidden status of cells — conditional formatting doesn't touch those settings.

While conditional formatting borrows many options from the Format Cells dialog box, it also brings its own bag of tricks. Features like data bars, color scales, and cell icons operate outside the traditional formatting menu, offering dynamic, visual ways to interpret your data at a glance. These tools don't just change how your data looks; they change how you see it.

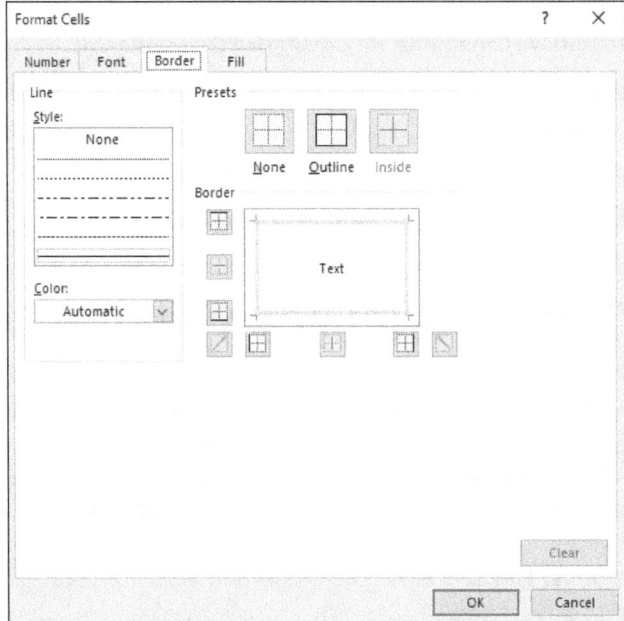

FIGURE 13-2:
Borders tab of
the Conditional
Formatting
version of the
Format Cells
dialog box.

Highlighting Cells Based on Value

The Home ⇨ Conditional Formatting ⇨ Highlight Cells Rules menu options let you spotlight data points — whether numbers, dates, or text — based on conditions that you choose. Think of it as giving a little extra jazz hands to the data that deserves attention! All the rules in this section allow you to enter values directly into the Conditional Formatting dialog box or reference a cell instead, making it easy to apply formatting dynamically.

REMEMBER

Rules in this section of the Conditional Formatting menu that accept text-based inputs are case-insensitive.

These rules take a fill-in-the-blank approach to flagging data:

>> **Greater Than:** Formats cells with values greater than your specified input — spotlighting the overachievers.

- **Numbers and dates:** Formats any number or date greater than the specified value. For example, entering 500 highlights values greater than, but not equal to, 500.

- **Text:** Formats any text that comes after the specified input alphabetically. For instance, entering M highlights words like Marketing or zebra.

However, in a series of letters from A to Z, only N through Z will be formatted because two or more characters starting with M or m are considered greater than a single letter.

>> **Less Than:** Formats cells with values less than your specified input — highlighting the underdogs.

- **Numbers and dates:** Formats any number or date less than the specified value. For example, entering 1/1/2026 highlights dates up through 12/31/2025.

- **Text:** Formats any text that comes before the specified input alphabetically. For instance, entering M highlights words like Lynx or aardvark. The number of characters doesn't matter — only the first letter is considered.

>> **Between:** Formats cells with values falling between two specified inputs — a nice middle-ground spotlight.

- **Numbers and dates:** Formats any number or date greater than or equal to the first value and less than or equal to the second value. For example, entering 400 and 500 highlights values between 400 and 500, including both.

- **Text:** Formats any text that starts with the first input, up to but not including text that begins with the second input. For instance, entering G and P highlights any text that starts with G, regardless of length, but stops before P.

>> **Equal To:** Formats cells with values exactly equal to your specified number — perfect for precise matches.

- **Numbers and dates:** Formats any number or date equal to the specified value.

  Excel uses a serial number format for both dates and times, so dates that contain a time component won't be an exact match. A cell with 7/1/2026 5:00 PM won't be formatted if you enter 7/1/2026 as the criterion — it's always 5:00 somewhere, just not necessarily in your dataset.

- **Text:** Formats cells that contain the exact text you specify. An input of Yippee ki-yay highlights YIPPEE KI-YAY if you're shouting or yippee ki-yay if you're whispering.

Text That Contains: Formats cells that contain the specified characters, whether it's a full or partial match. Perfect for situations where we can all be friends — even if it's just a partial match!

- **Numbers:** Formats any number (but not dates) that contains the specified sequence of digits. For example, entering 100 also highlights 1000 since it includes the same digit sequence, regardless of number formatting.

- **Text:** Formats cells that contain the specified sequence of characters — like the Terminator scanning for Sarah Connor — any match will do. Just as it targeted any Sarah Connor in the phone book, this rule highlights any cell containing your input, whether at the beginning, middle, or end. Entering Con highlights Connor, Connections, and beacon.

  Text That Contains is ideal when you don't want to be bothered by extra spaces. Since it looks for matches within the text, it ignores any leading or trailing spaces that may be lurking.

» **A Date Occurring:** No numbers or text here — just dates. Dynamic date ranges — such as Yesterday, Today, This Week, Next Month, and more — adjust each time you open the spreadsheet on a new day. This one's for those who like to roll with the changes!

» **Duplicate Values:** Highlights cells with values that show up two or more times within a range. Alternatively, choose Unique to give a shout out to values that appear just once in the range.

As you might expect, all the Highlight Cells Rules follow a similar process. This example demonstrates the Greater Than rule for either numbers or text:

1. **To format numbers, type 500 in cell D8, or m in cell A28 for text.**

2. **Select a range, such as D10:D20 for numbers, or A1:A26 for text.**

   To apply conditional formatting to multiple non-contiguous ranges, hold down Ctrl (Windows) or Cmd (macOS) while selecting the ranges before creating the rule. To adjust the ranges for an existing rule, see the "Navigating the rules manager" section later in this chapter.

3. **Choose Home ⇨ Conditional Formatting ⇨ Highlight Cells Rules ⇨ Greater Than.**

   In Excel for Windows, Greater Than dialog box appears, as shown in Figure 13-3. In Excel for macOS, the New Formatting Rule dialog box provides similar options for defining conditional formatting criteria.

4. **The Format Cells that are GREATER THAN field suggests a default value that is slightly greater than the midpoint, which you can adjust as needed:**

   - **Static input:** Type a number (or letter) of your choice.

     Excel provides a live preview of the conditional formatting, updating in real time if you change the input.

   - **Cell reference:** Select a cell that contains an input, such as D8 for numbers, or A28 for text.

     Excel provides a live preview of the conditional formatting based on the current cell value. After the rule is applied, the formatting updates in real time as the cell value changes.

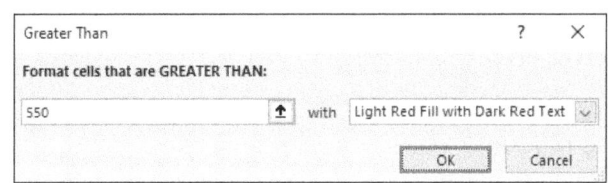

Greater Than   ?   ×

Format cells that are GREATER THAN:

550   ⬆   with   Light Red Fill with Dark Red Text ⌄

OK   Cancel

FIGURE 13-3:
The Greater Than
dialog box.

5. **To customize formatting, use the drop-down to select from five preset styles, or choose Custom Format to open the Format Cells dialog box.**

REMEMBER

Not all formatting options can be applied through conditional formatting, so don't be surprised if you can't find your favorite bells and whistles!

6. **If needed, configure formatting in the Format Cells dialog box, and then click OK.**

7. **Click OK again to apply the rule and close the Greater Than dialog box.**

Press Ctrl+Z (Windows) or Cmd+Z (macOS), or click Undo on the Quick Access Toolbar if you experience immediate regret. If you change your mind later, refer to the "Clearing Conditional Formatting" section later in this chapter for instructions on removing the formatting.

8. **If you used a cell reference, change the value in the referenced cell to see how the conditional formatting updates dynamically.**

Applying Top or Bottom Rules

Feel like playing favorites with your data? This one's strictly for numbers or dates — no text allowed. Head to Home ⇨ Conditional Formatting ⇨ Top/Bottom Rules to highlight the high achievers, call out the underperformers, or see who's stuck in the middle.

» **Top 10 Items:** Highlights the top 10 largest values (or latest dates) — but feel free to ratchet that number up or down to suit your whims.

» **Top 10%:** Highlights the top 10% (or any percentage you specify) of a list. In a list of twenty numbers (for example, change cell D1 to 20 to expand the sample data set), that means the two largest numbers (or latest dates) will be formatted (20 × 10% = 2).

» **Bottom 10 Items:** By default, this option highlights the 10 smallest values in a range — but you're free to pick any number of bottom feeders you want to call out.

>> **Bottom 10%:** The yang to Top 10's yin — identifies the lowest 10% (or any percentage you specify) of a list. In a list of fifty numbers (for example, change cell D1 to 50), the five smallest values (or earliest dates) get the spotlight (50 x 10% = 5).

>> **Above Average:** Excel calculates the average (mean) of the selected cells and then highlights any values (or dates, if you insist) that rise above it. Many folks think they're above average, but only a select few make the cut.

>> **Below Average:** This is going to sound mean (*rimshot!*), but any numbers (or dates, if you must) that fall below average get the treatment.

Applying Top/Bottom Rules follows the same process as the Greater Than example earlier in this chapter. Simply select your range, choose a rule, and adjust the default value if needed. See the previous section for step-by-step instructions.

Displaying Data Bars

Why did the spreadsheet bring a candy bar to the meeting? Because it wanted to sweeten the deal! I'm here all week, folks — or at least until you put this book back on the shelf. Seriously, though, Data Bars are calorie-free, bite-size charts that appear within worksheet cells, sized according to the underlying value. By default, Data Bars automatically sizes bars proportionately based upon the lowest and highest values in the selected range.

To give these concoctions a taste test:

REMEMBER

1. **Select a range, such as E10:E20.**

   You can layer more than one type of formatting, so feel free to select D10:D20, even if those cells already have Greater Than formatting applied. There's nothing wrong with wearing both a belt and suspenders.

2. **Choose Home ⇨ Conditional Formatting ⇨ Data Bars.**

   The Data Bars submenu appears, as shown in Figure 13-4.

3. **Browse built-in styles or go your own way:**

   ● **Apply a built-in style:** Hover over the fill options to see a live preview of the formatting — like sampling ice cream flavors before picking a scoop — then click one that suits your fancy or press Escape to call the whole thing off.

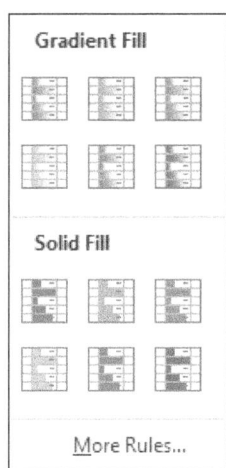

FIGURE 13-4:
The Data
Bars submenu.

TIP

Gradient Fill applies a color that fades from left to right, with longer bars representing higher values and shorter bars representing lower values. Solid Fill uses a uniform color intensity, adjusting only the bar length based on the cell's value.

- **Create a custom data bar:** Choose More Rules to open the New Formatting Rule dialog box, shown in Figure 13-5, where you can customize settings beyond the built-in options. Some basic tweaks to consider include:

  - **Show Bar Only:** Display just the data bars while hiding the numbers.

  - **Fill:** Select Solid Fill or Gradient Fill.

  - **Color:** Pick from theme and standard colors or choose More Colors for additional options.

  - **Border:** Defaults to No Border, but you can select Solid Border and pick a color.

  - **Negative Value and Axis:** Windows users must click Options for negative value and axis settings, while macOS users see them immediately.

  - **Bar Direction:** Defaults to Context, which typically flows from left to right, but you can switch it to right to left if needed.

TIP

The "Crafting Custom Rules" section later in this chapter digs into the depths of the New Formatting Rule dialog box.

4. **Click OK to apply the rule.**

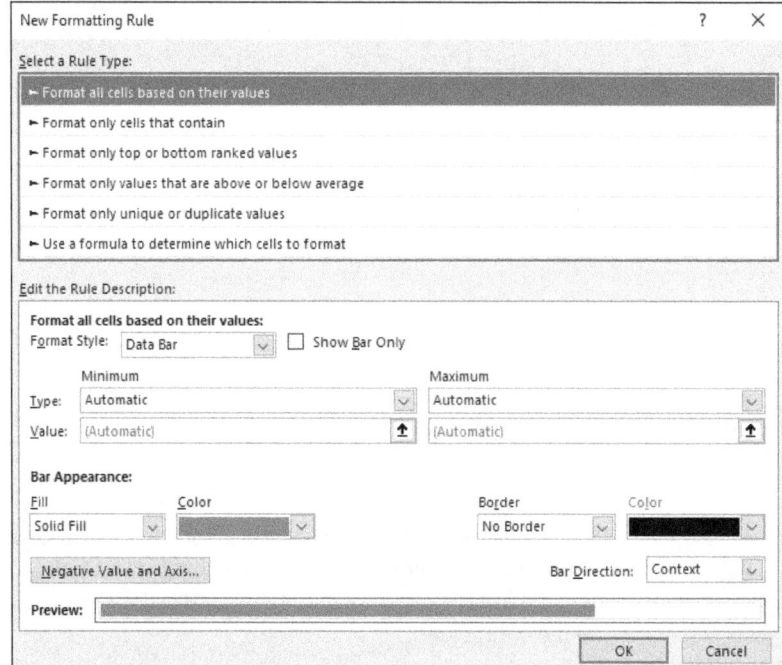

New Formatting Rule

Select a Rule Type:

► Format all cells based on their values

► Format only cells that contain

► Format only top or bottom ranked values

► Format only values that are above or below average

► Format only unique or duplicate values

► Use a formula to determine which cells to format

Edit the Rule Description:

Format all cells based on their values:

Format Style: Data Bar ☐ Show Bar Only

	Minimum	Maximum
Type:	Automatic	Automatic
Value:	(Automatic)	(Automatic)

Bar Appearance:

Fill: Solid Fill Color

Border: No Border Color

Negative Value and Axis... Bar Direction: Context

Preview:

OK Cancel

FIGURE 13-5: Data Bar settings in the New Formatting Rule dialog box.

Grading with Color Scales

"Do-re-mi-fa-so-la-ti-do!" Oops, wrong type of scale! Color Scales in Excel use gradients to visually represent data, making trends, patterns, and outliers easier to spot. Excel assigns specific colors to high and low values based on a predefined or custom color spectrum.

There are two types of Color Scales:

>> **Two-Color Scale:** Like Data Bars, this format assigns a color to the lowest and highest values in a data range, with a smooth gradient in between.

>> **Three-Color Scale:** Adds a midpoint (defaulting to the 50th percentile), allowing for a three-point gradient that further refines the visual hierarchy of your data. You can customize the midpoint using a specific value, percentage, or formula.

While you don't have to sort your data before applying Color Scales, it often helps. Sorting first ensures the colors flow in a smooth gradient rather than looking like chaotic confetti. Forget to sort? No problem — you can always sort afterward to fine-tune the visual impact.

Here's how to apply a predefined or custom color scale:

1. **Select a range, such as F10:F20.**

2. **Choose Home ⇨ Conditional Formatting ⇨ Color Scales.**

   The Color Scales submenu appears, as shown in Figure 13-6.

FIGURE 13-6: The Color Scales submenu.

3. **Browse built-in styles or craft your own look:**

   - **Apply a built-in style:** Hover over the Color Scale options to see a live preview of the formatting — like trying on different sunglasses to find the right vibe — then click the one that makes you say "Yes!" or press Escape if none of them are your scene.

   - **Create a custom scale:** Choose More Rules to open the New Formatting Rule dialog box, shown in Figure 13-7. The "Crafting Custom Rules" section later in this chapter provides a map to the Minimum and Maximum Type and Value fields, but you won't need a GPS for these settings:

     - **Format Style:** Defaults to 2-Color Style, choosing 3-Color Scale adds a Midpoint field to refine the gradient.

     - **Minimum Color:** Defines the color for the lowest values.

     - **Midpoint Color (if applicable):** Appears only in 3-Color Scale to set the transition shade between the lowest and highest values.

     - **Maximum Color:** Defines the color for the highest values.

4. **Click OK to apply the rule.**

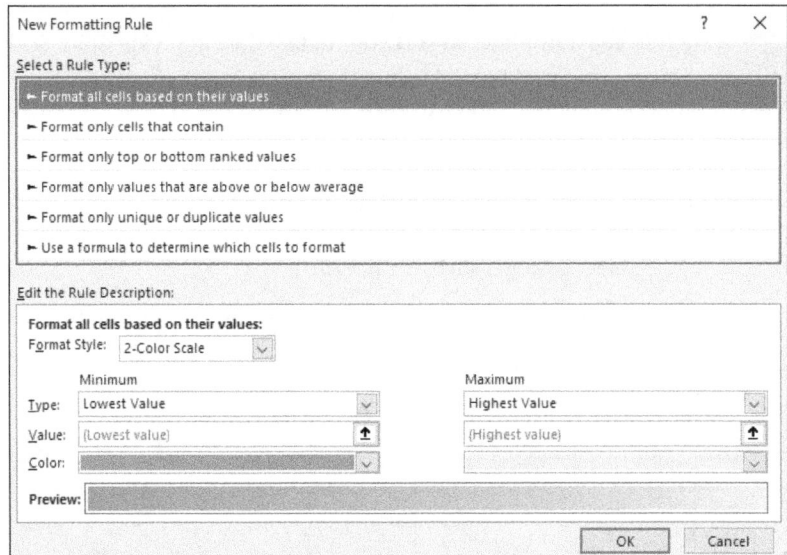

FIGURE 13-7:
2-Color Scale
settings in the
New Formatting
Rule dialog box.

Symbolizing with Icon Sets

Your data is good enough! It's smart enough! It's iconic! Or, at least it can be when you use the Icon Sets feature, which lets you choose from four types of icons to add visual cues and make patterns pop. The prebuilt icon sets are based on the percentage each cell's value contributes to the sum of the range, giving you a quick visual ranking of how each value stacks up across your data.

There are four types of icon sets:

» **Directional:** Sets of three, four, or five arrows point the way, perfect for indicating progress or changes.

» **Shapes:** Choose from three or four colorful circles to add a bit of flair and make comparisons stand out.

» **Indicators:** Three icons offer instant feedback. Two sets include checkmarks, exclamation marks, and Xs, while a third uses triangular flags to signal different statuses.

» **Ratings:** Rate your data with stars or represent strength with cell phone bars. You can also pick from two sets of five mini charts for a quick snapshot of trends.

Imagine, if you will, transforming raw numbers into a visual story — one where patterns and insights emerge at a glance:

1. **Select a range, such as G10:G20.**

2. **Choose Home ⇨ Conditional Formatting ⇨ Icon Sets.**

   The Icon Sets submenu appears as shown in Figure 13-8.

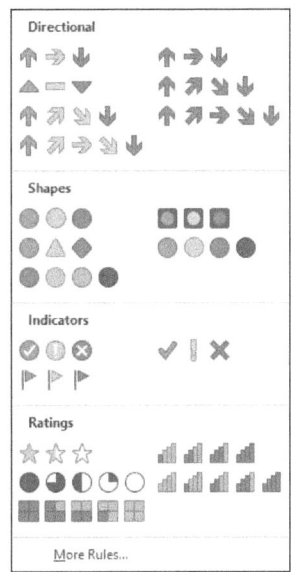

FIGURE 13-8:
The Icon
Sets submenu.

3. **Browse built-in styles or go the custom route:**

   - **Apply a built-in icon set:** Hover over the little pictures to see a live preview of the formatting — like test-driving a car before signing the papers — and then click one handles like a dream or press Escape to slam the brakes on this formatting.

   - **Create a custom scale:** Choose More Rules to open the New Formatting Rule dialog box, shown in Figure 13-9. The "Crafting Custom Rules" section later in this chapter dives deep into customizations, so this section keeps things in the shallow end:

     - **Reverse Icon Order:** Flips the order of icons displayed in the Icons column of the dialog box;

     - **Show Icon Only:** Hides the numbers and only shows the icons.

     - **Icon Style:** Select a prebuilt set as a starting point for further customization. The version of the New Formatting Rule dialog box shown in Figure 13-9 opens.

4. **Click OK to apply the rule.**

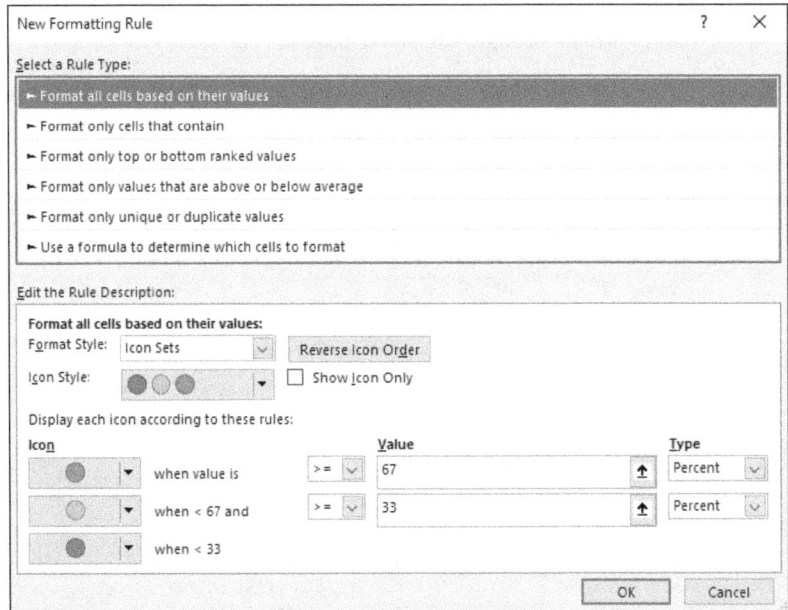

FIGURE 13-9:
The New
Formatting Rule
dialog box.

Crafting Custom Rules

Some custom rules are as simple as ordering a drip coffee to go — quick, straightforward, and no fuss. But it's also easy to veer into Venti, half-caf, quad-shot, ristretto, oat milk, two-pump sugar-free vanilla, one-pump caramel, extra-hot, no foam, light whip, with cinnamon powder on top territory.

When you need full control over your formatting, Excel lets you customize every detail with custom conditional formatting rules — because sometimes, only a made-to-order approach will do.

Setting rules that work for you

Here's how to have your conditional formatting your way:

1. **Select a range, such as H10:H20.**

2. **Choose Home ⇨ Conditional Formatting ⇨ New Rule.**

3. **In Windows, select a rule type and provide inputs when prompted, while macOS users must select Classic from the Style field, then choose a rule type.**

4. **Select a rule type and provide inputs when prompted:**

- **Format All Cells Based On Their Values:** This is the go-to option for Color Scales, Data Bars, and Icon Sets. By default, it applies a 2-Color Scale, but you can choose from other options like 3-Color Scale, Data Bar, or Icon Set. I'd need a lot more pages than I have available to break down all the nuances, but here's a quick rundown of the Type field choices you may encounter:

  - **Number:** Allows you to set specific values for formatting.

  - **Percent:** Formats values based on their percentage of the data range. For example, higher percentage values correspond to longer data bars, stronger icon indicators, or more intense color scaling.

REMEMBER

  It may sound contradictory, but the Number rule is often a better choice for formatting percentages, particularly for Data Bars. For example, to illustrate task completion percentages in a project, use the Number type to define a minimum of 0 and a maximum of 1.

  - **Formula:** Allows you to dynamically calculate a number value by using arithmetic or worksheet functions. This is useful when you want formatting to adapt based on other criteria.

  - **Percentile:** Useful for ranking values in a dataset, such as test scores, income brackets, or other scenarios where relative position matters. This is particularly helpful for Data Bars and Color Scales when analyzing distributions.

- **Format Only Cells That Contain:** Think of this as Highlight Cells Rules on steroids. Options include:

  - **Cell Value:** The second drop-down list includes all the options in the Highlight Cells submenu, plus Not Between, Not Equal To, Greater Than or Equal To (≥) and Less Than or Equal To (≤). Depending on your selection, one or two value fields will appear for input.

  - **Specific Text:** Defaults to Containing, which mirrors the Text That Contains option. You can also choose Not Containing, Beginning With, or Ending With, then enter a single value in the provided field.

  - **Dates Occuring:** An identical twin of the A Date Occurring rule on the Highlight Cells submenu.

  - **Blanks:** Welcome to the void — no inputs, no choices — just a way to shine a light on the gaps in your data.

TIP

  This type of conditional formatting adds a user-friendly touch, guiding users through expected inputs in unfamiliar spreadsheets. It helps ensure that no important data is overlooked, making the spreadsheet easier to navigate, more intuitive to use, and easier to audit!

- **No Blanks:** You can't tinker with this one either — the rule's name is also its criteria.

CROSS REFERENCE

- **Errors:** Houston, we have a problem! — this rule formats cells that contain error values, such as #N/A, #DIV/0!, #REF! — and yes, the list truly goes on. See the bonus chapter "Ten Frustrating Prompts" (available at www.dummies.com/go/excelfd).

TIP

Errors in spreadsheets can exist outside of what Excel detects. Always double-check your formulas and data to catch any potential issues that might slip under the radar!

- **No Errors:** There's implicit criteria here — as long as a cell doesn't contain an error value, it gets formatted — blank or not.

REMEMBER

The Errors and No Errors rules are based solely on cell contents and are not a replacement for the Error Checking indicator discussed in Chapter 10.

- **Format Only Top or Bottom Ranked Values:** Mirrors the Top 10 and Bottom 10 rules. Click % of the Selected Range to apply the Top 10% or Bottom 10% rules, then update the value field if needed.

- **Format Only Values That Are Above Or Below Average:** The Above and Below options mirror the Above Average and Below Average rules from the Top/Bottom Rules submenu, but that's just the beginning. You can also choose Equal or Above, Equal or Below, or take it even further — up to three standard deviations deep!

TECHNICAL STUFF

And now it's time to get out our pointy hats! Standard deviation measures how spread out the numbers in a data set are from the average. A small standard deviation means the numbers stick close to the average, while a large standard deviation means they're scattered far and wide. Use the STDEV.P function to calculate the standard deviation for an entire population, or STDEV.S for just a sample of the population.

- **Format Only Unique or Duplicate Values:** Exactly the same functionality as the Duplicate Values option on the Highlight Cells Rules submenu. So yes, you are seeing double.

- **Use a Formula to Determine Which Cells to Format:** The lone Format Values Where This Formula is True requires a formula that evaluates to TRUE or FALSE — no middle ground, no maybes. If the formula returns TRUE, your formatting is applied — otherwise no formatting for you!

REMEMBER

If the formula returns a number, text, or an error, Excel won't apply the formatting correctly.

5. **Click Format . . . (Windows) or select Custom Format from the Format With list (macOS).**

A feature-limited version of the Format Cells dialog box opens, but it includes a Clear button — something the standard dialog box lacks. If you need to eject all formatting choices and start over without closing the dialog box, this button has you covered.

6. **Apply formatting choices, and then click OK twice.**

The custom rule applies to the selected range, updating formatting dynamically based on the specified conditions.

TIP

In Windows, the Preview area of the New Formatting Rule dialog box displays "No Format Set" until you select one or more formatting options. If your rule is complex — or distractions abound — it's easy to click OK instead of Format. . . . The upcoming "Navigating the rules manager" section covers adjusting rules.

Designing formula-based rules

As you've seen, conditional formatting in Excel offers extensive customization. While there are some limitations to the types of formatting you can apply to cells, as covered in the "Decoding Conditional Formatting Options" section earlier in this chapter, the criteria you can set for applying that formatting are almost limitless. This flexibility enables you to create highly specific and targeted visual cues for your data. Let's look at two examples of formula-based rules that you can apply.

Formatting unlocked cells

By default, every cell within a worksheet is marked as Locked, which isn't an issue — until someone chooses Review ⇨ Protect Sheet (see Chapter 14) and puts the kibosh on free-range editing. This example demonstrates how to unlock input cells, while leaving sensitive cells — such as those containing formulas — locked. To ensure that no input stone goes unturned Conditional Formatting can highlight the unlocked cells, making it easy for you to check your work.

And we're off:

1. **Select cells D1:D5.**

2. **Choose Home ⇨ Format ⇨ Lock Cell.**

Ironically, the Lock Cell command unlocks cells as well — it's a toggle!

If you prefer more certainty about the locked status of a cell, choose Home ⇨ Format ⇨ Format Cells, then peek at the Locked checkbox on the Protection tab.

3. **Select cell A1.**

4. **Press Ctrl+Shift+End (Windows) or Cmd+Shift+End (macOS) to select from the active cell to the last used cell in in the worksheet.**

5. **Choose Home ⇨ Conditional Formatting ⇨ New Rule.**

   The New Formatting Rule dialog box opens.

6. **Choose Use a Formula to Determine Which Cells to Format.**

7. **Enter this formula: =CELL("protect",A1)=0, as shown in Figure 13-10.**

Be mindful when referencing worksheet cells when crafting custom rules — clicking on a cell instead of typing its address inserts an absolute reference (see Chapter 1), which can prevent the rule from working properly. For instance, =CELL("protect",$A$1)=0 applies formatting to the entire selected range based on the locked or unlocked status of cell A1, rather than evaluating each individual cell separately.

Chapter 17, Ten Timesaving Keyboard Shortcuts, covers how to toggle fields like Format Values Where This Formula is True into Edit mode, allowing you to use the arrow keys to navigate within the field without accidentally inserting unwanted cell references.

8. **Click Format . . . (Windows) or select Custom Format from the Format With list (macOS).**

   The conditional formatting version of the Format Cells dialog box opens.

FIGURE 13-10:
Use a Formula to Determine Which Cells to Format settings in the New Formatting Rule dialog box.

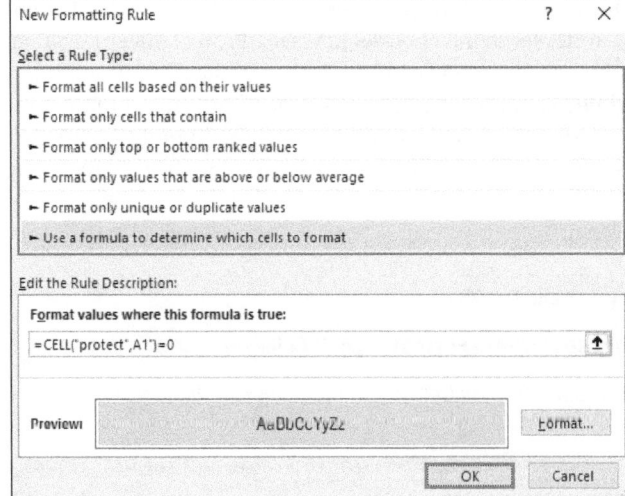

CELL FUNCTION

The CELL function is ideal for identifying esoteric aspects of your data that aren't accessible via the built-in rules. Here's a rundown on some of the available options that you can use in the *info_type* argument:

- **"filename":** Returns the path and file name of the workbook if it's saved; returns an empty string ("") if the referenced worksheet hasn't been saved.

- **"format":** Returns a code representing the cell's number format, such as "G" for General, ",2" for #,##0.00, etc.

- **"protect":** Returns 1 if the cell referenced is locked; otherwise, 0 if it is unlocked.

- **"type":** Indicates the cell contents type:
  - **"b" (blank):** The cell is empty.
  - **"l" (label):** The cell contains text.
  - **"v" (value):** The cell contains a numeric value.

---

9. **Choose a color from the Fill tab, along with any other formatting you wish, and then click OK twice.**

The formatting you chose should appear in cells D1:D5.

10. **Select cells D1:D5, then choose Format ⇨ Lock Cells.**

Cells D1:D5 are no longer formatted. The formatting adjusts dynamically, appearing or disappearing as you unlock or lock cells within the selected range. This responsiveness makes it easy to visually track cell protection status in real time.

REMEMBER

The locked status of a cell doesn't take effect until you protect the worksheet, as covered in the upcoming "Safeguarding conditional formatting" section and Chapter 14.

Extending formatting across columns

In the "Highlighting Cells Based on Value" section earlier in this chapter, I show that you can use numbers or cell references for conditional formatting rules. However, a limitation of that approach is that the formatting only applies to the cells you initially select. Conversely, a formula-based rule allows you to format multiple columns based upon the value of a single column providing more flexibility in applying conditional formatting across a broader range of data.

1. **Enter 500 into cell I8.**

2. **Select cells C10:I20.**

3. **Choose Home ➪ Conditional Formatting ➪ New Rule.**

   The New Formatting Rule dialog box opens.

4. **Choose Use a Formula to Determine Which Cells to Format.**

5. **Enter this formula: =$I10>$I$8, making special note of the $ signs.**

   $I10 is a relative reference to the first cell that contains a number. It is key to freeze the column, but not the row. $I$8 is an absolute reference to the input cell, and where it's key to freeze both the column and the row.

6. **Click Format . . . (Windows) or select Custom Format from the Format With list (macOS).**

   The conditional formatting version of the Format Cells dialog box opens.

7. **Choose a color from the Fill tab, along with any other formatting you wish, and then click OK twice.**

   The formatting adjusts dynamically, formatting cells in column C through I when the amounts within cells I10:I20 are greater than or equal to the value in cell I8.

REMEMBER

Conditional formatting rules apply in the order they are created, meaning earlier rules may override the one you just added. Some of the rules you created earlier in this chapter might take precedence, affecting how formatting is applied. An upcoming section covers how to adjust rule hierarchy to ensure higher-priority rules remain in effect or to prevent subsequent rules from overriding formatting when needed.

Removing Conditional Formatting

Conditional formatting can be like a flashy neon sign pointing out important data — useful until it's just screaming at you for no reason. When you're done basking in its glow, you can turn off the lights in several ways. Just be aware that it's also easy to accidentally wipe out conditional formatting, especially when copying and pasting data. If you need to delete individual rules, see the next section; the following options remove all rules at once:

» **Clear Rules:** Choose Home ➪ Conditional Formatting ➪ Clear Rules, and then choose one of the following:

- **Clear Rules from Selected Cells:** Requires selecting the affected range first

- **Clear Rules from Entire Sheet**: Removes all conditional formatting with no selection required

- **From This Table:** Available when any cell in an Excel table is selected (see Chapter 5)

- **From This PivotTable:** Available when any cell in a PivotTable is selected (see Chapter 12)

 » **Quick Analysis (Windows only):** Select a range, then click the Quick Analysis button or press Ctrl+Q, then choose Clear. . . on the Formatting tab.

» **Other approaches:** Tread carefully with these approaches — there's a high risk of unintended consequences:

- **Paste:** Copying a range of cells and then choose Home ⇨ Paste (applies formatting from the copied cells to the destination cells)

  See the upcoming "Preserving rules while copying/pasting" section for ways to paste data without accidentally wiping out conditional formatting.

TIP

- **Clear**: Choose Home ⇨ Clear ⇨ Clear Formats (removes all formatting, including conditional formatting, from the selected range)

  If you suddenly feel like you've made a grave mistake, rest easy — you can undo the removal of conditional formatting. Press Ctrl+Z (Windows) or Cmd+Z (macOS) or click Undo on the Quick Access toolbar.

Managing Conditional Formatting Rules

Conditional formatting may sometimes seem invisible, but behind the scenes, Excel keeps track of every rule applied across your worksheets. The Conditional Formatting Rules Manager acts as a control panel, giving you a centralized way to view, edit, delete, and reorder rules. This section begins with managing existing rules, including applying them to multiple ranges, before moving on to methods for preventing Excel from unexpectedly wiping out carefully crafted conditions during copy-paste actions.

Navigating the rules manager

Instead of hunting through scattered ranges to figure out what's driving your formatting, this tool lays everything out in an easy-to-read list. Use it to review, modify, or organize conditional formatting rules efficiently.

Here's how to manage existing rules for a selected range or any worksheet:

1. **To manage rules for a specific range — such as D1:D5 — select the range before opening the manager.**

   If you want to manage rules for an entire worksheet, skip this step.

TIP

   Choose Home ⇨ Find & Select ⇨ Conditional Formatting to quickly locate cells with conditional formatting on the active worksheet. This is useful for identifying which cells have rules applied, especially when troubleshooting unexpected formatting. If no such cells exist, Excel displays a No cells were found message.

2. **Choose Home ⇨ Conditional Formatting ⇨ Manage Rules.**

   The Conditional Formatting Rules Manager opens, as shown in Figure 13-11.

REMEMBER

   Don't panic if the rule list appears blank or incomplete — Excel defaults to showing rules for the current selection.

3. **If needed, select a worksheet from the Show Formatting Rules For list.**

   The rule list displays any conditional formatting rules in place and includes the following columns:

   - **Rules:** Displays the criteria for each rule, helping you identify the logic behind the formatting.

   - **Format:** Provides a preview of the applied formatting.

   - **Applies to:** Lists the ranges each rule covers, ensuring you know exactly where the formatting takes effect. A single rule can apply to multiple non-contiguous ranges — Excel separates them with commas (e.g., $A$1:$A$10, $D$1:$D$10). This allows you to enforce the same formatting across different areas without creating duplicate rules.

   - **Stop If True:** Allows you to stop one rule from overriding another. If a rule evaluates to TRUE, no rules below it in the list will apply.

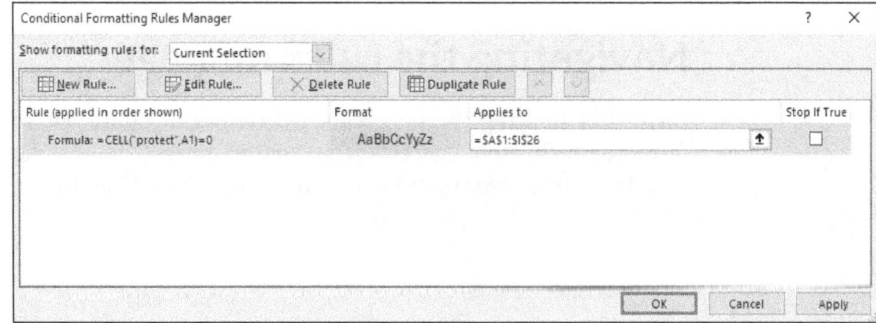

FIGURE 13-11:
The Conditional Formatting Rules Manager.

4. **Unless you're adding a new rule, select a rule from the list before clicking one of these buttons:**

- **New Rule (Windows) or + (macOS):** Opens the New Formatting Rule dialog box, where you can create a new conditional format from scratch, as discussed in the "Crafting Custom Rules" section earlier in this chapter.

- **Edit Rule:** Opens the Edit Formatting Rule dialog box, letting you tweak the conditions or formatting of the selected rule — similar to the process of creating a new rule.

  Double-click a rule to open the Edit Formatting Rule dialog box without clicking the Edit Rule button.

- **Delete Rule (Windows) or – (macOS):** Removes the selected rule without confirmation. You can only remove one rule at a time via the manager — see the "Removing Conditional Formatting" section earlier in this chapter to remove multiple rules at once from a range or worksheet.

  Deletions don't take effect until you click OK or Apply, and you can undo it by clicking Cancel. If the dialog box is already closed, press Ctrl+Z (Windows) or Cmd+Z (macOS), or use Undo on the Quick Access Toolbar.

- **Duplicate Rule:** Creates a copy of the selected rule, which you can then modify without affecting the original.

- **Up and Down Arrows:** Adjust the order of rules. Since conditional formatting applies from top to bottom, moving a rule up increases its priority, while moving a rule down makes it secondary to others. This is especially important when working with overlapping rules.

5. **To commit or abandon rule changes, click the corresponding button:**

- **Apply:** In Windows, saves rule changes without closing the dialog box.

- **OK:** Saves rule changes and closes the dialog box.

- **Cancel:** Discards rule changes and closes the dialog box.

Keeping conditional formatting intact

Conditional formatting can be unintentionally removed when copying and pasting data, especially on unprotected worksheets. Fortunately, Excel offers several methods to retain formatting during these actions.

Preserving rules while copying/pasting

To keep conditional formatting intact when pasting data, choose Home⇨ Paste drop-down and then one of these options:

>> **Formulas:** Inserts formulas without affecting conditional formatting.

>> **Formulas and Number Formatting:** Inserts formulas along with number formatting while keeping conditional formatting.

>> **Formatting:** Transfers only formatting (including conditional formatting) without modifying cell values.

>> **Merge Conditional Formatting:** Combines conditional formatting rules from both the copied and destination cells. This one is stealthy — it only appears as a Paste Special option when you've copied cells containing conditional formatting to the clipboard.

>> **Values:** Inserts only the values while retaining conditional formatting — Windows users can press Ctrl+Shift+V.

>> **Values and Number Formatting:** Inserts values along with number formatting (e.g., currency, dates, percentages) while keeping conditional formatting.

Alternatively, open the Paste Special dialog box:

1. **Home ⇨ Paste drop-down ⇨ Paste Special.**

2. **Choose the desired option, then click OK.**

   The Merge Conditional Formatting Option appears as All Merging Conditional Formats within the Paste Special dialog box.

TIP

Safeguarding conditional formatting

Although the paste options in the previous section are helpful, sometimes muscle memory — or just not knowing Excel's quirks — leads to reflexive actions that overwrite conditional formatting rules. To guard against this, protecting the worksheet provides a safety net. The steps in this example provide firsthand experience:

1. **Create some sample data in a blank worksheet:**

   a. **Enter these inputs:**

   - **A1:** 1

   - **A2:** 2

- **B1:** 100

- **B2:** 90

   b. **Select cells A1: B2, then drag the Fill Handle down to cell B10 to extend the series.**

2. **Apply conditional formatting:**

   a. **Select cells A1:A10.**

   b. **Choose Home ⇨ Conditional Formatting ⇨ Data Bars, and then select a prebuilt style.**

3. **Unlock the selected cells:**

   a. **Choose Home ⇨ Format ⇨ Format Cells or press Ctrl+1 (Windows) or Cmd+1 (macOS).**

   The Format Cells dialog box opens.

   b. **Go to the Protection tab, clear the Locked checkbox, and then click OK.**

4. **Enable worksheet protection:**

   a. **Choose Review ⇨ Protect Sheet.**

   The Protect Sheet dialog box opens.

   b. **Enter a password (optional), then click OK.**

   - **Windows:** If entering a password, type it the Password (Optional) field, click OK, confirm the password in the next dialog box, and click OK again.

   - **macOS:** If entering a password, type in both the Password and Verify fields, then click OK (that's called one and done).

      Users can only update unlocked cells — in this case A1:A10 — until worksheet protection is removed by choosing Review ⇨ Unprotect Sheet. See Chapter 14 for more details.

5. **Test by pasting data:**

   a. **Select cells B1:B10 and then choose Home ⇨ Copy or press Ctrl+C (Windows) or Cmd+C (macOS).**

   b. **Select cell A1 and then choose Home ⇨ Paste or press Ctrl+V (Windows) or Cmd+V (macOS).**

   The values from B1:B10 replace the contents in A1:A10, but the conditional formatting remains intact.

Chapter **14**

User-Proofing Excel Spreadsheets

xcel spreadsheets can feel like the Wild West — by default, users can type anything, anywhere, letting chaos reign. User-proofing is a matter of degrees, ranging from metaphorically fencing off certain cells to ensuring that your spreadsheets are truly stampede-proof. This chapter covers how to protect worksheets and workbooks to keep formulas and sensitive data safe while giving users peace of mind that they can't break anything. Of course, there are always exceptions, which you can grant via the Allow Edit Ranges feature. From there, the Data Validation feature delivers a one-two punch: control and documentation, all in one. Whether you're reining in careless clicks or nudging users toward better input, you'll have the tools to strike the right balance.

I'm guessing that back in the 1800s, folks said a daguerreotype is worth a thousand words — a two-bit word for the earliest photographs. In that spirit, here's how to open a locked-down Excel template — so you don't put the cart before the horse.

Windows users can work inside Excel:

1. **Choose File ⇨ New or press Ctrl+N to create a new workbook.**

2. **Right-click the worksheet tab.**

   Sure as shootin', the Insert dialog box appears.

3. **Activate the Spreadsheet Solutions tab.**

4. **Select Loan Amortization, and then click OK.**

   The Loan Amortization template shown in Figure 14-1 appears.

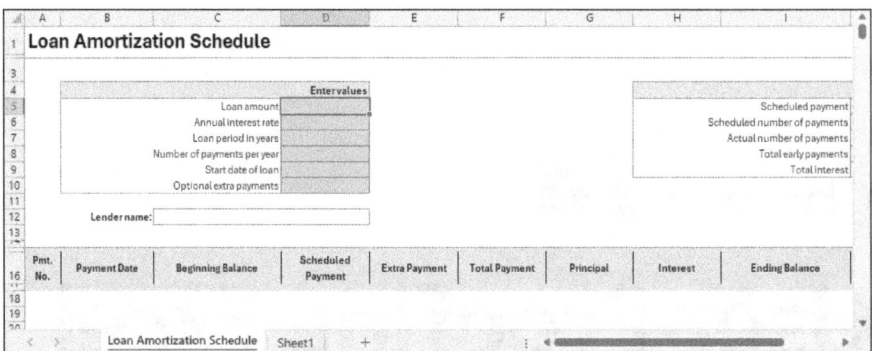

REMEMBER

Excel offers several built-in loan calculator and amortization templates, but only this specific one comes with worksheet protection enabled.

Meanwhile, those of you at the macOS ranch need to do these steps:

1. **Skedaddle over to** www.dummies.com/go/excelfd.

2. **Download the Chapter 14 Loan Amortization Schedule workbook.**

3. **Open the workbook in Excel.**

   Yer good to go if what's on your screen looks like Figure 14-1.

Alrighty then, let's reconnoiter:

1. **Click on cell A1 of the Loan Amortization Schedule worksheet.**

   No dice! It's like shooting blanks — this cell is locked down tight!

2. **Click on D10.**

   Yee haw! You've struck gold — an unlocked cell, ready for input! And you get to see a Data Validation input message to boot! Details on those are around the bend — but we still have some protection prospecting to do first.

TIP

That lovely shading in cells D5:D10 is pretty as a Kansas sunset, but it isn't just for show — it's a cue that those cells are fair game for input when worksheet protection is enabled. Just make sure to be consistent — someone left the paint off cells C13:D13, which means users may not realize it's open for business.

That's good stuff, but as we like to say around these parts, if one man can build a fence, another can cut the wire:

1. **Type Howdy! in cell D5.**

2. **Grab that there scroll bar on the right and give it a good yank.**

   Tarnation! Error values as far as the eye can see! Those rascally #VALUE! results are a sign of trouble brewing, but rest assured, by the end of the chapter, you'll be heading invalid inputs off at the pass.

REMEMBER

This template uses conditional formatting (Chapter 13) to hide some of the cells where you'll apply Data Validation later in the chapter. To stave off confusion and frustration, enter these inputs for average new car loans before you mosey on down the trail:

» **D5:** 50,000

» **D6:** 7%

» **D7:** 6

» **D8:** 12

» **D9:** 7/1/2026

Unlocking and Protecting Worksheet Cells

Left unprotected, worksheet cells are as drafty as the swinging doors of a saloon — anyone can stroll in and make changes, whether intentional or not. A misplaced keystroke can wipe out a formula, an accidental click can overwrite a crucial value, and before you know it, your carefully crafted workbook looks like it's been through a barroom brawl. Fortunately, Excel lets you lock things down, keeping your data intact while still allowing users to interact with the parts they need. Whether you're preventing innocent mistakes or fending off more deliberate meddling, worksheet protection helps you keep order without shutting the whole place down.

Claiming your home on the range

Just like a homesteader marking off land, Excel lets you put down stakes by deciding which cells stay protected and which are open for business. By default, every cell is marked as Locked, but that still leaves your worksheets as unprotected as a stagecoach with no shotgun rider.

The author of that new-fangled amortization schedule we were just eyeballing not only put on a belt — enabled worksheet protection so that locked cells can't be edited — but suspenders, too — you can't even put your mitts on them. I do thank that person kindly for at least leaving me a few unlocked cells to roam around in.

You're probably thinking, "Will you quit flapping your gums and get to it?" Fair enough. But first, we need to go backwards before we can go forward:

1. **To avoid feeling like a tumbleweed in a twister, activate this worksheet's sample workbook (shown in Figure 14-1).**

2. **Choose Review ⇨ Unprotect Sheet.**

   Ordinarily, this is where you might hit a password prompt, but this spreadsheet is an unmanned outpost — no lock, no key, just an open gate swinging in the wind.

3. **Click on cell A1.**

   Kapwing! The cell is now clickable and editable, in fact the entire worksheet is wide open to any lawless activity — there's simply no sheriff in town anymore.

   If you're hearing strains of Peggy Lee sing "Is That All There Is?" regarding worksheet protection, nope, that kind of thinking is fool's gold.

REMEMBER

Cells D5:D10 are already unlocked — here's how to expand that frontier further:

1. **Select one or more cells, e.g., E5:G12.**

2. **Choose Home ⇨ Format ⇨ Cells or press Ctrl+1 (Windows) or Cmd+1 (macOS).**

   The Format Cells dialog box appears, lookin' just as right as rain.

3. **Activate the Protection tab, clear the Locked checkbox shown in Figure 14-2, and then click OK.**

   You must unlock any cells that you want folks to be able to edit before enabling worksheet protection — much like settlers had to bust up the sod before planting their crops.

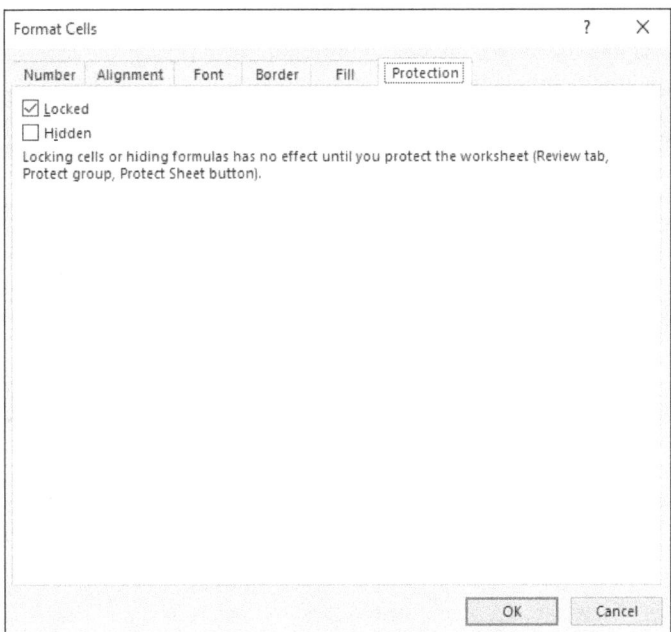

FIGURE 14-2:
The Protection
tab of the Format
Cells dialog box.

REMEMBER

You can lock and unlock cells as needed, just be sure to unprotect the worksheet before trying to stake your claim.

The Hidden checkbox in Figure 14-2 enables you to hide cell contents in plain sight — once a worksheet is protected, users can see cell values and formula results, but the formula bar will be as empty as a water trough in a drought.

**TECHNICAL
STUFF**

Making cell protection less of a chore

Now that you have the lay of the land, you might be thinking do I really have to keep opening that dang dialog box over and over again? Nope! You can shave off a couple of steps:

1. **Select a range of cells, e.g., H10:J13.**

2. **Choose Home ⇨ Format ⇨ Lock Cell.**

   The Locked setting of the cells is toggled off in this case — choose that command again to lock the cells back, which probably feels about as clear as mud.

   Keep your peepers peeled — macOS confirms a locked cell with a checkmark, but Windows plays it coy. The Lock Cell border vanishes when unlocked, and with the menu disappearing instantly, you might feel as uncertain as a gambler mid-hand.

CROSS REFERENCE

Chapter 13 covers using conditional formatting to color-code unlocked cells, making them easier to spot at a glance.

If that feels too high stakes or unwieldy, Windows offers a better approach:

1. **Choose Format on the Home tab, and then right-click Lock Cell.**

   A context menu generally appears whenever you right-click any element within Excel — like uncovering hidden treasure with just a click of your mouse.

2. **Choose Add to Quick Access Toolbar.**

   A Lock Cell icon appears on the Quick Access Toolbar. Unlike the version on the Format menu, a shaded background means this range is fenced off (locked) while no background means ripe for the taking (unlocked).

TIP

Click the icon to toggle the locked status of a cell faster than a greased pig. Windows users can ditch that varmint (a.k.a. mouse) by tapping Alt, then typing the shortcut that appears over the icon.

CROSS REFERENCE

I jaw about customizing the Quick Access Toolbar in Chapter 1.

It's a safe bet that number-filled cells (not formulas) are inputs that ought to be unlocked. To round 'em up quick, mosey over to Home ⇨ Find & Select ⇨ Go To Special, pick Constants, uncheck Text, Logicals & Errors, and then hit OK. Excel will lasso all numeric cells for you to mark as unlocked — if none turn up, it'll holler, No cells were found.

TIP

Securing worksheets

After you clear the Locked setting for any cells that users can freely edit, the next step is to protect the worksheet — which is like building walls around a frontier fort, keeping the settlers safe while still allowing trade at the front gate:

1. **Activate a single worksheet, such as Loan Amortization Schedule.**

REMEMBER

   Chapter 1 discusses using the group feature to make changes across multiple worksheets, but don't try that here unless you want to see the Protect Sheet command suddenly play opossum on you.

2. **Enable worksheet protection by choosing Review ⇨ Protect Sheet.**

   The Protect Sheet dialog box opens, as shown in Figure 14-3 for Windows users. The macOS version is similar but includes a rare gem of helpfulness: All cells are locked by default but can be formatted as unlocked.

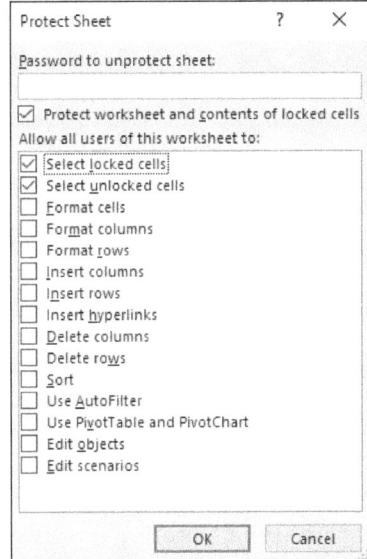

FIGURE 14-3:
The Protect Sheet
dialog box in
Excel
for Windows.

3. **If you want to keep the worksheet under lock and key, enter a case-sensitive password, or leave the field blank.**

   Protecting a worksheet without a password is like putting a split-rail fence around it; users can get through, but only purposefully.

REMEMBER

WARNING

   There's a blessing/curse trade-off to passwords: Sometimes, it's the only way to keep sensitive data safe, but when the password is unavailable or lost, users needing full access may feel like they've been handed a six-shooter with no bullets.

4. **If you filled in the password field and are using macOS, confirm the password in the Verify field — in Windows just hold your horses for a bit.**

5. **To set the boundaries for users, enable or clear checkboxes to permit or restrict functionality.**

   Two core settings are enabled by default:

   - **Select Locked Cells:** Think carefully before disabling this default setting. When turned off — as in this chapter's sample workbook — users can navigate between unlocked cells with the arrow keys, but they won't be able to scroll around the worksheet as usual without using the scroll bars — a sure-fire way to frustrate users.

   - **Select Unlocked Cells:** Disabling this option puts the worksheet into an untouchable state, so choose carefully here.

User creativity options include:

- **Format Cells:** Enabling this option allows users to cell formats such as colors, fonts, or number formatting. Leave it disabled if you want to maintain a consistent design.

- **Format Rows/Columns:** When turned on, users can adjust row heights, column widths, or hide/unhide rows and columns. Leave it disabled to prevent accidental layout changes.

To enhance interactivity, consider enabling these settings:

- **Use AutoFilter:** The setting name is a nod to the past, allowing users to work with existing filter buttons (see Chapter 4), though they cannot toggle the overall Filter feature on or off.

- **Use PivotTable and PivotChart:** The operative word here is "use" — users aren't allowed to create new reports or graphs (see Chapter 12), but when enabled, they can add, remove, or rearrange fields in existing ones.

6. **Click OK to enable worksheet protection.**

7. **Windows users confirm the password (if entered), while macOS users ride off into the sunset without interruption.**

Worksheet protection settings must be applied manually to each worksheet within a workbook. You can't copy these protection settings from one worksheet to another.

Disabling worksheet protection

When working through Excel's user interface, you can only unprotect one worksheet at a time:

1. **Activate a protected worksheet, such as Loan Amortization Schedule.**

2. **Choose Review ⇨ Unprotect Sheet.**

   This command effectively replaces Protect Sheet once a worksheet is secured, creating a "now you see it, now you don't" effect.

3. **Enter the password if prompted.**

Windows users can determine if any worksheets are protected by selecting File ⇨ Info. When applicable, Excel displays a list of protected sheets along with corresponding Unprotect links.

You have to type your password from scratch if you decide to protect the worksheet again — Excel can't be bothered to remember it for you.

Allowing protection overrides

Windows users can create password-protected areas that allow members of your posse, er, authorized users, to edit specific ranges of locked cells:

1. **Choose Review ⇨ Allow Edit Ranges.**

   The Allow Users to Edit Ranges dialog box opens.

   All users can access cells unlocked cells, while only users that know the password can change these cells.

2. **Click New.**

   The New Range dialog box opens.

3. **Type** Loan Summary **in the Title field or accept the default title.**

4. **Use the Refers To Field to choose one or more locked cell(s), such as** J5:J9.

5. **To require a password for editing the range, enter one in the Range Password field —** 123 **in this case. Otherwise, leave it blank to grant access based on specific users.**

   That is clearly not a secure password, but rather an easy one for you to retype in a minute.

6. **Click OK to close the New Range dialog box.**

   If you filled in the Range Password field, a Confirm Password dialog box appears.

7. **If prompted, confirm the password, in this case type** 123 **again.**

   Either way, the Allow Users to Edit Ranges dialog box reappears.

8. **Click Protect Sheet.**

   The Protect Sheet dialog box appears.

9. **Skip the password this time for demonstration purposes but ensure Select Locked Cells is enabled.**

10. **Click OK to enable worksheet protection.**

11. **Double-click on a locked cell that has permissions, such as J5.**

The Unlock Range dialog box appears (see Figure 14-4).

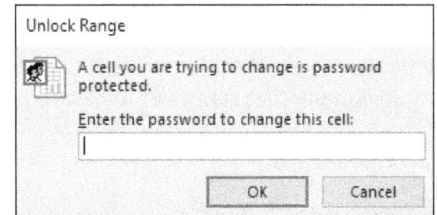

Unlock Range

A cell you are trying to change is password protected.

Enter the password to change this cell:

| OK | Cancel |

FIGURE 14-4:
The Unlock Range
dialog box.

12. **Enter the password — 123 in this case — and then click OK.**

You won't be prompted again during the current work session. Just tread carefully — there's a rattler — er, a formula — that you could easily step on in that cell.

Now that you have the low-down, take a quick gander at those other options in the Allow Users to Edit Ranges dialog box:

>> **New, Modify, or Delete:** Add, update, or remove ranges.

>> **Permissions. . .:** Grant edit rights to specific users based on local network or computer accounts — no password needed.

REMEMBER

You must set a range password or assign users — otherwise, no one will be able to edit the designated cells.

>> **Paste Permissions Information into a New Workbook:** Turn this checkbox on, and then click OK to send the details to a new workbook.

>> **OK:** Saves your changes now — but you'll need to protect the worksheet later.

>> **Cancel:** Discards changes.

>> **Apply:** Stores midstream changes, so you don't have to backtrack later.

Safeguarding Workbook Structure

By default, Excel users can freely:

>> Add or delete worksheets

>> Move or copy worksheets

» Hide or unhide worksheets

» Rename worksheets

» Change worksheet tab colors

Unlike worksheet protection, which offers granular permissions, workbook protection blocks all the above actions outright:

1. **Choose Review ⇨ Protect Workbook.**

   The Protect Structure and Windows dialog box (Figure 14-5) opens with a ghost town vibe. Protecting the structure isn't optional anymore — always leave that checkbox turned on — and the days of wrangling window placement are long gone.

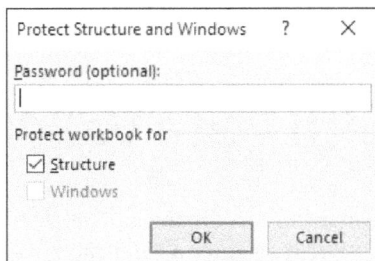

2. **To allow anyone to disable workbook protection later, leave the Password (Optional) blank — in this case, type XYZ.**

   Any password anywhere in Excel is *case-sensitive* — uppercase and lowercase matter!

REMEMBER

3. **Click OK — workbook protection would be enabled if the password field were left blank, but this time type XYZ again, and then click OK to enable protection.**

   Any commands related to the actions listed at the start of this section are disabled within Excel's ribbon and context menus. Normally, double-clicking a worksheet tab allows you to rename it, but with protection enabled, a prompt informs you: `Workbook is protected and cannot be changed`.

When you're ready to unprotect your workbook, you need to keep your wits about you:

1. **Notice the shaded background behind the Review ➪ Protect Workbook command, and then click it.**

   Excel sometimes pulls tricks on you like a card shark — in this case the Protect Workbook command holds onto its name like a leech, as opposed to Protect Sheet, which helpfully toggles to Unprotect Sheet.

2. **The Unprotect Workbook dialog box appears — in this case, enter XYZ — and then click OK.**

   This dialog box doesn't appear when you leave the Password (Optional) field blank when enabling workbook protection.

    As with worksheet protection, you have to type your password in again from scratch if you decide to enable workbook protection again.

   REMEMBER

Ensuring Accuracy with Data Validation

You can lead a horse to water, but you can't make it drink. Likewise, you can guide a user to a cell, but can you ensure they enter a valid value? With the Data Validation feature, the answer is a qualified yes. While some users might find a way to slip through the fence, most will stay happily within the corral.

Before diving into the details, make sure you have this chapter's sample workbook handy. If you followed the initial sequence at the start of this chapter, you saw how a single unexpected input can ignite a prairie fire of error values in your workbook. Blocking users from editing formulas with worksheet protection is one thing — ensuring valid inputs is another.

By default, every cell in a worksheet allows users to enter anything they wish, if it follows formula syntax rules. Data validation helps rein things in by enabling you to:

» Restrict cell inputs to specific criteria.

» Guide users with input messages.

» Respond to invalid inputs with error prompts.

 The downside of the Data Validation feature is that it only checks what users type into cells — anything pasted into a cell gets a free pass. See the "Protecting Data Validation Cells" and "Identifying Invalid Inputs" sections later in this chapter for ways to address this limitation.

WARNING

Setting boundaries with data validation

There are how-to examples later in this chapter, but if you're champing at the bit, choose Data ⇨ Data Validation now. The Allow field on the Settings tab of the Data Validation dialog box offers these options:

» **Any Value:** The equivalent of a bar brawl in a worksheet cell — anything goes when it comes to input.

» **Whole Number:** The equivalent of bellying up to a bar and ordering a whiskey — any brand will do, as long as it's a straight pour. Or to shoot straight, a restriction you might place on cell D7, Loan Period in Years, of the Loan Amortization Schedule worksheet.

» **Decimal:** This is where things can get frilly, like some finery from the mercantile. In cell D6, Annual Interest Rate, you could limit the user to entering a percentage, ensuring precise inputs.

REMEMBER

The Whole Number restriction howls like a wolf if your input includes decimal values (e.g., 3.14), while the Decimal restriction is cool with anything numeric (e.g., 3.14159).

» **List:** Nope, this doesn't mean that your wagon is leaning to the side, but rather a menu of valid choices that the user can choose from. For instance, cell C12, Lender Name, can yield a list of approved institutions.

» **Date:** This is not an invitation to the square dance, but rather a way to ensure that users enter a valid date, such as in D9, Start Date of Loan.

» **Time:** It's always high noon somewhere — this setting ensures that users don't try to knock the clock around. Standard time formats in Excel include:

- **12-hour format:** 2:30 p.m. (hours and minutes) or 2:30:00 p.m. (hours, minutes, and seconds)

- **24-hour format:** 14:30 (hours and minutes) or 14:30:00 (hours, minutes, and seconds)

REMEMBER

The Date restriction allows both dates and times (e.g., 7/1/2026 12:00 PM) if the input falls within the specified range. Conversely, the Time restriction only accepts time inputs — any associated date must be entered in a separate cell.

» **Text Length:** Limits the number of characters in a cell, kinda like the original 160-character limit for SMS texts.

WARNING

Unless the user keeps a count in their head, Excel doesn't offer any indication as to whether a text length restriction has been exceeded until the user presses Enter. This rule is best reserved for short inputs (e.g., six-digit ID numbers and such).

>> **Custom:** The gloves are off here — any bare-knuckle input rule that can be stated as a logical equation is fair game. If the formula evaluates to TRUE or 0 (zero), the user can proceed; anything else, including #VALUE! errors, sends the Data Validation deputy thundering in.

REMEMBER

Only one data validation restriction can be applied to a cell. However, data validation can be copied and pasted between cells.

Refining restrictions

The Settings tab of the Data Validation dialog box allows you to further refine permissible input once you select from the Allow field. For instance, most restrictions (Whole Number, Decimal, Date, Time, or Text Length) allow you to define inputs with the following criteria:

>> **Between/Not Between:** Define both a minimum and maximum value

>> **Equal To/Not Equal To:** Just one value needed

>> **Greater Than/Greater Than or Equal To:** Set a minimum value

>> **Less Than/Less Than or Equal To:** Set a maximum value

WARNING

Choose carefully when selecting Greater Than or Less Than versus their Equal To counterparts. It's easy to unintentionally block the lowest or highest allowed value simply by just by picking the wrong rule.

Depending on what you select in the Data field, fields labeled Minimum, Maximum, or Value will appear. Permissible entries include:

>> Inputs matching the allowed data type, such as 1 for Whole Number, .10 for Decimal, or 7/1/2026 for Date.

REMEMBER

Percentages, such as 10%, must be entered as decimal values — 0.10 in this case — in the Data Validation dialog box. Users can then enter percentages or decimal values in the worksheet cells.

>> Cell references that contain or evaluate to the allowed data type.

>> Formulas that evaluate to the allowed data type, such as =TODAY( ) to define allowable dates based on the current date.

The List restriction causes a Source field to appear, which accepts the following:

>> **Comma-separated list:** Ideal for options that (hopefully) won't change (e.g., January, February, March). The space after the comma is optional, so Excel won't complain if you enter Yes,No instead of Yes, No.

CROSS REFERENCE

Be sure to bone up on the difference between Enter and Edit modes in Chapter 18 to save yourself a heap of frustration when using the arrow keys to navigate within a list you enter.

>> **Cell reference:** Longer or dynamic lists are better suited to a range of cells that spans a single row or column, although referencing an Excel table (Chapter 5) eliminates future maintenance — new items added to the table will appear on the corresponding data validation list automatically.

REMEMBER

If you reference a normal range of cells (e.g., M2:M11), you'll need to manually update the Data Validation settings to include any additional items. If you try to outwit this limitation by extending the range to blank cells, a blank option will appear at the bottom of your data validation list.

>> **Formula:** A formula that evaluates to a list, such as the SORT function — e.g., =SORT(M2:M11) — covered in Chapter 9 — can further reduce Data Validation maintenance by keeping your lists automatically ordered.

The Custom restriction causes a Formula field to appear, which expects you to enter a formula that evaluates to TRUE or 0 (zero) when the user makes an acceptable input.

>> Although the Formula field accepts a cell reference (e.g., =A1), the rule will never evaluate to TRUE, causing all inputs to be rejected as invalid.

WARNING

The following checkboxes always or sometimes appear on the Settings tab:

>> **Ignore Blank:** This doesn't control whether users can leave a cell empty. Instead, it applies when a Data Validation rule references another cell — if the referenced cell is blank, Excel won't enforce the validation rule until that cell contains a value.

>> **In-Cell Drop-down:** This checkbox only appears when you choose List from the Allow list — clear it if you want to hide the drop-down list. Users will still be restricted to the designated inputs, but they'll have to type them manually.

>> **Apply These Changes to All Other Cells With the Same Settings:** Disabled when you create a new rule but allows modifications to apply to any other cells that have the same Data Validation settings.

Guiding with input messages

Data Validation lets you optionally create screen tips that can give users a heads up about a particular restriction. A quick exercise gives an immediate sense of things:

1. **Press Escape or click Close if the Data Validation dialog box is currently onscreen.**

2. **Select cell J10 of the Loan Amortization Schedule tab of this chapter's sample workbook.**

An input message appears — in this case offering guidance for recording extra loan payments.

3. **Select any other cell, such as J9.**

The input message vanishes.

TIP

Input messages can provide a nudge without restricting a user's inputs — you can type anything you want, such as Yahoo! in cell J10. To allow unrestricted input while still displaying an input message, leave the default Any Value rule in place on the Settings tab.

If you can't wait to see how to build an input message, choose Data ⇨ Data Validation, then select the Input Message tab, which contains two fields:

>> **Title (optional):** Up to 32 characters, which appear in bold on the input message.

>> **Input message (optional):** Up to 222 characters, although most users these days will stop reading long before that limit.

TECHNICAL
STUFF

The Show Input Message When Cell is Selected checkbox allows you to disable the data entry prompt, but if you don't want a prompt, just leave the Title and Input Message fields blank.

Responding with error alerts

I just had the craziest thought — hang with me here — did you know that sometimes users try to type something unexpected in a worksheet cell? Sheesh! Of course, it's often not intentional — see the "Identifying Invalid Inputs" section later in the chapter to see how to track down folks who flout the rules.

Data validation lets you allow users some room to roam — or not — based on the selection that you made from the Style field on the Error Alert tab of the Data Validation dialog box:

>> **Stop:** The most restrictive option, gives the user two choices:

- **Retry:** Edit the input.
- **Cancel:** Discard the input.

>> **Warning:** This prompt includes the question "Continue?" and gives the user a potential out:

- **Yes:** Override the rule and keep the entry.
- **No:** Edit the input.
- **Cancel:** Discard the input.

>> **Information:** The least restrictive option, allowing the user to acknowledge the rule before moving on. These are their choices:

- **OK:** Override the rule and keep the entry.
- **Cancel:** Discard the input.

The Error Alert tab also contains these fields:

>> **Title (optional):** Up to 32 characters, which appear in the title bar of the message dialog, defaults to Microsoft Excel if left blank.

>> **Error message (optional):** Up to 150 characters, which appear in the body of the message dialog box, and defaults to This Value doesn't match the data validation restrictions defined for this cell. if left blank.

The Show Error Alert After Invalid Data is Entered checkbox lets you disable the feedback prompt if you have nothing to say and don't want the default error message to appear.

Putting Data Entry Rules into Action

Now that you have a sense of what's possible with Data Validation, it's time to hobble the horses — er, place some restrictions in worksheet cells. The examples lead off by limiting a cell input to whole numbers. The second example shows how to create an in-cell drop-down list, and the third shows how to prevent users from entering the same value more than once. Each example illustrates a different error alert style, giving you hands-on experience with all three.

Requiring whole numbers

Here's how to only allow users to enter whole numbers in worksheet cells:

1. **If the worksheet is protected, choose Review ⇨ Unprotect Sheet.**

    See the "Disabling worksheet protection" section earlier in this chapter for more details.

2. **Select cells D7:D8 on the Loan Amortization Schedule tab of this chapter's sample workbook.**

    Cell D7 already contains data validation but D8 doesn't, so the prompt in Figure 14-6 asks whether you want to extend the rule.

3. **Click Yes.**

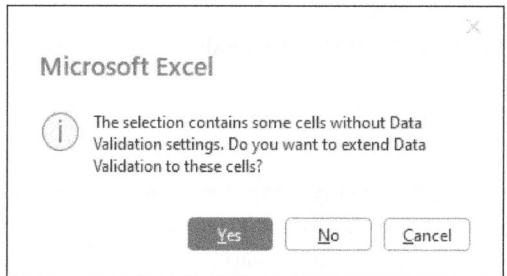

FIGURE 14-6:
The extend data valida-
tion prompt.

4. **Choose Data ⇨ Data Validation.**

    The Data Validation dialog box opens with the default setting of Any Value.

5. **The following settings carry over from the existing Data Validation rule:**

    - **Allow:** Whole Number (instead of the default Any Value)

    - **Data:** Between (the default setting)

    - **Minimum:** 1 (defaults to blank)

    - **Maximum:** 40 (defaults to blank)

6. **Craft an input message (which is missing from this template), as shown in Figure 14-7:**

   a. **Activate the Input Message tab.**

   b. **Type** `Enter a Valid Number` **in the Title field.**

   c. **Type** `Enter a whole number between 1 and 40.` **in the Input Message field.**

Be specific when crafting the title and input message for a data validation rule. Generic text like `Enter a number between 1 and 40` might mislead the users into thinking that decimals (e.g., `3.75`) are allowed, only to trigger an error. Clear feedback prevents frustration.

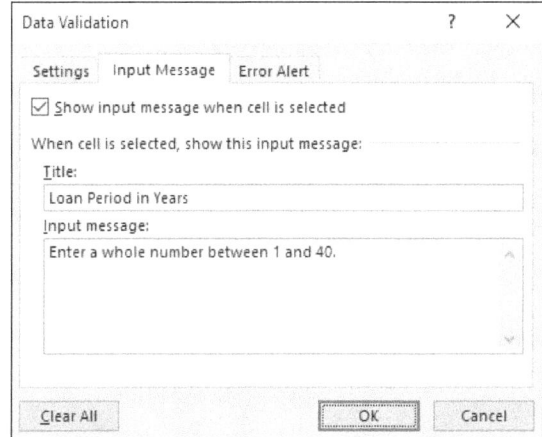

FIGURE 14-7:
The Input Message tab of the Data Validation dialog box.

7. **Modify the existing error alert, as shown in Figure 14-8:**

   a. **Activate the Error Alert tab.**

   b. **Accept the default style of Stop.**

   In this case, it doesn't make sense to let the user override the restriction, as doing so will likely result in formula errors elsewhere on the worksheet.

   c. **Replace "Years" in the Title field with Invalid Input — normally this field would be blank.**

   d. **Replace "Please enter a whole number of years from 1 to 40." With** `You must enter a WHOLE NUMBER between 1 and 40.` **in the Input Message field — usually blank a well.**

   In this case, using ALL CAPS helps emphasize a nuance of the expected input, making it harder to overlook.

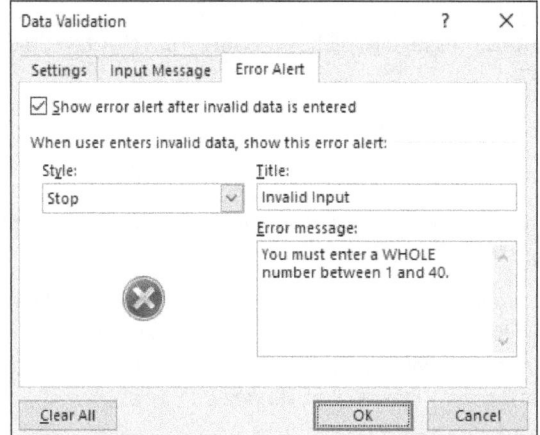

FIGURE 14-8:
The Error Alert
tab of the Data
Validation
dialog box.

8. **Click OK to apply the data validation rule.**

9. **Enter 4 in cell D7.**

The input is a whole number between 1 and 30, so the input is accepted.

10. **Type 12.5 in cell D8.**

The input is not a whole number, therefore the input is blocked, as shown in Figure 14-9.

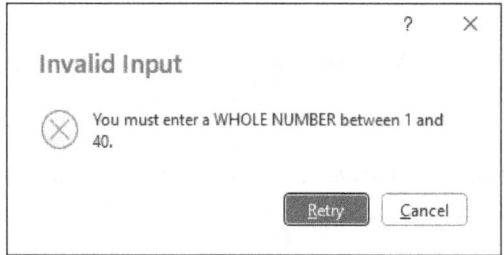

FIGURE 14-9:
The Stop style
error alert
dialog box.

Choosing from a list

Creating in-cell drop-down lists not only limits users to specific inputs but also simplifies data entry:

1. **Select cell C12.**

2. **Choose Data ⇨ Data Validation.**

3. Choose **List** from the **Allow** field.

4. **Type** `Cactus Creek Savings, Dusty Trail Trust, Silver Spur Bank` **in the Source field.**

5. **Craft an input message:**

   a. **Activate the Input Message tab.**

   b. **Type** `Lender Name` **in the Title field.**

   c. **Type** `Choose a lender from the list.` **in the Input Message field.**

6. **Create an error alert:**

   a. **Activate the Error Alert tab.**

   b. **Choose Warning from the Style list.**

   c. **Type** `Unexpected Input` **in the Title field.**

   d. **Type** `You typed an unexpected lender name.` **in the Error Alert field.**

7. **Click OK to apply the data validation rule.**

8. **You could click the drop-down button or press Alt+Down Arrow (Windows) or Option+Down Arrow (macOS) to display the list — but instead, type the letter** `S` **in cell C12.**

   The drop-down list displays Silver Spur Bank and Cactus Creek Savings because both contain at least one word that starts with S.

9. **Use your mouse or the arrow keys to navigate to your selection, then click or press Enter.**

   Silver Spur Bank appears in cell C12.

10. **Type** `Frontier Union Bank` **in cell C12, and then press Enter.**

11. **Choose Yes from the error message prompt shown in Figure 14-10.**

    Frontier Union Bank now appears in cell C12, illustrating how users can override Data Validation restrictions when permitted.

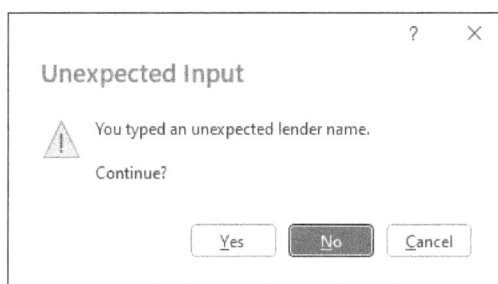

FIGURE 14-10:
The Warning style
error alert
dialog box.

Preventing duplicate entries

Here's how to prevent users from entering the same value more than once within a range of cells:

1. **Select cells E18:E25.**

2. **Choose Data ⇨ Data Validation.**

3. **Choose Custom from the Allow field.**

4. **Type** `=COUNTIF($E$18:$E25,E18)=1` **in the Formula field.**

The COUNTIF function determines the number of times that a value appears within a range of cells, and has the following arguments:

- **range:** One or more cells in which you want to search for the value specified in the *criteria* argument (in this case, $E$18:$E$28). The absolute reference ensures the search area remains fixed when applying the rule.

- **criteria:** The value that you want to count within the specified range (in this case, the value in cell E18, or the first cell within the *range* argument). The relative reference ensures the rule applies dynamically to each cell within the search area.

Chapter 2 compares absolute, mixed, and relative cell references.

CROSS
REFERENCE

5. **Craft an input message:**

    a. **Activate the Input Message tab.**

    b. **Type** `Unique Input Required` **in the Title field.**

    c. **Type** `Enter a unique amount.` **in the Input Message field.**

6. **Create an error alert:**

    a. **Activate the Error Alert tab.**

    b. **Choose Information from the Style list.**

    c. **Type** `Duplicate Value` **in the Title field.**

    d. **Type** `You entered a duplicate value.` **in the Error Alert field.**

7. **Click OK to apply the data validation rule.**

8. **Enter** `500` **in cell E18.**

The input is accepted because this is the only instance of 500 in the validation range.

REMEMBER

If cell E18 appears blank after you type 500, check the sample inputs for cells D5:D9 listed at the start of this chapter.

9. Enter 500 in cell E19.

10. Click OK on the error alert prompt shown in Figure 14-11.

500 now appears in E18 and E19, demonstrating once again how users can override Data Validation when permitted.

FIGURE 14-11:
The Information
style error alert
dialog box.

Protecting Data Validation Cells

As noted earlier in this chapter, users can bypass data validation restrictions, either accidentally or intentionally, by pasting data into validated cells. This means that worksheet protection is a crucial element of data validation. If the worksheet isn't protected, pasting may completely erase data validation settings, depending on how the user pastes. Conversely, on a protected worksheet, pasted values are accepted even if they're invalid, but the data validation rule remains intact.

Before enabling worksheet protection, ensure that all validated cells are formatted as unlocked:

1. Choose Home ➪ Find & Select ➪ Data Validation.

This selects all cells with Data Validation restrictions — if you've followed along with every example, that means D7, D9, C12, and E18:E25. If no cells have data validation, Excel displays the message No cells were found.

2. Choose Home ➪ Format ➪ Format Cells ➪ Protection, clear the Locked checkbox, and then click OK.

The "Unlocking and Protecting Worksheet Cells" section earlier in this chapter details how to specify worksheet cells — such as those without validation — before protecting the worksheet, as well as how to enable protection.

Identifying Invalid Inputs

As discussed earlier in this chapter, you can craft data validation that allow users to break the rules on purpose. In other cases, users may accidentally or deliberately paste values into validated cells — none the wiser because no error alert appears.

REMEMBER

Pasted values can erase Data Validation rules on unprotected worksheets, reducing or even eliminating any potential audit trail.

To audit and correct invalid inputs in data validation cells, follow these steps:

1. **If the worksheet is protected, choose Review ⇨ Unprotect Sheet.**

2. **Choose Data ⇨ Data Validation drop-down ⇨ Circle Invalid Data.**

If you've followed along with the examples, red circles will appear in cells C12 and E18:E25 — the zero values in cells E20:E25 are treated as invalid duplicates.

REMEMBER

If all data validation cells contain valid inputs — or if there aren't any on the active worksheet — Excel stays as quiet as a tumbleweed rolling through an abandoned town. No feedback, no fuss.

3. **To correct an invalid input, click on any cell that contains a red circle and make a correction.**

In some cases, Excel removes the red circle after the correction; in others, the circle may remain.

4. **To remove the red circles, either choose Data ⇨ Data Validation drop-down ⇨ Clear Validation Circles or save the workbook.**

Either action removes all data validation circles.

Removing Data Validation

If you change your mind about data validation, you can remove it easily:

1. **Select individual cells that contain data validation or go whole hog by choosing Home ⇨ Find & Select ⇨ Data Validation to select all validated cells on the active worksheet.**

2. **Click OK if the prompt shown in Figure 14-12 appears; otherwise click Clear All in the Data Validation dialog box.**

Cell contents and formatting will remain intact, but inputs will no longer be wrangled by Data Validation — it's a free-for-all now.

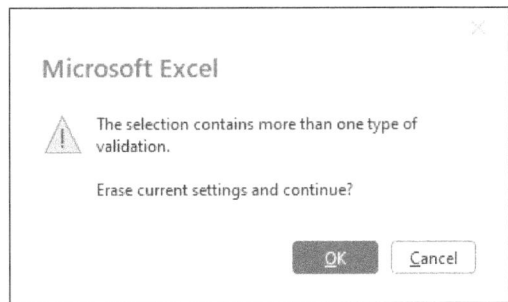

FIGURE 14-12:
The multiple types of validation prompt.

If you prefer a scorched earth approach, select one or more cells, then choose Home ⇨ Clear ⇨ Clear All to wipe out everything — cell contents, formatting, and, of course, any data validation rules. It's like erasing all traces of civilization from the spreadsheet frontier.

4

Automating Analysis

IN THIS PART . . .

Utilize Excel's AI tools to enhance productivity.

Simplify repetitive tasks using macros.

IN THIS CHAPTER

» **Streamlining tasks with Flash Fill**

» **Gaining Insights with Analyze Data**

» **Exploring Copilot Pro**

» **Connecting with Data Types**

» **Capturing data from images**

» **Collaborating with ChatGPT**

Chapter **15**

Accessing Artificial Intelligence

Working with artificial intelligence (AI) feels like learning a new dance while the music keeps changing — you're keeping up with the rhythm, but the steps never stay the same for long. Every step balances ground-breaking innovation against the risk of unintended consequences. In this chapter, I touch on foundational AI-driven features like Flash Fill, Analyze Data, and Data Types, alongside cutting-edge tools such as Copilot and Extracting Data from Pictures. Buckle up! This chapter provides an overview rather than an in-depth dive, because tools like Copilot are evolving rapidly and may already look different by the time you read this. As with many Excel features — and life itself — solving one problem often introduces new ones.

Automating with Flash Fill

Flash Fill in Excel is a tool that automates data entry by identifying patterns in your input and completing the remaining data for you. It is particularly effective for one-time tasks like splitting, combining, or formatting data consistently across rows.

Chapter 7 explores formula-based techniques for transforming and refor-matting text.

Here's how Flash Fill works:

>> **Pattern Recognition:** Flash Fill observes the patterns in your data entry. For instance, if you're extracting first names from a column of full names, typing a single example provides Excel with the pattern it needs to follow.

Flash Fill works only in blank columns adjacent to existing data and cannot directly modify the original data. If you're applying a pattern, like formatting Social Security numbers with dashes, use Flash Fill in a new column, then copy and paste the results over the original if needed.

>> **Auto-Filling Data:** After setting a pattern, type the first character or digit in the cell directly below the pattern cell. If Excel identifies a data entry pattern, it suggests completing the remaining cells in the column. Press Enter to accept the suggestions if they look correct.

>> **Manual Triggering:** If you type more than a single character in the next cell down from a pattern, Excel assumes that you don't want Flash Fill's assistance. In that case, or if Excel doesn't automatically apply Flash Fill, you can trigger it manually:

1. **Select the cell immediately beneath the cell that contains the data entry pattern.**

2. **Choose Data ⇨ Flash Fill or press Ctrl+E (Windows) or Cmd+E (macOS).**

Flash Fill processes data down one column at a time. If you're working with multiple columns, such as splitting first and last names, complete Flash Fill for the first column before moving to the next. Keep in mind that the command and shortcut are disabled when you select multiple pattern-setting cells.

Flash Fill is particularly useful for tasks like:

>> **Splitting data:** Separate components like first and last names or city, state, and postal code into distinct columns.

Excel tends to drop leading zeros from numbers, such as ZIP codes. To preserve these, type a single quote (') before the first digit when setting the pattern.

>> **Combining data:** Merge multiple elements, such as creating full names or combining city, state, and postal code into a single cell.

>> **Reformatting data:** Apply consistent formats, such as changing dates from "01-16-2027" to "January 16, 2027" or converting unformatted numbers like 123456789 into 123-45-6789.

Flash Fill simplifies tedious tasks, saving time and effort, but its effectiveness depends on clear patterns and adjacent blank columns for operation.

Exploring Insights with Analyze Data

The Analyze Data feature elevates the functionality of the Recommended Pivot-Tables and Recommended Charts features (see Chapter 12) to new heights. Unlike Copilot Pro (covered later in this chapter), you don't need to save your workbook to a specific location. However, an active internet connection is required since Analyze Data relies on cloud-based servers for its suggestions.

As the saying goes, a picture is worth a thousand words — so my editor will appreciate that I'm getting right to the demonstration:

1. **Create a sample data set:**

    ● **Windows:** Choose File ⇨ New, type Household Organizer in the search bar, press Enter, select the Household Organizer template, and click Create.

    ● **macOS:** Download the Chapter 15 Household Organizer workbook from www.dummies.com/go/excelfd and open it in Excel.

2. **To launch Analyze Data, select any cell within a list, such as cell B3 of the Budget worksheet in the Household Organizer template, and choose Home ⇨ Analyze Data.**

    The Analyze Data task pane opens, as shown in Figure 15-1, and includes the following sections — though in macOS, it might show up empty (that's AI, sigh):

    ● **Ask a Question About Your Data:** This field enables you to prompt the Analyze Data feature to create PivotTables and/or PivotCharts based upon natural language questions that you ask.

REMEMBER

Be as precise as possible when asking natural language questions. For example, a vague query like "top 5 amounts" might produce a PivotTable listing the top 5 amounts without including any context or identifying details, such as categories or descriptions.

- **Suggested Questions:** One or more prompts to help jump start your analysis. Click within the Ask a Question About Your Data field to see more suggestions, as well as a listing of recent questions that you've asked.

- **Settings button:** Displays a settings area from which you can fine-tune the analysis by excluding unwanted fields, and indicating whether a field is not a value, or if you want to Sum or Average the field. Click Update to apply the changes.

- **Discover Insights:** This section of the task pane typically comprises a combination of PivotTables and PivotCharts (see Chapter 12) that summarize elements of your data or point out extraordinary items. Depending upon the complexity of your data, a Show All link may appear at the bottom of the task pane that offers additional choices.

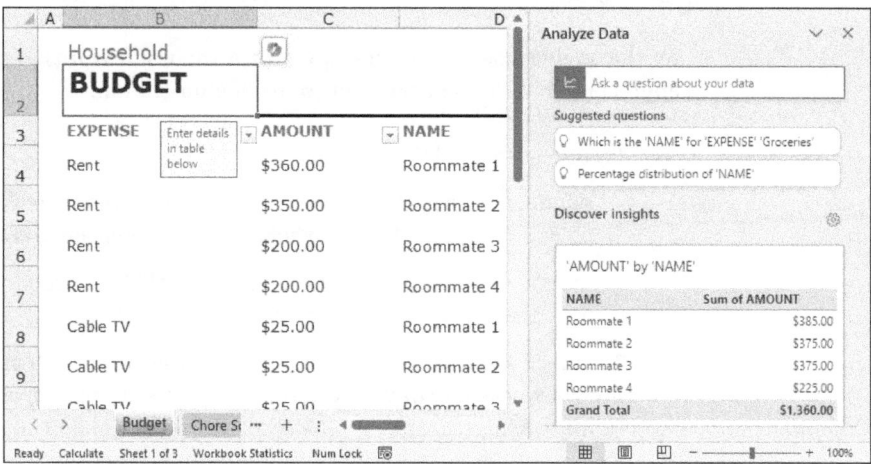

FIGURE 15-1:
The Analyze Data task pane.

The Analyze Data task pane notifies you if your dataset is either too small to generate meaningful reports or too large for the feature to process. While Microsoft hasn't disclosed an official cell limit, anecdotal evidence suggests a soft cap of approximately 1.5 million cells, calculated as the product of rows and columns in your dataset.

Introducing Copilot Pro

Copilot Pro is Excel's answer to Tony Stark's J.A.R.V.I.S. ("Just A Rather Very Intelligent System") — the ever-reliable AI assistant to Iron Man in the Marvel Cinematic Universe. For the uninitiated, Tony Stark is a billionaire genius, inventor, and superhero whose creations, like his iconic Iron Man suits, rely on cutting-edge technology powered by J.A.R.V.I.S. While I'm optimistic that Copilot Pro may one day match J.A.R.V.I.S.'s efficiency and adaptability, for now it often devolves into an exercise in frustration, channeling HAL from *2001: A Space Odyssey* with a resounding, "I'm sorry, Dave. I'm afraid I can't do that."

REMEMBER

Microsoft considers Copilot Pro a premium feature requiring an additional subscription. If you — or your employer — opt not to pay, the Copilot command won't appear on the Home tab of Excel's ribbon. However, you can access the browser-based version of Copilot at `copilot.microsoft.com` without a subscription. After your first couple of queries, you'll need to log in with your Microsoft account to continue using it.

WARNING

The website `www.copilot.com` belongs to a completely unrelated product. To stay safe and avoid confusion, always ensure the domain name includes `microsoft.com` when accessing resources related to Copilot.

Working with the Copilot Pro Task Pane

Keep in mind these limitations when working with Copilot Pro:

CROSS
REFERENCE

>> **Cloud requirement:** You must save your workbooks to OneDrive (see Chapter 18) or SharePoint. Copilot is unavailable in SharePoint workbooks that are currently checked out.

>> **AutoSave requirement:** You must enable the AutoSave option on Excel's Quick Access Toolbar to (see Chapter 1) to use Copilot Pro.

REMEMBER

The Home ⇨ Copilot command tab is always clickable but the Copilot task pane may stop you in your tracks with a reminder to turn on AutoSave. Similarly, certain context menus, which appear when you right-click on parts of the worksheet grid, include a Copilot command. If all options except Ask Copilot are disabled, it's likely that your workbook isn't saved to OneDrive or SharePoint, or AutoSave isn't enabled.

>> **Data limits:** Microsoft documentation specifies a limit of 2 million cells for CoPilot Pro. However, certain features, like Advanced Analysis with Python, may impose lower limits, such as 1 million cells.

>> **Processing delays:** Depending on the complexity of your request, Copilot Pro might take longer to process your data than it would to complete the task manually, or Copilot may metaphorically throw up its hands and say the equivalent of "I dunno."

>> **Excel table recommendation:** Early incarnations of Copilot required data to be formatted as an Excel table (see Chapter 5). That restriction has been softened, but Copilot may still recommend converting large datasets into a table for better functionality.

Despite its current quirks, Copilot Pro holds significant potential to become a powerful creative and analytical assistant for tasks that might otherwise feel daunting. AI tools often evolve in leaps and bounds, so while Copilot's current abilities may be a mixed bag, it's worth keeping an eye on its development — just don't forget that grain of salt. The Analyze Data feature discussed earlier provides a promising glimpse into the future capabilities Copilot might bring to the table.

Utilizing Data Types

The Data Types feature in Excel transforms basic text or numbers into connected data sources. Currently, Excel offers three main data types:

>> **Stocks:** Fields include price, volume, and market cap.

>> **Geography:** Fields include population, GDP, and capital city.

>> **Currencies:** Fields include price, 52-week high and low, and change percentage.

Here's how to use Data Types to return an exchange rate between two currencies:

1. **Enter a currency pair, such as GBP/USD, into a worksheet cell.**

2. **Convert the currency pair by selecting Data ⇨ Currencies.**

   As shown in Figure 15-2, the Insert Data icons, indicating the cell is now connected to a live data source.

3. **Select the cell containing the Data Type, then click Insert Data to display a Fields list shown in Figure 15-2. From this list, choose one or more fields, such as Price.**

A formula appears in the adjacent cell, e.g., =A1.Price.

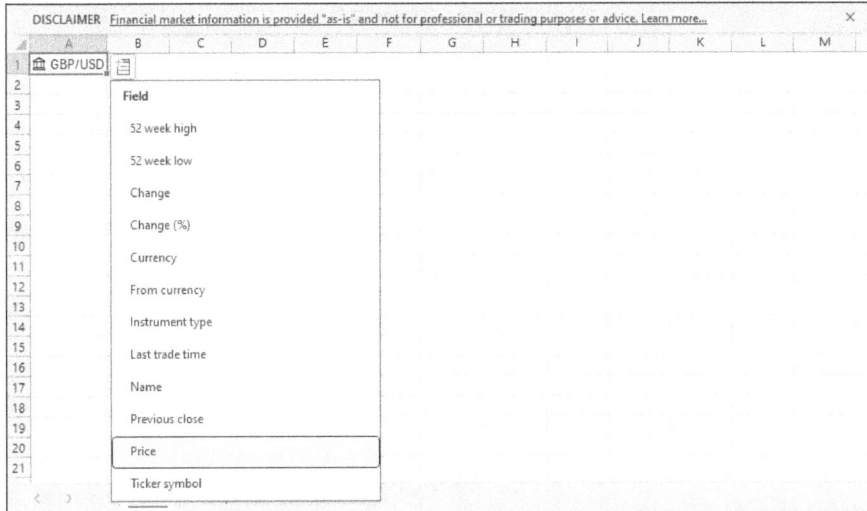

FIGURE 15-2: Data Type cell icon and the Insert Data field list.

Data Types refresh automatically, though the frequency depends on the provider. To manually refresh all Data Types, select Data ⇨ Refresh All. The Stocks and Geography Data Types work in a similar way: enter a ticker symbol or geographic location into a cell, then convert the input into a live connection. If Excel cannot identify the data, the Data Selector task pane appears, allowing you to specify or confirm the correct match. Cells that Excel cannot convert without clarification display a question mark icon, prompting you to use the Data Selector task pane for resolution.

Extracting Data from Pictures

The From Picture command uses optical character recognition (OCR) to extract text from the following file types:

» **AVI Image File Format**: *.avi

» **Graphics Interchange Format:** *.gif

» **High Efficiency Image File Format:** *.heif, *.heic; *.hif

» **Icon:** *.ico

» **JPEG File Interchange Format:** *.jpg, *.jpeg, *.jfif, *.jpe

» **Portable Network Graphics:** *.png

» **Scalable Vector Graphics:** *.svg

» **Tag Image File Format:** *.tif, *.tiff

» **Windows Bitmap:** *.bmp, *.dib, *.rle

» **Windows Metafile:** *.emf, *.emz, *.wmf, *.wmz

REMEMBER

Noticeably absent from this list is Portable Document Format (*.PDF). Data from PDF files can be extracted more elegantly using Power Query. For a detailed walk-through on this approach, check out the bonus chapter "Streamlining Data Trans-formation with Power Query" (available at www.dummies.com/go/excelfd).

Let's try a quick exercise to explore the current state of optical character recogni-tion (OCR) in Excel:

1. Create a sample image by choosing Insert ⇨ Text Box or Insert ⇨ Text ⇨ Text Box, and then use your mouse to draw a text box on the worksheet grid.

2. Type a question for the ages — Will I be able to extract this text? — into the text box.

3. Right-click the edge of the text box and select Save As Picture.

The Save As Picture dialog box opens.

4. Specify a name and location for the image, and then click Save.

5. To import text from a picture, click on cell A1 of a blank worksheet.

WARNING

Most Excel features warn you with a confirmation prompt, but From Picture goes nuclear and eliminates any data in the path of the import. Always use this feature in an unobstructed area of a worksheet, or even better, a completely blank worksheet.

6. Choose Data ⇨ From Picture ⇨ Picture From File.

The Picture From File dialog box opens.

7. **Select an image file, such as the picture that you just saved, and then click Import.**

   The Data From Picture task pane opens, as shown in Figure 15-3, with the following sections:

   - **Data Preview:** Displays the scanned image.

   - **Insert Data button:** Transfers the extracted text into the worksheet when clicked.

   - **Review button:** Enabled when text is flagged as questionable.

   - **Worksheet Preview:** Displays the text in a format similar to how it appears in worksheet cells. Click any cell in this section to zoom in and make corrections. Click Accept to confirm changes, or Close to leave the text as is.

     Although you can edit individual cells, Excel doesn't allow corrections where text merges from multiple columns or breaks inappropriately, as demonstrated here.

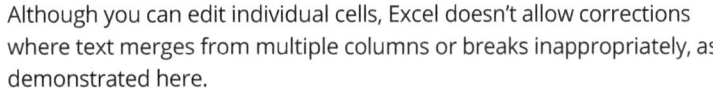

REMEMBER

8. **Click Insert Data to transfer the scanned information to your worksheet, and then click Insert Data again when prompted, "You are responsible for validating the accuracy of all data."**

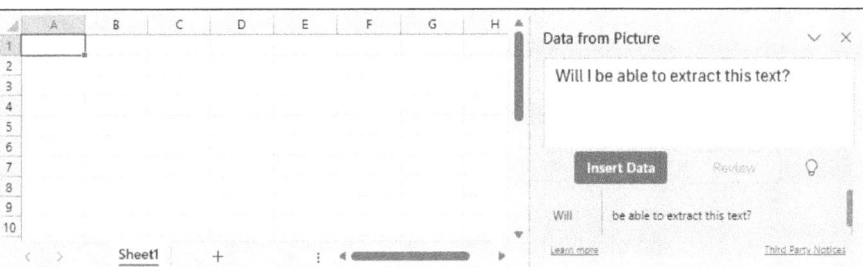

FIGURE 15-3:
The Data from Picture task pane.

Your text is now extracted into the worksheet. However, Excel interpreted the letter *I* as a column break, splitting the sentence Will I be able to import this? into two cells and omitting the letter *I* entirely. Results may vary, but many Excel features, including this one, often improve over time.

Interacting with ChatGPT

Let's step outside of Excel for a moment to explore possibilities with other AI platforms, such as ChatGPT. In my experience, AI excels at refining text and breaking down complex Excel formulas into digestible parts. However, using AI to write formulas or automate processes often produces mixed results, ranging from surprisingly effective to needing significant adjustments. Another factor to consider is the quality of the AI itself. Free platforms typically rely on older, less sophisticated models, which may limit their capabilities compared to premium options.

Deconstructing formulas and macros

One of the options in the Copilot Pro context menu is Explain This Formula, which promises to be a fantastic feature — once it works reliably. Perhaps I've been testing it with formulas that are too complex. In contrast, copying complex formulas from Excel and pasting them into ChatGPT (www.chatgpt.com) has never let me down. The key is to copy the formula from the formula bar or directly within the cell. If you copy the entire cell, you'll paste an image of the cell's value into ChatGPT, which does its best to describe the value rather than the formula itself. The explanations ChatGPT provides are an excellent troubleshooting tool. Recently, thanks to its clear breakdown, I quickly identified an issue I'd overlooked in a formula containing nested IF and VLOOKUP functions.

TIP

Chapter 10 discusses the Evaluate Formula feature, which lets you step through the calculation process within a formula. This can serve as a helpful companion to a written explanation, providing deeper insight into how the formula works.

Chapter 16 covers using macros to automate repetitive tasks in Excel. ChatGPT excels at explaining how macros work and deciphering the cryptic error messages often generated by Visual Basic for Applications (VBA). Instead of transcribing an error prompt manually, simply click on it and press Ctrl+C (Windows) or Cmd+C (macOS) to copy the message text to your clipboard. Paste it into an AI platform for analysis, or use a screen capture tool to take a screenshot of the error prompt and include it in your query.

Crafting formulas and code

AI platforms such as ChatGPT and Copilot can generate formulas and programming code based on the prompts you provide. However, it's essential to approach these tools with caution. A long-standing catchphrase to remember is "garbage in, garbage out" (GIGO) — coined by George Fuechsel, an early IBM programmer, to highlight that the quality of a computer's output depends entirely on the quality of its input.

CONNECTING EXCEL DIRECTLY TO CHATGPT

The free Excel Labs add-in introduces the LABS.GENERATIVEAI worksheet function, enabling ChatGPT integration directly into Excel for generating text-based outputs and insights without the need to copy prompts into your browser.

To access the Excel Labs add-in, open Excel and go to Home ⇨ Add-ins, then search for Excel Labs in the Office Add-ins store. Be aware of similarly named add-ins — the correct one is labeled "A Microsoft Garage project." Note that a ChatGPT API subscription is required to use this functionality.

AI can only act on the information you provide, so ensure your prompt is clear and detailed, including cell references and data descriptions. While AI can also write code to automate repetitive processes, the output is not foolproof. Generated code can contain errors or even cause data loss if not carefully reviewed. Always test AI-generated formulas and code in a controlled environment, such as a copy of your workbook, to identify and address potential issues before applying them to critical data.

IN THIS CHAPTER

» **Differentiating Excel's automation features**

» **Recording basic spreadsheet macros**

» **Fine-tuning macro security**

» **Reducing repetitive work**

» **Navigating the personal macro workbook**

Chapter **16**

Recording Macros

I f you thought macroeconomics was complicated, wait until you meet Excel macros! Unlike macroeconomic theories, which can leave your head spinning with supply and demand curves, Excel macros are here to simplify your life — no invisible hands required. Well, maybe a few invisible hands are at work, transcribing the actions you carry out into programming code that you can play back later.

Contrasting Code Versus Automation

Excel offers three different programming languages, but this chapter focuses solely on macros — specifically those written in VBA:

» **Visual Basic for Applications (VBA):** The granddaddy of Excel automation, VBA is a subset of the now-retired Visual Basic programming language. In Excel, VBA code is commonly referred to as macros.

For context, Excel also supports two other programming languages, which this chapter does not cover:

>> **TypeScript:** One of the new kids in town, TypeScript is a superset of JavaScript, widely used for web automation. Automation created in this language is known as Office Scripts, offering far greater cross-platform compatibility than VBA.

>> **Python:** The other newcomer, Python is one of the most popular programming languages worldwide, especially among data enthusiasts and data scientists. Chapter 15 touches on how you can use Copilot Pro to create reusable Python code on the fly.

Historically, recording or writing macros was the primary automation avenue available to Excel users. One of the significant advantages of Microsoft Excel 365 is the introduction of other powerful options:

>> **Dynamic array functions (Chapter 9):** These replace manual tasks like sorting and filtering with self-updating formulas, streamlining data transformation.

>> **Artificial intelligence (Chapter 15):** While AI has been part of Excel for over a decade, its development has been gradual. Copilot Pro, still in its early stages, promises to become an increasingly powerful assistant.

>> **Power Query (Bonus chapter "Automating Data Transformation with Power Query" (available at** www.dummies.com/go/excelfd**):** This tool provides a largely code-free way to create self-updating connections to external data sources and to rework data in ways that go beyond dynamic array functions.

Earlier in my career, before these features existed, I often encountered people who relied heavily on macros as a one-size-fits-all solution. Many would spend hours writing code to replicate functions that already existed but were simply unfamiliar to them.

Today, macros and scripts are just one of many robust automation tools in Excel, offering unparalleled flexibility and efficiency. The key is selecting the right tool for the job. As I often say, you can use a hammer to drive a screw into the wall, but the result won't be ideal. Sometimes, a hammer is exactly what you need; other times a screwdriver is the better choice. The same principle applies to Excel: knowing which feature to use ensures you get the job done effectively and efficiently.

Getting Started with the Macro Recorder

Think of Excel's Macro Recorder as actions-to-code, much like speech-to-text but for Excel. When enabled, the Macro Recorder translates most of your actions into programming code. I say most because there's a bit of unpredictability — some clicks or keystrokes may not be captured. Generally, actions that directly affect the worksheet or workbook are reliably converted into code. Staying patient and open-minded helps you master this basic automation feature and make the most of your efforts.

REMEMBER

Think of the Macro Recorder as a tasting menu for Excel automation. It offers a glimpse of what's possible, but any serious automation work in Excel requires rolling up your sleeves and working directly with programming code. Chapter 15 explores how AI might assist in writing code for you, subject to some significant caveats.

Understanding the risks of macros

Realizing you can turn the tables on Excel and have it do your bidding can be exhilarating, but remember the wise words from Spider-Man's 1962 comic book debut: "With great power comes great responsibility." If you choose to work with macros in Excel, keep the following constraints in mind:

>> **No Undo:** You cannot undo any actions carried out by a macro — or any actions performed prior to running a macro. Save your work frequently!

>> **No decision-making:** Recorded macros cannot make decisions, making the Macro Recorder suitable only for simple but repetitive tasks.

>> **Fragility:** Seemingly benign changes, like renaming a worksheet, can cause a macro to stop functioning.

REMEMBER

Unlike Excel formulas, which automatically update when worksheet names are changed, macros are static code. Structural changes in worksheets or workbooks require you to manually edit or re-record the macro.

>> **Keyboard shortcut conflicts:** Keyboard shortcuts assigned to macros can override Excel's built-in shortcuts or operating system shortcuts.

>> **File format limitations:** Macros are discarded in workbooks saved in the Excel Workbook (.xlsx) format. Use Excel Macro-Enabled Workbooks (.xlsm) or Excel Binary Workbooks (.xlsb) instead.

>> **Security concerns:** Macros can potentially contain malicious code, so adding macros to workbooks you share with others may cause concern or even be blocked by security settings.

>> **Platform limitations:** Macros created with VBA only work on desktop versions of Excel. They cannot be run in Excel for the Web, Google Sheets, or on mobile apps. Additionally, macros created in Excel for Windows may cause compatibility issues in Excel for macOS.

These constraints aren't meant to dissuade you from using macros but to help you understand their limitations.

Recording your first macro

Howdy! Let's start by recording a macro that types two simple words into a worksheet cell: Hello, World! This classic first exercise, widely used in programming, introduces key concepts without overwhelming the learner. Below, you walk through the start-to-finish process of recording and playing back an Excel macro, giving you a practical sense of how it works:

1. **Select any cell within a blank worksheet.**

2. **Choose View ⇨ Macros drop-down ⇨ Record Macro.**

    The Record Macro dialog box opens, as shown in Figure 16-1.

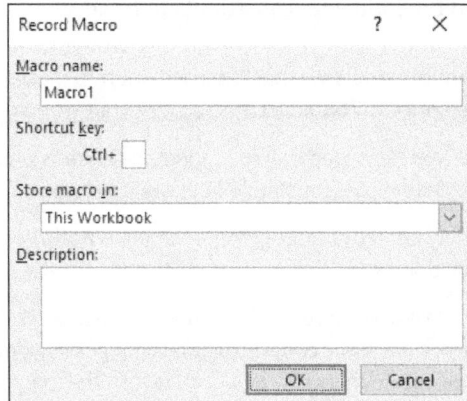

FIGURE 16-1:
The Record
Macro dialog box.

3. **Type HelloMacro into the Macro Name field.**

    Macro names are subject to the following constraints:

    ● The first character must be a letter.

    ● Numbers are allowed, but only from the second character onward.

    ● Spaces are not permitted, but underscores are allowed.

- No other punctuation or special characters can be used.

- Avoid reserved words like Sub, End, If, Then, or Excel feature names.

- Although you can reuse macro names, strive for unique names to avoid confusion and potential conflicts.

4. **Leave the Shortcut Key field blank for now.**

All will be revealed about shortcut keys later in this chapter.

5. **Select New Workbook from the Store Macro In list.**

Recorded macros can be stored in one of three locations:

- **This Workbook:** The macro is added to the currently active workbook and can only be used when that workbook is open. This is ideal for macros specific to a particular workbook.

- **New Workbook:** The macro is added to a new, blank workbook, with the same constraints as "This Workbook."

- **Personal Macro Workbook:** Saves the macro to a private workbook on your computer, allowing it to be played back in any open Excel workbook — but only on your computer. This is the best place to store general-purpose macros that you plan to use across multiple workbooks. Unlike regular workbooks, the Personal Macro Workbook is stored separately and loads automatically when Excel starts.

TIP

To keep macros in This Workbook or New Workbook, save the file as an Excel Macro-Enabled Workbook (.XLSM); otherwise, they'll be lost. If you modify macros in the Personal Macro Workbook, Excel prompts you to save changes when closing.

6. **Enter up to 255 characters in the Description field to document the macro's purpose or functionality.**

7. **Click OK to close the Record Macro dialog box and start recording.**

Since you selected New Workbook, Excel opens a blank workbook where your actions will be recorded. This is like hitting the record button on your phone — your screen won't be captured, but most of the actions you perform in Excel will be.

8. **Type the words `Hello, World!` in the active cell.**

9. **To stop recording, choose View ⇨ Macros ⇨ Stop Recording or click the square Stop Recording icon within Excel's Status Bar.**

TIP

The Stop Recording button remains hidden until you use the Macro Recorder for the first time. Once clicked, it becomes a Record Macro button for future use.

10. **(Windows only) Select an option in the Record Actions task pane:**

Even though this chapter focuses on VBA macros, Excel may still prompt you with options related to Office Scripts:

- **Save Script:** Saves a second copy of your macro as an Office Script.

- **Discard Script:** Discards the recorded Office Script.

- **Do Not Show Again:** Turn this checkbox on to stop Excel from creating Office Script versions of macros that you record.

  Once you select Do Not Show Again, this two-for-one option cannot be reenabled. However, this chapter does not cover Office Scripts, so you won't see any further discussion of them here.

WARNING

11. **To play your macro back, choose View ➪ Macros (Windows) or View ➪ Macros ➪ View Macros (macOS).**

The Macros dialog box opens.

12. **Click once on the HelloMacro macro and then click Run, or double-click the macro name to bypass the OK button.**

13. **The words** Hello, World! **should appear in a new cell.**

Managing Macro Security

Managing macro security in Excel can feel like trying to plug leaks in a dam with your fingers — fix one issue and another seems to pop up. Macros are powerful tools but carry risks, especially when dealing with workbooks from unknown or untrusted sources. To mitigate these risks, Excel prevents macros from being saved in .XLSX workbooks and requires them to be stored in a macro-enabled format — either .XLSM (Excel Macro-Enabled Workbook) or .XLSB (Excel Binary Workbook). Understanding and adjusting Excel's macro security settings is crucial for striking a balance between convenience and safety, ensuring your workflows remain efficient without opening the floodgates to potential issues.

Windows users have more granular control and encounter more prompts, whereas macOS users must often rely more on their judgment. The sections below walk you through saving macro-enabled workbooks, enabling trusted macros, and configuring security settings to strike the right balance between convenience and safety.

Saving macro-enabled workbooks

To preserve your code, a new or existing workbook must be saved in one of two specific formats:

1. **Activate a workbook that has one or more macros stored within it.**

2. **Choose File ⇨ Save As.**

   - Windows users see the Save As screen of Excel's Backstage View.

   - MacOS users are presented with a Save As dialog box.

3. **Select one of the macro-enabled formats from the File Type list:**

   - Excel Macro-Enabled Workbook (.xlsm)

   - Excel Binary Workbook (.xlsb)

     Excel Workbook files (.xlsx) and Excel Macro-Enabled Workbook files (.xlsm) are based on the XML format, a sibling of HTML — the predominant language used to build web pages. In contrast, Excel Binary Workbook files (.xlsb) are built on machine code, composed of 0s and 1s, resulting in a significantly smaller file size.

4. **Update the workbook name and/or file location if needed, then click Save.**

   If you modify macros in the Personal Macro Workbook, Excel prompts you to save changes when closing. For more details, see "Unpacking the Personal Macro Workbook" at the end of this chapter.

Enabling macro security

When you open a workbook containing macros in Excel for Windows, the security warning shown in Figure 16-2 appears. As Duran Duran famously put it, "The reflex is a lonely child" — and in Excel, the reflex often manifests as users compulsively clicking Enable Content, which can leave you stuck in a cycle, much like the song's enigmatic "waiting by the park."

By default, macros are disabled until you click Enable Content. Don't linger too long, though — the message bar prompt tends to vanish after a few minutes. If it disappears, the only way to restore it is to close the workbook and reopen it. And if that doesn't work, additional troubleshooting may be needed.

As the saying goes, "The road to hell is paved with good intentions." The Enable Content button is perfect for opening unfamiliar workbooks with caution but becomes a tedious hoop to jump through for workbooks containing macros you created yourself. Thankfully, Excel offers options to put that recurring prompt out to pasture.

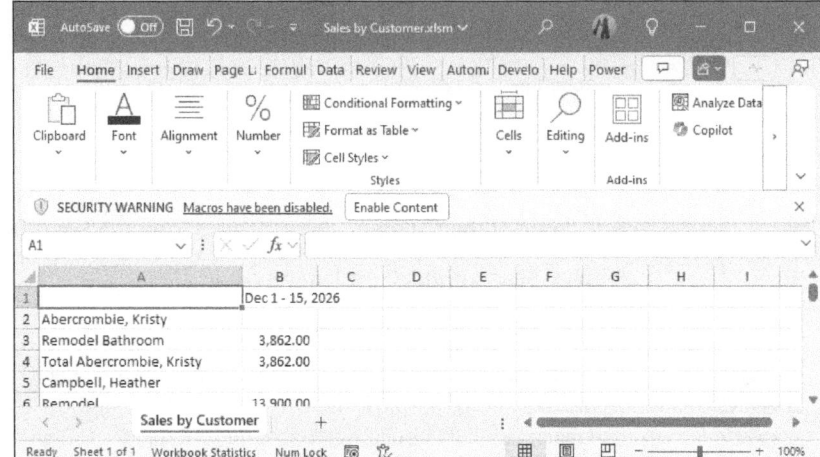

FIGURE 16-2:
A macro-related
security prompt
in Excel's
Message Bar.

Marking workbooks as trusted

Extraneous clicks take an imperceptible yet inexorable toll on us, both physically and emotionally. If there was a nail sticking out of the door frame of your front door and snagging your clothes every time you walked by, you wouldn't hesitate to nail that sucker back in. Conversely, many of us become inured to Pavlovian prompts that grab our sleeve in a similar fashion. Let's bring the hammer down on the Enable Content button in Excel for Windows:

1. **Open a workbook containing macros.**

   The Enable Content prompt appears unless you've already enabled the workbook during your current Excel session. If that's the case, you need to close Excel and reopen the workbook to see the prompt.

   WARNING

   Avoid clicking Enable Content on the Message Bar, because doing so disables the option to complete Step 2 for the current Excel session.

2. **Choose File ➪ Info ➪ Enable Content ➪ Enable Content.**

   Macros are now permanently enabled for this workbook, and the Enable Content prompt no longer appears whenever you open this workbook on this computer.

   REMEMBER

   This step must be repeated on each Windows computer where the workbook is opened.

Configuring Trust Center settings

Sure, marking a workbook as trusted is great, but have you heard about the Trust Center? It's like discovering that sliced bread isn't the greatest invention after all — bagels exist, and they're way more versatile. The Trust Center enables you to up your game by fine-tuning Excel's security settings on Windows devices:

1. **Choose File ⇨ Options ⇨ Trust Center.**

   The Trust Center section of the Excel Options dialog box opens.

2. **Click Trust Center Settings.**

   The Trust Center dialog box opens.

   REMEMBER

   If your computer is managed by an IT team, you may be restricted from adjusting some or all Trust Center settings.

3. **Choose Macro Settings.**

   The Macro Settings screen of the Trust Center dialog box appears, as shown in Figure 16-3. Most users won't need to make changes here, so this will be a quick stop.

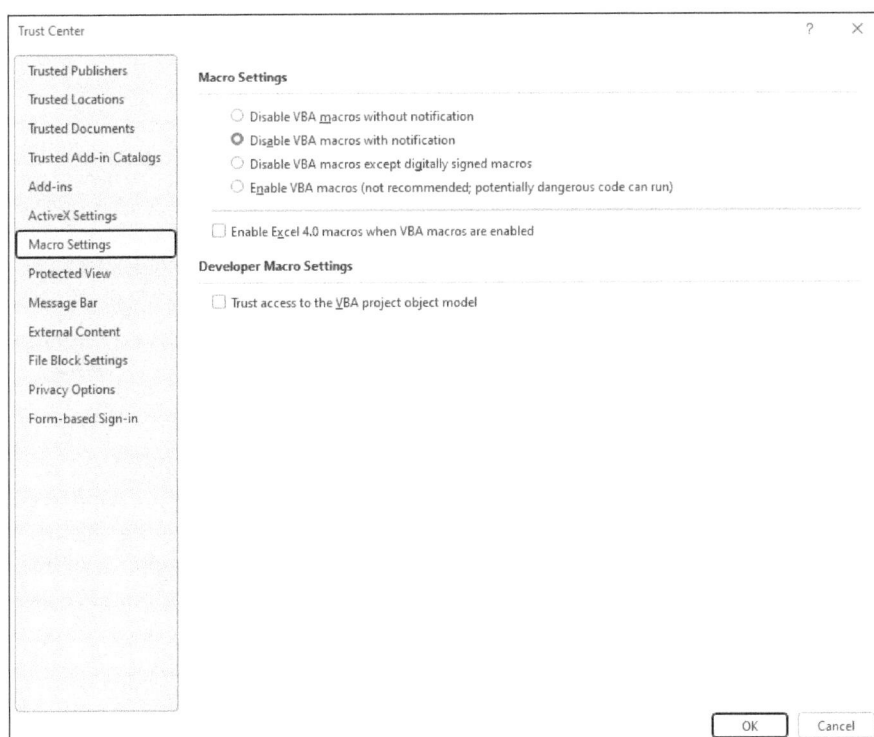

FIGURE 16-3: The Macro Settings section of the Trust Center dialog box.

4. **Set macros to "Disable VBA Macros with Notification."**

   This option permits Excel to display the Enable Content prompt on the Message bar. Alternatively:

   - The first option disables macros completely.

   - The third option enables macros only in digitally signed workbooks.

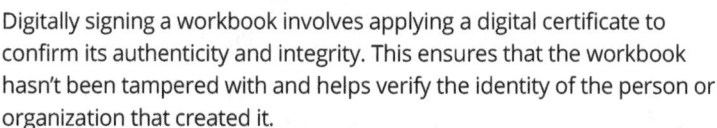

     Digitally signing a workbook involves applying a digital certificate to confirm its authenticity and integrity. This ensures that the workbook hasn't been tampered with and helps verify the identity of the person or organization that created it.

   - The fourth option? That's for those willing to answer Clint Eastwood's iconic question: "Do ya feel lucky, punk?" from *Dirty Harry*.

5. **Choose Trusted Locations in the sidebar.**

   The Trusted Locations section of the Trust Center appears.

6. **Click Add a New Location.**

   The Microsoft Trusted Location dialog box opens.

7. **Specify a trusted folder.**

   Use this dialog box to designate trusted folders on your computer or network. Workbooks containing macros from these locations bypass the Enable Content prompt.

   Check Subfolders of This Location Are Also Trusted to extend the trust to all subfolders.

8. **Click OK twice to close the Trust Center and Excel Options dialog boxes.**

Unblocking macros

This next feature may make you see red — literally. A red version of the Message Bar, shown in Figure 16-4, appears when Excel for Windows automatically flags emailed workbooks or downloaded files containing macros as "blocked." The twist? Unlike other security warnings in this chapter, clearing the block requires File Explorer unless you save the workbook to a trusted location, as discussed in the previous section.

To get unblocked in Windows (not an issue in macOS):

1. **Close the blocked workbook if it is open in Excel.**

2. **Use File Explorer to navigate to the folder where the workbook is saved.**

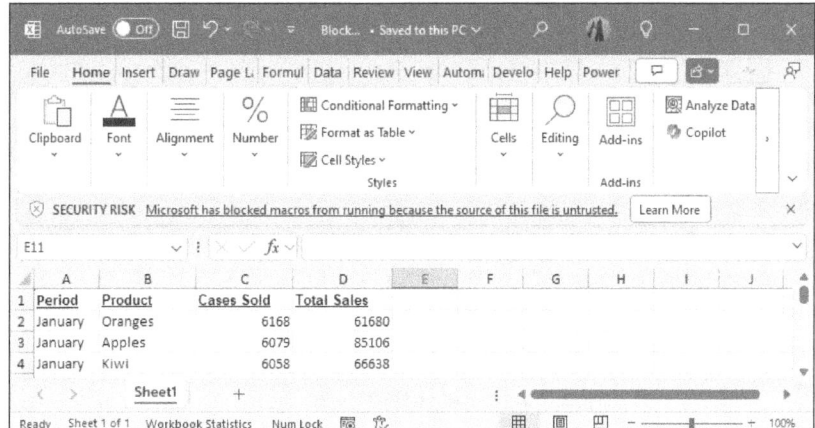

FIGURE 16-4:
The blocked
macros message
bar prompt.

3. **Right-click the workbook file and choose Properties.**

The Properties dialog box opens.

4. **Turn the Unblock checkbox off in the Security section of the General tab.**

5. **Click OK to close the dialog box and apply.**

The Unblock checkbox disappears from the Properties dialog box after you clear it and click OK or Apply.

REMEMBER

6. **Reopen the workbook in Excel and enable content if prompted.**

Maintaining Macros

After you've recorded a macro, you may need to edit or delete it as your needs change. The steps below guide you through modifying an existing macro or per-manently removing one.

Editing a macro involves the following steps:

1. **Choose View ⇨ Macros (Windows) or View ⇨ Macros ⇨ View Macros (macOS).**

The Macros dialog box opens.

2. **Select a macro (for example, HelloMacro from earlier in the chapter) and click Edit.**

The Visual Basic for Applications (VBA) Editor opens. This behind-the-scenes part of Excel is where macros reside in module sheets, editable like a Word document. Tread carefully — one stray keystroke can render a macro inoperable!

3. **Make necessary edits (for example, updating a worksheet name).**

4. **Save changes by choosing File ➪ Save.**

5. **Close the VBA Editor by clicking the Close button or choosing File ➪ Close and Return to Microsoft Excel.**

Deleting a macro requires these steps:

1. **Choose View ➪ Macros.**

   The Macros dialog box opens

2. **Select a macro and click Delete.**

3. **Click Yes to confirm that you wish to delete the macro.**

   Macro deletions cannot be undone.

WARNING

Streamlining Repetitive Tasks

Are you ready to create some code? I can't hear you! I said, *Are you ready to create some code?* That's more like it. This section features a small case study that demonstrates how to automate a helpful feature many users overlook and introduces three ways to simplify running macros. A second case study, in the upcoming "Taming the Macro Reference Beast" section, dives deeper into key considerations you'll want to keep in mind as you advance your skills.

Automating Center Across Selection

Our first macro kills two birds with one metaphorical stone by creating a macro that centers text across two or more columns — without using the dreaded Merge Cells feature. Since you're ready, let's dive in:

1. **Type** Report Heading **in cell A1 of a blank worksheet.**

2. **Type** Report Subheading **in cell A2.**

3. **Select cells A1:E2.**

   The goal here is to enter the contents of cells A1:A2 across columns A:E.

4. **Choose View ➪ Macros ➪ Record Macro, or if you're fancy, click the Macro Recording icon on Excel's Status Bar.**

   Either way, the Record Macro dialog box opens.

5. Type CenterTitle into the Macro Name field.

6. Leave the Shortcut Key field blank.

I know, the suspense must be killing you! I have to thicken the plot where I can — it's an Excel book, after all.

7. Select Personal Macro Workbook from the Store Macro In field.

This is a general-purpose macro you may want to use across all your Excel workbooks, so storing it in the Personal Macro Workbook keeps it accessible. For workbook-specific macros (e.g., copying and clearing cells), choose This Workbook or New Workbook.

8. Click OK to start the recording.

It's showtime! Let's just hope Beetlejuice isn't watching!

TIP

If you make a misstep while recording, don't panic. You can undo the action by clicking Undo on the Quick Access Toolbar or pressing Ctrl+Z (Windows) or Cmd+Z (macOS). To be clear, you can undo while recording, but you cannot undo when playing macros back. Feel free to use either your mouse or keyboard while recording — Excel transcribes actions the same way.

9. Choose Home ⇨ Format ⇨ Format Cells or press Ctrl+1 (Windows) or Cmd+1 (macOS) to open the Format Cells dialog box.

Alternatively, click the Alignment Settings button in the lower-right corner of the Alignment section on the Home tab.

10. Activate the Alignment tab of the Format Cells dialog box, and then select Center Across Selection from the Horizontal list.

11. Click OK to close the Format Cells dialog box and apply the formatting.

12. Click Stop Recording on the Status Bar or choose View ⇨ Macros drop-down ⇨ Stop Recording.

You now have a functional macro!

13. Now let's test your macro:

    a. Type Another Report Heading in cell K10.

    b. Type Another Report Subheading in cell K11.

    c. Select cells K10:Q11.

    d. Choose View ⇨ Macros (Windows) or View ⇨ Macros ⇨ View Macros (macOS).

The Macros dialog box opens.

e. Select the CenterTitle macro, and then click Run.

The text in cells K10:K11 should now be centered across cells K10:Q11.

TIP

To realign text that is centered across two or more cells, select the range and choose Home ➪ Align Left or Home ➪ Clear ➪ Clear Formats.

Assigning keyboard shortcuts to macros

If you were counting calories — err, I mean mouse clicks — at the end of the previous section, you might be thinking, wait a minute, it takes about as much effort to run the macro as it does to use the Format Cells dialog box. Right you are, grasshopper! But stick with me; we're about to cut through the clutter.

If you've been itching to learn about the mysterious Shortcut Key field in the Record Macro dialog box, your moment has arrived. Shortcut keys you assign to macros override Excel's built-in shortcuts or even your operating system's. For example, if you threw caution to the wind earlier by typing C into the Shortcut Key field — how bold of you! — you could now launch your CenterTitle macro anywhere in Excel by selecting a range of cells and pressing Ctrl+C (Windows) or Cmd+C (macOS). On the downside, you've effectively disabled your ability to copy to the clipboard. Eek!

WARNING

Think twice before assigning commonly used letters to keyboard shortcuts — you never know when someone else may open your workbook expecting one outcome (like pressing Ctrl+Z (Windows) or Cmd+Z (macOS) to undo) and instead experience a rude awakening when a macro suddenly starts running. Ask me how I know.

TECHNICAL
STUFF

Historically, the Macro Recorder couldn't replace an existing macro with an assigned keyboard shortcut, but thankfully that limitation has been lifted. Now, if only Microsoft would take it a step further by letting us edit macros in the Personal Macro Workbook without unhiding it first! To make it a reality, we need more folks to choose File ➪ Feedback ➪ Make a Suggestion and complete the online form. Together, we can make it happen!

Let's see how to assign — or unassign — keyboard shortcuts for macros:

1. **Choose View ➪ Macros (Windows) or View ➪ Macros ➪ View Macros (macOS).**

The Macros dialog box opens.

2. **Select a macro (e.g., CenterTitle), and then click Options.**

The Macro Options dialog box opens, as shown in Figure 16-5.

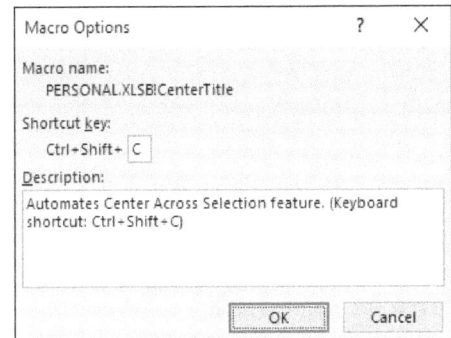

FIGURE 16-5:
The Macro
Options
dialog box.

3. **Manage the shortcut:**

   ● **Assign shortcut:** Type any letter from A to Z in the Shortcut Key field.

   In Windows, minimize overriding built-in shortcuts by typing a capital letter. In macOS, lowercase letters create Option+Cmd shortcuts, while uppercase letters use Ctrl+Shift.

   ● **Remove shortcut:** Clear the Shortcut Key field to unassign the shortcut.

4. **Use the Description field to document the shortcut (or lack thereof).**

   The contents of the Description field appear at the bottom of the Macros dialog box when you click on any macro in the list.

5. **Click OK to apply the change and close the Macro Options dialog box and Cancel to close the Macros dialog box.**

Keyboard shortcuts are efficient, but they come with risks. Beyond the possibility of overriding an Excel or operating system shortcut, there's also the challenge of remembering which shortcut you assigned to which macro. Unfortunately, Excel doesn't offer a way to generate a list of shortcut keys for your macros. The only option is to click the Options button for each macro, one by one, in the Macros dialog box.

Creating Quick Access Toolbar shortcuts

The world is full of risks, and thankfully, like a good neighbor, the Quick Access Toolbar (QAT) is there. Adding a shortcut for your macro provides insurance against certain keyboard shortcut risks:

>> **Visual cue:** Permanent icons let you run a macro with just a mouse click.

>> **Safer keyboard shortcut:** Windows users, rejoice! The QAT offers a safer way to assign shortcuts using the Alt key. Unfortunately, macOS users aren't invited to this party.

>> **Context specificity:** QAT icons can become a permanent fixture on your Excel screen or only appear when a specific workbook is active. As a bonus, workbook-specific toolbar buttons appear for other users on their computers, too.

Here's how to assign a Quick Access Toolbar shortcut to a macro:

1. **Choose File ⇨ Options ⇨ Quick Access Toolbar (Windows) or Excel ⇨ Preferences ⇨ Ribbon & Toolbar (macOS).**

   • **Windows:** The Quick Access Toolbar screen of the Excel Options dialog box opens.

   • **macOS:** The Quick Access Toolbar screen of the Excel Preferences dialog box opens.

2. **Customize the scope (Windows only):**

   • To tie the shortcut to a specific workbook, select it from the Customize Quick Access Toolbar drop-down.

   • Leave the field set to For All Documents (default) if you're assigning a shortcut to a macro in your Personal Macro Workbook.

3. **Select Macros from the Choose Commands From drop-down.**

4. **Select a macro from the list (e.g., PERSONAL.XLSB!CenterTitle) and click Add.**

5. **Click Modify.**

   The Modify Button dialog box opens.

6. **Apply optional customizations:**

   • **Choose a symbol:** Select a symbol to represent your macro.

   • **Update the Display Name:** Enter a name (spaces and punctuation are allowed).

     The Display Name appears as a screen tip when you hover over the QAT icon.

7. **Click OK twice to apply the changes.**

Your new shortcut now appears on the Quick Access Toolbar! If buyer's remorse strikes, simply right-click the shortcut and choose Remove. Windows users can tap the Alt key to reveal keyboard shortcuts for all QAT buttons.

If your keyboard has a number pad, tap (don't hold) the Alt key before typing the shortcut number; otherwise, an unexpected symbol might appear in the active cell. If you're prone to holding down the Alt key, use the number keys across the top of your keyboard instead.

Linking macros to shapes

It's time to get in shape — or, more specifically, link macros to objects like text boxes or pictures. This method works best for task-specific macros tied to specific workbooks. Linking a macro to a shape lets you assign a custom label, effectively creating a permanent on-screen button. This can make macros more accessible for casual or infrequent users of a particular spreadsheet.

Here's how to shape things up:

1. **To create a clickable shape, do the following:**

   a. **Choose Insert ⇨ Shapes or Insert ⇨ Illustrations ⇨ Shapes and then select a shape, such as Rounded Rectangles, from the shapes gallery.**

   b. **Drag your mouse over the worksheet grid, then release your left mouse button to create the shape.**

   c. **Double-click on the shape or right-click on the shape and then choose Edit Text to create a custom label.**

2. **To create a clickable text box, carry out these steps:**

   a. **Choose Insert ⇨ Text Box or Insert ⇨ Text ⇨ Text Box.**

   b. **Click inside the text box to add a custom label.**

3. **Right-click on the shape or text box and then choose Assign Macro.**

   The Assign Macro dialog box opens.

4. **Select a macro name from the list, and then click OK.**

Going forward, you can hover over the shape or text box and click it to launch the assigned macro.

Taming the Macro Reference Beast

This section offers advice on how to ask your relatives for references . . . hah! You're on your own there. But when it comes to Excel macros, how you reference cells can dramatically impact your results. Macros can store cell addresses in two ways: either as fixed (absolute) positions or as positions relative to where the macro starts. This is just one of countless ways Excel does exactly what you tell it to do, rather than what you intended. It can truly make you feel like there's a ghost in the machine.

Decoding absolute references in macros

Imagine recording a macro to format cells, only to discover later that it sometimes goes off the rails, carrying out actions in cells you never intended. Welcome to the world of absolute references in Excel macros. By default, the Macro Recorder locks in the exact cell locations used during recording, dutifully repeating the actions in those same spots. While this precision can be helpful, it often leads to unexpected surprises — like your perfectly formatted cells appearing in the wrong place, especially when you or someone else runs the macro on a different part of the worksheet. It can truly feel like your macro is possessed.

Which brings us to the movie *Beetlejuice*, where the titular ghost is summoned by saying his name three times in succession. Similarly, to banish him, his name must also be spoken three times — but that's covered later. For now, let's metaphorically invite Beetlejuice into our macro chat to explore the spectral situations that can arise when creating even a dead-simple macro. Don't worry — this phantom prankster won't haunt your macro for long.

1. **Select cell A1 within a blank worksheet.**

2. **Choose View ⇨ Macros drop-down ⇨ Record Macro, or if you're fancy, click the Macro Recording icon on Excel's Status Bar.**

Either way, the Record Macro dialog box opens.

3. **Type** BeetleMacro **into the Macro Name field.**

4. **Leave the Shortcut Key field blank, or fearlessly enter the lower-case letter *b*.**

The author of this book is not responsible for any emotional distress caused by losing the ability to bold text because you assigned this letter to a macro. Use with caution!

REMEMBER

Typing a capital B into the Shortcut Key field assigns Ctrl+Shift+B (Windows or macOS) to the macro, while typing a lowercase b assigns Ctrl+B or Option+Cmd+B, respectively.

5. **Select New Workbook from the Store Macro In field.**

Storing throwaway macros, like this one, in a new workbook makes them easy to discard — just close the workbook without saving when you're done. This helps avoid cluttering your Personal Macro Workbook.

6. **If the spirit moves you, type** `Beetlejuice, Beetlejuice, Beetlejuice` **into the Description field.**

7. **Click OK to start the recording.**

   Time to summon some macro mischief!

8. **Type** `Let the fun begin!` **in cell A1 then press Enter.**

   The cursor should move to cell A2.

9. **Type** `Until someone says 'Stop!'` **then press Enter.**

   The cursor should move to cell A3.

10. **Tap the Up arrow key once to return to cell A2.**

11. **Apply the following formatting:**

    - **Bold:** Press Ctrl+B (Windows) or Cmd+B (macOS) or select Home ⇨ Bold.

    - **Italics:** Press Ctrl+I (Windows) or Cmd+I (macOS) or select Home ⇨ Italics.

    - **Fill:** Select Home ⇨ Fill drop-down and then pick any color.

      If you need some mood music, I suggest "Any Colour You Like" from Pink Floyd's *Dark Side of the Moon*.

12. **Click Stop Recording on the Status Bar or choose View ⇨ Macros drop-down ⇨ Stop Recording.**

Now that the macro is complete, let's give it a whirl. The macro you created resides in a new workbook, but it can be executed within any open workbook if the containing workbook is also open. Here's how:

1. **Press Ctrl+N (Windows) or Cmd+N (macOS) to create a new workbook or choose File ⇨ New ⇨ Blank Workbook.**

2. **Ensure that cell A1 is selected.**

3. **Choose View ⇨ Macros or press Alt+F8 (Windows) or Fn+Option+F8 (macOS).**

   The Macros dialog box opens.

4. **Select BeetleMacro and then click Run.**

Well, well, well, it seems like there's nothing to see here! Cell A1 contains `Let the fun begin!` while cell A2 contains a formatted version of `Until someone says 'Stop!'`. Such is the fickle nature of recorded macros: If you recreate the exact conditions under which the macro was recorded, as Beetlejuice would say, "Dead-on perfect!"

But things aren't always as they appear:

1. **Press Shift+F11 (Windows) or Fn+Shift+F11 (macOS), click Insert Sheet, or choose Home ⇨ Insert ⇨ Insert Sheet.**

   A new worksheet appears within the workbook.

WARNING

   When testing macros, always use a blank worksheet or a fresh copy of the affected worksheet or workbook. This ensures you can clearly identify any changes made. Remember, macro actions cannot be undone, so proceed with caution.

2. **Select any cell *other* than A1, such as B13.**

3. **Choose View ⇨ Macros (Windows) or View ⇨ Macros ⇨ View Macros (macOS).**

   Alternatively, press Alt+F8 (Windows) or Fn+Option+F8 (macOS).

4. **Select BeetleMacro and then click Run.**

And suddenly the floor drops out. Cell B13 contains `Let the fun begin!`, while cell A2 contains the formatted version of `Until someone says 'Stop!'`. This illustrates how recorded macros default to absolute references. The macro applied formatting to the same absolute cell reference it recorded earlier (cell A2), even though you started the macro in B13. That's why things seem "off" — Excel is following your exact instructions, not your intention.

Let's go to the tape and see what happened:

 » Your cursor was already in cell A1, so the macro recorded that `Let the fun begin!` should appear in the active cell.

 » After typing in cell A1, you pressed Enter, which moved your cursor to cell A2. Here's where the disconnect started. In your mind, you may have thought, "I want `Until someone says 'Stop!'` to go in the next cell down." Excel, however, codified: "You moved to cell A2, so that's what I'll transcribe.

Sometimes, you'll feel like a nut and want the macro to act relative to where you are (relative references), and other times you won't — preferring the macro to follow the original script (absolute references). This flexibility is key to mastering macro recording. Hey, is anyone else suddenly craving chocolate?

Switching to relative references

Although it appears that the Macro Recorder wants to trap your cell references in leg irons, you can channel the musician Sting and declare, "Free, free, set them free!" By using relative references, you liberate your macros to act based on their starting position, giving them the flexibility to perform actions wherever you need them.

Now, let's set your macro free by switching to relative references so you can experience the difference firsthand:

1. **Press Shift+F11 (Windows) or Fn+Shift+F11 (macOS), click Insert Sheet, or choose Home ⇨ Insert drop-down ⇨ Insert Sheet.**

   A new worksheet appears within the workbook.

2. **Devilishly select any cell other than A1, such as D6.**

REMEMBER

   When creating general-purpose macros like this one, be mindful to pre-position the cursor *before* you start recording the macro. Conversely, if you want the macro to act on a specific cell, start in a different cell, and then, once recording begins, select the target cell and carry out your actions.

3. **Choose View ⇨ Macros drop-down ⇨ Use Relative References.**

   This setting ensures that Excel records "move down one cell" when you press Enter, instead of "move to cell A2."

4. **Choose View ⇨ Macros drop-down ⇨ Record Macro, or if you're fancy, click the Macro Recording icon on Excel's Status Bar.**

   Either way, the Record Macro dialog box opens.

5. **Type `BeetleMacro` into the Macro Name field.**

   In this case we're reusing the same macro name as before because our goal is to replace the existing macro.

6. **Engage with the Shortcut Key field, or don't.**

   No judgment here.

7. **Select This Workbook from the Store Macro In field.**

   Storing it here, as opposed to in a new workbook, ensures you don't create dueling macros, which could make you feel like your banjo just broke a string.

8. **If the spirit moved you earlier, type `Beetlejuice, Beetlejuice, Beetlejuice` again in the Description field.**

   Think of this second invocation as a sage smudge, banishing bad energy from your macro.

9. **Click OK to begin recording.**

One of two outcomes occurs:

- **A confirmation prompt appears:** Click Yes to overwrite the existing macro and proceed with the recording, as shown in Figure 16-6, or click No to return to the Record Macro dialog box.

- **No confirmation prompt appears:** This happens if you typed a variation of the macro name or chose to store the macro in a different workbook, either intentionally or accidentally. You can continue with the recording or stop the Macro Recorder and start over from Step 1 if needed.

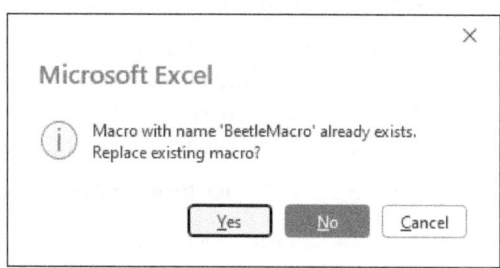

FIGURE 16-6:
The confirmation prompt for replacing an existing macro.

In the dialog box:

Microsoft Excel

ⓘ Macro with name 'BeetleMacro' already exists.
Replace existing macro?

Yes   No   Cancel

10. **Type** Things have a way of working out... **and press Enter.**

The cursor moves to cell D7.

11. **Type** ...if you just give them a chance!

The cursor moves to cell D8.

12. **Tap the Up arrow key once to return to cell D7.**

13. **Apply the following formatting:**

- **Bold:** Press Ctrl+B (Windows) or Cmd+B (macOS) or select Home ⇨ Bold.

- **Italics:** Press Ctrl+I (Windows) or Cmd+I (macOS) or select Home ⇨ Italics.

- **Fill:** Select Home ⇨ Fill drop-down and then pick any color.

14. **Click Stop Recording on the Status Bar or choose View ⇨ Macros drop-down ⇨ Stop Recording.**

And now, cue the extended drumroll (or, if you're not alone, consider air drumming to the iconic drum break from Phil Collins's "In the Air Tonight"). You're about to witness some macro magic:

1. **Press Shift+F11, click Insert Sheet, or choose Home ⇨ Insert ⇨ Insert Sheet.**

2. **Select any cell other than D6.**

   In this case, cell A1 is A-OK.

3. **Choose View ⇨ Macros or press Alt+F8 (Windows) or Fn+Option+F8 (macOS).**

   The Macros dialog box opens.

4. **Select BeetleMacro and then click Run.**

   And just like that, the ghost is gone! Your macro now works exactly as intended — no unexpected hauntings this time.

Feel free to run the macro on other cells, no matter where you go, the adage in the two cells rings true.

TIP There's so much more I could share with you about VBA macros, but my editor insists I stick to the basics. If you're eager to dive deeper, I highly recommend Dick Kusleika's *Microsoft 365 Excel VBA Programming For Dummies*. It's the perfect guide for taking your macro skills to the next level.

OPTIMIZING USE RELATIVE REFERENCES

The Use Relative References command functions as a toggle, much like Bold or Italics. However, it's far less intuitive to determine if it's enabled. When you select the command, the menu vanishes, leaving you to rely on a barely noticeable border around the command on the Macros drop-down menu — that's your clue it's turned on.

For a clearer indicator, in Windows right-click any ribbon tab and choose Customize Ribbon, or in macOS, choose Excel ⇨ Preferences ⇨ Ribbon and Toolbar. Enable the Developer tab by checking its box, then click OK. The Developer tab now appears in your ribbon, offering one-click access to starting and stopping macro recording, as well as a more visible Use Relative References command with shaded highlighting when enabled.

Once turned on, Use Relative References remains active until you exit Excel. You can toggle it on and off as needed, allowing a mix of absolute and relative references in the same macro.

Unpacking the Personal Macro Workbook

Ahem, pardon the intrusion — we're about to get personal here. Rest assured, your secrets are safe with me. The Personal Macro Workbook is a run-of-the-mill spreadsheet with two special traits:

>> **Self-launching:** The Personal Macro Workbook resides in a special startup folder, ensuring it opens automatically whenever Excel starts.

>> **Hidden:** The Personal Macro Workbook stays behind the scenes so it doesn't disrupt your workflow — or accidentally get closed. Closing it prevents access to any macros stored inside.

You may need to unhide the Personal Macro Workbook from time to time to carry out one or more of the following tasks:

>> **File backup:** Even with regular hard drive backups, it's a good idea to periodically back up this workbook manually. This also gives you the option to share your macros with colleagues or to a new device when it's time to upgrade your tech.

>> **Maintaining macros:** Excel inexplicably doesn't allow you to delete or edit macros that reside within the Personal Macro Workbook unless you first unhide the workbook. No other workbook is subject to this curious constraint.

Unhiding the Personal Macro Workbook

You may need to unhide the Personal Macro Workbook for tasks such as editing, backing up, or deleting macros:

1. **Choose View ⇨ Unhide Window (to the right of Freeze Panes in Excel for Windows).**

   The workbook version of the Unhide dialog box opens.

   If Unhide Window is disabled, the Personal Macro Workbook doesn't exist yet. It is created the first time you use the Macro Recorder.

REMEMBER

2. **Press Enter or click OK to unhide the workbook.**

   The Personal.xlsb workbook is now visible. While it includes a worksheet you can use to store information, its primary purpose is to act as a programming code repository.

3. **To edit or delete macros, see "Maintaining Macros" earlier in this chapter, or to back up the Personal Macro Workbook, do the following:**

   a) **Choose File ⇨ Save As.**

   b) **Save a copy the workbook in a new location.**

   c) **Close and then reopen Excel.**

   Always close and reopen Excel after backing up the Personal Macro Workbook to avoid accidentally working on the backup instead of the live copy.

4. **When you finish working with your macros, rehide the workbook by doing this:**

   a) **Activate the Personal.xlsb workbook.**

   b) **Choose View ⇨ Hide Window.**

   The Personal.xlsb workbook is now hidden.

5. **Save and close any unrelated workbooks in Excel.**

6. **Exit Excel, ensuring you click Save when prompted.**

   Keep an eye out for the prompt in Figure 16-7, which asks if you want to save changes to the Personal Macro Workbook. If you haven't made any changes worth saving, feel free to click Don't Save.

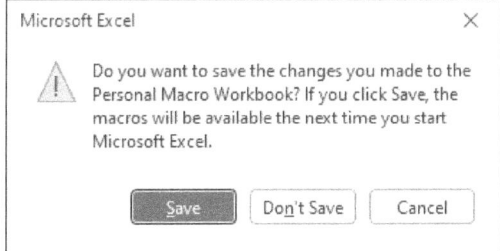

FIGURE 16-7:
The save prompt for the Personal Macro Workbook.

Transferring the Personal Macro Workbook to another computer

Follow these steps to transfer your Personal Macro Workbook to a new device:

1. **Create a backup of the workbook as described above and transfer the copy to the new device.**

2. **On the new device, use the Macro Recorder to create a basic macro (for example, HelloMacro from earlier in the chapter).**

3. **Unhide the Personal Macro Workbook:**

   a) **Choose View ⇨ Unhide Window.**

      The workbook version of the Unhide dialog box opens.

   b) **Press Enter or click OK to unhide the workbook.**

      The Personal.xlsb workbook appears onscreen.

4. **Choose File ⇨ Close to close the workbook and then click Yes to save changes.**

5. **Choose File ⇨ Open and select the backup copy of the workbook.**

6. **Save the workbook to the appropriate startup folder:**

   - **Windows:** C:\Users\<YourUsername>\AppData\Roaming\Microsoft\Excel\XLSTART

     The AppData folder is hidden by default. To access it, enable viewing hidden files and folders in File Explorer by checking Hidden Items in the View or Options tab.

   - **macOS:** ~/Library/Group Containers/UBF8T346G9.Office/User Content/Startup/Excel

7. **Choose View ⇨ Hide Window to hide the workbook.**

8. **Save and close the workbook and any unrelated workbooks in Excel.**

9. **Exit Excel, ensuring you click Save when prompted.**

You're now free to reopen Excel and revel in your newly transferred automation!

Recovering Discarded Macros

Muscle memory is a double-edged sword — sometimes our fingers move faster than our brains. Submitted for your approval (to borrow a line from Rod Serling of *The Twilight Zone*): A hapless Excel user staring at their screen in disbelief. They've reflexively clicked Save on the prompt in Figure 16-8 and now believe the macro they painstakingly created has vanished into the ether. But before panic sets in, there's a twist — this is The Twilight Zone, after all: As long as the workbook remains open in Excel, our mythical user can still recover their work and avoid a downward spiral into a cone of frustration.

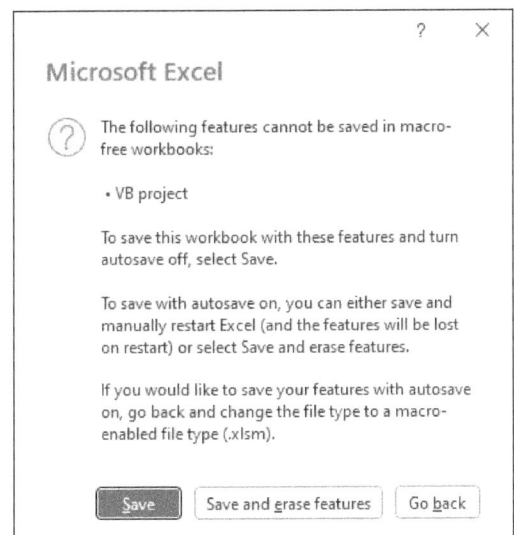

FIGURE 16-8:
The prompt that
asks if you want
to throw your
macro away.

Let's do a practice run so you can stay cool, calm, and collected should this ever happen to you:

1. **Choose View ⇨ Macros drop-down ⇨ Record Macro, or click the Macro Recording icon on Excel's Status Bar.**

    The Record Macro dialog box opens.

2. **Type** Redemption **into the Macro Name field.**

3. **Select New Workbook from the Store Macro In field.**

4. **Click OK to start the recording.**

    (No fluff or chitchat this time around.)

5. **Type some text into cell A1.**

    If you need inspiration, Arthur Brown famously sang, "I am the god of hellfire," in his song "Fire." In author-speak, that's foreshadowing for the triumph you'll feel in just a moment.

6. **To stop recording, choose View ⇨ Macros drop-down ⇨ Stop Recording or click the square Stop Recording icon within Excel's Status Bar.**

7. **Click the Save button on the Quick Access Toolbar, press Ctrl+S (Windows) or Cmd+S (macOS) or choose File ⇨ Save As.**

    - Windows users see the Save As screen of Excel's Backstage View.

    - MacOS users are presented with a Save As dialog box.

    In the immortal words of Fleetwood Mac, you can "Go Your Own Way."

8. **Choose a name and/or location for the workbook, then click Save.**

I suggest keeping the default name (e.g., Book1.xlsx) and saving it to your desktop for easy cleanup later.

9. **Since this is just a practice run, click Save when the chatty prompt in Figure 16-8 appears in Windows or Yes in the simpler macOS warning.**

Your workbook is saved but remains open in Excel.

In a real-world scenario, your best choice here is to click Go Back (Windows) or No (macOS). This avoids creating two copies of your workbook — something that can quickly cause confusion ("Where'd my macro go?"). More importantly, it ensures you don't inadvertently put your hard work at risk.

Clicking Save and Erase leaves you out in the cold. That option saves your workbook but then closes it, eliminating the loophole we're about to exploit.

10. **Now let out a good "oh no!" (just for practice, of course) as you verify your macro by choosing View ⇨ Macros.**

Like a trusty horse returning to the corral, good ole Redemption is right there, ready and waiting. Now get along, little dogie, and going forward use the Macro-Enabled Excel Workbook or Excel Binary Workbook formats for saving your work permanently.

5

The Part of Tens

Save time with ten keyboard shortcuts.

Master ten disaster recovery techniques.

IN THIS CHAPTER

» **Undoing and redoing tasks**

» **Saving and closing workbooks**

» **Selecting data and navigating worksheets**

» **Formula bar shortcuts**

» **Managing browser tabs**

Chapter **17**

Ten Timesaving Keyboard Shortcuts

Keyboard shortcuts are your secret weapon against the soul-crushing tedium of spreadsheet work. This chapter arms you with ten of my favorite Excel keyboard shortcuts — because who has time for menus? — along with an array of bonus shortcuts to turbocharge your efficiency.

REMEMBER

Depending upon your keyboard and operating system, you may have to press Fn to access the F1-F12 keys.

TIP

Psst! Want a stash of 50 Excel shortcuts? In Windows, choose File ⇨ New, type Shortcuts in the search box, and press Enter. Pick the Windows or macOS template. click the template, and boom — you've got a shortcut cheat sheet. In macOS, download the Chapter 17 Fifty Keyboard Shortcuts for macOS workbook from www.dummies.com/go/excelfd and open it in Excel. I can't even begin to explain why this isn't possible directly within Excel for macOS. For the full Monty, choose Help ⇨ Help (Windows) or Help ⇨ Excel Help (macOS), type Keyboard Shortcuts in Excel in the search field, and press Enter.

Undoing Actions

The Undo command on the Quick Access Toolbar is your personal time machine, letting you backtrack up to 100 missteps — er, purposeful actions — in Excel. Click it repeatedly, or slam Ctrl+Z (Windows) or Cmd+Z (macOS) like you're deleting evidence. Need a bigger rewind? The Undo drop-down menu lets you wipe out multiple blunders in one go.

TIP

Windows users can press Alt, followed by the number displayed in the screen tip for Undo, then use the down arrow to select their regrets — I mean, actions — to undo. Hit Enter and pretend it never happened.

REMEMBER

When editing text or a formula within a cell or the formula bar, Undo gets stingy — you can only reverse a single action. No multi-step rewinds here, so type carefully (or brace for regret). But wait, it gets worse: Certain actions wipe your Undo history clean. Delete, copy, or move a worksheet? Remove subtotals? There's no going back. You can still undo actions taken after these, but anything from before is lost to the spreadsheet void.

Repeating and Reversing Commands

Ah, the sneaky double life of Ctrl+Y (Windows) or Cmd+Y (macOS) — it's not just for redoing actions; it can also repeat them.

>> **Reversing:** Ever wish you could un-undo a brilliant-but-accidentally-reversed move? The Redo command, your digital do-over, restores up to 100 undone actions. Undo freely, ponder, then hit Ctrl+Y (Windows) or Cmd+Y (macOS) to march back. In Windows, the Redo drop-down lets you pick from 100 sequential actions. On macOS, you can redo 100 actions, but only one at a time. Just remember, Redo is disabled when there's nothing left to reverse.

TIP

Windows users can navigate the drop-down menu without touching the mouse. Just press Alt, followed by the number shown in the screen tip for Redo, and then use the down arrow to scroll through the list of actions. After you find the moment in time you want to revisit, press Enter to confirm your selection and watch Excel dutifully restore your past decisions up through that point.

>> **Repeating:** Unlike pasting, which becomes unavailable after performing another action that clears the clipboard, or redoing, which is limited to the number of undone actions available, repeating an action has no such constraints. You can repeat the last repeatable action to your heart's content

until you perform a different repeatable action, at which point Excel dutifully updates its memory to the new task. For example, if you apply a yellow highlight to cell A1, you can move to cell A5 and use the shortcut to apply the same formatting. However, you can't type `Excel is Fun` in cell A2 and then use the shortcut to insert that text elsewhere. To reuse content like this, you need to copy and paste.

Saving Smarter

 If I had a dollar for every Excel workbook that unexpectedly closed on me over the course of my career, I'd be drafting this book from my own secluded island. To save a workbook, use File ➪ Save, click Save on the Quick Access Toolbar, or keep your workflow uninterrupted by pressing Ctrl+S (Windows) or Cmd+S (macOS). For a better safety net, Chapter 18 covers saving to cloud-based drives, with OneDrive or SharePoint enabling the AutoSave (Chapter 1) feature.

 To open the Save As dialog box, select File ➪ Save As or press F12 (Windows) or Cmd+Shift+S (macOS).

TIP

Closing Workbooks Efficiently

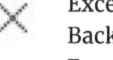 Excel's "death by a thousand cuts" is real, and Exhibit A is closing workbooks. Back in the good old days, there were two close buttons in Windows — one for Excel and one for the active workbook. Then came Excel 2013, merging them into a single button. Click Close with just one workbook open? Boom, Excel's gone. No problem if it's Miller Time, but otherwise, enjoy the relaunch ritual.

I dodge this nonsense by pressing Ctrl+W (Windows) or Cmd+W (macOS) to close just the active workbook, handling any Save prompt as needed. Excel stays open, ready for whatever is next.

Selecting Data Quickly

In Excel, the *current region* is the block of filled cells surrounding your selection, stopping at the first blank row or column. Think of it as a fenced-in area — your data stays together until a gap breaks the boundary.

To highlight the whole region in one move, select any cell in the data and press Ctrl+A (Windows) or Cmd+A (macOS). Excel selects everything connected, stopping at the blank rows and columns — like a digital coloring book that won't let you stray outside the lines. This trick is great for sorting, filtering, formatting, or copying data efficiently.

If you prefer using menus:

1. **Select any cell in your dataset.**

2. **Choose Home ⇨ Find & Select ⇨ Go To Special.**

   The Go To Special dialog box appears.

3. **Select Current Region and then click OK.**

TIP

In Windows, double-clicking the Current Region skips the extra click, instantly selecting the area and closing the dialog box — no extra button mashing required.

Duplicating Data Instantly

Sure, the Fill Handle is a great way to copy data, but have you tried these keyboard shortcuts?

TIP

» **Copy Down:** Select two or more cells and then press Ctrl+D (Windows) or Cmd+D (macOS) to fill the contents of the first row down the column(s).

Press Ctrl+' (Windows) or Cmd+' (macOS) to copy the contents — not the formatting — from the cell above.

» **Copy Right:** Select two or more cells and then press Ctrl+R (Windows) or Cmd+R (macOS) to transfer the contents of the first column across the row(s).

» **Fill a range:** Select multiple cells, enter or edit data in the first cell, and press Ctrl+Enter (Windows) or Cmd+Enter (macOS) to apply it to all selected cells at once.

Jumping to the Start of a Workbook

There's no place like home! Press Ctrl+Home (Windows) or Fn+Ctrl+Left Arrow (macOS) to jump to the top-left corner of the worksheet. If no panes are frozen, this means A1, but if panes are frozen, the first nonfrozen cell is selected, saving you from endless scrolling. See Chapter 4 for details on freezing and unfreezing rows and columns.

TIP

Pressing Home (Windows) or Fn+Left Arrow (macOS) moves you to either column A of the current row or the first nonfrozen column if panes are frozen.

Switching Between Enter and Edit Modes

Some keyboard shortcuts feel like a hall of mirrors — what they do depends on where you use them. The same shortcut can pull double (or triple) duty depending on the context. Before we get to the nitty-gritty of the shortcut, let's discuss editing modes, which apply within worksheet cells, the formula bar, and range input (RefEdit) fields within Excel dialog boxes. For simplicity, all three are considered a field:

>> **Edit Mode:** Actively editing a field, allowing navigation within the field using the arrow keys. Cells default to this mode — Edit appears in the Status Bar.

>> **Point Mode:** Used for highlighting and selecting cell ranges — dialog box fields and formula arguments default to this mode. Instead of typing a reference, you can click a cell or drag across a range. Point is displayed in the Status Bar when active.

>> **Enter Mode:** Dialog box fields sneakily switch to this mode when activated. Pressing an arrow key inserts a reference to an adjacent cell instead of moving the cursor. Enter appears on the Status Bar when this mode is active.

And now for a trip through the hall of mirrors, starting with a worksheet formula. If you're working within a worksheet formula:

1. **Create some sample data in a blank worksheet:**

   - **A1:** 100

   - **A2:** 100

2. **Type =SUM(into cell A3.**

   Enter appears in the status bar, signaling that you can use the arrow keys to select a range.

3. **Tap the Up Arrow key once to select cell A2, and then hold Shift while tapping Up Arrow again to select cells A1:A2.**

   Point mode becomes active.

4. **Type) to close the formula.**

Enter mode becomes active. Press an arrow key to save the formula and move to another cell, or press F2 (Windows) or Cmd+U (macOS) to switch to Edit mode, allowing you to navigate within the formula using the left and right arrow keys.

If you're working within a range input field in a dialog box in Windows:

1. **Select cells B1:B2, then Data ⇨ Line or Data ⇨ Sparklines ⇨ Line.**

The Sparklines dialog box opens.

2. **The Data Range field is activated and Enter appears on the status bar. Tap the Left Arrow key to select cell A1, hold Shift, then tap Down Arrow to cell A2.**

Point mode becomes active.

3. **Click in the Data Range field.**

Edit mode is activated.

4. **To navigate within the Data Range field, press F2 to switch to Edit mode.**

5. **Click OK to create sparklines (covered in more detail in Chapter 12) or click Cancel to move along.**

Excel seamlessly switches between these modes based on your actions, making it easy to unintentionally sabotage formulas and ranges — until you know what's happening behind the scenes.

Toggling Cell Reference Types

Chapter 2 covers the nuances of cell reference types in more detail, but don't sleep on the F4 (Windows) or Cmd+T (macOS) shortcuts, unless you *enjoy* manually inserting $ into your formulas. No matter where a cell or range reference appears — whether in a worksheet cell, the formula bar, or a range input field within a dialog box — this shortcut cycles through the following reference types:

>> **$A$1 (Absolute):** Locks both the column and row when the copying the formula.

>> **$A1 (Mixed):** Fixes the column, but the row shifts when copying.

>> **A$1 (Mixed):** Fixes the row, but the column shifts when copying.

>> **A1 (Relative):** Both the column and row adjust when copying.

REMEMBER

Want to lock down a range in a formula, like A1:A10? Hit the shortcut *immediately* after selecting it to transform it into $A$1:$A$10. Then type a comma or parenthesis, and then backspace. Now the shortcut gives you A1:$A$10, anchoring only the end. *Oops.* To fix it, click the argument name in the function screen tip, and then use the shortcut to apply the absolute reference correctly.

There's another hall of mirrors for Windows users:

>> Press F4 when navigating a worksheet to repeat the last action (a handy alternative to Ctrl+Y).

>> Press Ctrl+F4 to close the active window or workbook (instead of Ctrl+W).

>> Press Alt+F4 to shut down Excel entirely — you'll be prompted to save any unsaved workbooks. With that said, macOS users can press Cmd+Q to close Excel.

Breaking Up Long Formulas and Text

You can create a line break within Excel's formula bar or a worksheet cell by pressing Alt+Enter (Windows) or Ctrl+Option+Enter (macOS). This inserts a non-printable carriage return, allowing you to control how text appears within a single cell or the formula bar:

1. **Type** 2026 Product Sales **in cell A1 of a blank worksheet.**

The text overflows into column B.

2. **Select cell A1, then choose Home ⇨ Wrap Text.**

The text wraps onto multiple lines and will adjust automatically if the column width changes.

3. **In cell A3, manually enter line breaks:**

a) **Type** 2026, **then press Alt+Enter (Windows) or Ctrl+Option+Enter (macOS).**

b) **Type** Product, **then press the shortcut again.**

c) **Type** Sales, **and then press Enter.**

The text wraps onto three rows in the column and remains unaffected by column width changes.

This method is useful for creating structured text inside a single cell without relying on Wrap Text. You can insert line breaks within lengthy formulas the same way, making them much easier to read and understand.

TIP

You may need to resize the formula bar to see wrapped text or long formulas. Click the Expand Formula Bar button on the right or drag the bottom edge of the formula bar with your mouse to adjust its height.

TECHNICAL STUFF

Use `CHAR(10)` to force a line break within results generated by a formula, e.g., enter this formula `=2026&CHAR(10)& "Product "&CHAR(10)& "Sales"` then apply Wrap Text to display each part on a separate line within the same cell.

IN THIS CHAPTER

» **Stabilizing your Windows operating system**

» **Setting up automatic backups**

» **Reverting to earlier workbook states**

» **Implementing password security**

» **Reviewing the edits made to a workbook**

Chapter **18**

Ten Disaster Recovery Techniques

t takes only a small slip of the keyboard or mouse — or an ill-timed power outage — to cause your spreadsheet to vanish without being saved. Sometimes, it's just bad luck: Excel decides to test your patience with data corruption or inexplicable changes to critical workbooks.

The first three sections in this chapter represent a time-tested series of steps that are my go-to whenever anything odd surfaces in Excel, although the first two are Windows-specific. The other seven sections provide strategies to either recover from spreadsheet disasters or avoid them altogether — because prevention is way less stressful than damage control.

Deleting Temporary Files

Mac users can skip this section, but Windows users take note. Windows loves creating temporary files — little digital breadcrumbs left behind by the operating system and various applications to handle installations, updates, and other tasks. In theory, these files should vanish when their job is done. In reality? They pile up like forgotten leftovers in the back of the fridge. Over time, this clutter can make Excel unstable or even prone to crashing.

If Excel acts up, it's time to take out the trash, digitally speaking:

1. **Open the Start menu, type** `Disk Cleanup` **in the search bar, and then press Enter.**

   The Disk Cleanup: Drive Selection dialog box opens.

2. **Choose a drive from the list, typically C:, and then click OK.**

   A status window appears briefly, followed by the Disk Cleanup dialog box.

3. **Scroll down the list and choose Temporary Files.**

   REMEMBER

   Don't mix up *Temporary Internet Files* with *Temporary Files*. Temporary Internet Files help speed up web browsing but have no impact on Excel. You can delete them if you want, but it won't make Excel run any better.

4. **Scroll down the list and select Temporary Files.**

5. **Click OK to begin the Disk Cleanup process.**

   Another Disk Cleanup status window appears briefly and is then replaced by the Disk Cleanup dialog box.

6. **Click Skip if you are notified that any files are in use.**

I clear out my temporary files a couple of times a month to enhance Excel's stability. Here's a quicker method that I often use:

1. **Click Start, type** `%temp%`**, and then press Enter.**

   A File Explorer window opens to your Temporary Files folder.

2. **Click on any file within the folder, and then press Ctrl+A to select all temporary files and folders.**

3. **Press Delete on your keyboard to remove the selected files.**

   If some files are in use, click Skip to bypass them.

It's normal for some files to remain, as they may be in use by the operating system or active applications. The goal is to keep the number of files minimal — ideally in the dozens. When the number of temporary files starts reaching the thousands, strange behaviors can occur on your computer, potentially affecting performance and stability.

If you're familiar with auto-run batch files, you can automate this process by using the following DOS command to purge the temporary files folder every time you log in to your computer:

```
del /q /f /s %Temp%\*.*
```

Repairing Damaged Workbooks

Excel workbooks can sometimes harbor low levels of data corruption that manifests unpredictable glitches — like ghosts in the machine. A good next step is to use the repair utility that is built into Excel's Open dialog box — another Windows exclusive:

1. **Choose File ➪ Open ➪ Browse or press Ctrl+O.**

   The Open dialog box appears.

2. **Click *once* on the workbook that you wish to repair.**

   Avoid double-clicking, as doing so opens the workbook without repairing it.

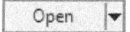

3. **Click the Open drop-down and then choose Open and Repair.**

4. **When prompted, click Repair.**

If the workbook isn't catastrophically damaged, a confirmation prompt reports that the repair was successful. Otherwise, you may be notified that the workbook cannot be repaired.

The Extract Data option in the Repair prompt strips all formatting from the workbook but preserves the formulas and data. However, in my experience, if Repair doesn't fix the issue, Extract Data doesn't either.

Windows users can choose Review ➪ Check Performance to open the Workbook Performance task pane. If prompted, click Optimize All to remove excess formatting, unneeded metadata, and unused styles — issues that can lead to frustration if left unchecked. Mac users aren't completely out in the cold — open your workbook in Excel for the Web and then choose Review ➪ Performance.

Checking for Updates

Microsoft 365 continuously updates itself, ensuring users always have the latest features, security patches, and performance improvements without manual installation. Updates occur in the background, delivering new tools, fixes, and protections automatically. Features roll out gradually, while critical security updates apply immediately. Business users benefit from admin controls that allow IT teams to manage update timing for compatibility. This self-updating model keeps Microsoft 365 modern, secure, and efficient with minimal user intervention.

With that said, sometimes patches don't install as expected, or an update fixes one issue while introducing new ones. If Excel is misbehaving, it's worth checking for updates to see if a fix is available:

>> **Windows:** Choose File ⇨ Account ⇨ Update Options ⇨ Check for Updates. If you don't see an Update Options button, ask your IT team for assistance. Otherwise, install any updates if prompted or wait while Excel installs them automatically.

>> **macOS:** Choose Help ⇨ Check for Updates to launch Microsoft AutoUpdate, and then click Update if updates are available. If Check for Updates doesn't appear on the Help menu, check the following:

- If you installed Excel via the Mac App Store, updates are managed there. Open the App Store, go to Updates, and then check for Excel updates.

- Download and install the latest version of Microsoft AutoUpdate from the Microsoft web site.

Tracking Modifications with Version Numbers

This deceptively simple trick has been my trusty sidekick throughout my career as a spreadsheet consultant. Whether I'm wrangling a personal project — like the webinar content manager I cobbled together 15 years ago — or teaming up on a client's automation tool, I always slap a version number onto the file name.

For example, I might christen the first draft of an Aged Receivable Analysis Tool as `Aged Receivable Analysis Tool 1.00.xlsx`. Each time I unleash a new iteration, I bump up the version number. This keeps everyone on the same page (at least the same spreadsheet), ensuring the latest version is easy to find, while leaving a paper trail (or fallback version) in case something in the fresh update goes sideways.

Backing Up to Cloud-Based Drives

One of the best ways to keep your spreadsheets from vanishing into the void is saving them to a cloud-based drive like OneDrive or SharePoint. Microsoft 365 users get 1 terabyte of OneDrive storage, so unless you're hoarding every spreadsheet you've ever made, space isn't a concern. Stashing your files in the cloud also unlocks AutoSave, which quietly saves your work as you go. And if you ever need to roll back to an earlier version — whether to recover lost data or unto a questionable decision — you can click the workbook name in Excel's title bar and select Version History to browse past versions side by side the current one.

REMEMBER

AutoSave only works with workbooks stored online. But don't worry — if your internet connection drops or you're off the grid, Excel saves your work locally and then syncs it back to the cloud after you're reconnected. Ages ago, Excel had an AutoSave add-in for local files, but that relic has long been retired.

Here's how to enable AutoSave:

1. **Toggle the AutoSave command on the Quick Access Toolbar.**

   The How Do I Turn On AutoSave dialog box appears.

2. **Select a location, such as OneDrive — Personal.**

   Your workbook is uploaded to the cloud.

After your workbook is safely in the cloud, it's wise to delete or rename any local copies — unless you enjoy the thrill of accidentally editing the wrong version and wondering why your boss can't see your updates. At that point, the File ⇨ Save and File ⇨ Save As commands consolidate into a single File ⇨ Save a Copy command, which lets you to save a workbook back to your device or local network.

WARNING

AutoSave doesn't work with password-protected Excel workbooks (discussed later in this chapter) because it requires real-time access, and because passwords must be entered manually, the feature is disabled. It also doesn't work with read-only files — workbooks that have been restricted to prevent accidental changes. If a file is marked as read-only, you need to save a copy or remove the restriction before AutoSave can kick in.

Ensuring Safety with Always Create Backup

I'm starting to feel like a broken record, but here's another tip that's just for the Windows users — because apparently, Excel loves playing favorites. If you prefer — or have no choice but — to keep your Excel workbooks tucked away on your device or local network, you can set up a limited safety net by preserving the last saved copy. This setting must be enabled one workbook at a time — no sweeping changes here — and the backup files cozy up in the same folder as the original. It's not the flashiest feature, and it's certainly not well-known, but when your workbook takes an unexpected nosedive, you'll be glad this unsung hero was quietly watching your back.

Enabling Always Create Backup

Here's how to set up an automatic backup for a workbook:

1. **Open the workbook that you wish to back up regularly.**

2. **Choose File ⇨ Save As ⇨ Browse (Windows) or press F12.**

   The Save As dialog box opens.

3. **Choose Tools ⇨ General Options.**

   The General Options dialog box opens.

4. **As shown in Figure 18-1, check the box labeled Always Create Backup.**

5. **Click OK to close the General Options dialog box.**

6. **In the Save As dialog box, specify a new name or file location if needed, and then click Save to finalize the backup setup.**

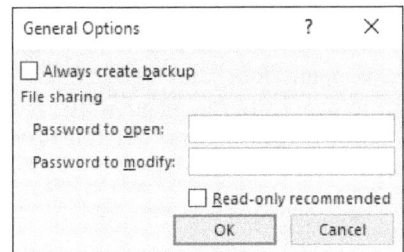

FIGURE 18-1:
The General
Options
dialog box.

To test this feature, save your workbook in the usual way — choose File ➪ Save, clicking the Save command on the Quick Access Toolbar, or smash Ctrl+S like it owes you money. A backup copy magically appears in the same folder as the active workbook and updates each time you save, like a trusty sidekick ready to bail you out of a spreadsheet disaster.

Accessing an automatic backup

Here's where things get a bit unusual. Excel automatically assigns the .XLK file extension to backups, but there's a small quirk when you try to open them:

1. **Choose File ➪ Open ➪ Browse or press Ctrl+O.**

   The Open dialog box appears.

2. **Select the backup workbook.**

   Backup workbooks have the prefix **Backup Of** and the .XLK extension, which may be hidden by your operating system.

3. **Click Yes when prompted, as shown in Figure 18-2.**

   Oddly, Excel doesn't recognize the .XLK extension it assigns, but you can safely open the backup workbook.

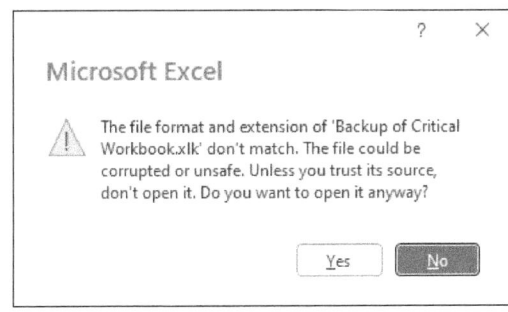

FIGURE 18-2:
Excel treats
workbook
backups as
potentially
malicious.

You can now work in the backup copy just as you would with any Excel workbook — and even keep it open alongside the active copy since they have different names. If you want to overwrite the original file with the backup, you need to close the live copy first — Excel won't let you pull a switcheroo while the original is still open.

Recovering Lost Work with AutoRecover

The AutoRecover feature helps protect your work against unexpected disasters like power outages, crashes, worksheet deletions, or that moment of panic when you close a workbook without saving. How Auto Recover works depends on your operating system:

>> **Windows:** Up to five backup copies are quietly created as you edit, giving you multiple restore points while you work. If you close the workbook without saving, Excel only retains the most recent backup.

>> **macOS:** Only one backup copy is saved if Excel crashes.

REMEMBER

Unsaved files typically linger on your hard drive for three to four days before Excel decides to clean house, so don't think of this is as a permanent archive. If you need to keep an AutoRecovered file, save it properly before it vanishes into the digital abyss.

Adjusting AutoRecover for better performance

If you use a Mac, skip onto the next section — this one's another Windows exclusive. By default, AutoRecover creates a backup every 10 minutes. However, in my experience, Excel seems to run on its own mysterious clock, often stretching that interval to 20 to 25 minutes, which feels like an eternity when you're deep in the trenches of spreadsheet work. If you don't want to gamble on Excel's timing, here's my recommendation for making AutoRecover a bit more reliable:

1. Choose File ➪ Options ➪ Save.

   The Save section of the Excel options dialog box appears.

2. **Lower the setting for Save AutoRecover Information Every 10 Minutes to every 2 or 3 minutes.**

   While cranking it down to one minute might seem like the ultimate safety net, it can actually backfire as your five backups will only cover the last 10 to 12 minutes of work. I find two minutes to be the sweet spot, giving me 20 to 25 minutes of protection. Excel's creative interpretation of time means it usually backs up my work every four or five minutes, striking a balance between protection and flexibility.

3. **Click OK to save your change and close the Excel Options dialog box.**

Accessing AutoRecover workbooks

If Excel crashes, the Document Recovery task pane automatically appears, listing workbooks with available AutoRecover copies. This kicks in when Excel detects an improper shutdown, giving you a chance to snatch your hard work back from the void.

TECHNICAL STUFF

You can't relaunch the Document Recovery task pane after it closes, but don't lose hope. You can try to manually recover files from these folders:

>> **Windows:** Navigate to C:\Users\<YourUserName>\AppData\ Local\Microsoft\ Office\UnsavedFiles or C:\Users\<YourUserName>\ AppData\Roaming\ Microsoft\Excel. Sometimes, AutoRecover files are stored in subfolders.

>> **macOS:** In Finder, choose Go ⇨ Go To Folder, and then enter ~Library/ Containers/com.microsoft.Excel/Data/Library/Preferences/AutoRecovery/.

Here's hoping that you uncover something more useful than digital dust bunnies lurking in the respective folder.

Accessing backups from the current work session

In Windows you can access up to five AutoRecover copies of your workbook during the current work session or the last AutoRecover copy if you closed without saving:

1. **Choose File ⇨ Info.**

   The Backstage view is displayed.

2. **If available, click on any time stamp next to the Manage Workbook command.**

   Each AutoRecover copy is opened separately from the live workbook, allowing you to compare versions. If no time stamps appear, AutoRecover hasn't (or didn't) back up your work yet.

Only the most recent AutoRecover copy is kept when you close a workbook without saving. Regardless of whether you choose to save or not, all other AutoRecover copies for that session are discarded.

Securing Workbooks with Passwords

In Chapter 14, I talk about locking down worksheets and workbook structure — because sometimes, you just don't want people messing with your stuff. Now, let's take it up a notch by limiting access entirely, with two levels of password protection. You can require a password to open the workbook, keeping out anyone that doesn't know the secret handshake — er, password. Or, you can allow users to open the workbook but restrict modifications, letting them view the contents but preventing edits unless they know the second level password. In the immortal words of MC Hammer, "You can't touch this."

Setting the VIP list

If you want to install velvet ropes and a bouncer outside your spreadsheet, here's how to keep out the uninvited entirely while ensuring only VIPs can make edits:

1. **Choose File ⇨ Save As ⇨ Browse (Windows) or File ⇨ Save As (macOS).**

2. **Click Tools ⇨ General Options (Windows) or Options (macOS).**

   The General Options dialog box appears in Windows, while the Save Options dialog box appears in macOS — because Excel likes to keep things just a little different across platforms.

Highfalutin' Windows users can choose File ⇨ Info ⇨ Protect Workbook ⇨ Encrypt with a Password to set a password to open — because nothing says exclusivity like encryption, even though this is basically the staff entrance for setting the password to open.

3. **Enter a case-sensitive password in either or both fields:**

   - **Password to open:** Think of this as checking IDs at the door — you'll only share this with people that you want to let inside the workbook.

   - **Password to modify:** You're in the club — er, workbook, but you'll need the 411 to start making edits.

     These are two separate password fields. If you're hot to trot and treat Password to Modify as a confirmation field, you'll be signing yourself (and everyone else) up for the joy of typing the password twice every time the workbook is opened — as if once weren't enough.

REMEMBER

4. **Click OK, and then confirm the password(s).**

   If your confirmation doesn't match the original, Excel sounds a metaphorical buzzer in the form of a "try again, pal" prompt — because even spreadsheets have standards.

5. **Save the workbook to lock things down.**

WARNING

   Forget the password, and Excel won't bail you out. Choose wisely, or risk locking even yourself out of your own fortress of data.

Revoking VIP access

So, you've decided to take down the velvet ropes and let everyone waltz into your workbook without needing the secret handshake — one for all and all for one! Here's how to remove the open and/or modify passwords and throw open the doors:

1. **Open the workbook from which you want to remove a password.**

2. **Choose File ➪ Save As ➪ Browse (Windows) or File ➪ Save As (macOS).**

   The Save As dialog box opens.

3. **Choose Tools ➪ General Options (Windows) or Options (macOS).**

   The General Options (Windows) — shown in Figure 18-1 — or Save Options (macOS) dialog box appears, ready to strip away the last remnants of exclusivity.

4. **Erase the Password to Open and/or Password to Modify fields, and then click OK.**

5. **Save the workbook to apply the password removal.**

   Excel needs official confirmation before it lets everyone in.

Auditing Edits with Show Changes

The Review ⇨ Show Changes or Review ⇨ Changes ⇨ Show Changes commands displays the Ch-ch-ch-ch-changes task pane (hat tip to David Bowie), where you can turn and face the strange — I mean review edits made to a selected a range or the entire worksheet. But don't expect this feature to work on locally stored workbooks — it only tracks changes for files saved to OneDrive or SharePoint. The task pane shows who edited each cell, along with the before and after values, so that you can channel your inner CSI investigator and piece together what happened — no red string required.

Storing Inputs with Scenario Manager

The Scenario Manager feature allows you to store and apply sets of up to 32 inputs, making it a powerful tool for exploring different possibilities without constant retyping. Part of Excel's What-If Analysis suite, it streamlines repetitive analysis and generates comparison reports to show how formulas respond to different inputs.

That said, I also consider Scenario Manager a secret weapon for disaster recovery, offering a quick way to restore overwritten inputs before you spiral into spreadsheet regret:

REMEMBER

1. **Select up to 32 input cells within a worksheet.**

    Scenarios only apply to the active worksheet — each sheet plays by its own rules.

2. **Choose Data ⇨ What-If Analysis ⇨ Scenario Manager.**

    The Scenario Manager dialog box appears.

3. **Click Add (Windows) or + (macOS) to create a new scenario.**

    The **New Scenario** dialog box appears.

4. **Enter a name in the Scenario Name field, such as** I want what I want.

5. **Confirm or select the input range in the Changing Cells field.**

6. **Click OK.**

    The Scenario Values dialog box appears.

7. **Confirm or enter values for each of the changing cells.**

8. **Click OK to save the scenario — because hey, you want what you want.**

It's not just a Cher song — you truly can turn back time (at least in Excel):

1. **Choose Data ⇨ What-If Analysis ⇨ Scenario Manager.**

   The Scenario Manager dialog box appears.

2. **Select a scenario from the list and click Show.**

   The changing cells specified in the scenario are overwritten with the stored values — like a spreadsheet time machine, but without the dramatic special effects.

REMEMBER

Don't panic if you open the Scenario Manager and don't see any scenarios — they may be hanging out in another worksheet. While each scenario is limited to 32 cells, there's no cap on the number of scenarios that you can create and apply across different areas of your workbook. So go ahead, build your alternate spreadsheet realities — and fallback positions — to your heart's content.

Index

C

Calculate Status option, 17
calculations
  about, 37, 52
  adding dates and times, 55
  adjusting options for, 257–258
  with AutoSum, 52
  with AVERAGE function, 56–57
  with AVERAGEIF function, 58–59
  cell references, 48–49
  conditional averages, 214–215
  finding smallest/largest values, 60
  operators, 37–42
  order of operations, 43–47
  replicating formulas, 49–51
  statistical functions, 56–60
  subtracting dates and times, 55
  with SUM function, 53–55
  weighted average, 57–58
capitalizing, with UPPER function, 164–165
Caps Lock Indicator option, 19
CELL function, 330–331
Cell Mode Indicator option, 17
cell references, 48–49, 353, 414–415
cells
  activating, 275
  applying styles, 67–70
  characters in, 10
  finding and replacing data in, 262–265
  finding characters in, 178–179
  formatting unlocked, 329–330
  highlighting based on value, 316–319
  linking, 40–42
  merging, 70–73
  navigating to, 270
  protecting, 341–348
  selecting, 275
  smart, 12
  unlocking, 341–348
Center Across Selection, 72–73, 390–392
centering, applying, 22
Change PivotTable Data Source dialog box, 304–305
CHAR function, 160, 185–186, 312

characters
  banned from worksheet names, 28
  counting, 180
  finding in cells, 178–179
  overwriting, 186–187
chart area, 286
chart elements, 287–288
chart filters, 288
chart styles, 288
chart title, 286, 287
charts
  about, 281–282
  creating, 282–283, 285–286
  creating templates, 292–293
  customizing, 286, 287–288
  deconstructing, 286
  maintaining, 288–289
  managing templates, 293–294
  moving, 289–291
  PivotTables, 296–309
  Recommended Charts, 283–284
  resizing, 289–291
  self-expanding, 129–130
  Sparklines, 294–296
  transferring formatting and elements, 291–292
ChatGPT, 375–377
CHOOSE function, 198–199
CHOOSECOLS function, 235–236
circular references, 253–254
cleaning text, with TRIM function, 169
clearing filters, 105
closing workbooks, 411
cloud-based drives, 421–422
co-authoring simultaneously, 33–34
code
  automation compared with, 379–380
  creating, 376–377
col_delimiter, 181
col_index_num, 138
collaborating
  about, 32
  co-authoring simultaneously, 33–34
  commenting, 34–35
  sharing workbooks, 32

Q

QUARTILE.EXC function, 109
QUARTILE.INC function, 109
Query tab, 14
question mark (?), 28, 207
Quick Access Toolbar (QAT)
  creating shortcuts, 393–395
  Custom Views shortcut, 277–278
  customizing, 14–16
  saving workbooks, 25
Quick Analysis feature, 113–114, 313–315

R

radar chart, 285
RANDARRAY function, 313
RANDBETWEEN function, 56
range operators, 40–41
range_lookup, 139, 142
ranges, navigating to, 270
rating icon sets, 324
Reapply command, 106
reapplying filters, 106
recalculating workbooks, 258
Recommended Charts, 283–284
Record Macro dialog box, 390–391, 396, 399, 405
recording macros
  about, 379
  absolute references in macros, 396–398
  assigning keyboard shortcuts to macros, 392–393
  automating Center Across Selection, 390–392
  code compared with automation, 379–380
  creating Quick Access Toolbar shortcuts, 393–395
  enabling macro security, 385–389
  linking macros to shapes, 395
  Macro Recorder, 381–384
  maintaining macros, 389–390
  managing macro security, 384–389
  Personal Macro Workbook, 402–404
  recovering discarded macros, 404–406
  relative references in macros, 398–401
  risks of macros, 381–382
  saving macro-enabled workbooks, 384–385

recovering
  discarded macros, 404–406
  lost work, 424–426
reformatting data, 369
#REF! error, 202, 212
refreshing PivotTables, 303–304
relative references, 48, 398–401
Remember icon, 5
Remove Duplicates dialog box, 102
removing. *See also* deleting
  conditional formatting, 332–333
  Data Validation, 362–363
  duplicates from multiple columns, 224
  duplicates with UNIQUE, 221–224
  extraneous spaces, 168–169
  slicers, 131–132
  subtotals, 113
  tracer arrows, 243–244
  watches, 256–257
renaming worksheets, 28
reordering worksheets, 271–272
repairing damaged workbooks, 419
repeating commands, 410–411
Replace Format button, 265
REPLACE function, 186–187
Replace tab, 262
replicating formulas, 49–51
reshaping data, 234–238
Resize Table command, 118
resizing
  charts, 289–291
  tables, 118
  text boxes, 75
resizing handles, 118, 291
restrictions, in Data Validation, 352–353
return_array, 149
reversing commands, 410–411
Review tab (ribbon), 12, 35
revoking VIP access, 427–428
ribbon, 11–14
RIGHT function, 180
ROW function, 50, 124
row_delimiter, 181

About the Author

David Ringstrom, CPA, is the president of Accounting Advisors, Inc., an Atlanta-based consulting and training firm he founded in 1991. David specializes in helping clients streamline repetitive business processes and has delivered over 2,500 live webinars on Microsoft Excel and related topics. He also owns Students Excel, an online platform designed to help accounting professors teach Excel more effectively. Throughout his career, David has authored hundreds of articles on spreadsheets and accounting software, with some published internationally. He has served as the technical editor for more than three dozen books, including *QuickBooks Desktop For Dummies*, *Quicken For Dummies*, and *Peachtree For Dummies*, and is the author or coauthor of eight books, including *QuickBooks Online for Dummies*, *Idiot's Guide to Introductory Accounting*, and *Exploring Microsoft Excel's Hidden Treasures*.

David lives in Atlanta, Georgia, with his children, Rachel and Lucas.

Author's Acknowledgments

I never imagined I'd have the opportunity to re-envision a marquee title like *Microsoft 365 Excel For Dummies*. This project marks the culmination of a long journey that traces back to the early 1990s when I voluntarily answered Lotus 1-2-3 questions on CompuServe. I share this to remind you: Stay focused on your goals, whatever they may be, because you can truly achieve them. I'm living proof.

I'd like to thank Rod Stephens for his technical editing prowess, Amy Handy for her meticulous copy editing, and Ted Cains for his guidance as project editor. Special thanks to Lindsey Berg, my publisher for *QuickBooks For Dummies*, for recommending me to Steve Hayes. Consulting, teaching, and writing about Excel are my passions, and it's been a pleasure to share so much of my hard-earned knowledge. I also want to thank you, the reader, for making this book possible, and extend my gratitude to the outstanding team at Wiley, who have brought six of my books to life so far. I also extend my unending gratitude to my chidren, Rachel and Lucas, for bearing with me on yet another book, and to Debra Kahraman . . . she knows.

Publisher's Acknowledgments

Executive Editor: Steve Hayes

Project Editor: Ted Cains

Copy Editor: Amy Handy

Technical Editor: Rod Stephens

Production Editor: Saikarthick Kumarasamy

Cover Image: © CGinspiration/Getty Images